T0207345

# Lecture Notes of the Institute for Computer Sciences, Social Informatics and Telecommunications Engineering 444

More information about this series at https://link.springer.com/bookseries/8197

Nguyen-Son Vo · Quoc-Tuan Vien ·
Dac-Binh Ha (Eds.)

# Industrial Networks and Intelligent Systems

8th EAI International Conference, INISCOM 2022
Virtual Event, April 21–22, 2022
Proceedings

*Editors*
Nguyen-Son Vo
Duy Tan University
Da Nang, Vietnam

Quoc-Tuan Vien
Middlesex University
London, UK

Dac-Binh Ha
Duy Tan University
Da Nang, Vietnam

ISSN 1867-8211 ISSN 1867-822X (electronic)
Lecture Notes of the Institute for Computer Sciences, Social Informatics
and Telecommunications Engineering
ISBN 978-3-031-08877-3 ISBN 978-3-031-08878-0 (eBook)
https://doi.org/10.1007/978-3-031-08878-0

This Springer imprint is published by the registered company Springer Nature Switzerland AG
The registered company address is: Gewerbestrasse 11, 6330 Cham, Switzerland

# Preface

We are delighted to introduce the proceedings of the 8th European Alliance for Innovation (EAI) International Conference on Industrial Networks and Intelligent Systems (INISCOM 2022). This conference brought together researchers, developers, and practitioners from around the world who are leveraging and developing industrial networks and intelligent systems. The focus of INISCOM 2022 was the state of the art in all areas of AI and 6G convergence in terms of models, technologies, and applications.

The technical program of INISCOM 2022 consisted of 19 full papers in oral presentation sessions at the main conference tracks. There were four conference tracks: Track 1 – Telecommunications Systems and Networks; Track 2 – Information Processing and Data Analysis; Track 3 – Industrial Networks and Intelligent Systems; and Track 4 – Security and Privacy. Aside from the high-quality technical paper presentations, the technical program also featured a keynote speech about "Communications in the 6G Era" given by Harish Viswanathan, Head of the Radio Systems Research Group at Nokia Bell Labs, USA.

Coordination with the steering chairs, Imrich Chlamtac and Trung Q. Duong, was essential for the success of the conference. We sincerely appreciate their constant support and guidance. It was also a great pleasure to work with such an excellent Organizing Committee team and we thank them for their hard work in organizing and supporting the conference. Particular thanks go to the Technical Program Committee (TPC), who completed the peer-review process for the technical papers and put together a high-quality technical program. We are also grateful to the conference manager, Natasha Onofrei, for the support and all the authors who submitted their papers to INISCOM 2022.

We strongly believe that INISCOM provides a good forum for all researchers, developers, and practitioners to discuss all science and technology aspects that are relevant to industrial networks and intelligent systems. We also expect that the future editions of INISCOM will be as successful and stimulating as this year's conference, as indicated by the contributions presented in this volume.

June 2022

Nguyen-Son Vo
Quoc-Tuan Vien
Dac-Binh Ha

Preface

# Organization

## Steering Committee

Imrich Chlamtac       University of Trento, Italy
Trung Q. Duong       Queen's University Belfast, UK

## Organizing Committee

### General Chair

Trung Q. Duong       Queen's University Belfast, UK

### General Co-chairs

Dac-Binh Ha       Duy Tan University, Vietnam
The-Anh Han       Teesside University, UK

### Technical Program Committee Chairs

Nguyen-Son Vo       Duy Tan University, Vietnam
Quoc-Tuan Vien       Middlesex University London, UK
Tuan Nguyen       University of Buckingham, UK
Dac-Binh Ha       Duy Tan University, Vietnam

### Sponsorship and Exhibit Chair

Hoa Le-Minh       Northumbria University, UK

### Local Chair

Hoa Le-Minh       Northumbria University, UK

### Workshops Chair

Chinmoy Kundu       University College Dublin, Ireland

**Publicity and Social Media Chairs**

| | |
|---|---|
| Antonino Masaracchia | Queen's University Belfast, UK |
| Tuan Nguyen | University of Buckingham, UK |

**Publications Chair**

| | |
|---|---|
| Nguyen-Son Vo | Duy Tan University, Vietnam |

**Web Chair**

| | |
|---|---|
| Van Nhan Vo | Duy Tan University, Vietnam |

**Posters and PhD Track Chair**

| | |
|---|---|
| Daniel Benevides da Costa | Federal University of Cearas, Brazil |

**Panels Chairs**

| | |
|---|---|
| Nguyen Gia Nhu | Duy Tan University, Vietnam |
| Berk Canberk | Istanbul Technical University, Turkey |

**Demos Chairs**

| | |
|---|---|
| Nguyen Quang Sang | Duy Tan University, Vietnam |
| Zoran Hadzi-Velkov | Ss. Cyril and Methodius University, Macedonia |

**Tutorials Chairs**

| | |
|---|---|
| Dang Viet Hung | Duy Tan University, Vietnam |
| Tuan Le | Middlesex University, UK |

## Technical Program Committee

| | |
|---|---|
| Ali Shahrabi | Glasgow Caledonian University, UK |
| Antonino Massarachia | Queen's University Belfast, UK |
| Cheng Yin | Queen's University Belfast, UK |
| Cong Hoang Diem | Hanoi University of Mining and Geology, Vietnam |
| Dac-Binh Ha | Duy Tan University, Vietnam |
| Dang Huynh | Queen's University Belfast, UK |
| Dao Thi-Nga | Le Quy Don Technical University, Vietnam |
| Huu Hung Nguyen | Le Quy Don Technical University, Vietnam |
| Huy T. Nguyen | Nanyang Technological University, Vietnam |
| Kien Dang | Ho Chi Minh City University of Transport, Vietnam |
| Kien Nguyen | Chiba University, Japan |

| Leandros Maglaras | De Montfort University, UK |
| Long Nguyen | Dong Nai University, Vietnam |
| Pham Ngoc Son | Ho Chi Minh City University of Technology and Education, Vietnam |
| Ta Minh Thanh | Le Quy Don Technical University, Vietnam |
| Tan Duy | Ho Chi Minh City University of Technology and Education, Vietnam |
| The Nghiep Tran | Le Quy Don Technical University, Vietnam |
| Toan Doan | Thu Dau Mot University, Vietnam |
| Truong Khoa Phan | University College London, UK |
| Tuan Nguyen | University of Buckingham, UK |
| Van-Ca Phan | Ho Chi Minh City University of Technology and Education, Vietnam |
| Van-Phuc Hoang | Le Quy Don Technical University, Vietnam |
| Xuan Nam Tran | Le Quy Don Technical University, Vietnam |
| Xuan Tung Truong | Le Quy Don Technical University, Vietnam |
| Yuanfang Chen | Hangzhou Dianzi University, China |

# Contents

**Industrial Networks and Intelligent Systems**

**Security and Privacy**

# Telecommunications Systems and Networks

# Rate Region and Achievable Rates of Full-Duplex Cognitive Radio NOMA Channels Under Imperfect Spectrum Sensing

Mohammad Ranjbar[1], Nghi H. Tran[1(✉)], Tutku Karacolak[2], and Shivakumar Sastry[1]

[1] Department of Electrical and Computer Engineering, University of Akron, Akron, OH, USA
{nghi.tran,ssastry}@uakron.edu
[2] School of Engineering and Computer Science, Washington State University Vancouver, Vancouver, USA
tutku.karacolak@wsu.edu

**Abstract.** This paper studies the rate region and the achievable rates of a non-orthogonal multi-access (NOMA) full-duplex (FD) cognitive radio (CR) channel in which multiple secondary users (SU) communicate to a base station under imperfect self-interference suppression (SIS) and spectrum sensing. Towards that goal, we first analyze the sensing performance, i.e., the probabilities of false alarm and miss-detection, of the considered NOMA FD CR channel under the assumption of non-time-slotted activity from the primary network. We use a Markov chain model to combine the sensing results under different sensing scenarios and derive the probability of collision between the primary and secondary networks under realistic imperfect spectrum sensing. Because of this sensing imperfection, the secondary channel is molded as a Gaussian-mixture (GM) channel. Due to the difficulty in obtaining the explicit expressions of the channel capacity and mutual information in GM, we propose new closed-form approximations of the rate region and the achievable rate for each of the users with arbitrarily small errors. These approximations are therefore helpful to analyze the rate region and to establish the achievable rates of the considered FD CR NOMA channel.

**Keywords:** Cognitive radio · Full-duplex · Gaussian-mixture interference · NOMA · Imperfect spectrum sensing

## 1 Introduction

Over the last decade, cognitive radio (CR) under the context of opportunistic spectrum access (OSA) has gained significant attention [7]. To date, most of the existing works under this line of research considered a single-user secondary network or a multi-user system but under orthogonal multiple access (OMA)

N.-S. Vo et al. (Eds.): INISCOM 2022, LNICST 444, pp. 3–19, 2022.
https://doi.org/10.1007/978-3-031-08878-0_1

schemes. While non-orthogonal multiple access (NOMA) schemes [3] provide significantly more benefits, the consideration of NOMA for CR poses significant challenges, especially under realistic conditions of imperfect sensing [15].

In CR with OSA, a SU periodically monitors the spectrum and opportunistically transmits over the spectrum holes. There has been an extensive literature on the analysis of OSA with regard to spectrum efficiency and throughput under the constraint of half-duplex (HD) communication, where an SU cannot sense and transmit simultaneously. With the recent development of full-duplex (FD) radio and self-interference suppression (SIS) [4,8], the integration of FD in CR has also been addressed [1,9]. For instance, the works in [1] considered the use of FD in a single-user CR that enables the SU to operate in different modes, such as transmit-and-sense (TS) and transmit-and-receive (TR) [1]. Such flexibility in operation helps improve spectrum sensing performance and/or throughput significantly. In [9], a "listen-and-talk" protocol based on FD was also proposed under TS framework for better spectrum utilization and sensing accuracy in CR.

In CR, even with FD capability, spectrum sensing is never perfect. When SU fails to detect the presence of the PU activity, miss-detection occurs, and both SU and PU suffer from interference. Under the practical assumption of finite input PU signals, it has been shown that the aggregate noise plus interference in the SU channel is Gaussian-mixture (GM) [10], which poses more challenges in the analysis. It is because the non-Gaussian characteristic leads to a totally different link and network behavior as compared to the Gaussian counterpart [12,14]. In our recent work in [13], we have studied the energy efficiency of a FD CR system under such non-Gaussian aggregate interference. However, the results were only obtained for a single-user scenario. To our knowledge, there does not exist any previous work in the literature that addresses the sensing performance and the corresponding transmission rates of a multi-user FD CR network under non-Gaussian aggregate interference.

Motivated by the above discussions, this paper studies the rate region and the achievable rates of a NOMA FD CR channel in which SUs communicate to a secondary base station (SBS) under imperfect SIS and spectrum sensing. In the considered NOMA, the SBS decodes the signal for each user by performing successive interference cancellation (SIC) [2]. With their FD capability, SUs can sense the channel while transmitting. We first analyze the sensing performance, i.e., the probabilities of false alarm and miss-detection, of the considered NOMA FD CR channel under the assumption of non-time-slotted activity from the primary network. We use a Markov chain model to combine the sensing results under different sensing scenarios and derive the probability of collision between the primary and secondary networks. Under imperfect spectrum sensing, we show that secondary channel is modeled as a Gaussian-Mixture channel. We then analyze the rate region of the considered FD CR NOMA channel and establish the achievable rates. Due to the lack of explicit expressions of both channel capacity and mutual information in GM channels, we develop new closed-form approximations with an arbitrary small error of the rate region and the achievable rate for each of the users.

## 2    System Model

In this work, we consider a cognitive multiple access channel where $N$ SUs opportunistically access the primary channel and communicate to a secondary base station (SBS). The SUs have SIS capability and they can work in FD mode. The quality of the SIS method at user $i$, $1 \leq i \leq N$, is represented by a zero-mean circularly symmetric Gaussian (CSCG) random variable $h_{ii}$ with variance $\sigma_{ii}^2$, which is the ratio of residual self-interference to the self-interference before suppression. Moreover, it is assumed that SUs always have data to transmit, i.e., saturated traffic.

To detect the white spectrum and avoid collision with the PU, the SUs take the samples of the channel with sampling frequency $f_s$ and make a decision about the PU activity every $N_s$ samples. This results in a time-slotted traffic with slot length of $\tau_s = \frac{N_s}{f_s}$. The SUs then report their sensing results to SBS and SBS makes a cooperative decision on the PU activity status. The entire sensing procedure will be explained further in the next section. It should also be noted that the PU activity is considered as non-time slotted, i.e., the PU can change its status any time. To take it into consideration, we introduce two new random variables $T_1$ and $T_0$ to represent the ON and OFF duration of the PU, respectively. These two random variables follow the probability distributions $f_{T_1}(\cdot)$ and $f_{T_0}(\cdot)$ and means $\tau_1$ and $\tau_0$, respectively. By assuming that $f_s$ is large enough, the PU state changes sufficiently slow, and we have $\tau_0 \gg \tau_s$ and $\tau_1 \gg \tau_s$.

### 2.1    Modes of Operation

With FD, the SUs can sense the channel and, simultaneously, transmit data. As a result, we can have two different modes of operation of SUs as follows:

1. *Sense-Only (SO)*: If the channel is sensed as busy, the SUs only sense the channel until the next sensing result.
2. *Transmit-Sense (TS)*: If the channel is sensed as idle, the SUs simultaneously transmit and sense for the next SU time slot.

### 2.2    Secondary Channels Under Imperfect Spectrum Sensing

In practice, sensing performance is characterized by probabilities of false alarm $P_f$ and miss-detection $P_m$. With FD, these sensing performance metrics are affected by the quality of SIS, and they will be analyzed further in the subsequent sections. In the case of false alarm or correct detection in the presence of the PU signal, SUs do not transmit, and the received signal at the SBS $y_r$ is either noise or noise plus interference from PU. Otherwise, all SUs will transmit. The input-output model of the SU channel can therefore be expressed as:

$$y_r = \begin{cases} \sum_{j=1}^{N} h_{jr} x_j + u_r, & H_0, \hat{H}_0 \\ \\ \sum_{j=1}^{N} h_{jr} x_j + u_r + w, & H_1, \hat{H}_0 \end{cases} \tag{1}$$

Here, $H_0/H_1$ denotes the hypothesis that the channel is free/busy while $\hat{H}_0/\hat{H}_1$ represents the hypothesis that the channel is sensed as idle/busy. For convenience, throughout the paper, we shall use sub-index 0 to indicate the PU, while sub-indices $1, 2, \ldots, N$ and sub-index $r$ to refer to the $N$ SUs and the SBS, respectively. Furthermore, in (1), $\boldsymbol{y}_r$ is the received signal at the SBS, $\boldsymbol{x}_j$ is the zero-mean transmitted signals from SU $j$ with variance $\sigma_j^2$. $\boldsymbol{u}_r$ is the additive noise at the SBS, which is modeled as CSCG random variable with zero mean and variance $\sigma_{u_r}^2$. Also, $\boldsymbol{h}_{jr}$ is a zero-mean circularly symmetric fading coefficient between SU $j$ and the SBS with variance $\sigma_{jr}^2$, and $\boldsymbol{w}$ is the PU interference at the SBS. It is clear that in the case of Gaussian $\boldsymbol{w}$, $\boldsymbol{u}_r + \alpha\boldsymbol{w}$ is a mixture of two Gaussian distributions. In a more realistic scenario, $\boldsymbol{w}$ and, hence, the aggregate noise plus interference are more accurately modeled as general GM random variables [11]. In this work, we adopt this model, and assume that $\boldsymbol{w}$ has the following PDF:

$$f_W(\boldsymbol{w}) = \sum_{i=1}^{p} \epsilon_i \mathcal{CN}(\boldsymbol{w}, 0, \sigma_{w,i}^2). \tag{2}$$

In (2), $\{\epsilon_i\}$ are the mixture probability with $\sum_{i=1}^{p} \epsilon_i = 1$, and $\mathcal{CN}(\boldsymbol{z}, \mu, \sigma^2)$ denotes a circularly symmetric complex Gaussian distribution with mean $\mu$ and variance per real dimension $\sigma^2/2$. Also, we assume all the links to be reciprocal, i.e., $\sigma_{ji}^2 = \sigma_{ij}^2$.

Given that, the model in (1) can be represented in an equivalent way as $\boldsymbol{y}_r = \beta \sum_{j=1}^{N} \boldsymbol{h}_{jr}\boldsymbol{x}_j + \boldsymbol{u}_r + \alpha\boldsymbol{w}$,, where $\beta$ and $\alpha$ are binary indicator random variables. Specifically, $\beta = 0$ corresponds to the event of sensing the channel as free and $\alpha = 1$ denotes the event that PU is active.

In the considered multi-user setup, the SBS can decode the signal for each SU by performing successive interference cancellation (SIC). To this end, it is essential to maintain the distinctness of the users' signals superimposed in the received signal $\boldsymbol{y}_r$. To apply SIC, the SBS should first setup a decoding order. Since each user experiences a different channel gain, the received signal power corresponding to the user with the largest $\sigma_{jr}^2\sigma_j^2$ is likely to be the strongest at the SBS. Without loss of generality, it is assumed that $\sigma_{1r}^2\sigma_1^2 \geq \sigma_{2r}^2\sigma_2^2 \geq \cdots \geq \sigma_{Nr}^2\sigma_N^2$. Having set up the decoding order, the SBS then decodes the first user signal by treating other signals as noise and then subtracts this decoded message from $\boldsymbol{y}_r$. In the next step, the second user signal is decoded from the modified received signal (without any interference from the first user) and the decoded signal is again removed by SIC. This procedure goes on until the last user signal is detected without any interference.

## 2.3   Achievable Rates

Assuming that the SBS has full knowledge of the channel gains $\vec{\boldsymbol{h}}_r = [\boldsymbol{h}_{1r}, \boldsymbol{h}_{2r}, \cdots, \boldsymbol{h}_{Nr}]$, the achievable rate at each user $j$ for a given set of power budget $\Sigma = \left[\sigma_1^2, \ldots, \sigma_N^2\right]$, is the average mutual information between the input signal and the received signal, which is

$$R_j\left(\Sigma\right) = \mathrm{E}_{\vec{h}_r}\left[I\left(y_r, \beta; x_j \mid \vec{h}_r\right)\right] = \mathrm{E}_{\vec{h}_r}\left[I\left(y_r; x_j \mid \beta, \vec{h}_r\right)\right]$$
$$= P\left(\beta = 1\right)\mathrm{E}_{\vec{h}_r}\left[I\left(y_r; x_j \mid \beta = 1, \vec{h}_r\right)\right]. \tag{3}$$

For simplicity, let $y_r^\beta = y_r \mid \beta = 1$ and $z_\beta = u + \left(\alpha \mid \beta = 1\right)w$. We then have $y_r^\beta = \sum_{j=1}^N h_{jr}x_j + z_\beta$, where $f_{Z_\beta}\left(z\right)$ can be defined as

$$P\left(\alpha = 0 \mid \beta = 1\right)\mathcal{CN}(z, 0, \sigma_{u_r}^2) + P\left(\alpha = 1 \mid \beta = 1\right)\sum_{i=1}^p \epsilon_i \mathcal{CN}(z, 0, \sigma_{w,i}^2 + \sigma_{u_r}^2)$$

$$= \sum_{i=1}^{p+1} \epsilon_{z,i} \mathcal{CN}(z, 0, \sigma_{z,i}^2). \tag{4}$$

Therefore, $R_j\left(\Sigma\right) = P\left(\beta = 1\right)\mathrm{E}_{\vec{h}_r}\left[I\left(y_r^\beta; x_j \mid \vec{h}_r\right)\right]$. Here, it is worth mentioning that $\alpha = 1 \mid \beta = 1$ corresponds to the event that there is collision between PU and SU, while $\alpha = 0 \mid \beta = 1$ is the event that SUs transmit without collision and $P\left(\beta = 1\right) = P\left(\hat{H}_0\right)$.

## 3  Sensing Performance Metrics

In this section, we shall focus on the sensing performance by studying the binary indicator random variables $\alpha$ and $\beta$. As mentioned earlier, $\alpha = 1$ corresponds to the event that PU is active and $\beta = 1$ is the event that SU decides to transmit. These two random variables are related to the following probabilities:

$$1 - P\left(\alpha = 0 \mid \beta = 1\right) = P\left(\alpha = 1 \mid \beta = 1\right) = \text{Probability of Collision,}$$

and

$$P\left(\beta = 1\right) = P\left(\hat{H}_0\right),$$

which are needed for the rate analysis.

Different from traditional HD CR, in the considered FD CR, the state of the system at each SU time slot depends on the sensing decision in the previous slot. Therefore, in this paper, we model the sensing decision status as a discrete-time Markov chain. To analyze this Markov chain, let $P_{10}$ and $P_{01}$ be the probabilities of PU going from ON to OFF and OFF to ON, respectively, during an SU slot, and they are given as $P_{10} = F_{\hat{T}_1}\left(\tau_s\right)$ and $P_{01} = F_{\hat{T}_0}\left(\tau_s\right)$. Because $\tau_0 \gg \tau_s$ and $\tau_1 \gg \tau_s$, it can be verified that $P_{10}$ and $P_{01}$ are small. Also, as PU activity is modeled as non-time slotted, we have two types of slots:

1. The slots in which the PU activity does not change.
2. The slots in which PU activity status changes.

It is then clear that the sensing performance in these two cases are different, and they need to be treated separately. For convenience, we shall use following notations:

1. $P_f^j$: The probability of false alarm while working at mode $j \in \{so, ts\}$ for slots in which PU activity status does not change.
2. $P_m^j$: The probability of miss-detection while working at mode $j \in \{so, ts\}$ for slots in which PU activity status does not change.
3. $P_f^{jc}$: The probability of false alarm while working at mode $j \in \{so, ts\}$ for slots in which PU activity status changes.
4. $P_m^{jc}$: The probability of miss-detection while working at mode $j \in \{so, ts\}$ for slots in which PU activity status changes.

We now model the sensing decision status at each decision instance as a discrete-time Markov chain with four different states as follows:

1. State $H_{00}$ representing $\hat{H}_0$ and $H_0$.
2. State $H_{01}$ representing $\hat{H}_0$ and $H_1$.
3. State $H_{10}$ representing $\hat{H}_1$ and $H_0$.
4. State $H_{11}$ representing $\hat{H}_1$ and $H_1$.

From $P_{10}$ and $P_{01}$ and the probabilities of false alarm and miss detection, we can obtain the state transition diagram of the sensing decision as in Fig. 1.

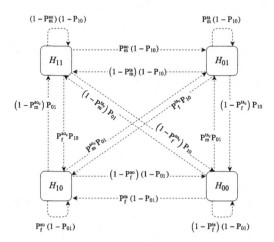

**Fig. 1.** The state transition diagram of the sensing status.

Given the proposed Markov chain, it is straightforward to verify that $P(\beta = 1) = P(H_{00}) + P(H_{01})$. In addition, we can find the collision probability and also the probability of collision-free transmission of SUs using this

Markov chain. To do that, let consider two scenarios in which collision happens in an SU slot:

1. When PU is present and SU fails to detect that the spectrum is occupied $H_{01}$. The probability of this scenario is the probability of $H_{01}$.
2. PU is not active and SU correctly senses the channel as free $H_{00}$. However, PU becomes active during SU transmission before the next sensing decision. The probability of this scenario is $P_{01}P(H_{00})$, which is relatively small.

Given these two scenarios, we can define the probability of collision during a time slot given that SU decides to transmit as

$$P_c = P(\alpha = 1 \mid \beta = 1) = \frac{P(H_{01}) + P_{01}P(H_{00})}{P(H_{00}) + P(H_{01})}. \tag{5}$$

Using the same argument, we can formulate the probability of collision-free transmission during a time slot as

$$P_{nc} = P(\alpha = 0 \mid \beta = 1) = \frac{(1 - P_{01})P(H_{00})}{P(H_{00}) + P(H_{01})} = 1 - P_c. \tag{6}$$

We now only need to find $P(H_{ij})$ using the steady state analysis of the Markov chain $\pi\mathbf{P} = \pi$ along with the constraint $\sum P(H_{ij}) = 1$, where $\pi$ (stationary distribution) and $\mathbf{P}$ (transition matrix) are given as

$$\pi = [P(H_{00}), P(H_{01}), P(H_{10}), P(H_{11})],$$

$$\mathbf{P} = \begin{bmatrix} (1 - P_{01})\left(1 - P_f^{ts}\right) & P_{01}P_m^{ts_c} & \left(1 - P_{01}P_f^{ts}\right) & P_{01}\left(1 - P_m^{ts_c}\right) \\ P_{10}\left(1 - P_f^{ts_c}\right) & (1 - P_{10})P_m^{ts} & P_{10}P_f^{ts_c} & (1 - P_{10})\left(1 - P_m^{ts}\right) \\ (1 - P_{01})\left(1 - P_f^{so}\right) & P_{01}P_m^{so} & \left(1 - P_{01}P_f^{so}\right) & P_{01}\left(1 - P_m^{so_c}\right) \\ P_{10}\left(1 - P_f^{so_c}\right) & (1 - P_{10})P_m^{so} & P_{10}P_f^{so_c} & (1 - P_{10})\left(1 - P_m^{so}\right) \end{bmatrix}. \tag{7}$$

After some manipulations, $P(H_{00})$ and $P(H_{01})$ are expressed as:

$$\begin{bmatrix} P(H_{00}) \\ P(H_{01}) \end{bmatrix} = \begin{bmatrix} \frac{(P_{01}+P_{10})(k_1-k_2)}{k_2} & -\frac{(P_{01}+P_{10})k_3}{k_2} \\ k_6 - \frac{k_4 k_1}{k_2} & k_7 + \frac{k_4 k_3}{k_2} \end{bmatrix}^{-1} \times \begin{bmatrix} -P_{10} + \frac{K_6 k_5}{k_2} \\ k_4 - \frac{k_4 k_5}{k_2} \end{bmatrix}, \tag{8}$$

where

$$k_1 = k_5 - (1 - P_{01})P_f^{ts}, \quad k_2 = 1 + k_5 - P_f^{so}(1 - P_{01}),$$
$$k_3 = -k_5 + P_{10}P_f^{ts_c}, \quad k_4 = -P_m^{so}(1 - P_{10}) + P_m^{so_c}P_{01},$$
$$k_5 = P_{10}P_f^{so_c}, \quad k_6 = k_4 + P_{01}\left(P_m^{ts_c} - P_m^{so_c}\right),$$
$$k_7 = k_4 - 1 - P_m^{so_c}P_{01} + P_m^{ts}(1 - P_{01}). \tag{9}$$

Given $P(H_{00})$ and $P(H_{01})$, we are now ready to calculate the false alarm and miss-detection probabilities. For simplicity, we consider energy-detection based sensing. With this sensing method, the energy of the received signal is calculated for a specific number of symbols and the result is compared with a threshold to determine whether the channel is busy or free. If $\boldsymbol{y}(n)$ is the received signal at a given SU, the energy is calculated as $M = \frac{1}{f_s \tau_s} \sum_{n=1}^{f_s \tau_s} |\boldsymbol{y}(n)|^2$. By comparing $M$ with a threshold, we can compute the false alarm and miss-detection probabilities of that user as $P_f = Pr\,[M > \epsilon \mid H_0]$ and $P_m = Pr\,[M < \epsilon \mid H_1]$.

As we discussed earlier, all SUs perform the sensing and then report their sensing results to the SBS. The SBS makes a cooperative decision on the PU activity. It is clear that SUs may report either their binary decision about presence of PU (hard decision) or their exact energy measurement (soft decision) to the SBS. In the case of hard decision, the SBS applies the $k$ out of $n$ rule, i.e., if $k$ or more SUs decides PU is active, the channel is assumed to be busy. Otherwise the channel is sensed as free. In the case of soft decision, the SBS uses the energy measurements of all the users to make the decision. Therefore, in the following, we calculate the sensing metrics for each user before extending the results to the cooperative sensing metrics using hard and soft decision methods.

### 3.1   Individual Sensing Performance

To calculate the probabilities of false alarm and miss-detection for each SU, it is noted that SU can be in TS or SO. While working in TS mode, the received signal at $i^{\text{th}}$ SU can be written as

$$
\boldsymbol{y}_i^{ts}(n) = \begin{cases} \sum_{j=1}^{N} \boldsymbol{h}_{ji}(n)\, \boldsymbol{x}_j(n) + \boldsymbol{u}_i(n), & H_0 \\ \sum_{j=0}^{N} \boldsymbol{h}_{ji}(n)\, \boldsymbol{x}_j(n) + \boldsymbol{u}_i(n), & H_1 \end{cases}, \tag{10}
$$

for $i = 1, \dots, N$. On the other hand, in the SO mode, the SUs do not transmit, and (10) can be simplified to

$$
\boldsymbol{y}_i^{so}(n) = \begin{cases} \boldsymbol{u}_i(n), & H_0 \\ \boldsymbol{h}_{0i}(n)\, \boldsymbol{x}_0(n) + \boldsymbol{u}_i(n), & H_1 \end{cases}. \tag{11}
$$

Now, as PU activity is non-time slotted, we have two different types of slots:

1. The slots in which the PU activity does not change.
2. The slots in which PU activity status changes.

In the following, we will analyze each of these cases. For that, we shall use $M_i^j$ to denote the energy received at user $i \in \{1, \dots, N\}$ while working in mode $j \in \{ts, so\}$ and $_iP_f^j$ and $_iP_m^j$ are the corresponding probabilities of false alarm and miss detection.

**The Slots in Which the PU Activity Does Not Change.** As SO is a special case of TS, we first find the probabilities of false alarm and miss-detection for user $i$ for the general form in (10) (TS mode). We will then use the results to find $_iP_f^{so}$ and $_iP_m^{so}$. To this end, we have the following propositions regarding the false-alarm and miss-detection probabilities of TS mode. Their proofs are rather straightforward, and we omit them for the brevity of the presentation.

**Proposition 1.** *Using the Central Limit Theorem, for the large number of samples* $(f_s \tau_s)$, *the distribution of* $M_i^{ts}$ *given* $H_0$ *can be approximated by Gaussian distribution with the following mean and variance*

$$E\left[M_i^{ts} \mid H_0\right] = \sum_{j=1}^{N} \sigma_{ji}^2 \sigma_j^2 + \sigma_{u_i}^2, \tag{12}$$

$$Var\left[M_i^{ts} \mid H_0\right] = \frac{1}{f_s \tau_s} \left\{ \sum_{j=1}^{N} E\left[|h_{ji}(n)|^4\right] E\left[|x_j(n)|^4\right] + 4 \sum_{j=1}^{N-1} \sum_{k=j+1}^{N} \sigma_{ji}^2 \sigma_{ki}^2 \sigma_j^2 \sigma_k^2 + \right.$$
$$\left. + E\left[|u_i(n)|^4\right] + 4\sigma_{u_i}^2 \sum_{j=1}^{N} \sigma_{ji}^2 \sigma_j^2 - \left(\sum_{j=1}^{N} \sigma_{ji}^2 \sigma_j^2 + \sigma_{u_i}^2\right)^2 \right\}. \tag{13}$$

**Proposition 2.** *Using the Central Limit Theorem, for the large number of samples* $(f_s \tau_s)$, *the distribution of* $M_i^{ts}$ *given* $H_1$ *can be approximated by Gaussian distribution with the following mean and variance*

$$E\left[M_i^{ts} \mid H_1\right] = \sum_{j=0}^{N} \sigma_{ji}^2 \sigma_j^2 + \sigma_{u_i}^2, \tag{14}$$

$$Var\left[M_i^{ts} \mid H_1\right] = \frac{1}{f_s \tau_s} \left\{ \sum_{j=0}^{N} E\left[|h_{ji}(n)|^4\right] E\left[|x_j(n)|^4\right] + 4 \sum_{j=0}^{N-1} \sum_{k=j+1}^{N} \sigma_{ji}^2 \sigma_{ki}^2 \sigma_j^2 \sigma_k^2 + \right.$$
$$\left. + E\left[|u_i(n)|^4\right] + 4\sigma_{u_i}^2 \sum_{j=0}^{N} \sigma_{ji}^2 \sigma_j^2 - \left(\sum_{j=0}^{N} \sigma_{ji}^2 \sigma_j^2 + \sigma_{u_i}^2\right)^2 \right\}. \tag{15}$$

Now, considering that in sensing mode, all SUs are silent. From (11), we can use the results of Propositions 1 and 2 to find the statistics of the received energy at user $i$ in the SO mode $M_i^{so}$ as

$$E\left[M_i^{so} \mid H_0\right] = \sigma_{u_i}^2, \, Var\left[M_i^{so} \mid H_0\right] = \frac{1}{f_s \tau_s} \left(E\left[|u_i(n)|^4\right] - \sigma_{u_i}^4\right), \tag{16}$$

$$E\left[M_i^{so} \mid H_1\right] = \sigma_{u_i}^2 + \sigma_{0i}^2 \sigma_0^2, \tag{17}$$

$$Var\left[M_i^{so} \mid H_1\right] = \frac{1}{f_s \tau_s} \left(E\left[|h_{0i}(n)|^4\right] E\left[|x_0(n)|^4\right] + E\left[|u_i(n)|^4\right] - \left(\sigma_{0i}^2 \sigma_0^2 - \sigma_{u_i}^2\right)^2\right). \tag{18}$$

As a result, the sensing metrics for user $i$ are calculated as

$$_iP_f^j = Q\left(\frac{\epsilon_i^j - E\left[M_i^j \mid H_0\right]}{\sqrt{Var\left[M_i^j \mid H_0\right]}}\right), \, _iP_m^j = 1 - Q\left(\frac{\epsilon_i^j - E\left[M_i^j \mid H_1\right]}{\sqrt{Var\left[M_i^j \mid H_1\right]}}\right), \tag{19}$$

for $j \in \{ts, so\}$ and $i = 1, \ldots, N$.

**The Slots in Which PU Activity Status Changes.** In this case, define two random variables $\hat{T}_1$ and $\hat{T}_0$ as the forward recurrence time for the ON and OFF periods of PU, respectively, which are observed at the sensing decision time. It can then be verified that the probability distributions of these two random variables are:

$$f_{\hat{T}_1}(t) = \frac{\int_t^\infty f_{T_1}(x)\,dx}{\tau_1}, f_{\hat{T}_0}(t) = \frac{\int_t^\infty f_{T_0}(x)\,dx}{\tau_0}. \tag{20}$$

The average forward recurrence time for ON and OFF periods of the slots with PU activity being changed are therefore calculated as

$$\mu_{\hat{T}_i} = \mathrm{E}\left[\hat{T}_i \mid \hat{T}_i < \tau_s\right] = \frac{\int_0^{T_s} t f_{\hat{T}_i}(t)\,dt}{F_{\hat{T}_i}(\tau_s)} = \frac{\int_0^{T_s} t\left[\int_t^\infty f_{T_i}(x)\,dx\right]dt}{\int_0^{T_s}\left[\int_t^\infty f_{T_i}(x)\,dx\right]dt}, \tag{21}$$

where $F(\cdot)$ denotes the cumulative distribution function (CDF).

Now, assuming that PU status changes after $\mu_{\hat{T}_i}$ seconds from the start of the frame. This is a reasonable assumption, as these slots rarely happen. While working in mode $j$, $j \in \{ts, so\}$, the energy received at $i^{\text{th}}$ SU when PU status changes from ON to OFF, $M_i^j \mid H_1 \rightarrow H_0$, and OFF to ON, $M_i^j \mid H_0 \rightarrow H_1$, can then be expressed as

$$M_i^j \mid H_1 \rightarrow H_0 = \frac{1}{f_s \tau_s}\left[\sum_{n=1}^{f_s \mu_{\hat{T}_1}}\left|\left[y_i^j(n) \mid H_1\right]\right|^2 + \sum_{n=f_s \mu_{\hat{T}_1}+1}^{f_s \tau_s}\left|\left[y_i^j(n) \mid H_0\right]\right|^2\right], \tag{22}$$

$$M_i^j \mid H_0 \rightarrow H_1 = \frac{1}{f_s \tau_s}\left[\sum_{n=1}^{f_s \mu_{\hat{T}_0}}\left|\left[y_i^j(n) \mid H_0\right]\right|^2 + \sum_{n=f_s \mu_{\hat{T}_0}+1}^{f_s \tau_s}\left|\left[y_i^j(n) \mid H_1\right]\right|^2\right]. \tag{23}$$

Using Central Limit Theorem, Levy-Cramer Theorem, Propositions 1 and 2, the results in (16–18), we then have:

$$\mathrm{E}\left[M_i^j \mid H_k \rightarrow H_{1-k}\right] = \frac{1}{\tau_s}\left\{\mu_{\hat{T}_k}\mathrm{E}\left[M_i^j \mid H_k\right] + \left(\tau_s - \mu_{\hat{T}_k}\right)\mathrm{E}\left[M_i^j \mid H_{1-k}\right]\right\}, \tag{24}$$

$$\mathrm{Var}\left[M_i^j \mid H_k \rightarrow H_{1-k}\right] = \frac{1}{\tau_s}\left\{\mu_{\hat{T}_k}\mathrm{Var}\left[M_i^j \mid H_k\right] + \left(\tau_s - \mu_{\hat{T}_k}\right)\mathrm{Var}\left[M_i^j \mid H_{1-k}\right]\right\}, \tag{25}$$

where $k = 0, 1$. That leads to the sensing metrics of $i^{\text{th}}$ SU working in mode $j$ of the slots that PU activity changes as:

$${}_iP_f^{jc} = Q\left(\frac{\epsilon_i^{jc} - \mathrm{E}\left[M_i^j \mid H_1 \rightarrow H_0\right]}{\sqrt{\mathrm{Var}\left[M_i^j \mid H_1 \rightarrow H_0\right]}}\right), \ {}_iP_m^{jc} = 1 - Q\left(\frac{\epsilon_i^{jc} - \mathrm{E}\left[M_i^j \mid H_0 \rightarrow H_1\right]}{\sqrt{\mathrm{Var}\left[M_i^j \mid H_0 \rightarrow H_1\right]}}\right). \tag{26}$$

Note that we use the sub-index $c$ to refer to the change of PU status.

## 3.2   Global (Cooperative) Sensing Performance

In this subsection, the focus is on the global sensing metrics. We shall first consider the hard decision based metrics before examining the soft decision ones.

**Hard Decision.** As we mentioned before, the global decision rule is implemented as $k$ out of $n$ rule. This rule includes simpler methods such as OR, AND and Majority rules as specific cases.

Let the set $\mathcal{S} = \{1, 2, 3, \ldots N\}$ represent the SUs. Also let $\mathcal{P}_k(\mathcal{S})$ be the set containing all subsets of $\mathcal{S}$ having $k$ or more elements. By assuming that all decisions are independent, the global false alarm and miss detection probabilities based on the $k$ out of $n$ rule are

$$P_f^j = \sum_{\mathcal{A} \in \mathcal{P}_k(\mathcal{S})} \prod_{i \in \mathcal{A}} {}_i P_f^j \prod_{i \in \bar{\mathcal{A}}} \left(1 - {}_i P_f^j\right), \tag{27}$$

and

$$P_m^j = 1 - \sum_{\mathcal{A} \in \mathcal{P}_k(\mathcal{S})} \prod_{i \in \mathcal{A}} \left(1 - {}_i P_m^j\right) \prod_{i \in \bar{\mathcal{A}}} {}_i P_m^j, \tag{28}$$

where $j \in \{ts, so, ts_c, so_c\}$ and $\bar{\mathcal{A}}$ is the complement of $\mathcal{A}$. Now, let consider the three special cases of OR, AND and Majority rules.

*OR Rule.* The SBS decides that PU is active if one or more SUs determine that PU is busy ($k = 1$).

$$P_f^j = 1 - \prod_{i=1}^{N} \left(1 - {}_i P_f^j\right) \quad \text{and} \quad P_m^j = \prod_{i=1}^{N} {}_i P_m^j. \tag{29}$$

*AND Rule.* The SBS decides that PU is active if all SUs sense the channel busy ($k = N$).

$$P_f^j = \prod_{i=1}^{N} {}_i P_f^j \quad \text{and} \quad P_m^j = 1 - \prod_{i=1}^{N} \left(1 - {}_i P_m^j\right). \tag{30}$$

*Majority Rule.* If more than half of SUs detect PU activity, the SBS decides that PU is active. So, the probabilities of false alarm and miss detection for majority rule can be obtained from (27) and (28) by setting $k = \left\lceil \frac{N}{2} \right\rceil$.

**Soft Decision.** For soft decision, the SBS decides the vacancy of the channel based on the following metric $M^j = \sum_{i=1}^{N} M_i^j$, $j \in \{ts, so\}$. Since $M_i^j$ is Gaussian, the mean and variance of $M^j$ under different hypothesis settings are

$$\mathrm{E}\left[M^j \mid \mathcal{H}\right] = \sum_{i=1}^{N} \mathrm{E}\left[M_i^j \mid \mathcal{H}\right], \mathrm{Var}\left[M^j \mid \mathcal{H}\right] = \sum_{i=1}^{N} \mathrm{Var}\left[M_i^j \mid \mathcal{H}\right], \tag{31}$$

for $j \in \{ts, so\}$ and $\mathcal{H} \in \{H_0, H_1, H_1 \rightarrow H_0, H_0 \rightarrow H_1\}$. As a result, $P_f$ and $P_m$ under the soft decision based method are calculated as

$$P_f^j = Q\left(\frac{\epsilon^j - \mathrm{E}\left[M^j \mid H_0\right]}{\sqrt{\mathrm{Var}\left[M^j \mid H_0\right]}}\right), \quad P_f^{j_c} = Q\left(\frac{\epsilon^j - \mathrm{E}\left[M^j \mid H_1 \rightarrow H_0\right]}{\sqrt{\mathrm{Var}\left[M^j \mid H_1 \rightarrow H_0\right]}}\right), \quad (32)$$

$$P_m^j = 1 - Q\left(\frac{\epsilon^j - \mathrm{E}\left[M^j \mid H_1\right]}{\sqrt{\mathrm{Var}\left[M^j \mid H_1\right]}}\right), \quad P_m^{j_c} = 1 - Q\left(\frac{\epsilon^j - \mathrm{E}\left[M^j \mid H_0 \rightarrow H_1\right]}{\sqrt{\mathrm{Var}\left[M^j \mid H_0 \rightarrow H_1\right]}}\right). \quad (33)$$

## 4   Rate Region and Achievable Rates

Given that the random variables $\alpha$ and $\beta$ and the sensing perfomance metrics have been fully characterized in the previous section, we will analyze the rate region and the achievable rate of each SU under NOMA with SIC in this section. To simplify the notations, hereafter, the use of $\boldsymbol{x} = x_1 + i x_2$ and $\boldsymbol{x} = [x_1, x_2]$ to indicate a 2-D vector is interchangeable.

### 4.1   Rate Region

The main results regarding the rate region are stated in the following proposition.

**Proposition 3.** *The convex hull of all $\{R_j\}_{j=1}^N$ satisfying*

$$R_j \leq P\left(\beta = 1\right)\left\{E_{\boldsymbol{h}_{jr}}\left[\Gamma_G\left(\left|h_{jr}\right|^2 \sigma_j^2\right)\right] - \Gamma_G\left(0\right)\right\}, \quad (34)$$

$$\sum_{j=1}^N R_j \leq P\left(\beta = 1\right)\left\{E_{\vec{\boldsymbol{h}}_r}\left[\Gamma_G\left(\sum_{j=1}^N \left|h_{jr}\right|^2 \sigma_j^2\right)\right] - \Gamma_G\left(0\right)\right\}, \quad (35)$$

*is an achievable rate region, where*

$$\Gamma_G\left(v\right) = -\log\left(\sum_{i=1}^{p+1} \frac{\epsilon_{z,i}}{\pi\left(\sigma_{z,i}^2 + v\right)}\right) + \frac{\left(\sum_{i=1}^{p+1} \frac{\epsilon_{z,i}}{2}\left(\sigma_{z,i}^2 + v\right)\right)\left(\sum_{i=1}^{p+1} \frac{\epsilon_{z,i}}{\pi\left(\sigma_{z,i}^2 + v\right)^2}\right)}{\sum_{i=1}^{p+1} \frac{\epsilon_{z,i}}{\pi\left(\sigma_{z,i}^2 + v\right)}}, \quad (36)$$

*and $\vec{\boldsymbol{h}}_r = [\boldsymbol{h}_{1r}, \boldsymbol{h}_{2r}, \cdots, \boldsymbol{h}_{Nr}]$.*

*Proof.* Let's first write the achievable rates in terms of mutual information between $\boldsymbol{y}_r$ and the user input signals as:

$$R_j \leq P\left(\beta = 1\right) E_{\vec{\boldsymbol{h}}_r}\left[I\left(\boldsymbol{x}_j; \boldsymbol{y}_r^{\beta} \mid \{\boldsymbol{x}_k\}_{k=1, k \neq j}^N, \vec{\boldsymbol{h}}_r\right)\right], \quad (37)$$

and

$$\sum_{j=1}^{N} R_j \leq P\left(\beta = 1\right) \mathrm{E}_{\vec{h}_r}\left[I\left(\{\boldsymbol{x}_k\}_{k=1}^{N}; \boldsymbol{y}_r^{\beta} \mid \vec{h}_r\right)\right]. \tag{38}$$

We then expand $I\left(\boldsymbol{x}_j; \boldsymbol{y}_r^{\beta} \mid \{\boldsymbol{x}_k\}_{k=1, k\neq j}^{N}, \vec{h}_r\right)$ as:

$$\mathrm{H}\left(\boldsymbol{y}_r^{\beta} \mid \{\boldsymbol{x}_k\}_{k=1, k\neq j}^{N}, \vec{h}_r\right) - \mathrm{H}\left(\boldsymbol{y}_r^{\beta} \mid \{\boldsymbol{x}_k\}_{k=1}^{N}, \vec{h}_r\right) = \mathrm{H}\left(\boldsymbol{h}_{jr}\boldsymbol{x}_j + \boldsymbol{z}_\beta \mid \boldsymbol{h}_{jr}\right) - \mathrm{H}\left(\boldsymbol{z}_\beta\right). \tag{39}$$

It is clear that by calculating $\mathrm{H}\left(\boldsymbol{h}_{jr}\boldsymbol{x}_j + \boldsymbol{z}_\beta \mid \boldsymbol{h}_{jr}\right)$ and setting $\boldsymbol{h}_{jr} = 0$, $\mathrm{H}\left(\boldsymbol{z}_\beta\right)$ can be obtained. In particular, we know that the PDF of $\boldsymbol{r}_j = \boldsymbol{h}_{jr}\boldsymbol{x}_j + \boldsymbol{z}_\beta$ given $\boldsymbol{h}_{jr}$ is given as $f_{R_j|H_{jr}}\left(\boldsymbol{y}\right) = \sum_{i=1}^{p+1} \epsilon_{z,i}\mathcal{CN}(\boldsymbol{y}, 0, \sigma_{z,i}^2 + |\boldsymbol{h}_{jr}|^2 \sigma_j^2)$.. Hence,

$$\mathrm{H}\left(\boldsymbol{h}_{jr}\boldsymbol{x}_j + \boldsymbol{z}_\beta \mid \boldsymbol{h}_{jr}\right) = -\sum_{i=1}^{p+1} \int_{\mathbb{R}} \epsilon_{z,i}\mathcal{CN}(\boldsymbol{y}, 0, \sigma_{z,i}^2 + |\boldsymbol{h}_{jr}|^2 \sigma_j^2) \log\left(f_{R_j|H_{jr}}\left(\boldsymbol{y}\right)\right) d\boldsymbol{y}. \tag{40}$$

There is no closed form solution of (40) due to the logarithm of a sum of Gaussian distributions [5,6]. In the following, our approach is to find an approximation achieving an arbitrary level of accuracy for the entropy of GM distribution using Taylor series expansion. Specifically, we use Taylor series to expand $\log\left(f_{R_j|H_{jr}}\left(\boldsymbol{y}\right)\right)$ over the mean vector of each Gaussian component which is 0 in this case. Thus, we have

$$\mathrm{H}\left(\boldsymbol{h}_{jr}\boldsymbol{x}_j + \boldsymbol{z}_\beta \mid \boldsymbol{h}_{jr}\right) =$$
$$-\sum_{i=1}^{p+1} \int_{\mathbb{R}} \epsilon_{z,i}\mathcal{CN}(\boldsymbol{y}, 0, \sigma_{z,i}^2 + |\boldsymbol{h}_{jr}|^2 \sigma_j^2) \sum_{|\alpha|\leq d} \frac{D^\alpha \log\left(f_{R_j|H_{jr}}\left(\boldsymbol{y}\right)\right)|_{\boldsymbol{y}=0}}{\alpha!} \boldsymbol{y}^\alpha d\boldsymbol{y}, \tag{41}$$

where $|\alpha| = \alpha_1 + \alpha_2$, $\alpha! = \alpha_1!\alpha_2!$, $\boldsymbol{y}^\alpha = y_1^{\alpha_1}y_2^{\alpha_2}$, and $D^\alpha f\left(\boldsymbol{y}\right) = \frac{\partial^{|\alpha|} f(\boldsymbol{y})}{\partial y_1^{\alpha_1} \partial y_2^{\alpha_2}}$. Moreover, $d$ is chosen based on the level of accuracy. It then follows that

$$\mathrm{H}\left(\boldsymbol{h}_{jr}\boldsymbol{x}_i + \boldsymbol{z}_\beta \mid \boldsymbol{h}_{jr}\right) = -\sum_{i=1}^{p+1} \sum_{\substack{|\alpha|\leq d \\ \alpha_1, \alpha_2 \in \mathcal{A}_e}}$$
$$\epsilon_{z,i} \frac{D^\alpha \log\left(f_{R_j|H_{jr}}\left(\boldsymbol{y}\right)\right)|_{\boldsymbol{y}=0}}{\alpha!} \left(\frac{\sigma_{z,i}^2 + |\boldsymbol{h}_{jr}|^2 \sigma_j^2}{2}\right)^{|\alpha|/2} (\alpha_1 - 1)!! (\alpha_2 - 1)!!, \tag{42}$$

where $\mathcal{A}_e$ denotes the set of even natural numbers and $a!! = a(a-2)$ $(a-4)\cdots 1$. As we will demonstrate shortly, the use of $d = 3$ can result in a highly accurate approximation. In this case, we have $\mathrm{H}\left(\boldsymbol{h}_{jr}\boldsymbol{x}_i + \boldsymbol{z}_\beta \mid \boldsymbol{h}_{jr}\right)$ as

$$- \log \left( f_{R_j | H_{jr}} \left( \boldsymbol{y} \right) \right) |_{y=0} - \sum_{i=1}^{p+1} \epsilon_{z,i} \left[ \frac{\partial^2 \log \left( f_{R_j | H_{jr}} \left( \boldsymbol{y} \right) \right)}{\partial y_1^2} \right] \Bigg|_{y=0} \frac{\sigma_{z,i}^2 + |h_{jr}|^2 \sigma_j^2}{2}.$$

$$(43)$$

Here, we have used the fact that $f_{R_j | H_{jr}} \left( \boldsymbol{y} \right)$ is symmetric with respect to $y_1$ and $y_2$, i.e., $\frac{\partial^2 \log \left( f_{R_j | H_{jr}} \left( \boldsymbol{y} \right) \right)}{\partial y_1^2} \Big|_{y=0} = \frac{\partial^2 \log \left( f_{R_j | H_{jr}} \left( \boldsymbol{y} \right) \right)}{\partial y_2^2} \Big|_{y=0}$. After some simple manipulations, we obtain

$$R_j \leq P \left( \beta = 1 \right) \left\{ \mathrm{E}_{h_{jr}} \left[ \Gamma_G \left( |h_{jr}|^2 \sigma_j^2 \right) \right] - \Gamma_G \left( 0 \right) \right\}, \qquad (44)$$

where

$$\Gamma_G \left( v \right) = - \log \left( \sum_{i=1}^{p+1} \frac{\epsilon_{z,i}}{\pi \left( \sigma_{z,i}^2 + v \right)} \right) + \frac{\left( \sum_{i=1}^{p+1} \frac{\epsilon_{z,i}}{2} \left( \sigma_{z,i}^2 + v \right) \right) \left( \sum_{i=1}^{p+1} \frac{\epsilon_{z,i}}{\pi \left( \sigma_{z,i}^2 + v \right)^2} \right)}{\sum_{i=1}^{p+1} \frac{\epsilon_{z,i}}{\pi \left( \sigma_{z,i}^2 + v \right)}}.$$

$$(45)$$

Finally, the sum-rate can be calculated using the following PDF of $y_r^\beta$

$$f_{Y_r | \vec{H}_r} \left( \boldsymbol{y} \right) = \sum_{i=1}^{p+1} \epsilon_{z,i} \mathcal{CN} (\boldsymbol{y}, 0, \sigma_{z,i}^2 + \sum_{j=1}^{N} |h_{jr}|^2 \sigma_j^2). \qquad (46)$$

Then following the same procedure in obtaining (44) earlier, we have

$$\sum_{j=1}^{N} R_j \leq P \left( \beta = 1 \right) \left\{ \mathrm{E}_{\vec{h}_r} \left[ \Gamma_G \left( \sum_{j=1}^{N} |h_{jr}|^2 \sigma_j^2 \right) \right] - \Gamma_G \left( 0 \right) \right\}. \qquad (47)$$

### 4.2   Achievable Rates of SUs

Based on the SIC NOMA described earlier, the received signal to decode the information of the $j^{\text{th}}$ user under SIC is given $y_{r,j}^\beta = \sum_{k=j}^{N} h_{kr} x_k + z_\beta$. By treating the signal of $k^{\text{th}}$ user with $k > j$ as noise for user $j$, we can write the achievable rate of $j^{\text{th}}$ user as

$$R_j = P \left( \beta = 1 \right) \mathrm{E}_{\vec{h}_r} \left[ I \left( x_j ; y_{r,j}^\beta \mid \vec{h}_r \right) \right]$$

$$= P \left( \beta = 1 \right) \mathrm{E}_{\vec{h}_r} \left[ \mathrm{H} \left( \sum_{k=j}^{N} h_{kr} x_k + z_\beta \mid \vec{h}_r \right) - \mathrm{H} \left( \sum_{k=j+1}^{N} h_{kr} x_k + z_\beta \mid \vec{h}_r \right) \right].$$

$$(48)$$

Using the same procedure that we found $\mathrm{H} \left( y_r^\beta \mid \vec{h}_r \right)$ in (47), we obtain

$$\mathrm{H} \left( \sum_{k=j}^{N} h_{kr} x_k + z_\beta \mid \vec{h}_r \right) = \Gamma_G \left( \sum_{k=j}^{N} |h_{kr}|^2 \sigma_j^2 \right). \qquad (49)$$

Note that $\text{H} \left( \sum_{k=j+1}^{N} \boldsymbol{h}_{jr} \boldsymbol{x}_j + \boldsymbol{z}_\beta \mid \vec{\boldsymbol{h}}_r \right)$ can be calculated using Taylor expansion. Finally, we can calculate the achievable rate $R_j$ as

$$R_j = P\left(\beta = 1\right) \text{E}_{\vec{\boldsymbol{h}}_r} \left[ \Gamma_G \left( \sum_{k=j}^{N} |\boldsymbol{h}_{kr}|^2 \sigma_k^2 \right) - \Gamma_G \left( \sum_{k=j+1}^{N} |\boldsymbol{h}_{kr}|^2 \sigma_k^2 \right) \right]. \quad (50)$$

## 5 Numerical Result

In this section, numerical results are provided to support our previous analysis and derivations. We use the sampling frequency of 1 MHz and the duration of each SU slot is assumed to be 1 ms. Moreover, $T_1$ and $T_0$ are modeled as exponential random variables with mean 100 ms. $\boldsymbol{u}$, $\boldsymbol{w}$ and fading coefficients are modeled as circularly symmetric Gaussian random variables with mean zero and variances per dimension 0.2, 0.3 and 1, respectively. For simplicity, we consider a 2-user channel. However, we would like to note that our results apply to any number of users. For the 2-user case, we assume both users use the same power $\sigma$. The sensing is performed using the soft decision method. While our analysis holds for any input signaling scheme, we will focus Gaussian input signals. In all simulations, SNR is defined as SNR $= \frac{\sigma^2}{\sigma_u^2}$.

In Fig. 2, we plot the rate regions of a two-user secondary network at SNR = 5 dB. Note that the rate region is calculated from (37) and (38) using Taylor expansion with $k = 3$. For comparison, the rate regions obtained by numerical integration are also provided. It can be seen from Fig. 2 that $k = 3$ provides accurate results that are very close to the numerical calculations. Note that the symmetry of the rate region comes from the fact that both users have the same power.

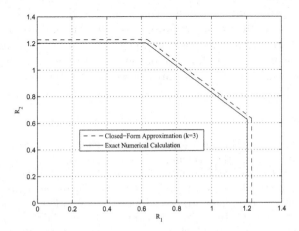

**Fig. 2.** Rate region of a 2-user channel using Gaussian input signals.

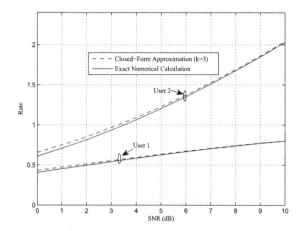

**Fig. 3.** The achievable rates with Gaussian signals.

In Fig. 3, the achievable rates versus SNR with SIC decoding for the two users are presented. Again, the accuracy of the closed-form approximations is clearly observed. Note that user 1 achieves a lower rate than user 2. This is because user 1 is assumed to be the first user to be detected. The fairness can certainly be improved by allocating power proportionally to the users.

## 6    Conclusion

This paper investigated the rate region and the achievable rates of a NOMA FD CR channel. Under the assumption of imperfect SIS and spectrum sensing, the sensing performance was first analyzed. Our method relied on a Markov chain model to combine the sensing results under different sensing scenarios and obtain the probability of collision between the SUs and PU. Due to the difficulty in obtaining the explicit expressions of the channel capacity and mutual information in GM, we then propose new closed-form approximations of the rate region and the achievable rate for each of the users with arbitrarily small errors. The rate region and the achievable rates were then established.

## References

1. Afifi, W., Krunz, M.: Incorporating self-interference suppression for full-duplex operation in opportunistic spectrum access systems. IEEE Trans. Wireless Commun. **14**(4), 2180–2191 (2015). https://doi.org/10.1109/TWC.2014.2382124
2. Ali, M.S., Tabassum, H., Hossain, E.: Dynamic user clustering and power allocation for uplink and downlink non-orthogonal multiple access (NOMA) systems. IEEE Access **4**, 6325–6343 (2016). https://doi.org/10.1109/ACCESS.2016.2604821
3. Di, B., Song, L., Li, Y.: Sub-channel assignment, power allocation, and user scheduling for non-orthogonal multiple access networks. IEEE Trans. Wireless Commun. **15**(11), 7686–7698 (2016). https://doi.org/10.1109/TWC.2016.2606100

4. Dinc, T., Chakrabarti, A., Krishnaswamy, H.: A 60 GHz CMOS full-duplex transceiver and link with polarization-based antenna and RF cancellation. IEEE J. Solid-State Circuits **51**(5), 1125–1140 (2016)

5. Durrieu, J.L., Thiran, J.P., Kelly, F.: Lower and upper bounds for approximation of the Kullback-Leibler divergence between Gaussian mixture models. In: ICASSP, IEEE International Conference on Acoustics, Speech and Signal Processing - Proceedings (Mc), pp. 4833–4836 (2012). https://doi.org/10.1109/ICASSP. 2012.6289001

6. Hershey, J.R., Olsen, P.A.: Approximating the Kullback-Leibler divergence between Gaussian mixture models. Acoust. Speech Signal Process. **4**(6), IV–317 (2007)

7. Hossain, E., Niyato, D., Han, Z.: Dynamic Spectrum Access and Management in Cognitive Radio Networks. Cambridge University Press, Cambridge (2009)

8. Kim, D., Lee, H., Hong, D.: A survey of in-band full-duplex transmission: from the perspective of PHY and MAC layers. IEEE Commun. Surv. Tutor. **17**(4), 2017–2046 (2015)

9. Liao, Y., Wang, T., Song, L., Han, Z.: Listen-and-talk: protocol design and analysis for full-duplex cognitive radio networks. IEEE Trans. Veh. Technol. **66**(1), 656–667 (2016). https://doi.org/10.1109/TVT.2016.2535483

10. Ozcan, G., Gursoy, M.C., Gezici, S.: Error rate analysis of cognitive radio transmissions with imperfect channel sensing. IEEE Trans. Wireless Commun. **13**(3), 1642–1655 (2014)

11. Ozcan, G., Gursoy, M.C., Gezici, S.: Error rate analysis of cognitive radio transmissions with imperfect channel sensing. IEEE Trans. Wireless Commun. **13**, 1642–1655 (2014). http://arxiv.org/abs/1310.1822

12. Ranjbar, M., Tran, N.H., Nguyen, T., Gursoy, M.C.: Capacity-achieving signals for point-to-point and multiple-access channels under non-Gaussian noise and peak power constraint. IEEE Access **6**, 30977–30989 (2018)

13. Ranjbar, M., Nguyen, H.L., Tran, N.H., Karacolak, T., Sastry, S., Nguyen, L.D.: Energy efficiency of full-duplex cognitive radio in low-power regimes under imperfect spectrum sensing. Mob. Netw. Appl. **26**(4), 1750–1764 (2021). https://doi. org/10.1007/s11036-021-01755-z

14. Vu, H.V., Tran, N.H., Gursoy, M.C., Le-Ngoc, T., Hariharan, S.: Capacity-achieving input distributions of additive quadrature Gaussian mixture noise channels. IEEE Trans. Commun. **63**(10), 3607–3620 (2015)

15. Yang, Z., Ding, Z., Fan, P., Al-Dhahir, N.: The impact of power allocation on cooperative non-orthogonal multiple access networks with SWIPT. IEEE Trans. Wireless Commun. **16**(7), 4332–4343 (2017). https://doi.org/10.1109/TWC.2017. 2697380

# Reconfigurable Intelligent Surfaces for Downlink Cellular Networks

Phuc Quang Truong$^{(\boxtimes)}$ and Ca Phan Van

Ho Chi Minh City University of Technology and Education,
Ho Chi Minh City, Vietnam
{phuctq,capv}@hcmute.edu.vn

**Abstract.** In this work, we propose a joint optimization of power allocation and phase shift for downlink RIS-aided cellular networks. In particular, the total network throughput was maximized under power consumption and QoS constraints. To tackle this problem, we consider power allocation procedure to solve the convex problem of power control coefficients optimization and Block Coordinate Descent (BCD)-based procedure to solve non-convex problem of RIS phase shift optimization. The numerical results are provided to illustrate the effectiveness of the proposed approach in terms of enhancing the coverage and the total network throughput.

**Keywords:** Reconfigurable intelligent surfaces · Power allocation · Phase shift optimization · Cellular network · Convex optimization

## 1 Introduction

Reconfigurable Intelligent Surfaces (RISs) are man-made panels that can be capable of configuring the properties of impinging electromagnetic waves based on Snell's law. RIS is the key technology enabling the 6th generation (6G) in the near future. With highlight features, RISs can work without energy source in case of reflecting incident signal only. Different from relaying or decoding and forwarding, RISs can response full-band and nearly not be affected by receiver noise [1]. Due to the potential advantages, RISs are not only the conceptual research but also they are deployed in practical scenarios [2]. The numerical results in [3] prove that RIS-aided wireless communication networks can achieve higher performance than traditional wireless networks.

In [4], the authors assumed the RIS-aided single cell wireless system with multi antennas at the access point (AP) and single antenna at K users. The RIS is equipped with N reflected elements which are controlled by the RIS-controller to switch either receiving mode or reflecting mode. In this case, the total transmit power at the AP is minimized by combining optimizing both active beamforming at the AP and passive beamforming with the user signal-to-interference-plus-noise ratio (SINR) constraints. To tackle this problem, both the semidefinite

Supported by Ho Chi Minh City University of Technology and Education, Vietnam.

N.-S. Vo et al. (Eds.): INISCOM 2022, LNICST 444, pp. 20–32, 2022.
https://doi.org/10.1007/978-3-031-08878-0_2

relaxation (SDR) and alternating optimization algorithms were applied. On the other hand, RIS-aided the wireless network including a base station (BS) with M antennas and K single-antenna users worked in two scenarios: multicasting and multi-user downlink communication. The authors proposed alternating direction method of multipliers (ADMM) algorithm to maximize the smallest signal-to-noise ratio (SNR) in passive beamforming problem [5].

In [6], the authors developed algorithm of low computational complexity to maximize the worst rate subject to the transmit power constraints by jointly designing the reflecting coefficient of RISs and transmit beamformers. In particular, the network of a multiple antenna AP transmitting to multiple single-antenna users, under both proper Gaussian signaling and improper Gaussian signaling with RIS-aided communication in case of without direct link from AP to users.

Recently, RIS-assisted unmanned aerial vehicle (UAV) communication becomes the promising technique to enhance the quality of communication. The scenario in [7] investigated a communication system consisting of a UAV, a ground user, and a RIS on building. Jointly UAV trajectory and passive beamforming at RIS were applied to maximize the average achievable rate of system. Furthermore, the application of UAV becomes more widen in numerous fields such as surveillance, disaster rescue mission, and geography exploration. Hence, the performance network and the quality of service need to enhance and ensure the connection between UAVs and users. In these cases, RIS-assisted multi-UAV networks plays an important role in supporting the connection from UAVs to users when the link is blocked by obstacles. In [8], deep reinforcement learning (DRL) approach was investigated to solve the continuous optimization problem that aimed to maximize the energy efficiency of UAVs networks. Similarly, DRL approach was proposed to maximize the network sum-rate in device-to-device (D2D) communications supported by RIS in [9].

Due to the significant benefits of both spectral efficiency and energy efficiency, non-orthogonal multiple access (NOMA) is the potential technique for future communication networks such as the beyond fifth-generation (B5G), 6G [10]. Thus, the combination of NOMA and RIS will help to enhance the coverage and energy efficiency. Particularly, an RIS-NOMA multi-input-single-output (MISO) system was investigated in [11] to maximize the sum-rate and minimize the total power consumption. To tackle this, the alternating successive convex approximation (SCA) and SDR based algorithms were proposed to solve the jointly transmit beamforming at the BS and passive beamforming at the RIS problems. In [12], the authors assumed that RIS-assisted the wireless power communication network to ensure the connection between a single-antenna BS and single-antenna users. To maximizing the throughput of the network, the authors combined optimizing the reflect beamforming of RIS and the time allocation for power transfer and information transmission BS and users in case of NOMA and time division multiple access (TDMA).

The multi RIS-assisted wireless network including a multi antennas AP and two groups of single antenna users was investigated in [13]. The authors aimed to minimize the transmit power at AP with the individual SINR constraint on information and energy harvesting at energy users.

In [14–16], the authors aimed to maximize the weighted sum rate at all users and the weighted sum power in a RIS-assisted wireless communication system via jointly optimizing the active beamforming at the transmitter and the reflect phase shift at the RISs. Nevertheless, the formulated problems are non-convex. Hence, in [16] the authors based on the fractional programming method to optimize active beamforming at BS and three low-complexity algorithms to solve the passive beamforming problem. Meanwhile, in [14] the authors utilized the sequential rank-one constraint relaxation approach to tackle the passive beamforming problem.

The main contributions of this work focus on extending coverage of the cellular networks by proposing the RIS technology to enhance the reliable of wireless networks, meanwhile the number of users increases rapidly. In particular, to tackle this problem, the joint power allocation at BS and phase shift optimization has been solved by both power allocation procedure in Algorithm 1 and BCD-based procedure in Algorithm 2.

The rest of the paper is organized as follows. We explain the system model of the proposed RIS-assisted downlink cellular network in Sect. 2. Meanwhile, Sect. 3 and Sect. 4 develop the problem statement, methodology and the joint power allocation and phase shift optimization, respectively. The simulation results are discussed in Sect. 5. Finally, the conclusion of the paper is provided in Sect. 6.

## 2   System Model

### 2.1   Network Model

In cellular networks, many user equipments (UEs) receive poor signal's quality from the BS because of shadowing and blocking effect. As illustrated in Fig. 1, we study the issue of throughput enhancement for downlink cellular networks with the assistance of RISs panels. Specifically, we assume that the UEs are devided into $M$ groups. And they are uniform randomly distributed in the coverage area. The set of UEs and the group of users are denoted as $\mathcal{K} = \{1, ..., K\}$ and $\mathcal{M} = \{1, ..., M\}$, respectively. The UEs are equipped with a single antenna.

The RISs are installed on the top of buildings, to work as small cell BS where each RIS is consisted of $N$ elements. The $m$-th group can cover a limited number of UEs, $\mathcal{K}_m = \{1, ..., K_m\}$ for $m \in \mathcal{M}$. The $(m, k)$-th UE demonstrates the $k$-th user in the $m$-th group.

The aim of this paper is to maximize the total throughput of cellular networks by exploiting the RIS technology to extend the coverage of wireless network and to serve many UEs with high QoS.

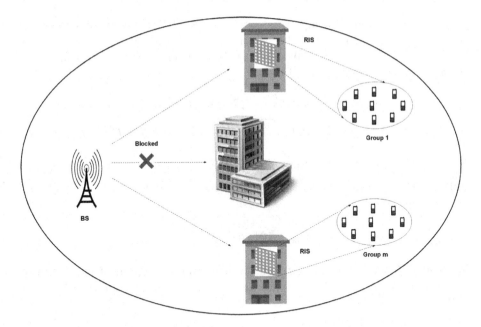

**Fig. 1.** An illustration of downlink RIS-aided cellular communications.

## 2.2 RIS-Aided Communication Models

To consider the assistance of RIS in communication models, we investigate the coordinate of the BS, the RISs and of all UEs as $(x_0, y_0, H_0)$, $(x_m, y_m, H_m)$, $m \in \mathcal{M}$ and $(x_k, y_k, 0)$, $k \in \mathcal{K}$, where $H_0$ and $H_m$ denote the height of the BS and the RIS altitude, respectively.

We focus on enhancing the links between the BS and the RISs. Thus, the path loss of the link from the BS to the $m$-th RIS follows the free-space path loss, i.e., line of sight (LoS), model as [17,18]

$$\beta_{0,m} = \beta_0 R_{0,m}^{-2}, \ m = 1, ..., M, \tag{1}$$

where we denote $\beta_0$ as the channel gain at reference position. In addition, $R_{0,m}$ is the distance between the BS and the $m$-th RIS, which is give by

$$R_{0,m} = \sqrt{d_{0,m}^2 + (H_0 - H_m)^2}, \tag{2}$$

As mention previous, we assign $d_{0,m} = \sqrt{(x_0 - x_m)^2 + (y_0 - y_m)^2}$.

In contrast, a more complicated non-LoS (NLoS) model is applied to the channel from the RIS to the UEs, which is usually affected by shadowing and blockage geometry. Thus, the path loss of the channel from the $m$-th RIS to the $(m, k)$-th UE is formulated as [19]

$$\beta_{m,k} = PL_{m,k} + \eta^{LoS} P_{m,k}^{LoS} + \eta^{NLoS} P_{m,k}^{NLoS}$$

$$= 10\alpha \log \left( \sqrt{d_{m,k}^2 + H_{U,m}^2} \right) + AP_{m,k}^{LoS} + B, \tag{3}$$

where $\eta^{LoS}$ and $\eta^{NLoS}$ are the average additional losses for LoS and NLoS, respectively, $A = \eta^{LoS} - \eta^{NLoS}$ and $B = 10\alpha \log(\frac{4\pi f_c R_{m,k}}{c}) + \eta^{NLoS}$. The distance path loss is given by

$$PL_{m,k} = 10 \log(\frac{4\pi f_c R_{m,k}}{c})^\alpha, \tag{4}$$

We denote $f_c$ and $c$ as carrier frequency in Hz and the speed of light in m/s, respectively. Where $\alpha \geq 2$ is the path loss exponent. The probability of LoS and NLoS is given by [20]

$$P_{m,k}^{LoS} = \cfrac{1}{1 + a \exp\left[-b\left(\arctan\left(\frac{H_{U,m}}{d_{m,k}}\right) - a\right)\right]}, \tag{5}$$

$$P_{m,k}^{NLoS} = 1 - P_{m,k}^{LoS}, \tag{6}$$

where both $a$ and $b$ are the constants of the environment.

Furthermore, we consider the effect of the phase shift matrix at the $m$-th RIS $\mathbf{\Phi}_m = diag[\phi_{1m}, \phi_{2m}, ..., \phi_{Nm}]$, here $\phi_{nm} = \alpha_{nm} e^{j\theta_{nm}}$ with $\alpha_{nm} \in [0, 1]$ and $\theta_{nm} \in [0, 2\pi]$ ($\forall n = 1, 2, ..., N$, $m \in \mathcal{M}$), that indicates the amplitude of the reflected signal and phase shift of the $n$-th reflecting element, respectively. We assign $\alpha_{nm} = 1$ because the reflecting element can not change the amplitude of reflecting signals [21]. Under this effect, the small scale fading coefficients, which are assumed as independent and identically distributed random variables with zero mean and unit variance, are used for the link from the BS to $m$-th RIS and the $m$-th RIS to the $(m, k)$-th UE, indicated by $\hat{h}_{0,m} \in \mathbb{C}^{N \times 1}$ and $\hat{h}_{m,k}^H \in \mathbb{C}^{1 \times N}$, respectively. The $H$ is the Hermitian conjugate operation.

Additionally, we denote $\mathbf{h}_{0,m} \in \mathbb{C}^{N \times 1}$ and $\mathbf{h}_{m,k}^H \in \mathbb{C}^{1 \times N}$ as the channel matrix between the BS and the $m$-th RIS and the $m$-th RIS to the $(m, k)$-th UE in the $m$-th group, respectively. Nevertheless, the cascaded channel matrix of the link between the BS and the $(m, k)$-th UE through the $m$-th RIS, $\mathbf{g}_{m,k} \in \mathbb{C}$, can be rewritten as [22]

$$\mathbf{g}_{m,k} = \mathbf{h}_{m,k}^H \mathbf{\Phi}_m \mathbf{h}_{0,m}, \tag{7}$$

where $\mathbf{h}_{0,m} = \sqrt{\beta_{0,m}} \hat{h}_{0,m}$ and $\mathbf{h}_{m,k}^H = \sqrt{\beta_{m,k}} \hat{h}_{m,k}^H$.

## 2.3  Transmission Schemes

As shown in Fig. 1, the BS transmits signal to its UEs with the reflection from RIS panel deployed on the top of buildings. With TDMA scheme, we have the signal at the $k$-th UE in the $m$-th group below

$$y_{m,k} = \sqrt{p_{m,k}}\mathbf{g}_{m,k}s_{m,k} + n_k, \tag{8}$$

where $p_{m,k}$ is the transmission power of the BS to the $(m,k)$-th UE; $s_{m,k}$ is information transmitted by the BS such that $||s_{m,k}||^2 \leq 1$; $n_k \sim \mathcal{CN}(0, \sigma_k^2)$ is the AWGN at the $(m,k)$-th UE.

Let $\boldsymbol{p}_0 = [\boldsymbol{p}_{0,m}]_{m=1}^M$, here $\boldsymbol{p}_{0,m} = [p_{m,k}]_{k=1}^{K_m}$, and $\boldsymbol{\Phi}_M = [\boldsymbol{\Phi}_m]_{m=1}^M$ denote the power control coefficients and the phase shifts of RISs, respectively, the received SNR at the $(m,k)$-th UE can be formulated as

$$\gamma_{m,k}\left(p_{m,k}, \boldsymbol{\Phi}_m\right) = \frac{p_{m,k}\left|\mathbf{g}_{m,k}\right|^2}{\sigma_k^2}. \tag{9}$$

## 2.4  Information Throughput

The information throughput of the $(m,k)$-th UE (in bps/Hz) can be expressed as

$$R_{m,k}\left(p_{m,k}, \boldsymbol{\Phi}_m\right) = \log_2\left(1 + \gamma_{m,k}\left(p_{m,k}, \boldsymbol{\Phi}_m\right)\right). \tag{10}$$

Hence, the total throughput of all the UEs in the network can be given by

$$R_{total}\left(\boldsymbol{p}_0, \boldsymbol{\Phi}_M\right) = \sum_{m=1}^M \sum_{k=1}^{K_m} R_{m,k}\left(p_{m,k}, \boldsymbol{\Phi}_m\right). \tag{11}$$

# 3  Problem Statement and Methodology

In this paper, we focus on maximizing the total throughput of downlink cellular networks. To tackle this problem, we jointly optimize $(\boldsymbol{p}_0)$ at the BS and $(\boldsymbol{\Phi}_M)$ of $M$ RISs given some power consumption and QoS constraints. The corresponding optimization problem is as follows:

$$\max_{\boldsymbol{p}_0, \boldsymbol{\Phi}_M} R_{total}\left(\boldsymbol{p}_0, \boldsymbol{\Phi}_M\right) \tag{12a}$$

$$\text{s.t.} \quad \sum_{m=1}^M \sum_{k=1}^{K_m} p_{m,k} \leq P_0^{\mathsf{max}}, m \in \mathcal{M}, \tag{12b}$$

$$R_{m,k}\left(p_{m,k}, \boldsymbol{\Phi}_m\right) \geq \bar{r}_{m,k}, \ m \in \mathcal{M}, \ k \in \mathcal{K}_m, \tag{12c}$$

$$0 \leq \theta_{nm} \leq 2\pi, \forall n = 1, 2, ..., N, \ m \in \mathcal{M}, \tag{12d}$$

where (12b) is used to limit the total power consumption of all RISs not greater than the maximum transmit power of the BS ($P_0^{\mathsf{max}}$). Meanwhile, (12c) is the QoS constraint at the $(m,k)$-th UE. And (12d) indicates the lower and upper bounds of the phase shifts when considering the $n$-th reflecting element of the $m$-th RIS.

# 4   Joint Power Allocation and Phase Shift Optimization

It is obvious that the problem (12) is non-convex with the non-convex functions of (12a) and (12c). Therefore, we iteratively optimize the power control coefficients of the BS and the phase shifts of RIS reflecting elements.

## 4.1   Power Control Coefficients Optimization

For any given $\boldsymbol{\Phi}_M$, (12) is equivalent to the following power control coefficients optimization problem

$$\max_{\boldsymbol{p}_0} R_{total}\left(\boldsymbol{p}_0\right) \tag{13a}$$

$$\text{s.t.}\quad (12\text{b}), (12\text{c}). \tag{13b}$$

To solve (13), we utilize the effective approximations and logarithm inequalities [23] based on the property of the convex function $f(z) = \log_2(1+\frac{1}{z}) \geq \hat{f}(z)$, where

$$\hat{f}(z) = \log_2\left(1 + \frac{1}{\bar{z}}\right) + \frac{1}{1+\bar{z}} - \frac{z}{(1+\bar{z})\bar{z}}, \tag{14}$$

$\forall z > 0, \bar{z} > 0$. Then, we can write

$$R_{m,k}\left(p_{m,k}\right) \geq \hat{R}_{m,k}^{(i)}\left(p_{m,k}\right), \ \forall k \in \mathcal{K}_m, \ \forall m \in \mathcal{M}, \tag{15}$$

where

$$z = \frac{\sigma_k^2}{p_{m,k}\left|\boldsymbol{g}_{m,k}\right|^2}, \ \bar{z} = z^{(i)} = \frac{\sigma_k^2}{p_{m,k}^{(i)}\left|\boldsymbol{g}_{m,k}\right|^2},$$

$$\hat{R}_{m,k}^{(i)}\left(p_{m,k}\right) = \log_2\left(1 + \frac{1}{\bar{z}}\right) + \frac{1}{1+\bar{z}} - \frac{z}{(1+\bar{z})\bar{z}}. \tag{16}$$

So far, (13) can be rewritten as (17) to yield the feasible points at the $i$-th iteration:

$$\max_{\boldsymbol{p}_0} \hat{R}_{total}^{(i)}\left(\boldsymbol{p}_0\right) \tag{17a}$$

$$\text{s.t.}\quad (12\text{b}), \tag{17b}$$

$$\hat{R}_{m,k}^{(i)}\left(\boldsymbol{p}_0\right) \geq \bar{r}_{m,k}, \ m \in \mathcal{M}, \ k \in \mathcal{K}_m, \tag{17c}$$

where $\hat{R}_{total}^{(\kappa)}\left(\boldsymbol{p}_0\right) = \sum_{m=1}^{M}\sum_{k=1}^{K_m} \hat{R}_{m,k}^{(\kappa)}\left(p_{m,k}\right)$.

Finally, we solve (17) by CVX tools [24] following the Algorithm 1. Particularly, we set up the values of $i = 0$, $\boldsymbol{\Phi}_M$, and $\varepsilon = 10^{-3}$. The number of iterations is $I_{max} = 20$. The output is the optimal power control coefficients $(\boldsymbol{p}_0^*)$.

---

**Algorithm 1.** Power allocation procedure

---

**Input:**
    $i = 0$, $\boldsymbol{\Phi}_M$, $\varepsilon = 10^{-3}$
    $I_{max} = 20$
  **while** (Divergence or $i \leqslant I_{max}$)
    Solve (17) for $(\boldsymbol{p}_0^{(i+1)})$ by CVX
    $i = i + 1$
  **end while**
  **Output:** $\boldsymbol{p}_0^*$

---

## 4.2 RIS Phase Shift Optimization

With the considering power control coefficients $\boldsymbol{p}_0$, the problem can be rewritten as

$$\max_{\boldsymbol{\Phi}_M} R_{total}\left(\boldsymbol{\Phi}_M\right) \tag{18a}$$

$$\text{s.t.} \quad (12c), (12d). \tag{18b}$$

Let $\boldsymbol{h}_{m,k}^H \boldsymbol{\Phi}_m \boldsymbol{h}_{0,m} = \psi_m^H \chi_{m,k}$ where $\psi_m = [\psi_m^1, ..., \psi_m^N]^H$ with $\psi_m^n = e^{j\theta_{nm}}$ ($\forall n = 1, 2, ..., N$), $\chi_{m,k} = diag(\boldsymbol{h}_{m,k}^H)\boldsymbol{h}_{0,m}$, and $a_k = P_0/\sigma_k^2$. With $|\psi_m^n|^2 = 1$, the constraint in (12d) becomes the unit-modulus constraint [4]. Then, the problem (18) is equivalently rewritten as

$$\max_{\psi_m, \, m \in \mathcal{M}} \sum_{m=1}^{M} \sum_{k=1}^{K_m} \log_2\left(1 + a_k \psi_m^H \chi_{m,k} \chi_{m,k}^H \psi_m\right) \tag{19a}$$

$$\text{s.t.} \quad \psi_m^H \chi_{m,k} \chi_{m,k}^H \psi_m \geq \left(2^{\bar{r}_{m,k}} - 1\right)/a_k, \tag{19b}$$

$$|\psi_m^n|^2 = 1, \forall n = 1, 2, ..., N, \; m \in \mathcal{M}. \tag{19c}$$

Nevertheless, (19) is non-convex. To make (19) become a convex optimization problem, we first denote $\mathbf{X}_{m,k} = \chi_{m,k}\chi_{m,k}^H$ and $\psi_m^H \mathbf{X}_{m,k}\psi_m = tr\left(\mathbf{X}_{m,k}\psi_m\psi_m^H\right) = tr\left(\mathbf{X}_{m,k}\boldsymbol{\Psi}_m\right)$ where $\boldsymbol{\Psi}_m = \psi_m\psi_m^H$ must satisfy $\boldsymbol{\Psi}_m \succeq 0$ and rank($\boldsymbol{\Psi}_m$)=1. And then, we relax the rank-one constraint of (19c) [6]. Thus, (19) is rewritten as

$$\max_{\psi_m, \, m \in \mathcal{M}} \sum_{m=1}^{M} \sum_{k=1}^{K_m} \log_2\left(1 + a_k tr\left(\mathbf{X}_{m,k}\boldsymbol{\Psi}_m\right)\right) \tag{20a}$$

$$\text{s.t.} \quad tr\left(\mathbf{X}_{m,k}\boldsymbol{\Psi}_m\right) \geq \left(2^{\bar{r}_{m,k}} - 1\right)/a_k, \tag{20b}$$

$$\boldsymbol{\Psi}_{m(n,n)} = 1, \forall n = 1, 2, ..., N, \; m \in \mathcal{M}, \tag{20c}$$

$$\boldsymbol{\Psi}_m \succeq 0. \tag{20d}$$

As a result, we can see that problem (20) is a convex semidefinite program (SDP) [4], which can be efficiently solved by using CVX. We proposed BCD-based method to solve problem (20) in Algorithm 2. Specifically, we assign $i = 0$,

$p_0$, $f_{m,k}^{(0)}$, and $\varepsilon = 10^{-3}$. The output of this algorithm is the optimal phase shift ($\boldsymbol{\Phi}_M^*$).

---

**Algorithm 2.** Phase shift searching procedure

---

**Input:**
$\quad i = 0$, $p_0$, $f_{m,k}^{(0)}$, $\varepsilon = 10^{-3}$
$\quad I_{max} = 20$
**while** (Divergence or $i \leqslant I_{max}$)
$\quad$ **for** $m = [1 : M]$
$\quad\quad$ Solve (20) for ($\boldsymbol{\Phi}_M^{(i+1)}$) by CVX
$\quad\quad f_{m,k}^{(i+1)}$
$\quad$ **end for**
$\quad i = i + 1$
**end while**
**Output:** $\boldsymbol{\Phi}_M^*$

---

Lastly, the Algorithms 1 and 2 are combined to solve the joint power allocation and phase shifts optimization.

## 5   Simulation Results

In this section, we investigate simulation results in Matlab to figure out the performance of the proposed method. We consider parameters of simulation as follows. The radius of circle coverage is 500 m. The radius of expanded deployment area is 2000m. In additional, we assume that the BS is located at $(0, 0, 30)$. The white power spectral density and QoS threshold are assigned to $\sigma^2 = -130$ dBm/Hz and $\bar{r}_{m,k} = 1$ bps/Hz, respectively. In term of the channel model, we set up the same as the settings in [23,25]. We conduct numerical results from our proposed method as in (12) i.e., optimal power allocation - optimal phase shift (OP-OPH), and the conventional methods i.e., optimal power allocation - random phase shift (OP-RPH), equal power allocation - random phase shift (EP-OPH), and equal power allocation - random phase shift (EP-RPH).

In Fig. 2 and Fig. 3, the total network throughput is plotted in two scenarios with the number of reflecting elements is fixed $N = 50$. In Fig. 2, we assume that the number of RISs and the number of UEs are $M = 4$ and $K = 20$, respectively. The number RISs is $M = 8$ and the number of UEs is $K = 30$ in Fig. 3. It is clear that the total network throughput rises when the transmit power at the BS increases. Specifically, when the number of RISs is increased, the total network throughput rises considerably. Moreover, in the consider method, the optimal phase shift can be more efficient than the others in all scenarios in Fig. 2 and Fig. 3.

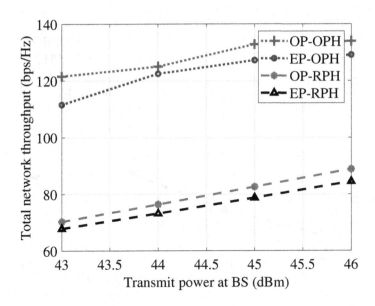

**Fig. 2.** Total throughput versus number of RISs ($M = 4$, $K = 20$, $N = 50$).

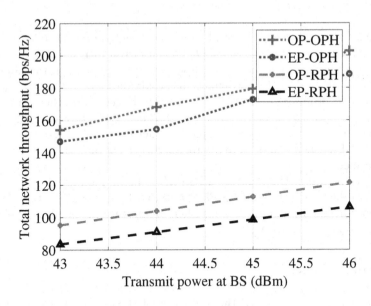

**Fig. 3.** Total throughput versus transmission power at BS ($M = 8$, $K = 30$, $N = 50$).

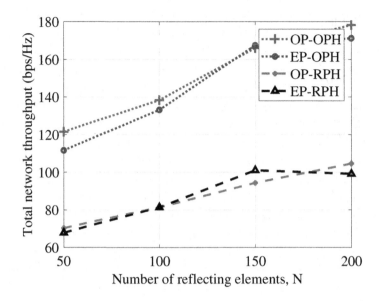

**Fig. 4.** Total throughput versus number of reflecting elements ($M = 4$, $K = 20$, $P_0^{max} = 43$ dBm).

Meanwhile, we illustrate the total network throughput versus different of RIS elements when $M = 4$, $K = 20$, and $P_0^{max} = 43$ dBm in Fig. 4. Clearly, as can be seen that the total network throughput grows steadily when the number of reflecting elements rises. In particular, the result shows that the total network throughput of proposed network is significantly larger than others in case the phase shift is optimized. As expected, the OP-OPH is the best method for RIS-aided downlink cellular network. Despite the fact that $P_0^{max}$ is fixed to 43 dBm, the OP-OPH method can achieve approximately much more 1,8 times than the EP-RPH method.

Finally, in case of the number of RIS $M = 4$, the number of user $K = 20$, and $P_0^{max} = 43$ dBm, the results in Fig. 2 and Fig. 4 prove that the total network throughput heightens about 1,5 times when we increase the number of reflecting elements from $N = 50$ to $N = 200$.

## 6   Conclusions

In this paper, we have studied the assistance of RIS for downlink cellular networks. Aiming to enhance the QoS of cellular network, the joint power allocation coefficients of BS and phase shifts of RIS optimization was applied. The numerical results demonstrated the efficiency of proposed system. The total network throughput achieved the highest in case both power and phase shift are optimized. Obviously, the coverage is expanded thanks to the RIS assisted, but not investigated in this paper.

# References

1. Basar, E., Di Renzo, M., De Rosny, J., Debbah, M., Alouini, M.-S., Zhang, R.: Wireless communications through reconfigurable intelligent surfaces. IEEE Access **7**, 116753–116773 (2019)
2. Wu, Q., Zhang, S., Zheng, B., You, C., Zhang, R.: Intelligent reflecting surface-aided wireless communications: a tutorial. IEEE Trans. Commun. **69**(5), 3313–3351 (2021)
3. Wu, Q., Zhang, R.: Towards smart and reconfigurable environment: intelligent reflecting surface aided wireless network. IEEE Commun. Mag. **58**(1), 106–112 (2020)
4. Wu, Q., Zhang, R.: Intelligent reflecting surface enhanced wireless network via joint active and passive beamforming. IEEE Trans. Wireless Commun. **18**(11), 5394–5409 (2019)
5. Huang, K.-W., Wang, H.-M.: Passive beamforming for IRS aided wireless networks. IEEE Wireless Commun. Lett. **9**(12), 2035–2039 (2020)
6. Yu, H., Tuan, H.D., Nasir, A.A., Duong, T.Q., Poor, H.V.: Joint design of reconfigurable intelligent surfaces and transmit beamforming under proper and improper gaussian signaling. IEEE J. Sel. Areas Commun. **38**(11), 2589–2603 (2020)
7. Li, S., Duo, B., Yuan, X., Liang, Y.-C., Di Renzo, M.: Reconfigurable intelligent surface assisted UAV communication: joint trajectory design and passive beamforming. IEEE Wireless Commun. Lett. **9**(5), 716–720 (2020)
8. Nguyen, K.K., Khosravirad, S., da Costa, D.B., Nguyen, L.D., Duong, T.Q.: Reconfigurable Intelligent Surface-assisted Multi-UAV Networks: Efficient Resource Allocation with Deep Reinforcement Learning (2021)
9. Nguyen, K.K., Masaracchia, A., Yin, C., Nguyen, L.D., Dobre, O.A., Duong, T.Q.: Deep Reinforcement Learning for Intelligent Reflecting Surface-Assisted D2D Communications (2021)
10. Ha, D.-B., Truong, V.-T., Lee, Y.: Performance analysis for RF energy harvesting mobile edge computing networks with SIMO/MISO-NOMA schemes. EAI Endorsed Trans. Ind. Netw. Intell. Syst. **8**(27), 4 (2021)
11. Fang, F., Xu, Y., Pham, Q.-V., Ding, Z.: Energy-efficient design of IRS-NOMA networks. IEEE Trans. Veh. Technol. **69**(11), 14088–14092 (2020)
12. Zhang, D., Wu, Q., Cui, M., Zhang, G., Niyato, D.: Throughput maximization for IRS-assisted wireless powered hybrid NOMA and TDMA. IEEE Wireless Commun. Lett. **10**(9), 1944–1948 (2021)
13. Wu, Q., Zhang, R.: Joint active and passive beamforming optimization for intelligent reflecting surface assisted SWIPT under QoS constraints. IEEE J. Sel. Areas Commun. **38**(8), 1735–1748 (2020)
14. Mu, X., Liu, Y., Guo, L., Lin, J., Al-Dhahir, N.: Exploiting intelligent reflecting surfaces in NOMA networks: joint beamforming optimization. IEEE Trans. Wireless Commun. **19**(10), 6884–6898 (2020)
15. Wu, Q., Zhang, R.: Weighted sum power maximization for intelligent reflecting surface aided SWIPT. IEEE Wireless Commun. Lett. **9**(5), 586–590 (2020)
16. Guo, H., Liang, Y.-C., Chen, J., Larsson, E.G.: Weighted sum-rate maximization for intelligent reflecting surface enhanced wireless networks. In: IEEE Global Communications Conference (GLOBECOM) 2019, pp. 1–6 (2019)
17. Nguyen, M., Nguyen, L.D., Duong, T.Q., Tuan, H.D.: Real-time optimal resource allocation for embedded UAV communication systems. IEEE Wireless Commun. Lett. **8**(1), 225–228 (2019)

18. Bor-Yaliniz, R.I., El-Keyi, A., Yanikomeroglu, H.: Efficient 3-D placement of an aerial base station in next generation cellular networks. In: IEEE ICC, pp. 1–5, May 2016

19. Mozaffari, M., Saad, W., Bennis, M., Debbah, M.: Efficient deployment of multiple unmanned aerial vehicles for optimal wireless coverage. IEEE Commun. Lett. **20**, 1647–1650 (2016)

20. Al-Hourani, A., Kandeepan, S., Lardner, S.: Optimal LAP altitude for maximum coverage. IEEE Wireless Commun. Lett. **3**(6), 569–572 (2014)

21. Xie, X., Fang, F., Ding, Z.: Joint optimization of beamforming, phase-shifting and power allocation in a multi-cluster IRS-NOMA network. IEEE Trans. Veh. Technol. **70**(8), 7705–7717 (2021)

22. Wu, Q., Zhang, R.: Beamforming optimization for wireless network aided by intelligent reflecting surface with discrete phase shifts. IEEE Trans. Commun. **68**(3), 1838–1851 (2020)

23. Nguyen, L.D., Tuan, H.D., Duong, T.Q., Dobre, O.A., Poor, H.V.: Downlink beamforming for energy-efficient heterogeneous networks with massive MIMO and small cells. IEEE Trans. Wireless Commun. **17**(5), 3386–3400 (2018)

24. Grant, M., Boyd, S.: CVX: MATLAB software for disciplined convex programming, version 2.1, March 2014. http://cvxr.com/cvx

25. Do-Duy, T., Nguyen, L.D., Duong, T.Q., Khosravirad, S., Claussen, H.: Joint optimisation of real-time deployment and resource allocation for UAV-aided disaster emergency communications. IEEE J. Sel. Areas Commun. **39**(11), 3411–3424 (2021)

# QoS-Aware Load Balancing Scheme in Dense Wi-Fi 6 WLANs

Elif Ak[1]([⊠])[iD] and Berk Canberk[2][iD]

[1] Computer Engineering Department, Istanbul Technical University, Istanbul, Turkey
`akeli@itu.edu.tr`
[2] Artificial Intelligence and Data Engineering Department,
Computer and Informatics Faculty, Istanbul Technical University, Istanbul, Turkey
`canberk@itu.edu.tr`

**Abstract.** Nowadays, increasing mobile and wireless usage demand accelerates new enhancements on IEEE 802.11 family to provide concurrent transmission and high efficiency. Thus, IEEE 802.11ax is released with the aim to improve overall throughput in dense WLANs considering the overlapping channel interference. However, the current WLANs suffer from uneven load distribution among the Access Points (AP). Because a station simply connects to the AP with the highest received signal strength indication (RSSI) in a legacy association way. And RSSI might not be the only criteria in the current WLANs due to the variety of application requirements and high date rates. Therefore, we propose a complete association scheme called Access Controller (AC) to manage admission, association, and adaptive carrier sensitivity control as a whole. The station from an overloaded AP is handed to a less loaded AP by considering various crucial metrics such as packet delivery ratio, fairness, RSSI, throughput, and round trip time. After effective load balancing, we adaptively tune the carrier sensitivity threshold to enhance concurrent transmission in IEEE 802.11ax WLANs. The results show that the proposed AC scheme outperforms in terms of fairness and per-station throughput in dense WiFi6 scenarios with over 500 stations.

**Keywords:** IEEE 802.11ax · Dense WLANs · QoS · Load balancing

## 1 Introduction

The IEEE 802.11ax task group has been newly realized the new promising amendment for High Efficiency (HE) Wireless Local Area Networks (WLANs) in 2020. One of the leading features of 802.11ax is Special Reuse (SR), which aims at improving throughput in dense scenarios with a high volume of access points (APs) and increased number of stations (STAs) per AP. The escalating necessity of dense AP deployment leads up Overlapping Basic Service Set (OBSS), where STAs can connect more than one AP with mostly similar signal strength. However, the current 802.11 standards give the responsibility of selecting an AP to the STAs. A STA simply selects an AP according to the strongest Received

© ICST Institute for Computer Sciences, Social Informatics and Telecommunications Engineering 2022
Published by Springer Nature Switzerland AG 2022. All Rights Reserved
N.-S. Vo et al. (Eds.): INISCOM 2022, LNICST 444, pp. 33–47, 2022.
https://doi.org/10.1007/978-3-031-08878-0_3

Signal Strenght Indicator (RSSI). However, the highest RSSI is not necessarily to be the best choice because the load of APs varies with BSS traffic flow and many other factors. The current unqualified AP selection mechanism causes an imbalance load among APs, fairness issues between STAs, and inefficient usage of resources. Despite RSSI being an essential criterion for selecting AP, divergent traffics, and data rate requirements of different applications imply the new definition of AP selection. Such a new definition should be supported with adaptive carrier sensitivity threshold (CST) because co-channel interference makes it challenging to balance STAs among APs [1].

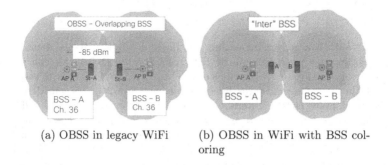

(a) OBSS in legacy WiFi    (b) OBSS in WiFi with BSS coloring

**Fig. 1.** Before and after BSS coloring is enabled [2]

Thanks to the new 802.11 amendment, namely WiFi6 (or formally IEEE 802.11ax), the term SR reveals BSS coloring implementation in WLANs. BSS color is 6 bits length data placed in frame preamble to determine the owner BSS of the frame without decoding the entire frame. The sensing frame with the same color means intra-BSS transmission; different color shows inter-BSS transmission. By recognizing the owner of the inter-BSS frame, concurrent intra-BSS transmission can continue. As seen in Fig. 1b, STA-A and STA-B are connected to different APs, naming AP-A and AP-B, respectively. However, both STAs are placed near the cell-edge of AP's ranges, and they sense their frames in case of concurrent transmission without BSS coloring. This was one of the challenging operations in legacy dense WLANs. On the other hand, when two BSS have different BSS colors, then STA-A and STA-B simply ignore each other's frame because they know their signals never be collied. Besides, BSS coloring enhancement enables STAs to adaptively tune CST by distinguishing OBSS packets with corresponding colors.

In dense deployment WLANs before the BSS coloring scheme, studies only propose STA-AP load balancing schemes without deploying adaptive CST. The problems mentioned above and BSS coloring enhancement motivate a new definition of load balancing mechanism in dense 802.11ax WLANs. Such a new definition of load balancing come with three research questions as follows: (i) how to integrate BSS coloring enhancement to deal with interference issue of OBSS, (ii) which STAs should be switched and how to select target AP, (iii) what criteria will be used to define the load of BSS. To point out these research questions, we propose a QoS-aware load balancing scheme runs in a centralized controller called Access Controller (AC) to increase concurrent transmissions and the efficiency of 802.11ax WLANs. The AC entity operates a load balancing mechanism enhanced with adaptive CST to adjust carrier sensing range dynamically. Then AC uses the global view of WLAN and takes network information from APs to select candidate STAs and re-associate to the target AP. Finally, the framework extensively defines the load for WiFi6 WLANs, considering various application requirements.

The rest of the paper gives the related works on AP selection, and load balancing in WLANs, then presents our contributions in Sect. 2. After that, the network model is presented in Sect. 3, and the proposed framework is introduced in Sect. 4. Moreover, the simulation parameters and evaluation results are discussed in Sect. 5. Finally, the summary of the proposed scheme is concluded in Sect. 6.

## 2   Literature Review

Different management operations are studied in IEEE 802.11 WLANs and one of the promising areas is to provide an enhanced association mechanism supported with adaptive CST. Many studies discuss association mechanisms for load balancing and adaptive CST separately. And few studies focus on both of them as a whole. Moreover, current studies propose various AP-STA association methods in place of the legacy strongest RSSI-based scheme. In that point, the proposed schemes are examined in two groups: centralized and STA-driven approaches.

The most practical STA-driven approach is the legacy strongest RSSI-based method which is also used in IEEE 802.11 WLANs. Within the STA-driven approaches, other studies use different metrics rather than RSSI. STAs can estimate the available bandwidth before the association procedure [3]. Or another study leverages interference of overlapping WLANs to select the most appropriate AP [1]. Kim et al. propose a scheme to measure the interference using external devices to find an AP with the least interference level [4]. Without deploying a centralized controller might accelerate the deployment time and decrease communication overhead. But STA-driven methods are lack global view information by nature.

Therefore, a centralized approach is another straightforward way to design an association mechanism. The centralized methods solve the load balancing problem either by managing the association & disassociation process or adjusting coverage area & sensitivity threshold adaptively. Some studies also use both methods in the same time [1].

Tang et al. [5] focus user demands to allocate bandwidth according to the users' requirement. Raschellà et al. [6] proposes a centralized controller based on SDN and considers the QoS requirements of the user's traffic. Gong and Yang [7] study aggregated throughput to balance load among APs in heterogeneous STAs. Peng et al. [8] analyze achievable normalized throughput and channel competition to select AP for association requests. Manzoor et al. [9] uses various metrics to define the load for AP selection and deploys a SDN model to monitor and control the WLAN.

Until now, none of the studies have analyzed load balancing issue in IEEE 802.11ax (or simply WiFi6) WLANs. Since WiFi6 comes with crucial enhancements such as BSS coloring, it should be taken separately in the design step. The studies [10] and [1] simulate the proposed approach in WiFi6 WLANs, but they do not use any specific features of WiFi6, which might help to design an association or adaptive CST mechanism.

Consequently, in order to fill explained gap and to provide a complete association mechanism with the aim of load balancing and fair channel access, we propose a novel Access Controller entity on the top of our design. And AC observes various metrics to run Decision Tree model to select candidate AP. The main contributions of this paper are summarized as follows:

- We propose the Access Controller entity as a centralized controller, which contains admission control, association control and adaptive CST tuning modules to form a complete association mechanism in IEEE 802.11ax WLANs.
- The admission control trains and tests the Decision Tree model with eight different categories to extensively analyze the load of the network.
- We introduce a new parameter, called as candidate strength parameter to select most appropriate STAs to shift between APs.
- Finally, we integrate adaptive CST mechanism with the proposed association procedure to provide fairness after load balancing and to adaptively tune CST for concurrent transmissions.

## 3   Network Architecture

In this study, we consider densely deployed WLAN scenarios where several APs' coverage areas are overlapped by building Overlapping Basic Service Set (OBSS). In order to model overlapped scenarios and consider orthogonal channels' negative effects [11], all APs are considered to operate in the same channel in 2.4 GHz band. Since using orthogonal channels affects the transmission quality between APs, this study only considers load balancing scheme between APs operates on same channel, not between channels. Moreover, APs are assumed to belong same WLAN service provider, which is the typical characteristic of dense WLANs. It is also worth mentioning that IEEE 802.11 standard supports the seamless roaming among the BSSs [12]. The STAs can be handover freely inside an Extended Service Set, which is a form of multiple BSS deployed by a single service provider in the infrastructure network.

All APs are connected to the centralized Access Controller (AC) through wired connection as seen in Fig. 2. The centralized controller has a global view on WLANs in which load metrics are collected from each AP thanks to *agent*. Collected metrics are then processed in the AC modules, naming *admission control* and *association control* to run proposed load-balancing scheme.

Each BSS has its own unique BSS color assigned by the service provider during WLAN deployment time without any collision. An example BSS coloring assignment is imitated in Fig. 2 by presenting AP's range with different colors.

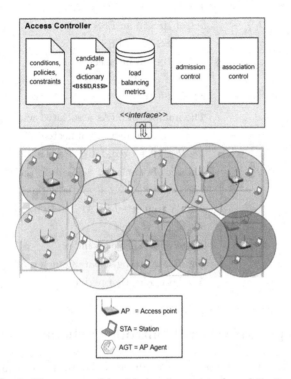

**Fig. 2.** The proposed load balancing network architecture

## 3.1 Problem Definition

We consider an ESS that involves $k$ interconnected BSSs and $N$ STAs. Let $\mathcal{B} = \{B_1, B_2, ..., B_k\}$ be the set of BSS in the dense WLAN, each BSS contains one AP, $AP_i$, where $i = 1, 2, ..., k$ and set of users, $\mathcal{U}_i$, belonging $B_i$. We assume the number of STAs which are associated with $AP_i$ is $n_i = |\mathcal{U}_i|$, and $N$ is the total number of STAs in WLAN, where $N = \sum_{i=1}^{k} n_i$. Also, it is known that APs have a maximum number of connected STA limit that the device handles whether a STA transmit data or not. Thus $c_i^{max}$ shows the maximum number of STAs that can associate to $AP_i$. All STAs have a candidate AP list, $\mathcal{C}$, and $\mathcal{C}_j$ shows $j-th$ STA's candidate AP list. That is, STA $j$ is within the coverage areas of APs in $\mathcal{C}_j$. Let $\mathcal{I}$ is the set of intersections of APs in the ESS. All notations used in the paper is listed in Table 1.

**Table 1.** Notations

| Symbol | Explanation |
|---|---|
| $\mathcal{I} = \{I_1, I_2, ..., I_m\}$ | Set of intersections of APs in the ESS |
| $N$ | Total # of STAs in WLAN |
| $\mathcal{B} = \{B_1, B_2, ..., B_k\}$ | Set of BSS in an ESS |
| $k$ | # of BSS in an ESS |
| $\mathcal{B}^i = \{B_r, B_{r+1}, ..., B_{r+p_i}\}$ | Set of BSS in intersection $I_i$ |
| $p_i$ | Number of APs (i.e. BSSs) in intersection $I_i$ |
| $AP_i$ | AP of $i^{th}$ BSS |
| $n_i = |\mathcal{U}_i|$ | The number of STAs associated with $AP_i$ |
| $c_i^{max}$ | Maximum number of connected STA limit of $AP_i$ |
| $\mathcal{C}_j$ | $j - th$ STA's candidate AP list |
| $\mathcal{U}_i$ | The set of connected STAs in $i^{th}$ BSS |
| $\mathcal{U}^i$ | The set of STAs in $i^{th}$ intersection, $I_i$ |
| $U_j^i$ | A STA connected to $AP_j$ and placed in the $I_i$ |
| $\mathcal{M} = \{M_1, M_2, ..., M_m\}$ | Set of DT models |
| $\mathcal{J} = \{J_1, J_2, ..., J_m\}$ | Set of Jain's Fairness Index |
| $\gamma$ | Candidate strength parameter |
| $T$ | AC data collection period |

## 4    The Proposed Access Controller Scheme

The Access Controller (AC) is the centralized server to monitor and control the ESS. STAs and their candidate APs list $\mathcal{C}$ are continuously observed, and changes are saved in the dictionary. A candidate AP is 3-tuple data with <*BSSID, RSSI,* $\gamma$> values recorded in the list $\mathcal{C}$ for each STA. BSSID is the unique value used in the BSS to assign an ID to each AP in the WLAN. This identifier is called a basic service set identifier (BSSID). The second value is Received Signal Strength Indicator (RSSI), which measures how well STA can hear a signal from an AP. The last value $\gamma$ is the proposed *candidate strength parameter* to show the strength of candidate AP for STA handover. Note that in this network architecture, all STAs and APs belong to the same ESS, thus they use the same extended basic service set identifier (ESSID). Three main modules of AC, naming Admission Control, Association Control, and Adaptive CST Control as follows.

### 4.1    Admission Control

The collected metrics are saved in the database of AC as also seen as *load balancing metrics* in Fig. 2. The dataset used as an input in DT algorithm, $X^{N \times F}$ contains $N$ samples, and $F$ features. In our complete DT-based admission control system, each intersection $I_i$ has own DT model trained with APs and STAs placed in the intersection $I_i$. Let $I_i$ is the $i-th$ intersection where $0 < i < m$. And suppose $p_i$ is the number of APs (i.e. BSSs) in intersection $I_i$, where $2 < p_i < k$ and $k$ is the number of APs in the ESS. Let $U_j^i$ shows a STA connected to $AP_j$ and placed in the $I_i$. In the light of these definitions, $M_i \subset \mathcal{M}$ is a DT model belongs to intersection $I_i$ with the $p_i$ APs, and trained with dataset $X_i^{N_i \times F_i}$. The features are basically: (i)RSSI values of $p_i$ APs in the intersection, (ii)$J_i$, (iii)number of STAs in each $p_i$ APs, (iv)packet delivery ratio (PDR) of $p_i$ APs, (v)bit error rate (BER) of $p_i$ APs, (vi)average loss rate of $p_i$ BSSs, (vii)normalized throughput of $p_i$ BSSs, (viii)average round-trip-time of $p_i$ BSSs, totally $7p_i + 1$ features. These features are as follows:

*RSSI* - Received Signal Strength Indicator (RSSI) is a measurement of how a STA receives the signal from the AP in the receiver's antenna during the packet transmission. RSSI value strongly depends on the distance. Thus, considering RSSI as the only metric for the AP association and load of BSS is not sufficient. Because usage of RSSI as only metric can not determine the interference on links [13]. Therefore, RSSI metric should be supported with other well-justified load criteria to measure the load of BSS acutely. RSSI value can be learnt from control packets during the association process. The value vary from 0 to $RSSI_{max}$ and the maximum value depends on the wireless card manufacturer. For example, Cisco cards use $RSSI_{max} = 100$, and they use $RSSI - 95 = dBm$ formula to transform RSSI value to power, and vice versa. While in Intel cards the RSSI value uses actual received power in the negative dBm scale. In this study, we refer the RSSI value to actual received power without applying any formula.

*Jain's Fairness Index* - Another criteria which we implemented in this study is well known Jain's fairness index introduced in [14]. $Th_i$ is the throughput of the $i^{th}$ intersection and $J_i \in \mathcal{J}$.

$$J_i = \frac{(\sum_{j=1}^{p_i} \frac{n_j}{c_j^{max}} max(Th_j))^2}{p_i \sum_{j=1}^{p_i} (\frac{n_j}{c_j^{max}} max(Th_j))^2} \tag{1}$$

Since each intersection has its own stationary set of APs, the aim is to balance the fairness index within the APs. In other words, each STA has only a limited chance to handover between APs (i.e. within the intersection). Therefore, considering fairness in ESS is inconvenient since we can not associate STAs to every APs. The value of Jain's index ranges from $1/p_i$ to 1. If all APs within the intersection $i$ is balanced, then the value will be 1. In the same way, the worst degree of load balancing is $1/p_i$, where $p_i$ is the number of APs in the intersection $i$.

*Number of STAs* - Even if a number of STAs is not a crucial value for BSS load determination, it is an important criterion to understand the number of connections on APs. Therefore, the number of STAs is also added to among DT model features like RSSI value. Since the number of associated STAs affects various network metrics such as throughput, rtt, loss rate etc.

*Packet Delivery Ratio (PDR)* - PDR is a ratio of correctly received packets to the total number of packets. It is mostly used to determine link quality and the load of BSS. And in the low data rates, PDR presents a strong correlation with RSSI value. However, with the higher data rates, the correlation is lost. Consequently, RSSI can not be used to estimate PDR value. Thus in this study, we include PDR as a feature in DT model.

*Bit Error Rate (BER)* - If there are various lengths of packet sizes in the ESS, the PDR metric may fail to observe link quality [13]. Therefore, we introduce another crucial metric to be used in DT model: bit error rate, or simply BER. BER is a ratio of the number of erroneous bits received over the total number of received bits. PDR metric also measures error packets, it makes a course-grained observation compared with BER. Thus, bit-level analysis is also important.

*Average Packet Loss Rate ($\widetilde{Lr}$)* - Another important criterion for load balancing decision is packet loss rate. Since packet loss rate dramatically affects the quality of service in real-time applications, the average packet loss rate of each BSS is calculated as follows,

$$\widetilde{Lr} = \frac{\sum_{i=0}^{n_i} Lr}{n_i} \tag{2}$$

$$Lr = 1 - (Lr - P_\epsilon * (1 - Pc)) \tag{3}$$

$P_\epsilon$ is the packet error rate and $P_c$ is the collision probability.

*Normalized Throughput ($\widehat{Th}$)* - In order to obtain normalized throughput of APs, we use Bianchi's model, which constructs a two-dimensional Markov model to analyze the saturated system throughput of a BSS in IEEE 802.11 with Distributed Coordination Function (DCF) mechanism. According to Bianchi's model [15], the normalized throughput of $i^{th}$ BSS is as follows;

$$\widehat{Th_i} = \frac{P_{ts} P_{tr} E[P]}{(1 - P_{tr})\sigma + P_{tr} P_{ts} T_s + P_{tr}(1 - P_{ts} T_c))} \tag{4}$$

where $P_{ts}$ and $T_{ts}$ is the probability and average time duration in the case transmission is successful. Also, $P_{tr}$ is the probability that there is at least one transmission within the given time, $T_c$ is the average time of collision, $\sigma$ is the slot duration.

The probability of having at least one transmission is calculated by $P_{tr} = 1 - (1 - \tau)^{n-1}$. And $\tau$ is probability that a STA attempts to transmits within the time duration.

*Average Round-Trip-Time (RTT)* - One of the aims of WiFi6 is to provide high efficiency in time-sensitive applications, such as high-quality videos, AR/VR applications, and real-time streaming. Therefore, round-trip-time plays a crucial role in determining this service differentiation and the load of APs.

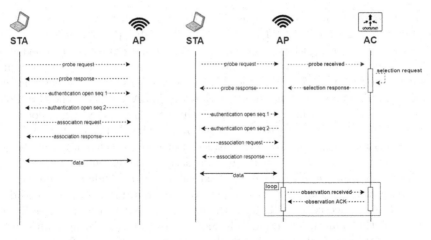

(a) Legacy way of association    (b) The proposed association procedure

**Fig. 3.** Two association methods

## 4.2 Association Control

**Legacy Way of Association.** In order to understand the contribution to the proposed Association Control mechanism, the two legacy ways of association in IEEE 802.11ax is shown in Fig. 3. Since in the passive scanning the STA sees each AP with their beacon packets, APs can not be chosen before the STA meet with the AP. Therefore, our proposed association scheme is based on the active scanning mechanism as presented in Fig. 3b. Red colors indicate the proposed control packets. In the association procedure, there are two cases: association of new STA and re-association of existing STA. The details of the two cases are as follows.

**The Proposed Association Procedure: New STA Association.** When a STA wants to connect to WLAN, it first sends a "probe request" and then waits for the "probe response". During this waiting time, AP sends "probe received" message through an *interface* of the proposed AC. Then, the AC selects an appropriate AP based on the DT output. Only the selected AP sends "probe response" message to the STA, unlike the legacy in which all APs hearing the probe request message response. After that, legacy authentication (if any) and association handshake are invoked.

**The Proposed Disassociation - Association Procedure: Existing STA Association.** One of the steps of load balancing is to consider existing STA-AP distribution. Since the load of BSS might change instantly, robust load balancing scheme should consider both new and existing STA associations as shown in Fig. 4.

*Trigger:* Load balancing for existing STAs differ from the new STA association. Because the trigger for new STA association is simply "probe request". On the other, there is no straightforward way to decide in what point the proposed algorithm should operate for existing STA association. Some of the studies use predefined period to balance load in the WLAN. Another frequently selected aspect is using Jain's index. If Jain's index within the WLAN exists some threshold, then the algorithm is run. However, one inclusive Jain's index might not mean that there is an imbalance situation in all overlapping WLANs. Therefore, we propose a new trigger point to only consider intersections which have imbalanced load problem. First, $\forall J_i \in \mathcal{J}$ is calculated. Second, the ascending ordered $\overline{\mathcal{J}}$ is obtained. Then, $J_j = min(\overline{\mathcal{J}})$ is selected so that worst balanced intersection will be the starting point. After selecting worst balanced intersection, candidate set of STAs is selected to shift from the associated AP to the new less loaded AP within the same intersection. The next step is re-calculating Jain's index for all intersections and processing in the same way. Note that after set of handovers, load of APs and Jain's index of intersections likely to change. In order to prevent "butterfly effect" caused by set of handovers, only one intersection is aimed to be balanced. If the same intersection is selected again after calculating Jain's fairness index one again, then second minimum Jain's index is processed. This process is continued until all intersections are balanced according to some predefined threshold, $T_f$.

*Candidate Strength Parameter:* In order to determine candidate STAs to be shifted from the current associated AP to the less loaded APs. Most studies simply select STAs which have less RSSI value. This also indicates a STA placed on the cell-edge is selected first for handover process. However, selecting STAs with low RSSI values is a similar idea to associate a STA with highest RSSI value. In other words, RSSI value shows poor performance in any association process because it is a weak metric stand-alone to define the load. We also propose a new metric named, candidate strength parameter, $\gamma$, to present a strength of a STA for handover process. Following formula shows the candidate strength parameter for $i^{th}$ STA to handover to less loaded $AP_j$.

$$\gamma_i = \frac{\overline{P_j} + \overline{T_j}}{2} + RSSI_{i,j} \tag{5}$$

where $\overline{P_j}$ and $\overline{T_j}$ is the normalized packet loss rate and throughput in $AP_j$. The value of $\gamma$ varies $-1$ to $2$, where minimum value indicates a STA is shifted to the $AP_j$.

*Candidate APs:* Note that the proposed *gamma* parameter is only calculated for STAs which has selected less loaded $AP_j$ in own candidate APs list. The candidate APs of $i^{th}$ STA, $C_i$, defines the set of APs in which covers the STA with acceptable link quality. Let $T_r$ is the RSSI value threshold to determine acceptable link quality in between STA and AP. The APs having the RSSI value above the threshold are considered as the appropriate candidates for association.

In this study, we use $T_r = \{-70, -75, -80\}$ different thresholds to evaluate the performance.

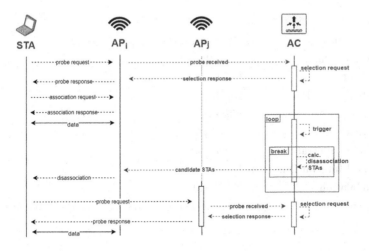

**Fig. 4.** The proposed disassociation - association procedure

### 4.3 Adaptive CST Control

In the scope of AC decision scheme, adaptive CST tuning is another module to decrease overlapping co-channel interference between APs. AP loading scheme without adaptive CST tuning is prone to OBSS interference, which considerably affects QoS of STAs and transmission quality. Therefore, AC first initialized all BSS with default CST, which is $-82$ dBm for 20 Mhz channel and increments 3 dB with the channel is doubled. Each new association attempt first runs DT model with the given input. Then association and authentication packets are sent to the AP according to new association decision. Finally Adaptive CST Control algorithm is triggered according to mechanism described in [16] to provide fair channel contention in dense WLANs. Since edge-cell STAs are most vulnerable to unfair channel access followed by low throughput, adaptive tuning of CST value is crucial part of the AC scheme. In the work [16], we alternated the $UpdatePeriod_\alpha$ value, used in local scale update period, with the new association timer. By this way, BSS and STAs scale own CST value to decrease co-channel interference caused from OBSS.

## 5   Evaluation

The ns-3 [16] network simulator is used in this experiment due to adaptive features for IEEE 802.11ax networks. We also used 20Mhz channels with overlapping WLANs with same channel. In this section, we evaluate the performance of our proposed AC scheme in dense WiFi6 WLANs in terms of the average

**Table 2.** Simulation parameters

| Parameter | Value |
| --- | --- |
| Number of APs | 19 |
| Number of STAs | 570 |
| STA density | 30 STAs per AP |
| Channel Band | 2.4 GHz |
| Mobility | Exists as described |
| AP/STA Tx Power | 20/15 dBm |
| Number of antennas | SISO |
| Packet | 1464 bytes |
| Beacon Interval | 102.4 ms |
| Guard Interval Duration | 1.6 us |
| Modulation | 256-QAM |
| Management | All APs belong to the same management entity |

throughput per STA, and average Jain's Fairness Index. We used the indoor Small BSSs Scenario for dense WLANs [17] proposed by IEEE 802.11ax Task Group (TGax). Other simulation parameters can be found in Table 2.

The ML model is trained using 61000 samples and tested over 18100 samples. Since each intersection has at most 4 APs, the number of labels vary 2 to 4. We use ID3 decision tree model. Thus we split dataset according to Information Gain (i.e. Entropy) value. Moreover, we prefer to use Cost Complexity Pruning (CCP) technique.

## 5.1   Results

In order to compare the performance of the proposed AC scheme, we used three baselines. RSSI-based association mechanism is the traditional way in IEEE 802.11 WLANs explained before. Percentage based scheme is another candidate method discussed by IEEE task group [17]. According to percentage based association STA associations are divided into three group with defined percentages. X% of STAs are associated with the strongest AP, then Y% of STAs are associated with the second-strongest AP, so on so fort. And final baseline is random association scheme in which STAs are randomly chosen and associated to the less loaded AP.

We perform 50 simulations for each method with same conditions to observe the performance of each baselines. Since there are two different associations way, half of simulations implement new STA associations; other half for existing STA associations. Then average of each test results are calculated to plot the final result.

Figure 5a shows the variation of the Jain's fairness index with increasing number of STAs. When the number of STAs increase, it is clear to observe

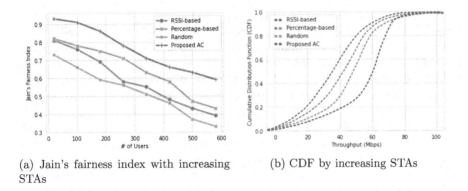

(a) Jain's fairness index with increasing STAs

(b) CDF by increasing STAs

**Fig. 5.** Comparison with baseline methods

dramatic decline due to ascending channel competitions. As it is expected AC scheme gives superior result thanks to adaptive CST mechanism, which directly aims to increase fair transmission between STAs. Another observation is that RSSI-based scheme gets higher Jain's index compared to random scheme. This results also shows the importance of RSSI metric in the association and load determination. But it also shows it has shortfall by comparison with the proposed AC scheme.

Figure 5b plots the cumulative distribution function of the total network throughput when the number of STAs is 20 per APs. The results is the average from 50 simulation runs, with half of them is new STA association and other half is the result of existing STA association. It can be observed that the percentage gain of the proposed AC scheme is quite large. Because the proposed AC scheme can find the STA-AP association set by using various critical metrics. Therefore, the proposed scheme can not only provide fairness balance among BSSs but also increases QoS.

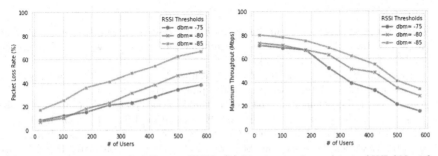

(a) Packet loss rate of different RSSI thresholds

(b) Maximum throughput of WLAN with different RSSI thresholds

**Fig. 6.** Analysis of RSSI threshold used by STA's to form candidate AP list for handover

The last experiment set measures the effect of the network with changing RSSI thresholds, $T_r$. Since RSSI threshold directly affects the possible associations of a STA (i.e. candidate AP list), it most likely have an impact on the network and transmission performance. Consequently, Fig. 6a shows worst packet loss rate performance in $T_r = -85$ dbm. When lower $T_r$ values, number of options for STAs to associate APs increases. Then with the adaptive CST mechanism, packet loss rate tends to increase. However, the throughput results present exact opposite implications. Figure 6 indicates that having larger candidate AP list does not affect the maximum throughput in the WLAN. In other words, higher values of threshold has a negative impacts on maximum throughput and leads to inefficient usage of the network. Therefore, this analysis shows that lower values of the threshold which is used for creating candidate APs list is suggested.

## 6   Conclusion

This study provides a complete association management scheme including adaptive carrier sensitivity considering both new STA association and existing STA association. In order to monitor underlying ESS, the proposed access controller (AC) takes related QoS and network parameters from APs via an interface and builds a decision tree model. The features are carefully selected and particular decision models are trained for each overlapping areas (i.e. intersections). After that we introduce a new metric called as candidate strength parameter to select a set of STAs for re-association. Finally we evaluate the proposed AC scheme with three baselines: legacy RSSI-based association, percentage based association, and random disassociation. Then we compare the various RSSI thresholds to observe the system performance. The results show that the proposed AC scheme gains 6% and 14% improvement in Jain's fairness index and throughput, respectively.

## References

1. Kim, Y., et al.: AP selection algorithm with adaptive CCAT for dense wireless networks. In: 2017 IEEE Wireless Communications and Networking Conference (WCNC), pp. 1–6. IEEE (2017)
2. Wi-Fi 6 BSS Coloring and Spatial Reuse White Paper. https://www.cisco.com/c/en/us/products/collateral/wireless/white-paper-c11-743702.pdf
3. Dai, Y., Xu, D., Zhan, Y.: Towards optimal access point selection with available bandwidth estimation. In: 2017 IEEE International Conference on Internet of Things (iThings) and IEEE Green Computing and Communications (GreenCom) and IEEE Cyber, Physical and Social Computing (CPSCom) and IEEE Smart Data (SmartData), pp. 762–769. IEEE (2017)
4. Kim, H., Lee, W., Bae, M., Kim, H.: Wi-fi seeker: a link and load aware AP selection algorithm. IEEE Trans. Mob. Comput. 16(8), 2366–2378 (2016)
5. Tang, H., Yang, L., Dong, J., Ou, Z., Cui, Y., Wu, J.: Throughput optimization via association control in wireless LANs. Mob. Netw. Appl. 21(3), 453–466 (2016)

6. Raschella, A., Bouhafs, F., Seyedebrahimi, M., Mackay, M., Shi, Q.: Quality of service oriented access point selection framework for large Wi-Fi networks. IEEE Trans. Netw. Serv. Manag. **14**(2), 441–455 (2017)
7. Gong, D., Yang, Y.: AP association in 802.11 n WLANs with heterogeneous clients. In: 2012 Proceedings IEEE INFOCOM, pp. 1440–1448. IEEE (2012)
8. Peng, M., He, G., Wang, L., Kai, C.: AP selection scheme based on achievable throughputs in SDN-enabled WLANs. IEEE Access **7**, 4763–4772 (2018)
9. Manzoor, S., Chen, Z., Gao, Y., Hei, X., Cheng, W.: Towards QoS-aware load balancing for high density software defined Wi-Fi networks. IEEE Access **8**, 117623–117638 (2020)
10. Cao, F., et al.: User association for load balancing with uneven user distribution in IEEE 802.11 ax networks. In: 2016 13th IEEE Annual Consumer Communications & Networking Conference (CCNC), pp. 487–490. IEEE (2016)
11. Farej, Z.K., Ali, O.K.M.: An algorithm for load balancing of the extended service set WLAN. In: 2020 1st Information Technology to Enhance e-learning and Other Application (IT-ELA), pp. 48–53. IEEE (2020)
12. Feirer, S., Sauter, T.: Seamless handover in industrial WLAN using IEEE 802.11 k. In: IEEE 26th International Symposium on Industrial Electronics, pp. 1234–1239, June 2017 (2017)
13. Vlavianos, A., Law, L.K., Broustis, I., Krishnamurthy, S.V., Faloutsos, M.: Assessing link quality in IEEE 802.11 wireless networks: which is the right metric? In: IEEE 19th International Symposium on Personal, Indoor and Mobile Radio Communications, pp. 1–6 (2008)
14. Chiu, D.-M., Jain, R.: Analysis of the increase and decrease algorithms for congestion avoidance in computer networks. Comput. Netw. ISDN Syst. **17**(1), 1–14 (1989)
15. Bianchi, G.: Performance analysis of the IEEE 802.11 distributed coordination function. IEEE J. Sel. Areas Commun. **18**(3), 535–547 (2000)
16. Ak, E., Canberk, B.: Two-scale AI-driven fair sensitivity control for 802.11 ax networks. In: GLOBECOM 2020–2020 IEEE Global Communications Conference, pp. 1–6. IEEE (2020)
17. Merlin, S., et al.: TGax Simulation Scenarios. doc. IEEE 802.11-14/0980r14 (2015). https://mentor.ieee.org/802.11/dcn/14/11-14-0980-16-00ax-simulation-scenarios.docx

# Performance Analysis of Intelligent Reflecting Surface-Aided Mobile Edge Computing Network with Uplink NOMA Scheme

Dac-Binh Ha[1,2(✉)], Van-Truong Truong[1,2], and Van Nhan Vo[2,3]

[1] Faculty of Electrical-Electronic Engineering, School of Engineering and Technology,
Duy Tan University, Da Nang 550000, Vietnam
hadacbinh@duytan.edu.vn, truongvantruong@dtu.edu.vn
[2] Institute of Research and Development, Duy Tan University,
Da Nang 550000, Vietnam
vonhanvan@dtu.edu.vn
[3] Faculty of Information Technology, School of Computer Science,
Duy Tan University, Da Nang 550000, Vietnam

**Abstract.** This paper investigates the system performance of an intelligent reflecting surface-assisted mobile edge computing (MEC) network under Nakagami-$m$ fading channel with an uplink non-orthogonal multiple access (NOMA) scenarios. The considered system consists of an access point (AP), two NOMA users, i.e., a cell-center user and a cell-edge user, and a two-dimensional passive element array of the intelligent reflecting surface (IRS). Specifically, we consider the IRS to act as a relay to help cell-edge users offload tasks to the AP. We derive closed-form expressions of the successful computation probability (SCP) to evaluate the system performance. Furthermore, we analyze the ceiling SCP when the system operates in the high-SNR regime to clarify the system further. Finally, we investigate the impact of critical system parameters on the behavior of this considered system to look insight into the performance. The simulation results confirm the accuracy of our analysis.

**Keywords:** Intelligent reflecting surface · Mobile edge computing · MEC server · Non-orthogonal multiple access · Successful computation probability · Uplink NOMA

## 1 Introduction

Many sensor nodes (SN) and machines were connected via wireless links in the Fourth Industrial Revolution era. However, since these nodes typically have limited computing capabilities, they cannot complete tasks that require large amounts of computation in instantaneous time, not responding in real-time [1]. In order to address this issue, servers with small-scale data centers, which usually are co-located with the access points (APs) or base station (BS), can be deployed

© ICST Institute for Computer Sciences, Social Informatics and Telecommunications Engineering 2022
Published by Springer Nature Switzerland AG 2022. All Rights Reserved
N.-S. Vo et al. (Eds.): INISCOM 2022, LNICST 444, pp. 48–61, 2022.
https://doi.org/10.1007/978-3-031-08878-0_4

at the edge of the network, delivering compute resources that help mobile devices complete a task. Therefore, these resource-intensive nodes can offload their tasks to APs for computing and obtain the results in real-time requirements via wireless links. This approach is mentioned as mobile edge computing (MEC) [2].

In addition, the non-orthogonal multiple access (NOMA) technique has been proposed to be integrated into MEC systems to increase the number of connections, and enhance spectrum efficiency and energy efficiency [3–6]. Zhow et al. in [3] investigates the NOMA MEC system and the problem of optimizing computational performance in two schemes, i.e., partial offloading and local computation. Meanwhile, the work [6] investigate the NOMA-MEC model in the wireless sensor network (WSN). The results show that the NOMA-MEC network performance is significantly superior to the traditional OMA method. However, NOMA MEC models still have many problems to be studied [7,8], such as user pairing issues or resource allocation issues. For instance, the more significant the difference in channel gain of the cell-center user and the cell-edge user, the higher the overall sum capacity, but the cell-edge user may encounter a risk of achieving a meager offloading success rate, reducing the overall performance of the system.

Therefore, integrating relaying and cooperative communication schemes into the NOMA-MEC network can help improve cell-edge user performance [9–12]. Indeed, relay-aided transmission models have been indicated to increase transmission reliability, network coverage, and achievable rate. Specifically, the authors in [12] presented promising NOMA-MEC-based relaying architectures and analyzed their advantages for both uplink and downlink. However, [13] stated that the drawbacks in current network technology are that it can only handle the transmitter and receiver, not the environment in between.

Recently, intelligent reflecting surfaces (IRS), which consist of a two dimensional passive element array, has been proposed as an effective solution to enhance the performance of next-generation wireless communication networks [14–16]. Each element of IRS can independently incur some change to the incident signal, e.g., the phase, amplitude, frequency, or even polarization. Therefore, an IRS intelligently configures the wireless environment to aid the transmissions between the base station and far users when direct links have low qualities. There have been several studies on independently integrating IRS with MEC [17,18], and IRS with NOMA [19–21], to maximize the advantages of these techniques.

Obviously, the integration of IRS into NOMA-MEC systems opens up a potential research direction, contributing to realizing the future MEC network [22–24]. Zhou et al. propose a two-user IRS-NOMA-MEC model with a novel NOMA time-sharing scheme that allows the system to switch using NOMA or TDMA. The authors investigate the system with two scenarios where the computing power of the MEC server is finite and infinite. Wang et al. studied a massive users NOMA-MEC IoT model with the help of multiple reflecting elements IRS. The authors state the problem of maximizing energy efficiency and propose a semidefinite programming relaxation algorithm to solve this non-convex problem. In the work [25], Li et al. consider an IRS wireless-powered NOMA MEC IoT network. Specifically, IoT devices (IDs) can harvest energy from a power station directly and through a reflected channel via IRS. The ID then uses the collected energy to offload the task to the AP using the uplink NOMA protocol. Simulation results clarified the effect of the IRS on the system in the absence of its use.

Motivated by [21], this paper considers an IRS-aided NOMA MEC network in which a cell-center user and an IRS-aided cell-edge user intend to offload their tasks to a MEC AP. The main contributions of our work are as follows:

- We investigate a MEC system model and IRS-NOMA protocol for this system.
- We derive the closed-form expressions for the successful computation probability (SCP) and ceiling in the high-SNR regime.
- To look insight into the behavior of this system, we investigate the impact of critical system parameters on the system performance.

The other parts of our paper is organized as follows. The system model of MEC based on IRS-NOMA protocol is described in Sect. 2. In Sect. 3, SCP is analyzed, closed-form expression is obtained. The numerical results and discussion are provided in Sect. 4. Finally, the conclusions and future works are presented in Sect. 5.

## 2   System Model

Let us consider an IRS-aided mobile edge computing NOMA network as shown in Fig. 1. In which, two resource-constrained mobile devices (MD), i.e., $U_1$ and $U_2$, offload their computation-intensive tasks to MEC with the support of IRS. More specifically, $U_1$ is the near user, i.e., the cell-center user, which can offload its tasks to AP directly. While $U_2$ is the far user, i.e., the cell-edge user, which needs assistance from the IRS for offloading because there is no direct channel from $U_2$ to AP due to large distances or/and blocking objects. The edge computing server, specifically the MEC server, is located at the AP. Suppose these two devices are connected by high data-rate optical fiber [17]. The IRS consisted of $N$ passive reflecting elements placed in the cell to assist the users' computation offloading. Assumed that the element spacing of the IRS is large enough so that the small-scale fading associated with two different, reflecting elements is independent. We assumed that all devices are equipped with a single antenna and operate in the half-duplex mode under Nakagami-$m$ fading.

Our proposed model is especially suitable for intelligent communication systems in IoT applications or smart factories [26,27]. For instance, SNs or machines in IoT systems will have difficulty communicating with APs in urban environments due to obstructions. However, the IRS deployed on the buildings will solve this problem by supporting the communication by creating a possible connection between both ends.

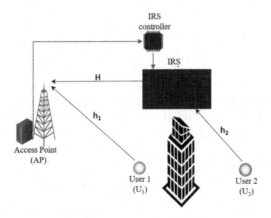

**Fig. 1.** System model

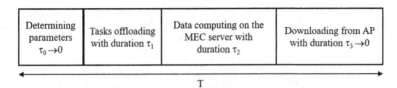

| Determining parameters $\tau_0 \to 0$ | Tasks offloading with duration $\tau_1$ | Data computing on the MEC server with duration $\tau_2$ | Downloading from AP with duration $\tau_3 \to 0$ |
|---|---|---|---|

T

**Fig. 2.** Time flow chart for uplink IRS-aided NOMA MEC network

Assumed that $U_1$ and and $U_2$ have $L_1$ and $L_2$ bit tasks, respectively, that need to be processed. However, these tasks cannot be processed locally within the maximum allowable delay due to the computational limitations of MDs. Therefore, $U_1$ and $U_2$ offload their tasks to the AP, and the MEC server will assist in the processing. The channel state information (CSI) of all channels in proposed system is assumed perfectly known at MEC AP [6, 28, 29]. Note that the AP-$U_1$ link is assumed to be NLoS, while the links of AP-IRS and IRS-$U_2$ can be either LoS or NLoS for different scenarios. The small-scale fading vectors of the links of AP-IRS, AP-$U_1$ and $U_2$-IRS denoted by $\mathbf{H} \in \mathbb{C}^{1 \times N}$, $\mathbf{h_1} \in \mathbb{C}^{1 \times 1}$ and $\mathbf{h_2} \in \mathbb{C}^{N \times 1}$, respectively. More specifically, they are $\mathbf{H} = [h_{01}, h_{02}, ..., h_{0N}]$, $\mathbf{h_1} = [h_{11}]$ and $\mathbf{h_2} = [h_{21}, h_{22}, ..., h_{2N}]^T$, respectively.

We continued to propose an offloading protocol, called the IRS-NOMA scheme, for the MEC network, as shown in Fig. 2.

- In the first phase, namely the parameter determining phase, the MDs $U_1$ and $U_2$ estimate the CSI at the beginning of each communication in period $\tau_0$.
- In the second phase, namely the offloading phase, $U_1$ and $U_2$ are paired together and apply the uplink NOMA technique to offload their tasks to the MEC server during period $\tau_1$. Based on the principle of NOMA, the received signal of offloading tasks at AP is expressed as:

$$y = \mathbf{h_1}\sqrt{\frac{\rho P_U}{d_1{}^{\alpha_1}}}s_1 + \mathbf{H\Phi h_2}\sqrt{\frac{(1-\rho)P_U}{d_{21}{}^{\alpha_2}d_{22}{}^{\alpha_2}}}s_2 + n, \tag{1}$$

where $P_U$ denotes the total transmit power of MD; $\rho$ represents the power allocation ratio; $s_i$ denotes for the offloading task of the $i^{th}$ user, $i \in \{1,2\}$; $d_1$, $d_{21}$ and $d_{22}$ denote the horizontal distances from AP to $U_1$, from AP to IRS and from IRS to $U_2$, respectively; $\alpha_1$ stands for the path loss exponent of the link from AP to $U_1$; $\alpha_2$ represents the path loss exponent of the link from AP to IRS and from $U_2$ to IRS; $n \sim \mathcal{CN}(0, \sigma^2)$ denotes the additive white Gaussian noise (AWGN) at AP; $\mathbf{\Phi} \overset{\Delta}{=} \text{diag}\left[\beta_1 e^{j\theta_1}, \beta_2 e^{j\theta_2}, ..., \beta_N e^{j\theta_N}\right]$, $j = \sqrt{-1}$, is a diagonal matrix with $\beta_n \in [0,1]$ is the amplitude-reflection and $\theta_n \in [0, 2\pi)$ is the phase-shift variable of the $n^{th}$ element of IRS.

- In the third phase, namely the computing phase, according to the uplink NOMA concept, AP first decodes the signal of $U_1$ by treating the signal from $U_2$ as interference and then subtracts $s_1$ from $y$ to obtain $s_2$. Hence, the signal-to-interference-plus-noise ratio (SINR) and the signal-to-noise ratio (SNR) at AP to decode $s_i$ are respectively written as

$$\gamma_{U_1} = \frac{\rho\gamma_U\eta|h_{11}|^2}{(1-\rho)\gamma_U\mu|\mathbf{H\Phi h_2}|^2 + 1} = \frac{\rho\gamma_U\eta X}{(1-\rho)\gamma_U\mu Y + 1}, \tag{2}$$

$$\gamma_{U_2} = (1-\rho)\gamma_U\mu|\mathbf{H\Phi h_2}|^2 = (1-\rho)\gamma_U\mu Y, \tag{3}$$

where $\gamma_U \overset{\Delta}{=} \frac{P_U}{\sigma^2}$ is the transmit SNR of users, $\eta \overset{\Delta}{=} d_1{}^{-\alpha_1}$, $\mu \overset{\Delta}{=} (d_{21}d_{22})^{-\alpha_2}$, $X \overset{\Delta}{=} |h_{11}|^2$, $Y \overset{\Delta}{=} |\mathbf{H\Phi h_2}|^2$. In this phase, these tasks are accomplished on the MEC server in period $\tau_2$.
- Finally, in the last phase, namely the result returning phase, AP returns the computation results to users during period $\tau_3$.

The time flow chart for the uplink IRS-aided NOMA MEC network is as Fig. 2, in which $\tau_0$, as well as $\tau_3$ are assumed very small compared to transmission time and thus are ignored [3,29].

Note that $h_{0n}$, $h_{11}$ and $h_{2n}$, $n \in \{1, 2, .., N\}$, follow the Nakagami-$m$ fading model with fading parameters, $m_H$, $m_{h1}$ and $m_{h2}$, respectively, i.e., the probability density function of them is given by

$$f(x) = \frac{2m^m x^{2m-1}}{\Gamma(m)}e^{-mx^2}, \tag{4}$$

where $\Gamma(.)$ is the gamma function, $m \in \{m_H, m_{h1}, m_{h2}\}$. Note that the NLoS condition is achieved when $m = 1$ is set, while the LoS condition is attained when $m > 1$ [30].

## 3    Performance Analysis

This section presents the performance analysis based on the criterion of successful computation probability (SCP). The SCP, denoted by $\Omega_s$, is used as a vital metric to describe the performance of a MEC system [6, 28, 29]. By definition, $\Omega_s$ is the probability that all tasks are successfully offloaded, computed, and feed-backed to the MDs within the maximum allowable system delay $T > 0$, which is expressed as

$$\Omega_s = \Pr\left(\tau_1 + \tau_2 \leq T\right), \tag{5}$$

where

$$\tau_1 = \max\left\{\frac{L_1}{B\log_2(1+\gamma_{U_1})}, \frac{L_2}{B\log_2(1+\gamma_{U_2})}\right\}, \tag{6}$$

in which $B$ denotes the channel bandwidth.

$$\tau_2 = \frac{\xi(L_1 + L_2)}{f}, \tag{7}$$

where $\xi$ and $f$ denote the number of CPU cycles needed for executing each bit and the CPU-cycle frequency of the MEC server, respectively.

Similar to [21], we adjust the parameters of the IRS to obtain the best channel quality for $U_2$, i.e., to maximize $|\mathbf{H\Phi h_2}|$. Note that,

$$|\mathbf{H\Phi h_2}| = |\sum_{n=1}^{N} \beta_n h_{0n} h_{2n} e^{j\theta_n}|, \tag{8}$$

thus, the phase-shift variables of all $h_{0n} h_{2n} e^{j\theta_n}$ are set to be the same, e.g., $\theta_n = \theta^* - \arg(h_{0n} h_{2n})$, where $\theta^*$ is an arbitrary constant, $\theta^* \in [0, 2\pi)$. For simplicity, we assume that $\beta_n = 1, \forall n$. Therefore, after deploying the optimal phases $\theta_n$, we have

$$Y = |\mathbf{H\Phi h_2}|^2 = \left(\sum_{n=1}^{N} |h_{0n}||h_{2n}|\right)^2 \tag{9}$$

According to [21], we implement the cummulative density function (CDF) and probability function (PDF) of the random variable $Y$ as follows:

$$F_Y(x) = e^{-\frac{\lambda}{2}} \sum_{i=0}^{\infty} \frac{\lambda^i \gamma\left(i + \frac{1}{2}, \frac{x}{2N(1-\nu)}\right)}{i! 2^i \Gamma\left(i + \frac{1}{2}\right)}, \tag{10}$$

$$f_Y(x) = e^{-\frac{x}{2N(1-\nu)} - \frac{\lambda}{2}} \sum_{i=0}^{\infty} \frac{\lambda^i x^{i-\frac{1}{2}}}{i! 2^{2i+\frac{1}{2}} \Gamma\left(i + \frac{1}{2}\right) [N(1-\nu)]^{i+\frac{1}{2}}}, \tag{11}$$

where

$$\nu = \frac{1}{m_H m_{h2}} \left[\frac{\Gamma\left(m_H + \frac{1}{2}\right)}{\Gamma(m_H)}\right]^2 \left[\frac{\Gamma\left(m_{h2} + \frac{1}{2}\right)}{\Gamma(m_{h2})}\right]^2, \tag{12}$$

$\lambda = \frac{N\nu}{1-\nu}$, and $\gamma(.,.)$ is the lower incomplete gamma function.

We continue to introduce the following two Lemmas to evaluate the proposed system performance.

**Lemma 1.** The closed-form expression of the SCP, i.e., $\Omega_s$, for the considered IRS NOMA MEC system based on the proposed IRS-NOMA scheme under quasi-static Nakagami-$m$ fading is as follows:

$$\Omega_s = e^{-\frac{\gamma_1^{th}}{\rho\eta\gamma_U} - \frac{\lambda}{2}} \sum_{i=0}^{\infty} \frac{\lambda^i \Gamma\left(i + \frac{1}{2}, \frac{\gamma_1^{th}\gamma_2^{th}}{\rho\eta\gamma_U} + \frac{\gamma_2^{th}}{2N(1-\nu)(1-\rho)\mu\gamma_U}\right)}{i! 2^{2i+\frac{1}{2}} \Gamma\left(i + \frac{1}{2}\right) \left[\frac{N(1-\nu)(1-\rho)\mu\gamma_1^{th}}{\rho\eta} + \frac{1}{2}\right]^{i+\frac{1}{2}}}, \quad (13)$$

where $\gamma_1^{th} = 2^{\frac{L_1}{BT'}} - 1$, $\gamma_2^{th} = 2^{\frac{L_2}{BT'}} - 1$, $T' = T - \frac{\xi(L_1+L_2)}{f}$, and $\Gamma(.,.)$ is the upper incomplete gamma function.

*Proof.* Expanding definition (5) with formulas (6), (7), we have:

$$\Omega_s = \Pr\left(\tau_1 + \tau_2 \leq T\right)$$

$$= \Pr\left(\max\left\{\frac{L_1}{B\log_2(1 + \gamma_{U_1})}, \frac{L_2}{B\log_2(1 + \gamma_{U_2})}\right\} + \frac{\xi(L_1 + L_2)}{f} \leq T\right)$$

$$= \Pr\left(\gamma_{U_1} > 2^{\frac{L_1}{BT'}} - 1, \gamma_{U_2} > 2^{\frac{L_2}{BT'}} - 1\right)$$

$$= \Pr\left(\frac{\rho\gamma_U\eta X}{(1-\rho)\gamma_U\mu Y + 1} > \gamma_1^{th}, (1-\rho)\gamma_U\mu Y > \gamma_2^{th}\right)$$

$$= \Pr\left(X > \frac{\gamma_1^{th}[(1-\rho)\gamma_U\mu Y + 1]}{\rho\gamma_U\eta}, Y > \frac{\gamma_2^{th}}{(1-\rho)\gamma_U\mu}\right)$$

$$= \int_a^{\infty} \left\{1 - F_X\left(\frac{\gamma_1^{th}[(1-\rho)\gamma_U\mu t + 1]}{\rho\gamma_U\eta}\right)\right\} f_Y(t)dt$$

$$\overset{(1)}{=} \int_a^{\infty} e^{-\frac{\gamma_1^{th}[(1-\rho)\gamma_U\mu t + 1]}{\rho\gamma_U\eta}} e^{-\frac{t}{2N(1-\nu)} - \frac{\lambda}{2}} \sum_{i=0}^{\infty} \frac{\lambda^i t^{i-\frac{1}{2}}}{i! 2^{2i+\frac{1}{2}} \Gamma\left(i + \frac{1}{2}\right) [N(1-\nu)]^{i+\frac{1}{2}}} dt$$

$$= e^{-\frac{\gamma_1^{th}}{\rho\gamma_U\eta} - \frac{\lambda}{2}} \sum_{i=0}^{\infty} \frac{\lambda^i}{i! 2^{2i+\frac{1}{2}} \Gamma\left(i + \frac{1}{2}\right) [N(1-\nu)]^{i+\frac{1}{2}}} \int_a^{\infty} e^{-\left[\frac{(1-\rho)\mu\gamma_1^{th}}{\rho\eta} + \frac{1}{2N(1-\nu)}\right]t} t^{i-\frac{1}{2}} dt$$

$$\overset{(2)}{=} e^{-\frac{\gamma_1^{th}}{\rho\gamma_U\eta} - \frac{\lambda}{2}} \sum_{i=0}^{\infty} \frac{\lambda^i \Gamma\left(i + \frac{1}{2}, \frac{(1-\rho)\mu\gamma_1^{th}a}{\rho\eta} + \frac{a}{2N(1-\nu)}\right)}{i! 2^{2i+\frac{1}{2}} \Gamma\left(i + \frac{1}{2}\right) \left[\frac{N(1-\nu)(1-\rho)\mu\gamma_1^{th}}{\rho\eta} + \frac{1}{2}\right]^{i+\frac{1}{2}}}.$$

where $T' = T - \frac{\xi(L_1+L_2)}{f}$, $\gamma_1^{th} = 2^{\frac{L_1}{BT'}} - 1$, $\gamma_2^{th} = 2^{\frac{L_2}{BT'}} - 1$, $a = \frac{\gamma_2^{th}}{(1-\rho)\mu\gamma_U}$, step (1) is obtained by substituting $F_X(x) = 1 - e^{-x}$ and (11), step (2) is obtained by applying the result of Eq. (3.381–3) in [31]. This concludes our proof.

**Lemma 2.** The SCP, i.e., $\Omega_s$, for the considered IRS NOMA MEC system based on the proposed IRS-NOMA scheme under quasi-static Nakagami-$m$ fading when operating in a high transmit SNR regime, approaches the ceiling as follows:

$$\Omega_s^\infty = e^{-\frac{\lambda}{2}} \sum_{i=0}^{\infty} \frac{\lambda^i}{i! 2^{2i+\frac{1}{2}} \left[ \frac{N(1-\nu)(1-\rho)\mu\gamma_1^{th}}{\rho\eta} + \frac{1}{2} \right]^{i+\frac{1}{2}}}. \tag{14}$$

*Proof.* When $\gamma_U \rightarrow \infty$, $\lim\limits_{\gamma_U \rightarrow \infty} e^{-\frac{\gamma_1^{th}}{\rho\eta\gamma_U}} \rightarrow 1$ and $\lim\limits_{\gamma_U \rightarrow \infty} \Gamma\left(i + \frac{1}{2}, \frac{\gamma_1^{th}\gamma_2^{th}}{\rho\eta\gamma_U} + \right.$ $\left. \frac{\gamma_2^{th}}{2(1-\rho)b\gamma_U} \right) \rightarrow \Gamma\left(i + \frac{1}{2}\right)$. Thus, the upper bound of $\Omega_s$ can be obtained as (14). This concludes our proof.

# 4   Numerical Results and Discussion

In this section, we provide the numerical results and discussions of SCP-based system performance. Table 1 summarizes the Monte-Carlo simulation parameters to be used in the next part of this manuscript [21].

**Table 1.** Simulation parameters

| Parameters | Notation | Typical values |
|---|---|---|
| Environment | | Nakagami-$m$ |
| Nakagami fading parameters | $m_H$, $m_{h2}$ | 3, 1.5 |
| Distances | $d_1$, $d_{21}$, $d_{22}$ | 10 m, 40 m, 10 m |
| Path-loss exponents | $\alpha_1$, $\alpha_2$ | 3.5, 2.5 |
| Number of IRS' elements | $N$ | 18, 24, 30 |
| The transmit power | $P_U$ | 10–40 dB |
| The CPU-cycle frequency of MEC server | $f$ | 1 GHz |
| The number of CPU cycles of MEC server for executing each bit | $\rho$ | 5 |
| The channel bandwidth | $B$ | 300–800 MHz |
| The threshold of latency | $T$ | 1 s |
| The total data bits of user tasks | $L$ | 0.5–1.5 Mbits |
| The length of U$_1$'s task | $L_1$ | 0.4 L Mbits |
| The length of U$_2$'s task | $L_2$ | 0.6 L Mbits |

## 4.1   The Impact of the Average Transmit SNR and the Number of IRS Elements

Figure 3 depicts the curves of successful computation probability $\Omega_s$ been subject to the average transmit SNR ($\gamma_U$) and the different number of IRS elements ($N$). When the $\gamma_U$ increase, $\Omega_s$ increases. When $\gamma_U$ rises too high above 35 dB, $\Omega_s$ gradually approaches saturation value. Another observation in Fig. 3 is that when $N$ increases, $\Omega_s$ increases. It is consistent with the fact that when the number of IRS elements increases, it means $U_2$ will be better supported for offloading, leading to improved performance of the whole system.

However, the effects of $N$ on SCP are clearly observable only in cases where $\gamma_U$ has a low value. In the opposite case, as observed in the accompanying small figure, increasing $N$ can improve $\Omega_s$ very little, only about 0.1 %. To put it more simply, the IRS NOMA MEC system can be designed with a low number of IRS elements when the transmitting power of the devices is large enough.

The key fact to remember is that the SCP can be improved by increasing the transmit power and/or the number of IRS elements.

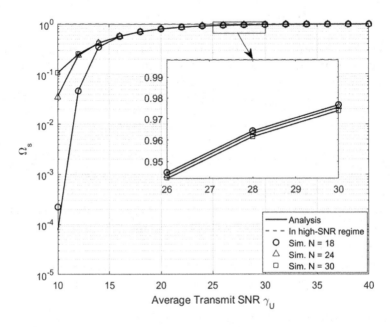

**Fig. 3.** $\Omega_s$ vs. average transmit SNR $\gamma_U$ with different $N$.

## 4.2   The Impact of the Task Length and the Bandwidth

In this experiments, we investigate the impact of the task length ($L$) and the bandwidth ($B$) on $\Omega_s$, which are depicted as Fig. 4 and Fig. 5, respectively. We can observe that $\Omega_s$ increases when $L$ decreases. It is consistent with the formulas (6) and (7), when $L$ decreases, the time to offload and calculate the tasks decreases, leading to the probability that the tasks are completed within the time $T$ allows increase. However, the effect of $L$ on $\Omega_s$ is only clearly observed when ($\gamma_U$) is low.

The result from Fig. 5 shows that when we increase the bandwidth, system performance is improved. The formula (6) could explain this result: As $B$ increases, $\tau_1$ decreases, meaning less time is needed to offload tasks, leading to improved $\Omega_s$. We conclude that the SCP of proposed system can be improved by increasing the bandwidth and/or decreasing the task length.

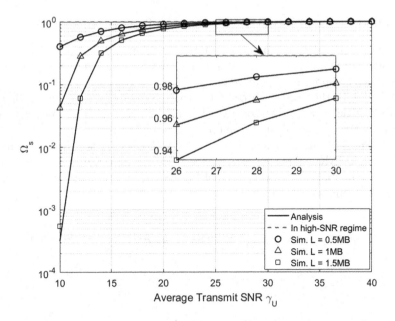

**Fig. 4.** $\Omega_s$ vs. average transmit SNR $\gamma_U$ with different task length $L$.

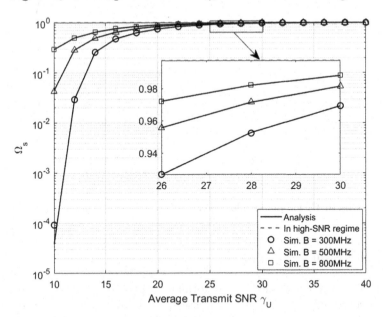

**Fig. 5.** $\Omega_s$ vs. average transmit SNR $\gamma_U$ with different bandwidth $B$.

### 4.3    The Impact of Power Allocation Coefficient

The curves in Fig. 6 demonstrate the impact of power allocation coefficient ($\rho$) on $\Omega_s$ with different transmit power levels. Again, this figure shows that the system's SCP responds as $\gamma_0$ increases.

According to the form of three SCP curves, we state that $\Omega_s$ increases when $\rho$ increases from 0 to $\rho^*$. In contrary $\Omega_s$ falls when $\rho$ increases from $\rho^*$ to 1, where $\rho^*$ is the optimal value for maximization of $\Omega_s$.

From Fig. 3, 4 and 5, when $\gamma_U \to \infty$ the ceiling of $\Omega_s$ is nearly 1. It means that in a high-SNR regime, $\Omega_s$ approaches 1. Referring to the views of the above results, we can state that the agreement between simulation and analysis results is good, confirming our analysis's accuracy.

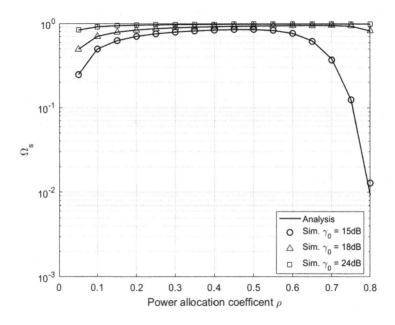

**Fig. 6.** $\Omega_s$ vs. power allocation coefficient $\rho$ with different $\gamma_U$.

## 5    Conclusion

In this paper, we have studied the performance of an IRS-assisted NOMA MEC system. Accordingly, we propose a 4-phase IRS-NOMA protocol for the system, including the parameter determining, offloading, computing, and result returning phases. We derive the closed-form expressions of successful computation probability and its ceiling in the high-SNR regime. Furthermore, the impacts of critical system parameters, such as the transmit SNR, the number of IRS elements, the task length, bandwidth, and the power allocation coefficient on the behavior of this considered system, have been evaluated to look insight into the performance.

In order to improve the system performance, we can increase the transmit SNR, number of IRS elements, and bandwidth or decrease the task length or select the optimal power allocation coefficient. We will focus on the multiple users wireless power transfer of this IRS NOMA MEC system in future work.

# References

1. Pham, Q.V., Fang, F., Ha, V.N., Piran, M.J., Le, M., Le, L.B., Hwang, W.J., et al.: A survey of multi-access Edge Computing in 5G and beyond: fundamentals, technology integration, and state-of-the-art. IEEE Access **8**, 116974–117017 (2020)
2. Mao, Y., You, C., Zhang, J., Huang, K., Letaief, K.B.: A survey on mobile edge computing: the communication perspective. IEEE Commun. Surv. Tutor. **19**(4), 2322–2358 (2017)
3. Zhou, F., Wu, Y., Hu, R.Q., Qian, Y.: Computation efficiency in a wireless-powered mobile edge computing network with NOMA. In: IEEE International Conference on Communications (ICC), 20–24 May 2019, Shanghai, China (2019)
4. Ding, Z., Fan, P., Poor, H.V.: Impact of non-orthogonal multiple access on the offloading of mobile edge computing. IEEE Trans. Commun. **67**(1), 375–390 (2019)
5. Wang, F., Xu, J., Ding, Z.: Multi-antenna noma for computation offloading in multiuser mobile edge computing systems. IEEE Trans. Commun. **67**(3), 2450–2463 (2019)
6. Truong, V.T., Ha, D.B., So-In, C., et al.: On the system performance of mobile edge computing in an uplink NOMA WSN with a multiantenna access point over nakagami-$m$ fading. IEEE/CAA J. Automatica Sinica **9**(4), 668–685 (2022)
7. Akbar, A., Sobia Jangsher, F.A.B.: NOMA and 5G emerging technologies: a survey on issues and solution techniques. Comput. Netw. **190**, 107950 (2021). https://doi.org/10.1016/j.comnet.2021.107950
8. Maraqa, O., Rajasekaran, A.S., Al-Ahmadi, S., Yanikomeroglu, H., Sait, S.M.: A survey of rate-optimal power domain NOMA with enabling technologies of future wireless networks. IEEE Commun. Surv. Tut. **22**(4), 2192–2235, 107950 (2020)
9. Duong, T.Q., Bao, V.N.Q.: Performance analysis of selection decode-and-forward relay networks. Electron. Lett. **44**(20), 1206–1207 (2008)
10. Fan, L., Zhang, S., Duong, T.Q., Karagiannidis, G.K.: Secure switch-and-stay combining (SSSC) for cognitive relay networks. IEEE Trans. Commun. **64**(1), 70–82, 107950 (2015)
11. Truong, V.T., Vo, M.T., Lee, Y., Ha, D.B.: Amplify-and-forward relay transmission in uplink non-orthogonal multiple access networks. In: 2019 6th NAFOSTED Conference on Information and Computer Science (NICS), pp. 1–6 (2019). https://doi.org/10.1109/NICS48868.2019.9023818
12. Li, D., Li, B., Qin, N., Jing, X., Du, C., Wan, C.: The research of NOMA-MEC network based on untrusted relay-assisted transmission in power internet of things. IOP Conf. Ser. Earth Environ. Sci. **634**, 012052 (2021)
13. Di Renzo, M., et al.: Reconfigurable intelligent surfaces vs. relaying: differences, similarities, and performance comparison. IEEE Open J. Commun. Soc. **1**, 798–807, 012052 (2020)
14. Alghamdi, R.: Intelligent surfaces for 6G wireless networks: a survey of optimization and performance analysis techniques. IEEE Access **8**, 202795–202818, 012052 (2020). https://doi.org/10.1109/ACCESS.2020.3031959

15. Dai, L.: Reconfigurable intelligent surface-based wireless communications: antenna design, prototyping, and experimental results. IEEE Access **8**, 45913–45923, 012052 (2020). https://doi.org/10.1109/ACCESS.2020.2977772

16. Chen, Z., Ma, X., Han, C., Wen, Q.: Towards intelligent reflecting surface empowered 6g terahertz communications: a survey. China Commun. **18**(5), 93–119 (2021). https://doi.org/10.23919/JCC.2021.05.007

17. Bai, T., Pan, C., Deng, Y., Elkashlan, M., Nallanathan, A., Hanzo, L.: Latency minimization for intelligent reflecting surface aided mobile edge computing. IEEE J. Sel. Areas Commun. **38**, 2666–2682 (2020)

18. Chu, Z., Xiao, P., Shojafar, M., Mi, D., Mao, J., Hao, W.: Intelligent reflecting surface assisted mobile edge computing for internet of things. IEEE Wireless Commun. Lett. **10**(3), 619–623, 012052 (2021). https://doi.org/10.1109/LWC.2020.3040607

19. Yang, G., Xu, X., Liang, Y.: Intelligent reflecting surface assisted non-orthogonal multiple access. In: 2020 IEEE Wireless Communications and Networking Conference (WCNC), pp. 1–6 (2020). https://doi.org/10.1109/WCNC45663.2020.9120476

20. Zheng, B., Wu, Q., Zhang, R.: Intelligent reflecting surface-assisted multiple access with user pairing: NOMA or OMA? IEEE Commun. Lett. **24**(4), 753–757 (2020). https://doi.org/10.1109/LCOMM.2020.2969870

21. Cheng, Y., Li, K.H., Liu, Y., Teh, K.C., Vincent Poor, H.: Downlink and uplink intelligent reflecting surface aided networks: NOMA and OMA. IEEE Trans. Wireless Commun. **20**(6) (2021). https://doi.org/10.1109/twc.2021.3054841

22. Zhou, F., You, C., Zhang, R.: Delay-optimal scheduling for IRS-aided mobile edge computing. IEEE Wireless Commun. Lett. **10**, 740–744 (2021). https://doi.org/10.1109/LWC.2020.3042189

23. Chen, G., Wu, Q., Chen, W., Ng, D.W.K., Hanzo, L.: IRS-aided wireless powered MEC systems: TDMA or NOMA for computation offloading? 2108.06120 (2021)

24. Wang, Q., Zhou, F., Hu, H., Hu, R.Q.: Energy-efficient design for IRS-assisted MEC networks with NOMA. In: 2021 13th International Conference on Wireless Communications and Signal Processing (WCSP) (IEEE), pp. 1–6 (2021)

25. Li, X., Xie, Z., Chu, Z., Menon, V.G., Mumtaz, S., Zhang, J.: Exploiting benefits of IRS in wireless powered NOMA networks. IEEE Trans. on Green Commun. Netw. **6**(1), 175–186 (2022). https://doi.org/10.1109/TGCN.2022.3144744

26. Okogbaa, F.C., et al.: Design and application of intelligent reflecting surface (IRS) for beyond 5G wireless networks: a review. Sensors **22**(7), 2436 (2022)

27. Chu, Z., Xiao, P., Shojafar, M., Mi, D., Mao, J., Hao, W.: Intelligent reflecting surface assisted Mobile Edge Computing for Internet of Things. IEEE Wireless Commun. Lett. **10**(3), 619–623 (2020)

28. Truong, V.T., Ha, D.B., Lee, Y., Nguyen, A.N.: On performance of cooperative transmission in Uplink Non-orthogonal Multiple Access wireless sensor networks. In: Proceedings of the 4th International Conference on Recent Advance in Signal Processing, Telecommunications and Computing (SigTelCom) (IEEE), pp. 56–60 (2020)

29. Ye, Y., Lu, G., Hu, R.Q., Shi, L.: On the performance and optimization for MEC networks using uplink NOMA. In: IEEE International Conference on Communications Workshops (ICC Workshops), Shanghai, China (IEEE) (2019)

30. Nguyen, A.N., So-In, C., Ha, D.B., Truong, V.T. et al.: Performance analysis in UAV-enabled relay with NOMA under Nakagami-$m$ fading considering adaptive power splitting. In: 2021 18th International Joint Conference on Computer Science and Software Engineering (JCSSE) (IEEE), pp. 1–6 (2021)
31. Gradshteyn, I., Ryzhik, I.: Table of Integrals, Series, and Products. Elsevier Academic Press (2007)

# Performance Analysis of RF Energy Harvesting NOMA Mobile Edge Computing in Multiple Devices IIoT Networks

Van-Truong Truong[1,2], Dac-Binh Ha[1,2], Tien-Vu Truong[3],
and Anand Nayyar[4(✉)]

[1] Faculty of Electrical-Electronic Engineering, Duy Tan University,
Da Nang 550000, Vietnam
truongvantruong@dtu.edu.vn, hadacbinh@duytan.edu.vn
[2] Institute of Research and Development, Duy Tan University,
Da Nang 550000, Vietnam
[3] Faculty of Information Technology, Duy Tan University, Da Nang, Vietnam
truongtienvu@dtu.edu.vn
[4] Science and Technology Department, Duy Tan University, Da Nang, Vietnam
anandnayyar@duytan.edu.vn

**Abstract.** This paper considers the efficient offloading and computation design for radio frequency energy harvesting (RF EH) uplink non-orthogonal multiple access (NOMA) industrial Internet of Thing (IIoT) network. Specifically, the system contains multiple energy-constrained devices classified into two clusters and a MEC server deployed in a wireless access point (AP). We propose a four-phase communication protocol, namely EOCD, consisting of EH, task offloading, task computation, and information feedback transmission. Cluster head (CH) scheme is applied based on the channel information state to harvest RF energy from the AP in the first phase. In the second phase, CHs offload their workload to the AP using NOMA. The AP decodes the information signal and supports the computation of offload tasks in the third phase. Finally, AP feedbacks the result to each CH. Accordingly, we derive the closed-form expressions for the successful computation probability (SCP) of the considered system and CHs. We use Monte Carlo simulations to verify the results of the mathematical analysis. The numerical results demonstrate the effects of critical system parameters such as the time switching ratio, the transmit power, the number of devices in the cluster, and the task length of our proposed EOCD scheme compared to the conventional orthogonal multiple access (OMA) schemes.

**Keywords:** Mobile edge computing · Non-orthogonal multiple access · Uplink NOMA · Successful computation probability · Multiple devices

© ICST Institute for Computer Sciences, Social Informatics and Telecommunications Engineering 2022
Published by Springer Nature Switzerland AG 2022. All Rights Reserved
N.-S. Vo et al. (Eds.): INISCOM 2022, LNICST 444, pp. 62–76, 2022.
https://doi.org/10.1007/978-3-031-08878-0_5

# 1   Introduction

In recent years, Industry 4.0 has been effectively deployed in many industries such as automobile manufacturing, oil and gas exploitation, and warehouse management. Accordingly, the concept of IIoT was born with the leverage and reality of IoT in the context of industrial transformation and focused on guaranteeing real-time performance [1,2]. In IIoT paradigm, there are a massive number of mobile devices or machines connected and synchronized within the density network [3,4]. Moreover, many IIoT applications sponsored by local users can be very computation-intensive and latency-critical, e.g., smart factory, virtual reality, remote surgery, and autonomous car [5]. However, the finite battery life and the limited computation capacity of these devices pretend vital challenges. Mobile edge computing (MEC) is proposed, which enables edge users offload their task to MEC servers deployed at the edge network, can address the challenges mentioned above [6–8]. Moreover, the robust resource MEC servers can support energy or caching to ensure edge devices performance [9–11]. Therefore, the design of the MEC model needs a combination of the allocation of radio communication resources and devices computing resources, which is a complex problem and attracts much research attention [12]. Moreover, to further enhance the MEC offloading efficiency, a new multi-function MEC paradigm has been proposed, in which the MEC servers can employ different radio access networks (RANs) for wireless power charging and offloaded-task computing [13].

Since non-orthogonal multiple access (NOMA) outperforms compare to OMA in terms of spectral efficiency, supporting massive connectivity, and reduce latency [14], many researchers have proposed and evaluated system performance with NOMA MEC models [15–18]. For instance, Zhu *et al.* in [16] proposed a multi-user task offloading model in a NOMA MEC network. Specifically, a base station (BS) equipped with a MEC server assists $N$ users with different task requests. The users are divided into $L$ pairs, and each pair is allocated a time slot to offload the task using uplink NOMA. The authors proposed a matching-based user grouping algorithm and optimal power and time allocation that minimizes system energy consumption and delay. In [18], Xue *et al.* proposed the NOMA MEC multi-user multi-server system. The authors use the Lagrangian multiplier method to determine the optimal transmission power allocation to help the system achieve maximum offloading efficiency.

In addition, in an effort to develop a RAN system with self-sufficient devices, the radio frequency energy harvesting (RF EH) technique has been proposed [19]. This technique allows users to receive wireless power in the frequency bands from 3 KHz -3 GHz from BS or wireless access point (AP). Accordingly, edge users will be assured of energy for the computation and offloading processes, improving system performance. For instance, Vo *et al.* in [20] proposes a relay-based IoT network model using RF EH technique. The relays use power-splitting-based relaying for the EH process and forward information from a multi-antenna BS to the IoT sensor. The results show that this approach helps to improve system performance in terms of outage probability and throughput. More realistically, Vyas *et al.* in [21] proposed an RF EH prototype with an adaptive duty cycle determination method for scavenging wireless power from TV signals at the distance of 6.5 km from the source.

However, the research on the design of multiple devices RF EH NOMA MEC networks has not been considered in the previous works. This motivated us to propose an RF EH and information transmission based devices selection and NOMA for multiple devices MEC IIoT systems. Accordingly, we analyze system performance by deriving the analytical expressions for successful computation probability (SCP) of system and each user. Our main contributions are as follows:

- We study the multiple devices RF EH NOMA MEC IIoT network over Rayleigh fading channel. Accordingly, we propose the four phase system protocol with CH approach, namely EOCD, to ensure the real-time performance.
- We derive the closed-form expression of successful computation probability (SCP) for the whole system and two CHs. Furthermore, we provided numerical results to investigate the impact of the network parameters, i.e., transmit power, time switching ratio, task length, bandwidth, to verify RF EH NOMA deployment's effectiveness in the MEC network.
- We compare the system performance between the EOCD and OMA scheme to clarify the outstanding performance of our proposed scheme.

The remainder of this paper is organized as follows. In Sect. 2, we introduce the system model and communication protocol for the multiple devices RF EH NOMA MEC IIoT systems. In Sect. 3, we perform the performance analysis in terms of SCP of whole system and each CHs. Section 4 presents simulation results and some discussion. Section 5 concludes the paper with future scope.

## 2  System Model

We consider an RF EH NOMA-aided computation offloading in a multiple IIoT devices (ID) MEC network as illustrated in Fig. 1. Specifically, a hybrid MEC server deployed in an access point $(AP)$ to provide wireless power and offloading services for multiple IDs. The IDs are classified into two clusters, i.e., **A** and **B** to oversee different tasks in a smart factory. The cluster **A** has $M$ IDs, denoted by $A_m, (m = 1, ..., M)$, which performs tasks of length $L_{A_m}$. Whereas cluster **B** has $N$ IDs, denoted by $B_n, (n = 1, ..., N)$, performing tasks of length $L_{B_n}$.

Due to the characteristics of working in IIoT networks with a dynamic environment and mission-critical applications, IDs require an uninterrupted supply of energy and regular collection of ambient data, and timely delivery of control decisions [1,20]. Thus, the IDs in the network are equipped with hardware to harvest the RF energy of the $AP$ to ensure continuous and seamless operation [9,22]. Since the computational capabilities of these IDs are limited, the users are assumed to offload their computationally intensive tasks to the hybrid MEC server. Furthermore, for reliability and redundancy, we assume each cluster monitors the same events and executes the same tasks, i.e., $L_{A_m} = L_1$ and $L_{B_n} = L_2$. All devices are assumed to be equipped with a single antenna and operate in the half-duplex mode [7,9].

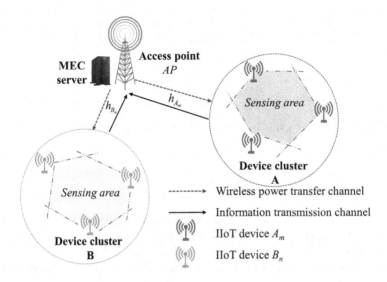

**Fig. 1.** Multiple devices RF EH NOMA MEC IIoT system model

## 2.1 Proposed Methodology

In this section, we propose a novel communication and offloading protocol, namely EOCD, for the proposed system. Following [8,9], we design a protocol that combines the offloading, communication, and computing processes in the NOMA MEC IIoT network to ensure energy and latency constraints.

Because $AP$ and IDs are in the same MEC system with a short transmission distance, we assume $AP$ has the full channel state information (CSI) of the system [8,9]. Before the communication takes place, $AP$ sends a pilot signal to the IDs, and estimates the CSI of all links $\nu - AP, \nu \in \{A_n, B_m\}$. Based on the information collected, the $AP$ selects the cluster head (CH) for each cluster so that the channel from the $AP$ to each CH has the largest signal-to-noise ratio (SNR). The CHs representing the cluster send all their collected information to the $AP$. In the scope of this paper, we assume that the communication process between IDs and their CH has been resolved [23], and do not consider here.

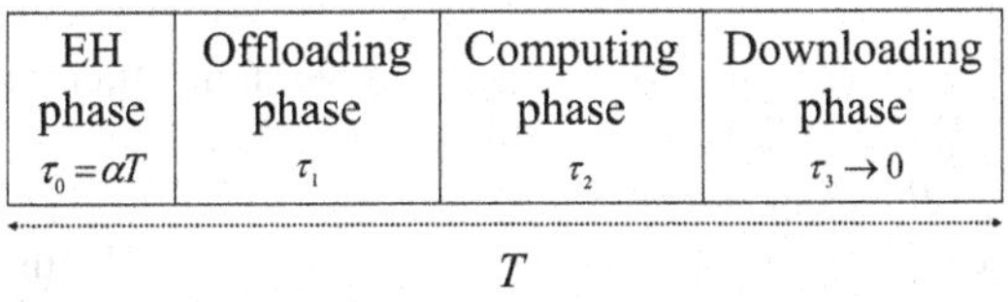

| EH phase | Offloading phase | Computing phase | Downloading phase |
|---|---|---|---|
| $\tau_0 = \alpha T$ | $\tau_1$ | $\tau_2$ | $\tau_3 \to 0$ |

$T$

**Fig. 2.** Time flow chart of system protocol EOCD for proposed system

Let $A^*$ and $B^*$ be the CH of the cluster **A** and **B**, respectively. The formulas describe the indices of the CHs for communication as follows:

$$A^* = \arg \max_{1 \leq m \leq M} \{g_{A_m}\},$$
$$B^* = \arg \max_{1 \leq n \leq N} \{g_{B_n}\}. \tag{1}$$

The channel power gains of the CHs for communication as follows:

$$g_{A^*} = \max_{1 \leq m \leq M} \{g_{A_m}\},$$
$$g_{B^*} = \max_{1 \leq n \leq N} \{g_{B_n}\}. \tag{2}$$

Let $g_\nu, \nu \in \{A^*, B^*\}$ denotes the channel power gain of links $\nu - AP$. We assume that the links from $AP$ to IDs are independent and modeled as Rayleigh fading channels. Thus $g_\nu$ are random variables that follow an exponential distribution. Accordingly, the probability density function (PDF) and cumulative distribution function (CDF) of $g_\nu$ are, respectively,

$$F_{g_\nu}(x) = \left(1 - e^{-\frac{x}{\lambda_\nu}}\right)^L = \sum_{l=0}^{L} \binom{L}{l} (-1)^l e^{-\frac{lx}{\lambda_\nu}}, \tag{3}$$

$$f_{g_\nu}(x) = \sum_{l=1}^{L} \binom{L}{l} \frac{(-1)^{l+1} l}{\lambda_\nu} e^{-\frac{lx}{\lambda_\nu}}, \tag{4}$$

where $L \in \{M, N\}$.

The system protocol EOCD, whose time flow chart is shown in Fig. 2, is divided into four phases in transmission time block $T$, as follows:

– *Phase 1 - EH phase:*
  During this phase, $A^*$ and $B^*$ harvest RF energy from the $AP$ for the period $\tau_0 = \alpha T$, where $\alpha$ denotes the time switching ratio, i.e., $0 < \alpha < 1$, and $T$ stands for the threshold of latency. If the system is integrated with optimization algorithms, $AP$ will calculate the EH time so that the system's performance is maximized. The energy obtained by the CHs in this process is:

$$E_\nu = \eta P_0 g_\nu \alpha T, \tag{5}$$

  where $0 < \eta \leq 1$ stands for the energy conversion efficiency of the energy receiver [9,24], $P_0$ denotes the transmit power of $AP$.
– *Phase 2 - Task offloading phase:*
  This phase takes place in the period $\tau_1$, in which CHs use all the energy collected in *Phase 1* to send their task to $AP$ using uplink NOMA. Thus, the received superposition signal at $AP$ is as follows:

$$y_{AP} = h_{A^*} \sqrt{P_{A^*}} x_A + h_{B^*} \sqrt{P_{B^*}} x_B + n_{AP}, \tag{6}$$

where $h_\nu$ denotes the channel coefficient of the link $\nu - AP$, $x_\nu$ stands for the offloading task of the CH $\nu$, $\nu \in \{A^*, B^*\}$, $n_{AP} \sim \mathcal{CN}(0, \sigma^2)$ represents the AWGN at the $AP$. The transmit power of CHs is as follows

$$P_\nu = \frac{E_\nu}{(1-\alpha)T - \tau} = aP_0 g_\nu, \tag{7}$$

where $a \triangleq \frac{\eta\alpha T}{(1-\alpha)T-\tau}$, $\tau$ stands for the computing time at hybrid MEC server defined as follows:

$$\tau = \frac{\rho(L_1 + L_2)}{f}, \tag{8}$$

where $\rho$ denotes the number of required CPU cycles for each input bit, and $f$ is the CPU-cycle frequency of hybrid MEC server.

– *Phase 3 - Data computing phase:*

In this phase, the $AP$ uses successive interference cancellation (SIC) to decode the superimposed signal to obtain useful signals from the CHs [15–17]. The $AP$ decodes the higher-power level signal first and treat the lower-power level signal as noise. Continuing, the $AP$ discards the decoded signal and receives the rest one. In this context, at $AP$ exist two signal decoding scenarios described as follows:

- In the case the channel power gain of link $A^* - AP$ is better than channel power gain of link $B^* - AP$, i.e., $g_{A^*} > g_{B^*}$, $AP$ applies SIC technique to decode $x_A$ by treating the message $x_B$ as noise. Then $AP$ obtains $x_B$ by subtracting $x_A$ from received signal $y_{AP}$. Hence, the signal-to-interference-plus-noise ratio (SINR) and the SNR for the $AP$ to decode $x_\nu, \nu \in \{A, B\}$ are written as:

$$\gamma_{11} = \frac{a\gamma_0 g_{A^*}^2}{a\gamma_0 g_{B^*}^2 + 1}, \tag{9}$$

$$\gamma_{12} = a\gamma_0 g_{B^*}^2, \tag{10}$$

where $\gamma_0 = \frac{P_0}{\sigma^2}$.

- In the opposite case, i.e., $g_{A^*} < g_{B^*}$, the SINR and SNR for the $AP$ to decode $x_\nu, \nu \in \{A, B\}$ are written as:

$$\gamma_{22} = \frac{a\gamma_0 g_{B^*}^2}{a\gamma_0 g_{A^*}^2 + 1}, \tag{11}$$

$$\gamma_{21} = a\gamma_0 g_{A^*}^2. \tag{12}$$

The achievable channel capacity from CHs $A^*$ and $B^*$ to the $AP$ is as:

$$\begin{cases} C_{11} = (1-\alpha)B\log(1+\gamma_{11}), \\ C_{12} = (1-\alpha)B\log(1+\gamma_{12}), & g_{A^*} > g_{B^*} \\ C_{21} = (1-\alpha)B\log(1+\gamma_{21}), \\ C_{22} = (1-\alpha)B\log(1+\gamma_{22}), & g_{A^*} < g_{B^*} \end{cases} \tag{13}$$

where $B$ denotes the channel bandwidth.

Then, these tasks are executed on the hybrid MEC server in duration $\tau_2$.

- *Phase 4 - Downloading phase:*
  Finally, in the last phase, CHs download the results from $AP$ during $\tau_3$. $\tau_3$ is assumed very small compared to transmission time and thus is neglected [25].

## 3    Performance Analysis

Following [8,9,25], the successful computation probability (SCP), denoted by $\phi_s$, of the RF EH NOMA MEC IIoT system is defined as the probability that the cluster's tasks are completed within the maximum delay time allows $T > 0$. Thus, we derive the formula of SCP as follow:

$$\phi_s = \Pr(\max(t_1, t_2) + \tau \le T) \tag{14}$$

where $t_1$ and $t_2$ are the transmission latency of $A^*$ and $B^*$, respectively and calculated as follows:

$$\begin{cases} t_1 = \frac{L_1}{C_{11}}, t_2 = \frac{L_2}{C_{12}}, & g_{A^*} > g_{B^*} \\ t_1 = \frac{L_1}{C_{21}}, t_2 = \frac{L_2}{C_{22}}, & g_{A^*} < g_{B^*} \end{cases} \tag{15}$$

We derive the SCP of two CHs and whole system as three Lemma.

**Lemma 1.** The closed-form expression of the SCP of CH $A^*$, denoted by $\phi_s^{A^*}$, for this considered system over quasi-static Rayleigh fading is as follow:

$$\phi_s^{A^*} = \begin{cases} \sum_{MN} \left\{ \frac{n}{\lambda_{B_n}} \frac{\pi}{K} \sum_{i=1}^{K} \exp\left(-\frac{m}{\lambda_{A_m}}\sqrt{\Psi_1} - \frac{n}{\lambda_{B_n}}\ln\frac{1}{x_i}\right)\sqrt{\frac{1-\phi_i}{1+\phi_i}} \right. \\ \left. + \frac{m\lambda_{B_n}}{m\lambda_{B_n}+n\lambda_{A_m}}\exp\left[-b_1\left(\frac{m}{\lambda_{A_m}}+\frac{n}{\lambda_{B_n}}\right)\right] \right\}, \gamma_{th1} < 1 \\[2em] \sum_{MN} \left\{ \frac{n}{\lambda_{B_n}}\frac{\pi c_1}{2K}\sum_{i=1}^{K}\exp\left(\frac{m}{\lambda_{A_m}}\sqrt{\Theta_1}-\frac{n}{\lambda_{B_n}y_i}\right)\sqrt{1-\phi_i^2} \right. \\ + \frac{n\lambda_{A_m}}{m\lambda_{B_n}+n\lambda_{A_m}}\exp\left[-c_1\left(\frac{m}{\lambda_{A_m}}+\frac{n}{\lambda_{B_n}}\right)\right] \\ \left. + \frac{m\lambda_{B_n}}{m\lambda_{B_n}+n\lambda_{A_m}}\exp\left[-b_1\left(\frac{m}{\lambda_{A_m}}+\frac{n}{\lambda_{B_n}}\right)\right] \right\}, \gamma_{th1} > 1 \end{cases} \tag{16}$$

where $\sum_{MN} \triangleq -\sum_{m=1}^{M}\sum_{n=1}^{N}\binom{M}{m}\binom{N}{n}(-1)^{m+n+1}$, $\Psi_1 = \gamma_{th1}\left(\ln^2\frac{1}{x_i}+\frac{1}{a\gamma_0}\right)$, $x_i = \frac{\phi_i+1}{2}$, $\phi_i = \cos(\frac{2i-1}{2K}\pi)$, $\gamma_{th1} = 2^{\frac{L_1}{(1-\alpha)B\Omega_1}}-1$, $\Omega_1 = (1-\alpha)T-\tau_1$, $\tau_1 = \frac{\rho L_1}{f}$, $c_1 = \sqrt{\frac{\gamma_{th1}}{a\gamma_0(1-\gamma_{th1})}}$, $\Theta_1 = \gamma_{th1}y_i^2+\frac{1}{a\gamma_0}$, $y_i = \frac{\phi_i+1}{2}c_1$, $b_1 = \sqrt{\frac{\gamma_{th1}}{a\gamma_0}}$, $K$ is the complexity-vs-accuracy trade-off coefficient.

*Proof.* See the Appendix A.

**Lemma 2.** The closed-form expression of the SCP of CH $B_n^*$, denoted by $\phi_s^{B^*}$, for this considered system over quasi-static Rayleigh fading is as follow

$$\phi_s^{B^*} = \begin{cases} \sum\limits_{MN} \left\{ \frac{m}{\lambda_{A_m}} \frac{\pi}{K} \sum\limits_{i=1}^{K} \exp\left(-\frac{n}{\lambda_{B_n}}\sqrt{\Psi_2} - \frac{m}{\lambda_{A_m}}\ln\frac{1}{x_i}\right)\sqrt{\frac{1-\phi_i}{1+\phi_i}} \right. \\ \left. + \frac{n\lambda_{A_m}}{m\lambda_{B_n} + n\lambda_{A_m}}\exp\left[-b_2\left(\frac{m}{\lambda_{A_m}} + \frac{n}{\lambda_{B_n}}\right)\right] \right\}, \gamma_{th2} < 1 \\[2em] \sum\limits_{MN} \left\{ \frac{m}{\lambda_{A_m}} \frac{\pi c_2}{2K} \sum\limits_{i=1}^{K} \exp\left(\frac{n}{\lambda_{B_n}}\sqrt{\Theta_2} - \frac{m}{\lambda_{A_m}y_i}\right)\sqrt{1-\phi_i^2} \right. \\ + \frac{m\lambda_{B_n}}{m\lambda_{B_n} + n\lambda_{A_m}}\exp\left[-c_2\left(\frac{m}{\lambda_{A_m}} + \frac{n}{\lambda_{B_n}}\right)\right] \\ \left. + \frac{n\lambda_{A_m}}{m\lambda_{B_n} + n\lambda_{A_m}}\exp\left[-b_2\left(\frac{m}{\lambda_{A_m}} + \frac{n}{\lambda_{B_n}}\right)\right] \right\}, \gamma_{th2} > 1 \end{cases} \quad (17)$$

where $\sum\limits_{MN} \triangleq -\sum\limits_{m=1}^{M}\sum\limits_{n=1}^{N} \binom{M}{m}\binom{N}{n}(-1)^{m+n+1}$, $\Psi_2 = \gamma_{th2}\left(\ln^2\frac{1}{x_i} + \frac{1}{a\gamma_0}\right)$, $x_i = \frac{\phi_i+1}{2}$, $\phi_i = \cos(\frac{2i-1}{2K}\pi)$, $\gamma_{th2} = 2^{\frac{L_2}{(1-\alpha)B\Omega_2}} - 1$, $\Omega_2 = (1-\alpha)T - \tau_2$, $\tau_2 = \frac{\rho L_2}{f}$, $c_2 = \sqrt{\frac{\gamma_{th2}}{a\gamma_0(1-\gamma_{th2})}}$, $\Theta_2 = \gamma_{th2}y_i^2 + \frac{1}{a\gamma_0}$, $y_i = \frac{\phi_i+1}{2}c_2$, $b_2 = \sqrt{\frac{\gamma_{th2}}{a\gamma_0}}$, $K$ is the complexity-vs-accuracy trade-off coefficient.

*Proof.* The proof of Lemma 2 is similar to the proof of Lemma 1.

**Lemma 3.** The closed-form expression of the SCP of the considered system over quasi-static Rayleigh fading, denoted by $\phi_s$, is as follow

$$\phi_s = \begin{cases} \sum\limits_{MN} \left\{ \frac{n}{\lambda_{B_n}} \frac{\pi}{K} \sum\limits_{i=1}^{K} \exp\left(-\frac{m}{\lambda_{A_m}}\sqrt{\Psi} - \frac{n}{\lambda_{B_n}}(b-\ln z_i)\right)\sqrt{\frac{1-\phi_i}{1+\phi_i}} \right. \\ \left. + \frac{m}{\lambda_{A_m}} \frac{\pi}{K} \sum\limits_{i=1}^{K} \exp\left(-\frac{n}{\lambda_{B_n}}\sqrt{\Psi} - \frac{m}{\lambda_{A_m}}(b-\ln z_i)\right)\sqrt{\frac{1-\phi_i}{1+\phi_i}} \right\}, \gamma_{th} > 1 \\[2em] \sum\limits_{MN} \left\{ \exp\left[-c\left(\frac{m}{\lambda_{A_m}} + \frac{n}{\lambda_{B_n}}\right)\right] + \frac{n}{\lambda_{B_n}} \frac{\pi}{2K}(c-b) \sum\limits_{i=1}^{K} \exp\left(-\frac{m}{\lambda_{A_m}}\sqrt{\Theta} - \frac{n}{\lambda_{B_n}}t_i\right) \right. \\ \left. \times \sqrt{1-\phi_i^2} + \frac{m}{\lambda_{A_m}} \frac{\pi}{2K}(c-b) \sum\limits_{i=1}^{K} \exp\left(-\frac{n}{\lambda_{B_n}}\sqrt{\Theta} - \frac{m}{\lambda_{A_m}}t_i\right)\sqrt{1-\phi_i^2} \right\}, \gamma_{th} < 1 \end{cases}$$
$$(18)$$

where $\sum\limits_{MN} \triangleq -\sum\limits_{m=1}^{M}\sum\limits_{n=1}^{N} \binom{M}{m}\binom{N}{n}(-1)^{m+n+1}$, $\Psi = \gamma_{th}\left((b-\ln z_i)^2 + \frac{1}{a\gamma_0}\right)$, $\gamma_{th} = 2^{\frac{L}{(1-\alpha)B\Omega}} - 1$, $\Omega = (1-\alpha)T - \tau$, $\tau = \frac{\rho L}{f}$, $b = \sqrt{\frac{\gamma_{th}}{a\gamma_0}}$, $c = \sqrt{\frac{\gamma_{th}}{a\gamma_0(1-\gamma_{th})}}$, $\Theta = \gamma_{th}\left(t_i^2 + \frac{1}{a\gamma_0}\right)$, $z_i = \frac{\phi_i+1}{2}$, $\phi_i = \cos(\frac{2i-1}{2K}\pi)$, $t_i = \frac{(\phi_i+1)(c-b)}{2} + b$, $K$ is the complexity-vs-accuracy trade-off coefficient.

*Proof.* The proof of Lemma 3 is similar to the proof of Lemma 1.

## 4   Numerical Results and Discussion

In this section, we present numerical results to confirm the accuracy of the theoretical results obtained for SCP. Unless otherwise specified, the system parameters are as follow: $P_0 = 10$ dB, $\alpha = 0.4$, $\eta = 0.6$, $\rho = 10$, $f = 1$ GHz, $B = 100$ MHz, $T = 10$ ms, $M = 3$, $N = 2$.

Figures 3a and 3b depict the SCP of each CH and whole system under the effect of time switching ratio ($\alpha$) with different average transmit SNR ($\gamma_0$). We find that as $\gamma_0$ increases, the SCP for each CH and the whole system increases. In other words, increasing transmit power can help improve system performance. In addition, this figures show that $\alpha$ massively influences the SCP. If $\alpha$ is too small or too large, the system's SCP has a low value. Specifically, when $\alpha$ gradually increases from 0, the system's SCP tends to increase and reach maximum value. However, as $\alpha$ continues to grow too large, SCP drops. It can be explained that when $\alpha$ is low, CHs do not gather enough energy to function, resulting in low SCP. Nevertheless, when EH time is too large, i.e., $\alpha$ gets closer to 1, the offloading and computation processes no longer have enough time to complete, resulting in tasks that cannot be completed in time maximum allowable delay and SCP reduces.

We continue to compare the proposed system performance in two schemes, NOMA and OMA. In all three cases, the results show that the system operating under the NOMA scheme has significantly higher performance when operating under the OMA scheme.

Figures 4a and 4b depict the SCP of each CH and whole system under the effect of average transmit SNR ($\gamma_0$) with different time switching ratios ($\alpha$). The obtained results once again confirm the observations in the above experiments. We observe that when $\gamma_0$ increases, that is, increases the transmit power of the $AP$, the system performance increases. However, when $\gamma_0$ grows too large, the system's SCP and CHs tend to saturate. Therefore, it is necessary to consider the design of the $AP$'s transmits power appropriately while ensuring system performance in the proposed system. In all three investigating cases with different $\alpha$, the SCP of the OMA scheme is much lower than the corresponding NOMA scheme. The curves are only asymptotic when $\gamma_0$ is very large. It proves the advantage of the NOMA-based system that we propose.

Figures 5a and 5b depict the impact of the number of IDs $(M, N)$ on the SCP of the whole system and CHs. In Figs. 5a, we examine the system performance with five cases: the simplest case with one ID in each cluster, i.e., $(M, N) = (1, 1)$, (ii) increase the number of IDs in cluster **A**, i.e., $(M, N) = (3, 1)$, (iii) increase the number of IDs in cluster **B**, i.e., $(M, N) = (1, 3)$, (iv) increase the number of IDs in two cluster, i.e., $(M, N) = (3, 3)$, and (v) $(M, N) = (4, 4)$. The results show that increasing the number of IDs can significantly improve system performance. Specifically, the largest difference between the worst case (i) and the best case (v) is up to 60 %. It is consistent with the operating protocol of the system when the IDs are selected as the CH with the best transmission channel, thereby obtaining the most energy and participating in the most effective offloading process.

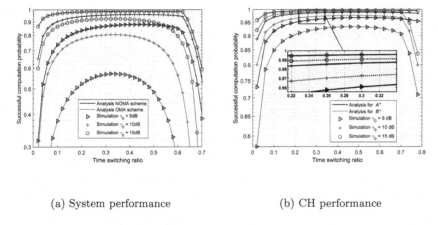

(a) System performance                    (b) CH performance

**Fig. 3.** The impact of time switching ratio on SCP with the different average transmit SNR.

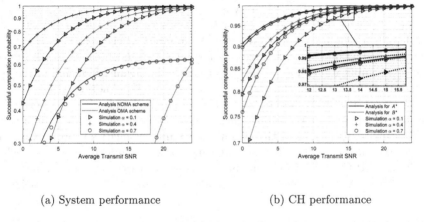

(a) System performance                    (b) CH performance

**Fig. 4.** The impact of average transmit SNR on SCP with the different time switching ratio.

However, when we compare the results in case (iv) and case (v), we notice that the performance improvement slows down as we continue to increase the number of IDs in each cluster. Furthermore, the effect of $(M, N)$ on SCP is evident when $\gamma_0$ is low; this effect decreases as the transmit power increases. Another observation while we set the total number of users in the two clusters to be equal, i.e., case (ii) and case (iii), their system SCP is equal. It shows that the role of clusters in our proposed system is the same. The results obtained in Figs. 5b also give the same conclusion as above.

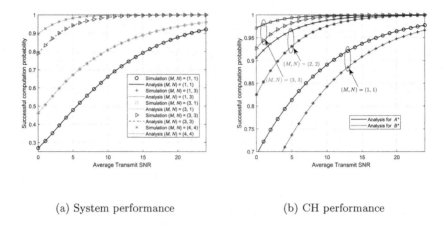

(a) System performance                    (b) CH performance

**Fig. 5.** The impact of average transmit SNR on SCP with the different number of IDs

Figure 6 depicts the SCP of the whole system under the effect of the length of task $(L_1, L_2)$ with different bandwidth $B$. We observed that the more significant task length, the lower the performance of the system. The reason is that as $L$ is more considerable, according to the formulas (8) and (15), the task offload time and computation time at the $AP$ are more significant, resulting in $AP$ not enough time to complete the task and respond to CHs. Another observation is that $B$ has a significant hold on SCP. The larger the bandwidth, the better the system performance. It is entirely consistent with the formula (13); a high value of $B$ means that the greater the achievable channel capacities from CHs to $AP$, the shorter the offloading time in enhancement system performance. Thus, when designing a MEC model, it is clear that the characteristics of the offloading tasks and channel bandwidth should be considered to achieve the required efficiency.

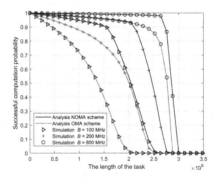

**Fig. 6.** The impact of the length of task on system SCP with the different bandwidth

The simulation results (Simulation) and analytical calculations (Analysis) are consistent in the above experiments, showing our research's correctness.

# 5 Conclusion

In this paper, we have proposed a novel network MEC IIoT scenario in which we used RF EH and NOMA for offloading tasks of multiple IDs to $AP$. Specifically, the IDs in each cluster select CHs to harvest the energy and offload their tasks over the Rayleigh fading channel. We derive the SCP of the whole system and two CHs and use them to evaluate system performance. The simulation results have shown that the EOCD scheme outperforms the existing OMA strategy, thus marking it an assuring candidate for carrying the functionality of the MEC IIoT scenarios. Specifically, system performance can be enhanced by implementing the following methods: (i) increase the transmit power of $AP$, (ii) increase the number of IDs in the clusters. Computational and theoretical results coincide, proving the accuracy of our study.

In future studies, we will investigate the system in the general case when the AP is equipped with many antennas. Furthermore, we will propose low complexity algorithms to find the optimal time switching ratio to help SCP reach its maximum value.

**Acknowledgments.** Van-Truong Truong was funded by Vingroup JSC and supported by the Master, PhD Scholarship Programme of Vingroup Innovation Foundation (VINIF), Institute of Big Data, code VINIF.2021.TS.049.

## Appendix A: Proof of Lemma 1

Here, from equation (14) we derive the closed-form expression of $\phi_s^{A^*}$ as (A-0).

$$\phi_s^{A^*} = \Pr\left(t_1 + \tau_1 \le (1-\alpha)T\right) \tag{A-0}$$

$$= \underbrace{\Pr\left(g_1 > g_2, \gamma_{11} \ge \underbrace{2^{\frac{L_1}{(1-\alpha)B\Omega_1}} - 1}_{\gamma_{th1}}\right)}_{I_1} + \underbrace{\Pr\left(g_1 < g_2, \gamma_{21} \ge 2^{\frac{L_1}{(1-\alpha)B\Omega_1}} - 1\right)}_{I_2}.$$

Using the properties of CDF and PDF, we implement $I_1$ as (A-1).

$$I_1 = \Pr\left(g_1 > g_2, \frac{a\gamma_0 g_1^2}{a\gamma_0 g_2^2 + 1} > \gamma_{th1}\right)$$

$$= \begin{cases} \underbrace{\int_0^\infty \left[1 - F_{g_1}\left(\sqrt{\gamma_{th1}\left(x^2 + \frac{1}{a\gamma_0}\right)}\right)\right] f_{g_2}(x)\,dx, \gamma_{th1} < 1}_{I_{11}} \\[4mm] \underbrace{\int_0^{c_1}\left[1 - F_{g_1}\left(\sqrt{\gamma_{th1}\left(x^2 + \frac{1}{a\gamma_0}\right)}\right)\right] f_{g_2}(x)\,dx}_{I_{12}^a} + \underbrace{\int_{c_1}^\infty [1 - F_{g_1}(x)] f_{g_2}(x)\,dx, \gamma_{th1} > 1}_{I_{12}^b} \end{cases}$$

$$\tag{A-1}$$

Using the Gaussian-Chebyshev quadrature method, we easily calculate $I_{11}$ as (A-2).

$$
\begin{aligned}
I_{11} = &-\sum_{m=1}^{M}\sum_{n=1}^{N}\binom{M}{m}\binom{N}{n}(-1)^{m+n+1}\frac{n}{\lambda_2}\frac{\pi}{K} \\
&\times \sum_{i=1}^{K}\exp\left(-\frac{m}{\lambda_1}\sqrt{\gamma_{th1}\left(\ln^2\frac{1}{x_i}+\frac{1}{a\gamma_0}\right)}-\frac{n}{\lambda_2}\ln\frac{1}{x_i}\right)\sqrt{\frac{1-\phi_i}{1+\phi_i}},
\end{aligned}
\tag{A-2}
$$

where $x_i = \frac{\phi_i+1}{2}$, $\phi_i = cos(\frac{2i-1}{2K}\pi)$, $K$ is the complexity-vs-accuracy trade-off coefficient. Using the same method, we calculate $I_{12}^a$ and $I_{12}^b$ as (A-3) and (A-4), respectively.

$$
\begin{aligned}
I_{12}^a = &-\sum_{m=1}^{M}\sum_{n=1}^{N}\binom{M}{m}\binom{N}{n}(-1)^{m+n+1}\frac{n}{\lambda_2}\frac{\pi c_1}{2K} \\
&\times \sum_{i=1}^{K}\exp\left(\frac{m}{\lambda_1}\sqrt{\gamma_{th1}y_i^2+\frac{1}{a\gamma_0}}-\frac{n}{\lambda_2 y_i}\right)\sqrt{1-\phi_i^2},
\end{aligned}
\tag{A-3}
$$

where $y_i = \frac{\phi_i+1}{2}c_1$, $\phi_i = cos(\frac{2i-1}{2K}\pi)$, $K$ is the complexity-vs-accuracy trade-off coefficient.

$$
I_{12}^b = -\sum_{m=1}^{M}\sum_{n=1}^{N}\binom{M}{m}\binom{N}{n}(-1)^{m+n+1}\frac{n\lambda_1}{m\lambda_2+n\lambda_1}\exp\left[-c_1\left(\frac{m}{\lambda_1}+\frac{n}{\lambda_2}\right)\right].
\tag{A-4}
$$

Next, we focus to derive the closed-form expression of $I_2$ as (A-5).

$$
\begin{aligned}
I_2 = &\Pr\left(\underbrace{\sqrt{\frac{\gamma_{th1}}{a\gamma_0}}}_{d_1} < g_1 < g_2\right) = \int_{d_1}^{\infty}\left[F_{g_1}(x)-F_{g_1}\left(\sqrt{\frac{\lambda_{th1}}{a\gamma_0}}\right)\right]f_{g_2}(x)\,dx \\
= &-\sum_{m=1}^{M}\sum_{n=1}^{N}\binom{M}{m}\binom{N}{n}(-1)^{m+n+1}\frac{m\lambda_2}{m\lambda_2+n\lambda_1}\exp\left[-d_1\left(\frac{m}{\lambda_1}+\frac{n}{\lambda_2}\right)\right].
\end{aligned}
\tag{A-5}
$$

This concludes our proof.

# References

1. Hou, X., Ren, Z., Yang, K., Chen, C., Zhang, H., Xiao, Y.: IIoT-MEC: a novel mobile edge computing framework for 5G-enabled IIoT. In: Proceedings of Wireless Communications and Network Conferences (WCNC), pp. 1–7. IEEE, Marrakesh, Morocco (2019)

2. Krishnamurthi, R., Kumar, A., Gopinathan, D., Nayyar, A., Qureshi, B.: An overview of IoT sensor data processing, fusion, and analysis techniques. Sensors **20**(21), 6076 (2020)

3. Chettri, L., Bera, R.: A comprehensive survey on Internet of Things (IoT) toward 5G wireless systems. IEEE Internet Things J. **7**(1), 16–32 (2019)

4. Elkashlan, M., Duong, T.Q., Chen, H.: Millimeter-wave communications for 5G–part 2: applications [Guest Editorial]. IEEE Commun. Mag. **53**(1): 166–167 (2015)

5. Mao, Y., You, C., Zhang, J., Huang, K., Letaief, K.B.: A survey on mobile edge computing: the communication perspective. IEEE Commun. Surv. Tut. **19**(4), 2322–2358 (2017)

6. Mach, P., Becvar, Z.: Mobile edge computing: a survey on architecture and computation offloading. IEEE Commun. Surv. Tut. **19**(3), 1628–1656 (2017)

7. Truong, V.T., Ha, D.B.: Secured scheme for RF energy harvesting mobile edge computing networks based on NOMA and access point selection. In: Proceedings of 7th NAFOSTED Conference on Information and Computer Science, pp. 7–12. IEEE, Ho Chi Minh City, Vietnam (2020). https://doi.org/10.1109/NICS51282.2020.9335833

8. Ha, D.-B., Truong, V.-T., Ha, D.-H.: A novel secure protocol for mobile edge computing network applied downlink NOMA. In: Vo, N.-S., Hoang, V.-P. (eds.) INISCOM 2020. LNICST, vol. 334, pp. 324–336. Springer, Cham (2020). https://doi.org/10.1007/978-3-030-63083-6_25

9. Truong, V.-T., Vo, M.-T., Ha, D.-B.: Performance analysis of mobile edge computing network applied uplink NOMA with RF energy harvesting. In: Vo, N.-S., Hoang, V.-P., Vien, Q.-T. (eds.) INISCOM 2021. LNICST, vol. 379, pp. 57–72. Springer, Cham (2021). https://doi.org/10.1007/978-3-030-77424-0_6

10. Yang, Z., Liu, Y., Chen, Y., Tyson, G.: Deep reinforcement learning in cache-aided MEC networks. In: ICC IEEE International Conference on Communication (ICC), pp. 1–6. IEEE, Shanghai, China (2019). https://doi.org/10.1109/ICC.2019.8761349

11. Tam, H.H.M., Tuan, H.D., Nasir, A.A., Duong, T.Q., Poor, H.V.: MIMO energy harvesting in full-duplex multi-user networks. IEEE Trans. Wirel. Commun. **16**(5), 3282–3297 (2017)

12. Sabella, D., Vaillant, A., Kuure, P., Rauschenbach, U., Giust, F.: Mobile-edge computing architecture: the role of MEC in the Internet of Things. IEEE Consum. Electron. Mag. **5**(4), 84–91 (2016)

13. Malik, R., Vu, M.: Energy-efficient joint wireless charging and computation offloading in MEC systems. IEEE J. Sel. Topics Signal Process. **15**, 1110–1125 (2021)

14. Wei, Z., Guo, J., Ng, D.W.K., Yuan, J.: Fairness comparison of uplink NOMA and OMA. In: Proceedings of IEEE 85th Vehicle Technology Conference, pp. 1–6. (IEEE) (VTC Spring) (2017)

15. Zhou, F., Wu, Y., Hu, R.Q., Qian, Y.: Computation efficiency in a wireless-powered Mobile Edge Computing network with NOMA. In: Proceedings IEEE International Conference on Communication (ICC), pp. 1–7. IEEE, Shanghai, China (2019). https://doi.org/10.1109/ICC.2019.8761172

16. Zhu, J., Wang, J., Huang, Y., Fang, F., Navaie, K., Ding, Z.: Resource allocation for hybrid NOMA MEC offloading. IEEE Trans. Wireless Commun. **19**(7), 4964–4977 (2020)

17. Fang, F., Xu, Y., Ding, Z., Shen, C., Peng, M., Karagiannidis, G.K.: Optimal resource allocation for delay minimization in NOMA-MEC networks. IEEE Trans. Commun. **68**(12), 7867–7881 (2020)

18. Xue, J., An, Y.: Joint task offloading and resource allocation for multi-task multi-server NOMA-MEC networks. IEEE Access **9**, 16152–16163 (2021)
19. Sidhu, R.K., Ubhi, J.S., Aggarwal, A.: A survey study of different RF energy sources for RF energy harvesting. In: Proceedings of International Conference on Automatic, Computer and Technological Management (ICACTM), pp. 530–533. IEEE, London, UK (2019). https://doi.org/10.1109/ICACTM.2019.8776726
20. So-In, C., Tran, H., Tran, D.D., Heng, S., Aimtongkham, P., Nguyen, A.N., et al.: On security and throughput for energy harvesting untrusted relays in IoT systems using NOMA. IEEE Access **7**, 149341–149354 (2019)
21. Vyas, R., Nishimoto, H., Tentzeris, M., Kawahara, Y., Asami, T.: A battery-less, energy harvesting device for long range scavenging of wireless power from terrestrial TV broadcasts. In Proceedings of IEEE/MTT-S International Microwave Symposium on Digest, pp. 1–3. IEEE, Montreal, QC, Canada (2012). https://doi.org/10.1109/MWSYM.2012.6259708
22. Rauniyar, A., Engelstad, P., Osterbo, O.N.: RF energy harvesting and information transmission based on NOMA for wireless powered IoT relay systems. Sensors **18**(10), 3254 (2018)
23. Al-Baz, A., El-Sayed, A.: A new algorithm for cluster head selection in LEACHs protocol for wireless sensor networks. Int. J. Commun. Syst. **31**(1), e3407 (2018)
24. Dac-Binh, H., Duc-Dung, T., Vu, T.H., Een-Kee, H.: Performance of amplify-and-forward relaying with wireless power transfer over dissimilar channels. Elektronika ir Elektrotechnika J. **21**(5), 90–95 (2015)
25. Ye, Y., Hu, R.Q., Lu, G., Shi, L.: Enhance latency-constrained computation in MEC networks using uplink NOMA. IEEE Trans. Commun. **68**(4), 2409–2425 (2020)

# Design and Performance Evaluation of Full-Duplex Relay Node in LoRaWAN-Based System

Van-Truyen Phan[1,2], Xuan-Tung Truong Minh[2,3], and Van-Truong Truong[1,2(✉)]

[1] Faculty of Electrical-Electronic Engineering, Duy Tan University, Da Nang 550000, Vietnam
{phanvantruyen,truongmxuantung,truongvantruong}@dtu.edu.vn
[2] Institute of Research and Development, Duy Tan University, Da Nang 550000, Vietnam
[3] Mechanical Engineering Faculty, Duy Tan University, Da Nang 550000, Vietnam

**Abstract.** In recent years, wireless sensor network (WSN) has attracted much attention from researchers and the industry. In particular, low power wide-area wireless network (LPWAN) protocols are widely applied in many fields thanks to their effective cost, long range, and energy efficiency. This study proposed a hardware design for a full-duplex relay node (FDRN) for relaying data from sensor nodes (SN) to the LoRaWAN gateway. Accordingly, we proposed the LLC-RTOS algorithm based on FreeRTOS to simultaneously receive, convert, and transmit LoRaWAN signals at FDRN. We proposed a novel LPWAN model based on LoRaWAN for application in WSNs by joining FDRN to the traditional 4-layer LoRaWAN model. Finally, we use the practical method to evaluate the system performance based on the packet loss percentage (PLP), and received signal strength indicator (RSSI) under three scenario: (a) single SN communicated with gateway via FDRN, (b) multiple SNs communicated with gateway via FDRN, and (c) multiple SNs communicated with gateway via multiple FDRNs. The obtained results show the efficiency of the FDRN design and the proposed model when the system can achieve a PLP less than 0.1% and RSSI 100 dBm within a 4 km communication range.

**Keywords:** LoRa · LoRaWAN · Full-duplex relay node · Wireless sensor network · LoRaWAN server · Application server

## 1 Introduction

In recent years, the outstanding development of Industry 4.0 has created the impetus for the development of intelligent systems in almost all fields of industry, agriculture, healthcare, transportation, and civil [1]. The trend of the Internet

© ICST Institute for Computer Sciences, Social Informatics and Telecommunications Engineering 2022
Published by Springer Nature Switzerland AG 2022. All Rights Reserved
N.-S. Vo et al. (Eds.): INISCOM 2022, LNICST 444, pp. 77–90, 2022.
https://doi.org/10.1007/978-3-031-08878-0_6

of Things (IoT) has opened up many advantages for the research, construction, and deployment of intelligent networks globally, in which wireless sensor network (WSN) plays a critical role [2].

Several low power wide-area network (LPWAN) communication technologies such as LoRa and Sigfox are being applied in WSNs due to their effective cost, long-range, and energy efficiency [3,4]. LoRa enables low data rate transmission over a covered area of up to 10 km with several mA peak broadcast currents [5]. Excellent customization at the physical layer allows LoRa to support communication between sensor nodes (SNs). However, because of customization, node-to-node (N2N) communication in LoRa networks is not integrated into the global pattern, so LoRa communication is not accessible to standardized and maintained LoRaWAN Gateways from LoRa Alliance.

Meanwhile, LoRaWAN is an open network protocol that provides connections between LPWAN gateways and IoT end-devices according to LoRa Alliance standards. The study [6] by Erturk et al. present the 4-layers standard architecture of LoRaWAN networks, as Fig. 1. In particular, the end node (EN) supporting LoRaWAN is a sensor or actuator that is wirelessly connected to the LoRaWAN network through gateways using LoRa modulation technology. ENs are mostly battery operated and perform functions to digitize physical or environmental information [7]. The LoRaWAN gateway connects to the ENs via the IP backbone to receive the devices LoRa modulated RF data and forward to the server in the LoRaWAN network. The network server plays the role of managing the entire network and establishes a secure 128-bit AES connection for data transmission and control. The network server ensures the authenticity of every sensor on the network and the integrity of the messages. Finally, the application servers are responsible for securely processing, managing, and interpreting data received from the sensors and generating downlink payloads to the ENs.

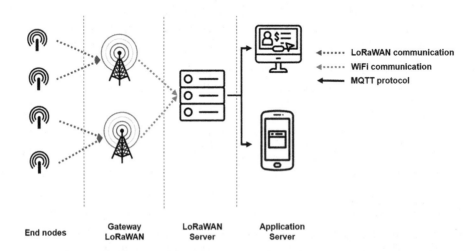

**Fig. 1.** The LoRaWAN network architecture

Data is formatted in a unique standard that makes it easy to synchronize with the LoRaWAN network server and application Server. However, the standard LoRaWAN model is only suitable for star network architectures, where SNs connect directly to one or more LoRaWAN gateways and cannot send messages to each other. It poses significant practical deployment challenges for WSN applications, where multiple LoRaWAN gateways must be designed to manage large numbers of nodes distributed over a wide range. The system's scalability is limited when the gateway must be placed at a location with backhaul access to the network server [8]. Moreover, the information forwarding mechanism between nodes in the WSN serves for data routing, cluster head selection, leading to reduce the information traffic transmitted to the gateway, saving energy, and increasing the network's lifetime. Therefore, ensuring device-to-device communication in the LoRaWAN network is interested in researchers learning and proposing solutions [9–12].

For instance, Daniel *et al.* in [9] proposes to solve the problem of scaling a LoRaWAN network by using multiple gateways that coordinate data forwarding. The gateways communicate over a standard LoRaWAN network and have a built-in routing table, which updates through each data relay loop. The authors propose a protocol that works based on the tunneling technique. The gateways deployed the Hybrid Wireless Mesh Protocol and Ad-hoc OnDemand Distance Vector Routing for data forwarding. The results show that the larger the number of data hops in the system, the higher the delay time, but it can still respond in real-time with a delay of approximately 1.58 s for the 3-step routing process. Truong *et al.*'s solution to utilize the Zigbee multi-hop network with LoRa in [11] is also worth noting. The authors propose a hybrid Zigbee and LoRa network to leverage Zigbee's N2N communication to complement the LoRaWAN network disadvantage. The proposed model can be applied in 3 case studies: air quality monitoring, agricultural monitoring, and Internet of underwater Thing monitoring.

Even so, securing N2N communication in LoRaWAN is still a matter of research, thus prompted us to carry out this study. In this paper, we aim at a circuit that relays data between ENs in a real-time response LoRaWAN network. The main contributions of this paper are as follows:

- We designed the LoRa – LoRaWAN full-duplex relay node (FDRN) hardware, ensuring N2N communication in the LoRaWAN network. Accordingly, we proposed a novel LoRaWAN network model consisting of 5 device layers, in which the SN layer communicating with the relay node is added to expand the data collection area of the WSN system.
- We proposed to use the FreeRTOS in the FDRN board, namely LLC-RTOS, for LoRa data acquisition and processing.
- We evaluated system performance based on the packet loss percentage (PLP), and the received signal strength indicator (RSSI) index following the distance of devices and the data rate.

The remainder of this paper is organized as follows. Section 2 presents the system model for N2N communication and the novel extended LoRaWAN model, which outlines the hardware and software design of FDRN. The experimental results under actual conditions and discussion are presented in Sect. 3. Section 4 concludes the paper and presents the future work.

## 2   System Design

### 2.1   The Hardware of FDRN

The FDRN designed is highlighted in Fig. 2, which includes two LoRa Ra–02 SX1278 modules operating in the 433 MHz band that communicates with the Atmega328P MCU via Serial Peripheral Bus (SPI) protocol. SPI is a full-duplex synchronous communication standard in the architecture of one master (MCU) and many slaves (Ra-02), using connections Serial Clock (SCK), Master Input Slave Output (MISO), Master Output Slave Input (MOSI), and Slave Select (SS). SCK is the synchronous clock pin for the communication generated by the master; each SCK clock indicates 1 bit of incoming or outgoing data. MISO transmits the data from the slaves to the MCU, while the MOSI operates in the opposite direction. Finally, SS is used to select the slave to communicate with; each slave is communicated with the master via a separate SS pin. If the MCU pulls the particular Ra-02 SS into low, communication will occur.

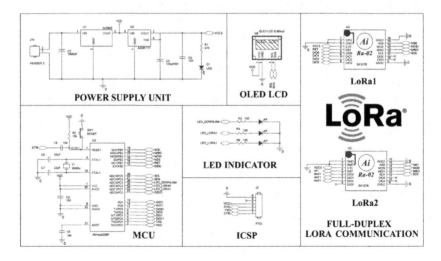

**Fig. 2.** The FDRN hardware design

The OLED module is connected to MCU via Inter-Integrated Circuit (I2C) protocols, displaying receiving and transmitting LoRa packet information. I2C is a simple synchronous serial communication protocol developed by Philips Semiconductors for data transfer between an MCU and multiple salves. I2C devices use only two signaling lines, Serial Clock Line (SCL) and Serial Data Line (SDA). The transmitted data is sent over the SDA wire and synchronized with the clock signal from the SCL. To prevent short-circuit occurring when devices simultaneously pull signals to high and low logic level, both I2C bus lines act as open drain drivers. That is, to put it more simply, any device connected to the I2C network can drive SDA and SCL low logic levels but cannot drive them high one. That's said, a 10 kΩ pull-up resistor deployed in the OLED module is used for each bus line to keep them high logic level by default.

Three LEDs indicate the transmit, receive, and error signals. The circuit works under 5 V and 3.3 V voltage regulation, powered by two 5500 mAh LiPo batteries. Ra-02 modules operate with 3.3 V power, while the rest are powered with 5 V. Thus, the MCU operating at 5 V TTL logic can be compatible with other 5 V TTL devices or 3.3 V TTL/CMOS devices without any logic level converter. The 433 MHz antennas with 10cm long Ipex connectors are distributed around the edges of the circuit to amplify with the 3 dBi gain signal. Figure 3 is FDRN prototype, which is manufactured follow industrial printed circuit board standards.

**Fig. 3.** The FDRN prototype

## 2.2   The Software of FDRN

We propose using the LoRa to LoRaWAN conversion based on FreeRTOS, namely LLC-RTOS, for FDRN to forward data from the SN to the LoRaWAN gateway, as Algorithm 1.

We use the Sandeep LoRa [13] library for SN data acquisition and the LoRaWAN-MAC-in-C (LMIC) provided by IBM for LoRaWAN connectivity [14]. The MCU sets up the appropriate IO, SPI, and I2C ports and sends commands to start the Ra-02 modules when the system is powered up. The parameters specific to LoRa and LoRaWAN networks are set, including operation frequency $(f)$, spreading factor $(SF)$, code rate $(CR)$, and bandwidth $(BW)$. FDRNs start their operation by sending a *join request* message with 8 bytes unique application identifier, 8 bytes unique device identifier, and 2 bytes random attract replay to the LoRaWAN server in the *join procedure*. This

**Algorithm 1.** LoRa to LoRaWAN conversion based on FreeRTOS (LLC-RTOS)

1: **Setup**: Library LoRa and LoRaWAN
2: **Setup**: IO port, SPI port, I2C port
3: **Setup**: LoRa and LoRaWAN parameter: $f = 433$ MHz, $SF = 7$, $CR = 1$, and $BW = 125$ KHz.
4: **Setup**: RTOS Preemptive scheduling and Tasks
5: Send *join request* to LoRaWAN server
6: Wait until get *join accept* from LoRaWAN server
7: Joint LoRaWAN network with secure connection
8: Setting up FreeRTOS tasks and Preemptive scheduling
9: **while** True **do**
10:     **if** SN ID available **then**
11:         Run algorithm for LoRa SN data acquisition
12:         Decompress the LoRa data
13:         Convert data to LoRaWAN format
14:         Run algorithm for sending data to LoRaWAN gateway
15:         LED indicator and OLED display
16:     **else**
17:         Drop message

process ensures the security of the communication process, as only authorized devices can participate in the network. After using secure *matching keys* to check the legitimacy of the FDRNs, the LoRaWAN server initializes the *session keys*, i.e., Network Session Key and Application Session Key, in response to the *join accept* message to the FDRN via normal downlink. Next, FDRN decrypts the *join accept* message and receives the session key to join the LoRaWAN network. Next, the FDRN establishes a LoRa network to communicate with the SNs, based on the previously agreed IDs allocated to the SNs of the declared communication frequency band. Due to the highly customizable characteristics of using LoRa raw data, security setup operations are not used.

Accordingly, the first Ra-02 module holds the role of communicating with SNs using LoRa, while the rest module communicates with the Dragino gateway according to the LoRaWAN standard. FreeRTOS integrated on the MCU is responsible for initiating and executing tasks, including LoRa data acquisition (Task 1) as Algorithm 2, saving LoRa raw data into 64 bytes memory (Task 2), LoRa to LoRaWAN packet format conversion (Task 3), display packet information on OLED (Task 4), and LoRaWAN packet delivery (Task 5).

Algorithm 2 describes the process by which the FDRN receives data from SNs. Each LoRa module always has two methods of receiving information: single receive mode (SRM) and Continuous receive mode (CRM). However, due to the use of battery power at FDRN, we use SRM with alternate Standby mode, ensuring maximum energy savings. In this mode, the Ra-02 module continuously searches for the preamble, a particular signal used to detect incoming LoRa signals, during the time slot with a length from 4 to 1023 LoRa symbols. Otherwise, the LoRa signal is fully detected and received, the RxDone interrupt is initiated after the payload block, and Cyclic Redundancy Check (CRC) is performed. The Ra-02 then returns to the Standby state and waits for the next slot. In the event that a preamble signal is not detected at the end of the time slot cycle, the Ra-02 initiates the RxTimeout interrupt and returns to Standby mode. Furthermore, since the communication period of the SNs to the FDRN is fixed, the SRM can still ensure a shallow packet loss rate.

---

**Algorithm 2.** LoRa single receive mode for SN data acquisition algorithm

---
1: Start
2: Wait for Interrupt request (IRQ)
3: **if** RxTimeout IRQ **then**
4:     Go to Standby mode
5:     Go to End
6: **if** RxDone IRQ **then**
7:     Go to Standby mode
8:     **if** Payload CRC detect error **then**
9:         Goto End
10:    **else**
11:        Read SN data
12: End

---

After the data from the SNs is saved into the FIFO data buffer, preprocessing is performed. For the convenience of processing and decompression, data from sensors will be formated with JavaScript Object Notation (JSON), where the *key* being the sensor information and the *value* is the value that the sensor read. The FDRN checks the sensor information against the pre-conventional ID. If the SN's ID belongs to the device group managed by the FDRN, it will decompress the data. This process is indicated by *LoRa receiving* LED. Information about the packet such as packet sequence, and sensing data, is displayed on the OLED, and saved to memory. If the ID belongs to another device group, FDRN automatically drops that packet and continues to consider the next packet. If the data counter is not continuous, the FDRN detects the lost packet and indicates by the *data drop* LED.

We continue to describe the process of sending data to the Dragino gateway in Algorithm 3. Sensor data is stored in the FIFO buffer of the second Ra-02 module. Note that the data in the FIFO buffer cannot be erased when the transmission ends unless the device goes into an Sleep state or a new message sequence arrives. TxDone interrupt signals occurred when each successful packet was sent to the gateway. This process is indicated by *LoRaWAN sending* LED. Ra-02 continues to check if there is still data to send; if there is, the whole process is performed again; if not, the module enters the Standby state.

**Algorithm 3.** Sending data to LoRaWAN server algorithm

1: Start
2: Write data in FIFO buffer
3: Wait for TxDone IRQ
4: **if** New transmit data is available **then**
5:     Go to Start
6: **else**
7:     Go to End
8: End

Under The Thing Network Fair Use Policy, we limit the uplink airtime to 30 s per day per FDRN. In other words, the real-time constraints in LoRaWAN are not too strict. However, the data collected from the SNs have higher requirements when each environmental data update occurs in a 1 s cycle. Based on that, we apply Preemptive scheduling to the system and set the priority levels in the execution of tasks are as follows: Task 1 has the highest priority, followed by Task 2, Task 3 and Task 4 have the same priority at the 3rd level, and Task 5 has the lowest priority. The CPU of MCU always controls the tasks with the highest priority; when an Interrupt service routine (ISR) is generated, the system will pause the executing task, complete the ISR, then the system executes the task with the highest priority at the time. The system then resumes the interrupted tasks. So, in preemptive mode, the system can respond to urgent tasks such as collecting IoT data promptly.

### 2.3   The Novel LoRaWAN Architecture

In this section, we propose the novel LoRaWAN architecture, in which five layers of devices are coordinated to work in a comprehensive system, as shown in Fig. 4. Specifically, four LoRa32 modules [15] act as SNs for receiving signals from the surrounding environment and communicate with the Dragino LoRaWAN gateway through the help of two FDRNs. We use The Things Network (TTN) as the LoRaWAN Server and TagoIO as the Application Server.

The first layer contains SNs, i.e., LoRa32 modules, which are battery operated and responsible for digitizing environmental parameters thanks to the sensor system. LaRa32 is accompanied by unique identifiers for activation when participating in the LoRa network, and at the same time, ensuring the safety of packets when transmitted in the network. The second layer includes FDRNs, which are responsible for receiving signals from two SNs, encrypting data according to an ID of SNs, and formatting data following to LoRaWAN standard. Next, the data is packed and forwarded to the LoRaWAN Gateway.

The third layer is LoRaWAN Gateway, i.e., Dragino LG01N. It is an opensource LoRaWAN Gateway, which allows converting LoRaWAN wireless data from FDRNs to LoRaWAN Server through an IP backbone, such as WiFi, Ethernet, 3G, or 4G connection [16]. In fact, LG01N operates entirely at the physical layer and is also a LoRa data relay. It checks the data integrity of each incoming

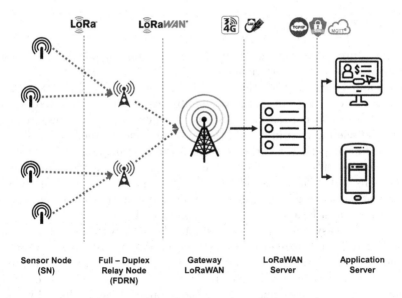

**Fig. 4.** The novel LoRaWAN architecture

LoRa RF message. The LoRa message is dropped if the CRC is incorrect. If CRC is true, the LG01N forwards them to the LoRaWAN Server, along with some metadata such as the received message RSSI, and the timestamp. LG01N is equipped with Dragino HE Linux module with OpenWrt operating system, communicating with LoRa module via Atmega328P processor. Using Message Queuing Telemetry Transport (MQTT) communication protocol, the LG01N is suitable for low-bandwidth IoT devices.

The fourth layer is LoRaWAN Server, i.e., TTN [17]. It is an infrastructure to store the data of the LoRaWAN network globally, with an ecosystem consisting of 21.5 thousand LoRaWAN Gateways are operating at the same time, covering over 151 countries and territories. TTN establishes a secure 128-bit AES connection for end-to-end data transfer, i.e., from FDRN to Applications in the Cloud and vice versa. TTN ensures the authenticity of every sensor and the integrity of all messages. While the TTN cannot see or access application data, it performs essential roles, including checking device addresses, validating frames, and managing frame counters. Furthermore, TTN decodes data through the Payload Decoder algorithm to obtain Raw Payload packets and forwards them to the appropriate application servers. In the case of downlink LoRa setup, TTN queues payloads coming from the Application Server to SN connected to the network.

The application server TagoIO is the last layer in our proposed LoRaWAN architecture. TagoIO is an IoT cloud platform, translates raw value from TTN into parameters users can connect and interact with [18]. The data on TagoIO will be displayed in the form of a Dashboard, supported on desktop and smartphone to help users easily monitor data anytime, anywhere.

## 3    Experiment Results and Discussion

This section presents experiment scenarios for the proposed LoRaWAN system and evaluates the system performance using the PLP, and RSSI. PLP is a parameter commonly used to check the bit error rate in the communication process and is measured by ratio of the total number of incorrectly received bits and total number of transmitted bits. RSSI is an index to measure the strength of the signal at the receiver; in theory, the larger this parameter, the better.

In the first experiment, we investigated the system performance with the different number of SNs and FDRNs. We carried out the following three scenario examinations as Fig. 5. Specifically, in the first experiment (a), the LoRaWAN communication network consisting of one SN and one FDRN was investigated. FDRN is fixed at a location that has line-of-sight (LoS) connection to gateway is available for easy and secure connection. We set up the SN at 10 m away from the FDRN and increased the distance until 6 km. At each location, the SN sends 1000 packets with a sequence number to the FDRN. The process of data statistics is handled by the TagoIO Dashboard with direct link to TTN. In the experiment (b), the system performance parameters are evaluated when the FDRN serves two SNs, placed in symmetrical positions across the FDRN. And in the last experiment (c), the network of two FDRNs and four SNs communicating with each other was investigated.

Figure 6 describes the interface for statistics data from Dashboard TagoIO. The interface includes function blocks that allow observation of transmission distance parameters, packet sequence number, RSSI per packet, packet status, average RSSI statistics, and the number of packets lost during communication.

Figure 7 shows the impact of the number of SN and FDRN on the PLP over different distances. Observing the left side of Fig. 7, when the distance between devices is between 10 m and 300 m, scenario (c) performs the worst when the PLP is approximately 17%, followed by scenario's PLP (b) reaching approx 5%, while scenario (a) has no packet loss. It shows that when LoRa devices are distributed too close together, they will affect the received signal at FDRN. The more complex the system with more SNs and FDRNs, the more significant the impact. When the devices are far away enough, the PLP drops to approximately zero. However, when the transmission distance increases more than 5 km, the SN is entirely unable to communicate with the FDRN causing the PLP to increase to 100%.

Figure 8 shows the impact of SN and FDRN on the RSSI of FDRN over different distances. We use the built-in function provided by [13] to measure the RSSI. We use scenarios (a) and (b) in this experiment. The results show that RSSI decreases with distance, and case (b) have a higher RSSI than case (a) by 5 to 7 dBm, that is, the received signal strength at FDRN in case (b) is better. It shows that when using multiple SNs at the same frequency resource, the received signal strength at FDRN can be enhanced. Therefore, if there is a requirement for packet accuracy, we can designate multiple SNs in the same

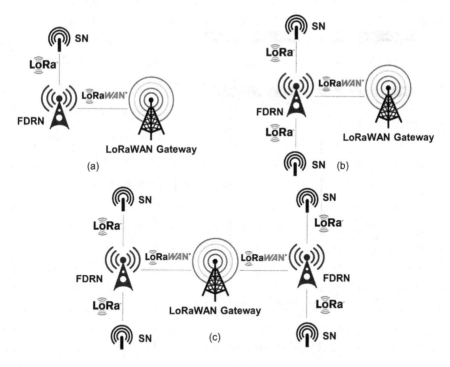

**Fig. 5.** Scenario examinations (a), (b), and (c)

monitored area, and these SNs simultaneously send signals to the FDRN to enhance RSSI. However, Fig. 7 shows that the PLP of the case (b) is higher than case (a) when the distance is from 0 to 300 m. It can be explained as when the distance between the SNs is relatively close; the SNs will affect each other when transmitted on the same frequency. It is the biggest drawback in the LoRa communication network compared to LoRaWAN when the self-frequency hopping mechanisms of LoRaWAN cannot be applied in LoRa communication.

When the distance between the SNs is large enough, the RSSI gradually decreases with the distance but still ensures a reasonable level, i.e., from −30 to −70 dBm, and the signal can be received and appropriately decoded at the FDRN. When the distance is approximately 5 km, the RSSI measured in case (a) reaches saturation with an inferior performance of −138 dBm. It means that the received signal is purely noise in the frequency 433 MHz, and the necessary LoRa data cannot be suitably decoded. While in (b), the saturation RSSI event reached a value of approximately −130 dBm and occurred at a distance of 4.5 km.

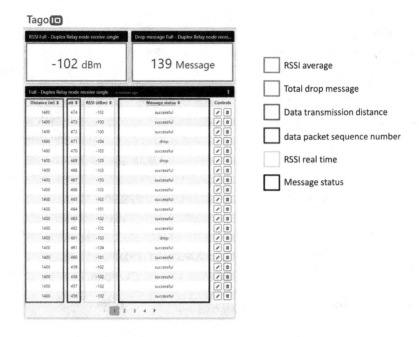

**Fig. 6.** TagoIO dashboard interface

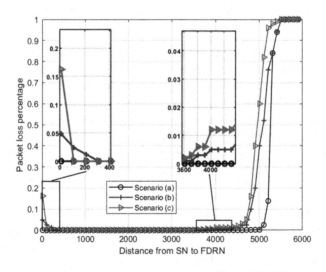

**Fig. 7.** The impact of the distance and number of SN and FDRN to the packet loss percentage

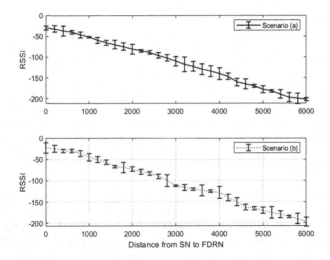

**Fig. 8.** The impact of the number of SN and FDRN to the RSSI

## 4   Conclusion and Future Work

This paper designs the hardware and software for the LoRa - LoRaWAN FDRN in the WSN network. In which, the MCU communicates with two LoRa Ra02 modules, integrated with FreeRTOS to simultaneously perform the tasks of acquiring data from the SNs, converting LoRa data format to LoRaWAN, storing and displaying data, and transmitting data to the LoRaWAN gateway. Accordingly, we propose a new LoRaWAN model with five layers operating synchronously, adding D2D communication between SN and FDRN layers to the traditional LoRaWAN model. Finally, we evaluate system performance in terms of RSSI and PLP according to the number of SNs, the number of FDRNs, and the distance between devices in the network by experimental method. The proposed system can work well within the communication range of 4 km and achieve a PLP of less than 0.1%.

In future studies, we will design SNs that integrate listen before talk capabilities to ensure that SNs can communicate with FDRN more effectively. At the same time, we will study the expansion system with multiple LoRaWAN gateways that support multiple FDRNs and SNs.

## References

1. Raj, A., Prakash, S.: Internet of everything: a survey based on architecture, issues and challenges. In: Proceedings of the 5th IEEE Uttar Pradesh Section International Conference on Electrical, Electronics and Computer Engineering (UPCON), Gorakhpur, India, pp. 1–6. IEEE (2018)
2. Shahraki, A., Taherkordi, A., Haugen, O., Eliassen, F.: A survey and future directions on clustering: from WSNs to IoT and modern networking paradigms. IEEE Trans. Netw. Serv. Manag. **18**(2), 2242–2274 (2020)

3. Olatinwo, D.D., Abu-Mahfouz, A., Hancke, G.: A survey on LPWAN technologies in WBAN for remote health-care monitoring. Sensors **19**(23), 5268 (2019)

4. Liya, M., Arjun, D.: A survey of LPWAN technology in agricultural field. In: Proceedings of the Fourth International Conference on IoT in Social, Mobile, Analytics and Cloud, pp. 313–317 (IEEE) (2020)

5. Zourmand, A., Hing, A.L.K., Hung, C.W., AbdulRehman, M.: Internet of Things (IoT) using LoRa technology. In: Proceedings of the IEEE International Conference on Automatic Control and Intelligent Systems, Selangor, Malaysia, pp. 324–330. IEEE (2019)

6. Erturk, M.A., Aydin, M.A., Buyukakkaclar, M.T., Evirgen, H.: A survey on LoRaWAN architecture, protocol and technologies. Future Internet **11**(10), 216 (2019)

7. Tokmakov, D., Asenov, S., Dimitrov, S.: Research and development of ultra-low power LoraWan sensor node. In: Proceedings of the IEEE XXVIII International Scientific Conference Electronics, Sozopol, Bulgaria, pp. 1–4. IEEE (2019)

8. Codeluppi, G., Cilfone, A., Davoli, L., Ferrari, G.: LoRaFarM: a LoRaWAN-based smart farming modular IoT architecture. Sensors **20**(7), 2028 (2020)

9. Lundell, D., Hedberg, A., Nyberg, C., Fitzgerald, E.: A routing protocol for LoRa mesh networks. In: Proceedings of the IEEE 19th International Symposium on "A World of Wireless, Mobile and Multimedia Networks" (WoWMoM), Chania, Greece, pp. 14–19 (2018). https://doi.org/10.1109/WoWMoM.2018.8449743

10. Osorio, A., Calle, M., Soto, J.D., Candelo-Becerra, J.E.: Routing in LoRaWAN: overview and challenges. IEEE Commun. Mag. **58**(6), 72–76 (2020)

11. Truong, V.-T., Nayyar, A., Showkat, A.L.: System performance of wireless sensor network using LoRa-zigbee hybrid communication. Comput. Mater. Continua **68**(2), 1615–1635 (2021). https://doi.org/10.32604/cmc.2021.016922. http://www.techscience.com/cmc/v68n2/42201

12. Cotrim, J.R., Kleinschmidt, J.H.: LoRaWAN mesh networks: a review and classification of multihop communication. Sensors **20**(15), 4273 (2020)

13. Mistry, S.: Arduino LoRa library (2021). https://github.com/sandeepmistry/arduino-LoRa. Accessed 27 Dec 2021

14. IBM, Kooijman, M., Moore, T., Won, C., Rose, F.: MCCI LoRaWAN LMIC library (2021). https://www.arduino.cc/reference/en/libraries/mcci-lorawan-lmic-library/. Accessed 27 Dec 2021

15. Wang, J., Yi, S., Zhan, D., Zhang, W.: Design and implementation of small monitoring wireless network system based on LoRa. In: Proceedings of the IEEE 4th Advanced Information Technology, Electronic and Automation Control Conference (IAEAC), Chengdu, China, vol. 1, pp. 296–299. IEEE (2019)

16. Van Truong, T., Nayyar, A., Masud, M.: A novel air quality monitoring and improvement system based on wireless sensor and actuator networks using LoRa communication. PeerJ Comput. Sci. **7**, e711 (2021)

17. Coutaud, U., Heusse, M., Tourancheau, B.: LoRa channel characterization for flexible and high reliability adaptive data rate in multiple gateways networks. Computers **10**(4), 44 (2021)

18. Lee, S.L., Darsono, A.M.: Enhancement of smart street light monitoring system based on LoRa technology. In: INOTEK 2021, vol. 1, pp. 67–68 (2021)

# Throughput Optimization for NOMA Cognitive Radios with Multi-UAV Assisted Relay

Le-Mai-Duyen Nguyen[1,2], Van Nhan Vo[2,3(✉)], Tran Thi Thanh Lan[2,3],
Nguyen Minh Nhat[2,3], Anand Nayyar[2,3], and Viet-Hung Dang[2,3]

[1] Faculty of Electrical-Electronic Engineering, Duy Tan University,
Da Nang 550000, Vietnam
nguyenlmaiduyen@duytan.edu.vn
[2] Institute of Research and Development, Duy Tan University,
Da Nang 550000, Vietnam
vonhanvan@dtu.edu.vn, {tranthithanhlan,nguyenminhnhat,
anandnayyar,dangviethung}@duytan.edu.vn
[3] Faculty of Information Technology, Duy Tan University, Da Nang 550000, Vietnam

**Abstract.** In this paper, we investigate the throughput optimization for the non-orthogonal multiple access (NOMA) cognitive radio (CR) system with multi-unmanned aerial vehicle (UAV) assisted relays. We propose the communication protocol as follows: in the first phase, a secondary transmitter (ST) transmits the signals to the first UAV relay (UR) using non-orthogonal multiple access (NOMA); meanwhile, a ground base station (GBS) communicates with a primary receiver (PR) under the interference of the ST. In the second phase, the first UR applies the decode-and-forward (DF) technique to transfer the signals to the second UR. Simultaneously, the GBS communicates with PR under the interference of the first UR. Similarly, in the next phase, the UR forwards the signals, while the PR receives the information from the GBS without the interference. In the last two phases, the UR and the SRs receive the signals under the GBS's interference. Accordingly, the outage probability of the primary network and the throughput of the secondary network is analyzed. Moreover, we propose constraint genetic algorithm (CGA) aided obtaining UR's configurations to optimize the throughput of the secondary network under the constraints of the system performance of the primary network.

**Keywords:** Cognitive Radio (CR) · Non-Orthogonal Multiple Access (NOMA) · Unmanned Aerial Vehicle (UAV) · Continuous Genetic Algorithm (CGA) · UAV Relay (UR)

## 1 Introduction

The cognitive radio (CR) is widely regarded as a potential solution for addressing the issues of spectrum scarcity, which have been exacerbated by the enormous

N.-S. Vo et al. (Eds.): INISCOM 2022, LNICST 444, pp. 91–104, 2022.
https://doi.org/10.1007/978-3-031-08878-0_7

development of wireless data traffic of the fifth generation (5G) communication systems [9]. More specifically, CR allows public access to the underutilized spectral bands in order for unlicensed (cognitive) users to exploit the licensed spectrum from an opportunistic point of view, thus economically increasing overall spectral efficiency [10].

On the other hand, the above requirements for 5G systems, especially spectrum efficiency and huge connectivity, non-orthogonal multiple access (NOMA) can be a supplement solution for CR technique because it demonstrates the capacity to boost connection if there are restricted radio resources available [14]. In NOMA, the whole bandwidth may be used simultaneously by each user with different power levels [13].

For example, the authors in [4] investigated a relaying scheme in the cooperative NOMA CR with a primary transmitter (PT), a primary receiver (PR), a secondary transmitter (ST), a relay, and two secondary receivers (SRs). The closed-form expressions for outage probability (OP) are derived for evaluating the system performance of the two SRs over both Rayleigh fading and Nakagami-$m$ fading. For extension, Z. Xiang *et al.* considered a NOMA CR network with a a PT, a ST, multiple PRs, and multiple SRs. The authors concluded that the NOMA and CR combination can reduce the mutual interference among signals and improve the system throughput for massive users [14].

However, the large-scale connections with obstacle issues in CR networks lead to the reduction of system throughput. Thus, unmanned aerial vehicle (UAV) assisted relay is an effective means of improving the system performance. Thanks to the ability of overcoming obstacles and the flexibility to shift postures, UAV increases the possibility of line-of-sight (LoS) [6,11]. For example, L. Sboui *et al.* investigated the achievable rates of a CR with a UAV assisted relay. The authors derived the expression of the power maximizing both primary and secondary rates to analyze the system performance. They concluded that the UAV assisted relay may be used in conjunction with CR technology to increase both rates by using the flexibility, independence, and other quality of service (QoS) of UAVs [11].

Meanwhile, D. Chi-Nguyen *et al.* focused on a CR network where UAV is used as a relay to bridge the communication from a ST to a SR. Then, an optimization algorithm is proposed to achieve an optimal secrecy rate for the UAV CR network. The numerical results showed that the algorithm can achieve a fast coverage rate and optimize the UAV path [3]. It is noted that the interference from primary network to secondary network was not considered in this work. Therefore, B. Ji *et al.* investigated the interference issue of a cooperative transmission mechanism for a CR network, in which the primary network and the secondary network shared a dedicated radio frequency (RF) source with decode-and-forward (DF) UAV selection. The numerical results of the simulation verified the mechanism's efficiency and the calculation correctness [5].

However, based on the above survey, no existing work using multi-hop UAV relay (UR) in NOMA CR networks has studied the system performance optimization of the secondary network under the constraint OP of the primary network. This work will overcome those mentioned drawbacks with following primary contributions:

– We investigate a NOMA CR system, in which the ground base station (GBS) sends the signals to the PR using orthogonal multiple access (OMA) and the ST, with the help of multiple URs, transmits the information to the IoT destinations (IDs) using NOMA.
– We propose the communication protocol for the considered system and analyse the system performance at the primary and secondary networks.
– We propose to apply a CGA for resource allocation optimization of the URs such that the PR can decode the signals from the GBS.

## 2  System Model and Communication Protocol

### 2.1  System Model and Channel Assumptions

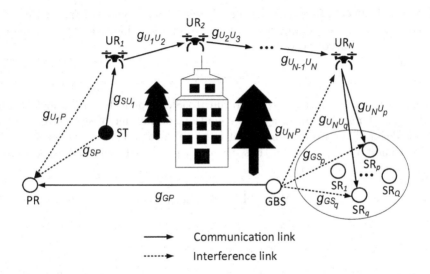

**Fig. 1.** A NOMA CR Internet of Things (IoT) architecture.

This paper aims to investigate the disturbed communication in a disaster situation when the GBS is no longer available for transferring the information to the IDs in the existing CR. Thus, let us consider a NOMA CR as shown in Fig. 1 in which primary users (PUs) (GBS and PR) licensed the spectrum by using OMA principle. Meanwhile, secondary users (SUs) ((ST, URs, and IDs, i.e., $D_p$ and $D_q$) try to utilize the licensed spectrum by using NOMA technique for their communication provided that their transmit power does not interrupt the communication of the PUs. The GBS, PR, ST, IDs, URs are equipped with single antennas. Here, the channel gains and distances of GBS-PR, ST-PR, ST-UR$_1$, UR$_1$-PR, UR$_n$-UR$_n+1$, UR$_N$-$D_p$, UR$_N$-$D_q$, GBS-UR$_N$, GBS-$D_p$, and GBS-$D_p$ links are denoted by $g_{GP}$, $g_{SP}$, $g_{SU_1}$, $g_{U_nU_{n+1}}$, $g_{U_ND_p}$, $g_{U_ND_p}$, $g_{GU_N}$, $g_{GD_p}$, and

$g_{GD_q}$; and $d_{GP}$, $d_{SP}$, $d_{SU_1}$, $d_{U_nU_{n+1}}$, $d_{U_ND_p}$, $d_{U_ND_p}$, $d_{GU_N}$, $d_{GD_p}$, and $d_{GD_q}$, respectively, where $N$ is the number of the URs and $n \in \{1, \ldots, N\}$.

Here, all channel gains are identically independent distributed (i.i.d) and remain constants for the duration of one packet. In particular, for the ground-to-ground communication, the channel gains are modeled as the gains of Rayleigh fading channels, i.e., random variables (RVs) distributed following an exponential distribution. Thus, the probability density function (PDF) and cumulative distribution function (CDF) of the channel gains are formulated as follows [6]:

$$f_{g_a}(x) = \frac{1}{\Omega_a} \exp\left(-\frac{x}{\Omega_a}\right), \tag{1}$$

$$F_{g_a}(x) = 1 - \exp\left(-\frac{x}{\Omega_a}\right), \tag{2}$$

where $a \in \{SP, GP, GD_p, GD_q\}$ is an RV with a mean value of $\Omega_a = \mathbf{E}[a]$.

For the air-to-ground and ground-to-air communication, the path loss models are expressed as absolute values

$$\overline{L}_b = \beta_b d_b^{\eta_b}, \tag{3}$$

where $b \in \{SU_1, U_ND_p, U_ND_q\}$. According to [8], a ground-to-air channel is more likely to be dominated by either LoS conditions or non-line-of-sight (NLoS) conditions depending on the environment (e.g., sub-urban, urban, or dense-urban). Here, we assume that $\eta_b = 2$; thus, the quantity $\beta_b$ is formulated as $\beta_b = 10^B$ [2], in which $B$ is defined as

$$B = \frac{10 \log_{10}(4\pi f/c)^2 + \omega_{NLoS}}{10} + \frac{\omega_{LoS} - \omega_{NLoS}}{10 + 10\varphi \exp\left[-\psi\left(\frac{180}{\pi}\theta - \varphi\right)\right]}, \tag{4}$$

where $\theta$ is the UR elevation angle with respect to either the GBS, ST, or IDs; $\varphi$ and $\psi$ are constants that depend on the environment [12]; and $\omega_{LoS}$ and $\omega_{NLoS}$ are environment and frequency dependent parameters that represent the excess path losses of the LoS link and NLoS link, respectively [12]. For the air-to-air communication, the path loss can be expressed as [2]

$$\overline{L}_{U_nU_{n+1}} = \beta_{U_nU_{n+1}} d_{U_nU_{n+1}}^{\eta_{U_nU_{n+1}}}, \tag{5}$$

where $\beta_{U_nU_{n+1}} = \left(\frac{4\pi f}{c}\right)^2$.

Furthermore, the ground-to-air, air-to-ground, and air-to-air channel gains follow Nakagami-$m$ distributed fading environment with fading severity parameter $m$ [7], i.e., RVs following a Gamma distribution. Thus, the PDF and CDF of channel gain $g_\alpha$ are formulated as follows [6]:

$$f_{g_\alpha}(x) = \left(\frac{m_\alpha}{\Omega_\alpha}\right)^{m_\alpha} \frac{x^{m_\alpha - 1}}{\Gamma(m_\alpha)} \exp\left(-\frac{m_\alpha x}{\Omega_\alpha}\right), \tag{6}$$

$$F_{g_\alpha}(x) = 1 - \sum_{j=0}^{m_\alpha - 1} \left(\frac{m_\alpha x}{\Omega_\alpha}\right)^j \frac{1}{j!} \exp\left(-\frac{m_\alpha x}{\Omega_\alpha}\right). \tag{7}$$

where $\alpha \in \{b, U_n U_{n+1}\}$, $g_\alpha$ is a RV with a mean value $\Omega_\alpha = \mathbf{E}\left[|g_\alpha|^2\right]$ and $\Gamma(\cdot)$ is the Gamma function. In addition, due to the complex environment, the imperfect channel state information (CSI) is considered for all channels, i.e., $g_a = \tilde{g}_a + e_a$ and $g_\alpha = \tilde{g}_\alpha + e_\alpha$, where $\tilde{g}_a$ and $\tilde{g}_\alpha$ are the channel coefficients estimated by using the minimum mean square errors (MMSEs) for $g_a$ and $g_\alpha$, respectively; and $e_a, e_\alpha \sim \mathcal{CN}(0, \Omega_e)$, with $\Omega_e$ being the correctness of the channel estimation and $\mathcal{CN}(0, \Omega_e)$ being a scalar complex Gaussian distribution with zero mean and variance $\Omega_e$ [1].

## 2.2  Communication Protocol

The basic idea of a NOMA CR is that the GBS with the transmitted power $P_P$ sends the signal to the PR on an orthogonal frequency band in the primary network. For the secondary network, the ST may sense the frequency band from the GBS to transmit the signals to $D_p$ and $D_q$ with the help of the URs by applying NOMA principle. Specifically, there are $(N + 1)$ phases for signal transmission from the GBS to the IDs as follows:

- In the first phase, the ST transmits the superimposed signal $x_S$ to $D_p$ and $D_q$, where $x_S = \sqrt{\mu_p}x_p + \sqrt{\mu_q}x_q$, $\mu_p + \mu_q = 1$, and $\mu_p < \mu_q$. Therefore, the received signal at the first UR can be written as

$$y_{U_1} = \sqrt{\frac{P_S}{\bar{L}_{SU_1}^\theta}} \left(\sqrt{\mu_p}x_p + \sqrt{\mu_q}x_q\right) g_{SU_1} + n_{U_1}, \tag{8}$$

where $n_{U_1} \sim \mathcal{CN}(0, N_0)$. The received signal-to-interference-plus-noise ratios (SINRs) at the first UR for decoding $x_p$ and $x_q$ are formulated as

$$\gamma_{U_1}^{(p)} = \frac{\mu_p P_S \tilde{g}_{SU_1}}{\bar{L}_{SU_1}(P_S \Omega_e + N_0)}, \tag{9}$$

$$\gamma_{U_1}^{(q)} = \frac{\mu_q P_S \tilde{g}_{SU_1}}{\bar{L}_{SU_1}\left(\frac{\mu_p P_S \tilde{g}_{SU_1}}{\bar{L}_{SU_1}} + P_S \Omega_e + N_0\right)}. \tag{10}$$

Meanwhile, the GBS broadcasts the signal $x_P$ to the PR by using OMA principle. It is noted that the ST interferes the PR on the orthogonal frequency band due to the broadcast nature. Thus, the received signal at the PR in the first phase can be written as

$$y_P^{(1)} = \sqrt{\frac{P_P}{d_{GP}^\theta}} g_{GP} x_P + \sqrt{\frac{P_S}{d_{SP}^\theta}} g_{SP} x_S + n_P^{(1)}, \tag{11}$$

where $n_P^{(1)} \sim \mathcal{CN}(0, N_0)$. Therefore, the received SINR at the PR is formulated as

$$\gamma_P^{(1)} = \frac{P_P \tilde{g}_{GP}}{d_{GP}^\theta \left[\frac{P_S \tilde{g}_{SP}}{d_{SP}^\theta} + (P_S + P_P) \Omega_e + N_0\right]}. \tag{12}$$

– In the second phase, the first UR uses the DF to decode and forward the signal from ST to the second UR. Thus, the received signal at the second UR can be written as

$$y_{U_2} = \sqrt{\frac{P_{U_1}}{\bar{L}_{U_1 U_2}^\theta}} \left(\sqrt{\mu_p^{(1)}} x_p + \sqrt{\mu_q^{(1)}} x_q\right) g_{U_1 U_2} + n_{U_2}, \tag{13}$$

where $n_{R_2} \sim \mathcal{CN}(0, N_0)$. Therefore, the received SINRs at the second UR for decoding $x_p$ and $x_q$ are formulated as

$$\gamma_{U_2}^{(p)} = \frac{\mu_p^{(1)} P_{U_1} \tilde{g}_{U_1 U_2}}{\bar{L}_{U_1 U_2} (P_{U_1} \Omega_e + N_0)}, \tag{14}$$

$$\gamma_{U_2}^{(q)} = \frac{\mu_q^{(1)} P_{U_1} \tilde{g}_{U_1 U_2}}{\bar{L}_{U_1 U_2} \left(\frac{\mu_p^{(1)} P_{U_1} \tilde{g}_{U_1 U_2}}{\bar{L}_{U_1 U_2}} + P_{U_1} \Omega_e + N_0\right)}. \tag{15}$$

Furthermore, due to the short distance from the first UR to the PR, the interference of the UR affects the received signal at the PR as follows:

$$y_P^{(2)} = \sqrt{\frac{P_P}{d_{GP}^\theta}} g_{GP} x_P + \sqrt{\frac{P_{U_1}}{d_{U_1 P}^\theta}} g_{U_1 P} x_S + n_P^{(2)}, \tag{16}$$

where $n_P^{(2)} \sim \mathcal{CN}(0, N_0)$. Therefore, the received SINR at the PR in the second phase is formulated as

$$\gamma_P^{(2)} = \frac{P_P \tilde{g}_{GP}}{d_{GP}^\theta \left[\frac{P_{U_1} \tilde{g}_{U_1 P}}{\bar{L}_{U_1 P}^\theta} + (P_{U_1} + P_P) \Omega_e + N_0\right]}. \tag{17}$$

– Similarly, in the $n$-th phase $(2 < n < N)$, the $(n-1)$-th UR decodes and forwards the signal from the $(n-2)$-th UR to the $n$-th UR. Thus, the received signal at the $n$-th UR can be written as

$$y_{U_n} = \sqrt{\frac{P_{U_{n-1}}}{\bar{L}_{U_{n-1} U_n}^\theta}} \left(\sqrt{\mu_p^{(n-1)}} x_p + \sqrt{\mu_q^{(n-1)}} x_q\right)$$

$$\times g_{U_{n-1} U_n} + n_{U_n}, \tag{18}$$

where $n_{U_n} \sim \mathcal{CN}(0, N_0)$. Then, the received SINRs at the $n$-th UR for decoding $x_p$ and $x_q$ are formulated as

$$\gamma_{U_n}^{(p)} = \frac{\mu_p^{(n)} P_{U_{n-1}} \tilde{g}_{U_{n-1}U_n}}{\bar{L}_{U_{n-1}U_n}\left(P_{U_{n-1}}\Omega_e + N_0\right)}, \tag{19}$$

$$\gamma_{U_n}^{(q)} = \frac{\mu_q^{(n)} P_{U_{n-1}} \tilde{g}_{U_{n-1}U_n}}{\bar{L}_{U_{n-1}U_n}\left(\frac{\mu_p^{(n)} P_{U_{n-1}} \tilde{g}_{U_{n-1}U_n}}{\bar{L}_{U_{n-1}U_n}} + P_{U_{n-1}}\Omega_e + N_0\right)}. \tag{20}$$

For the primary network, the received signal at the PR in the $n$-th phase is written as

$$y_P^{(n)} = \sqrt{\frac{P_P}{d_{GP}^\theta}} g_{GP} x_P + n_P^{(n)}, \tag{21}$$

where $n_P^{(n)} \sim \mathcal{CN}(0, N_0)$. The received SINR at the PR in the $n$-th phase is

$$\gamma_P^{(n)} = \frac{P_P \tilde{g}_{GP}}{d_{GP}^\theta \left(P_P \Omega_e + N_0\right)}. \tag{22}$$

– In the $N$-th and $(N+1)$ slots, the $N$-th UR and the IDs are affected by the interference of the GBS because of the broadcast nature. Thus, the received signals at the $N$-th UR, $D_p$, and $D_q$, respectively, become

$$y_{U_N} = \sqrt{\frac{P_{U_{N-1}}}{\bar{L}_{U_{N-1}U_N}}} g_{U_{N-1}U_N} x_S + \sqrt{\frac{P_P}{d_{GU_N}^\theta}} g_{GU_N} x_P$$
$$+ n_{U_N}, \tag{23}$$

$$y_{D_p} = \sqrt{\frac{P_{U_N}}{\bar{L}_{U_N}}} g_{U_N} x_S + \sqrt{\frac{P_P}{d_{GD_p}^\theta}} g_{GD_p} x_P + n_{D_p}, \tag{24}$$

$$y_{D_q} = \sqrt{\frac{P_{U_N}}{\bar{L}_{U_N D_q}}} g_{U_N D_q} x_S + \sqrt{\frac{P_P}{d_{GD_q}^\theta}} g_{GD_q} x_P + n_{D_q}, \tag{25}$$

where $n_{U_N}, n_{D_p}, n_{D_q} \sim \mathcal{CN}(0, N_0)$. Accordingly, the SINRs at $U_N$, $D_p$, and $D_q$ for decoding the $p$-th and $q$-th signals are

$$\gamma_{U_N}^{(p)} = \frac{\mu_p^{(N-1)} P_{U_{N-1}} \tilde{g}_{U_{N-1}U_N}}{\bar{L}_{U_{N-1}U_N}\left[\begin{array}{c}\frac{P_P \tilde{g}_{GU_N}}{\bar{L}_{GU_N}} + N_0 \\ + \left(P_P + P_{U_{N-1}}\right)\Omega_e\end{array}\right]}, \tag{26}$$

$$\gamma_{U_N}^{(q)} = \frac{\mu_q^{(N-1)} P_{U_{N-1}} \tilde{g}_{U_{N-1}U_N}}{\bar{L}_{U_{N-1}U_N} \left[ \frac{\mu_p^{(N-1)} P_{U_{N-1}} \tilde{g}_{U_{N-1}U_N}}{L_{U_{N-1}U_N}} + N_0 \\ + \frac{P_P \tilde{g}_{GU_N}}{\bar{L}_{GU_N}} + \left(P_P + P_{U_{N-1}}\right) \Omega_e \right]}, \tag{27}$$

$$\gamma_{D_p}^{(p)} = \frac{\mu_p^{(N)} P_{U_N} \tilde{g}_{U_N D_p}}{\bar{L}_{U_N D_p} \left[ \frac{P_P \tilde{g}_{GD_p}}{d_{GD_p}^\theta} + \left(P_P + P_{U_N}\right) \Omega_e + N_0 \right]}, \tag{28}$$

$$\gamma_{D_q}^{(q)} = \frac{\mu_q^{(N)} P_{U_N} \tilde{g}_{U_N D_q}}{\bar{L}_{U_N D_q} \left[ \frac{\mu_p^{(N)} P_{U_N} \tilde{g}_{U_N D_q}}{\bar{L}_{U_N D_q}} + \frac{P_P \tilde{g}_{PD_q}}{d_{PD_q}^\theta} \\ + \left(P_P + P_{U_N}\right) \Omega_e + N_0 \right]}. \tag{29}$$

Similar to the $n$-th phase, the received signals at the PR in the $N$-th and $(N+1)$-th phase are not affected by the interference from the GBS. In other words, the received SINRs at the PR in the $(N+1)$-th phase are

$$\gamma_P^{(N)} = \gamma_P^{(N+1)} = \gamma_P^{(n)}. \tag{30}$$

According to the DF definition, the end-to-end SINRs for decoding the signals at the $p$-th and $q$-th ID are as follows:

$$\gamma_{E2E}^{(p)} = \min\left\{\gamma_U^{(p)}, \gamma_{D_p}^{(p)}\right\}, \tag{31}$$

$$\gamma_{E2E}^{(q)} = \min\left\{\gamma_U^{(q)}, \gamma_{D_q}^{(q)}\right\}, \tag{32}$$

where $\gamma_U^{(p)} = \min\limits_{n\in\{1,...,N\}} \gamma_{U_n}^{(p)}$ and $\gamma_U^{(q)} = \min\limits_{n\in\{1,...,N\}} \gamma_{U_n}^{(q)}$.

## 3   System Performance Analysis and Problem Formulation

In this section, the system performance of the NOMA CR is analyzed. Then, the problem formulation is defined in which the ST and the URs need to control their power allocations for satisfying that the communication from the GBS to the PR does not degrade and the throughput of the secondary network is maximized.

In order to guarantee the above conditions, the OP of the PR in all phases should be smaller than a predefined threshold, $\varepsilon_P$, i.e.,

$$\mathcal{O}_P = \Pr\left\{C_P < \gamma_P\right\} \leq \varepsilon_P, \tag{33}$$

where $\gamma_P$ is the outage threshold at the PR and $C_P$ is the channel capacity of the GBS-PR link with the bandwidth system $(W)$ as follows:

$$C_P = \min_{n\in\{1,...,N+1\}} C_P^{(n)}$$

$$= \min_{n\in\{1,...,N+1\}} \frac{W}{N+1} \log\left(1 + \gamma_P^{(n)}\right). \tag{34}$$

Furthermore, the OP of the secondary network is formulated as follows:

$$\mathcal{O}_S = \Pr\left\{ C_S^{(p)} < \gamma_S \text{ or } C_S^{(q)} < \gamma_S \right\}, \tag{35}$$

where $\gamma_S$ is the outage threshold at the IDs and $C_S^{(p)}$ and $C_S^{(q)}$ is the channel capacities of the ST-$D_p$ and ST-$D_q$ links as follows:

$$C_S^{(p)} = \frac{W}{N+1} \log\left(1 + \gamma_{E2E}^{(p)}\right), \tag{36}$$

$$C_S^{(q)} = \frac{W}{N+1} \log\left(1 + \gamma_{E2E}^{(q)}\right). \tag{37}$$

Then, the throughput of the secondary network is defined as follows:

$$\mathcal{T}_S = (1 - \mathcal{O}_S)\,\gamma_S. \tag{38}$$

The objective is to maximize the throughput of the secondary network subject to the requirements of the OP of the primary network. In particular, we optimize the power allocation factors at the URs, i.e., $\mu_p$, $\mu_p^{(n)}$, and the altitudes of the URs. Then, the optimization problem can be formulated as follows:

$$\max_{\mu_p, \mu_p^{(n)}, h_n} \{\mathcal{T}_S\}, \tag{39}$$

$$\text{s.t. } P_S \leq P_{\max}, \tag{40}$$

$$\mathcal{O}_P^{(n)} \leq \varepsilon_P, \tag{41}$$

$$\mu_p + \mu_q = 1, \tag{42}$$

$$\mu_p^{(n)} + \mu_q^{(n)} = 1, \tag{43}$$

$$n \in \{1, \ldots, N+1\}, \tag{44}$$

where $P_{\max}$ is the maximum transmit power of the ST.

## 4  CGA Aided Optimum Power Allocation and URs' Altitudes

The given problem in (39)–(44) is a nonlinear optimization problem which can be solved by optimization methods including calculus-based, exhaustive search, and sub-optimal search. Calculus-based is suitable for convex objective functions but not applicable for non-convex and multi-optima ones. Meanwhile, exhaustive search takes high computational cost and long run time with high dimension search space. Therefore, in this work, we apply Continuous Genetic Algorithm (CGA), a heuristic sub-optimal optimization method, which can deal with non-convex function and high dimension input. The searched parameters are power allocations and the altitudes of UAVs which try to maximize the system throughput.

---

**Algorithm 1.** Continuous Genetic Algorithm

---

1: **Initialize**
2: $t = 0$, $\lambda$, $r_c$, $r_m$, and $T$
        \\$T$ is the maximum number of generation iterations
3: Generate initial population $\mathbf{d}_k^{(t)}$, $k = 1, \ldots, \lambda$
4: **for** $(t = 1$ to $T)$ **do**
5:    **for** $(k = 1$ to $\lambda)$ **do**
6:        Evaluate fitness of chromosome $k$:  $\mathbf{f}_k^{(t)} = \mathcal{T}_S$
        as in (38)
7:    **end for**
8:    Reproduce chromosomes based on their fitnesses
9:    Apply crossover by pairing the parents with $r_c$
10:   Apply mutation to offspring with $r_m$
        \\New population is formed
11: **end for**
12: Output the best chromosomes

---

CGA algorithm is an improved variation of genetic algorithm (GA) that can deal with the problem with a large number of continuous variables and is applied as presented in Algorithm 1. In which, the input of the algorithm is the objective function defined in (39) and algorithm controlling parameters. Specifically, CGA considers a chromosome as a vector of real values, thus is efficient in continuous domains. The $k$-th chromosome at the $t$-th generation is

$$\mathbf{d}_k^{(t)} = [\mu_p, \mu_p^{(n)}, h_n], \tag{45}$$

where $n \in \{1, \ldots, N + 1\}$. The algorithm begins with random chromosomes in initial population $\mathbf{d}_k^{(0)}$. Then, each chromosome in the population is evaluated by an objective function and the selection step chooses the good ones for reproduction to maintain the population size $\lambda$. In the crossover step, most of chromosomes are recombined in pairs with a crossover rate $r_c$ to create new pairs of chromosomes, called offsprings. Specifically, when CGA chooses a pair of individuals $\mathbf{d}_i^{(t)}$, $\mathbf{d}_j^{(t)}$, it reproduces two new candidates $\mathbf{d}_i^{(t+1)}$, $\mathbf{d}_j^{(t+1)}$ as

$$\mathbf{d}_i^{(t+1)} = (1 - u)\mathbf{d}_i^{(t)} + u\mathbf{d}_j^{(t)}, \tag{46}$$

$$\mathbf{d}_j^{(t+1)} = (1 - u)\mathbf{d}_j^{(t)} + u\mathbf{d}_i^{(t)}, \tag{47}$$

where $u$ is a uniform random value satisfies $0 < u < 1$.

In order to escape from local optima, the mutation step is used to pick several chromosomes at a low mutation rate and modifies them randomly by adding a random value to each entry of the parent chromosomes. This value is governed by a Gaussian distribution whose mean is 0 and scale is $r_m$. The purpose of this step is to maintain genetic diversity within the population because gene pool tends to become more and more homogeneous over many generations. Chromosomes evolve through generations as a loop consisting of selection, crossover, and mutation steps in searching space or population. The best chromosome is the output of the optimization process:

$$\mathbf{d}^* = [\mu_p^*, \mu_p^{(n)^*}, h_n^*]. \tag{48}$$

## 5  Numerical Analysis

In this section, numerical results are presented to analyze the OP of the considered NOMA CR and the convergence of Algorithm 1. Without loss of generality, we investigate the considered system with the following system parameters [1,2]. We set the fading parameters to $m_\alpha = 2$, the system bandwidth to $W = 100$ MHz, the number of the URs to $N = 3$, the thresholds of the IDs and PR for successfully decoding their signals are $\gamma_S \in \{3, 5, 7\}$ and $\gamma_P = 10$. Furthermore, we investigate the UR operating in an urban environment with the parameters $\varphi = 9.6177$, $\psi = 0.1581$, $\omega_{\text{LoS}} = 1$, and $\omega_{\text{NLoS}} = 20$ [6].

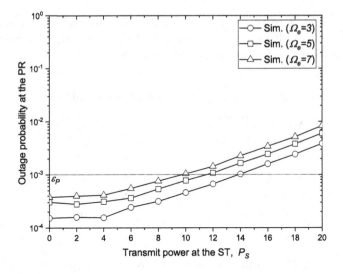

**Fig. 2.** Impact of the transmit power at the ST and the channel estimation error on the OP of the primary network.

In Fig. 2, we plot the impact of the transmit power at the ST and the channel estimation error on the OP at the PR. It is observed that when we increase $P_S$ and $\Omega_e$, the OP at the PR increases. This is because the high transmit power of the ST and channel estimation error lead the larger interference at the PR. Figure 3 illustrates the throughput of the secondary network for different values of the last UR's altitude and outage threshold $\gamma_S$. We can see that $T_S$ reaches

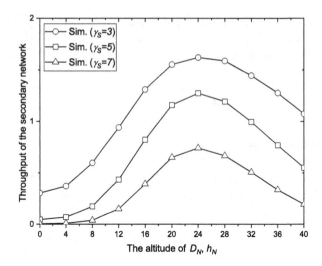

**Fig. 3.** Impact of the altitude of the last UR and the outage threshold $\gamma_S$ on the OP of the secondary network.

the optimal point once $h_N$ goes to a specific value. The reason is when the $N$-th UR flies with high altitude, the probability of the LoS is high. However, if the altitude is very high, the path-loss becomes large.

**Table 1.** Convergence comparison details

| Average generation number to reach 95% maximum value | $r_c = 0.3$ | $r_c = 0.5$ | $r_c = 0.7$ |
|---|---|---|---|
| $r_m = 0.1$ | 38 | 22 | 12 |
| $r_m = 0.2$ | 66 | 53 | 30 |
| $r_m = 0.3$ | 73 | 67 | 57 |

Next, for CGA optimization part, the results are presented with different combinations of population size $\lambda = \{20, 50, 100\}$, crossover rate $r_c = \{0.3, 0.5, 0.7\}$, and mutation scale $r_m = \{0.1, 0.2, 0.3\}$. Specifically, Fig. 4 portrays the convergence of Algorithm 1 within 60 generations ($T = 60$). Three curves present the mean fitness values over generations for three population sizes of 20, 50, and 100, respectively. It can be seen that the simulation curves all converge after a number of generations, implying that CGA works well with our above mentioned nonlinear optimization problem. Besides, $\lambda = 100$ gives better convergence than $\lambda = 50$ and $\lambda = 20$, or the convergence is more stable with higher population sizes. This is obviously the trade-off between convergence stability and computational cost. It is also remarked from Fig. 4 that all three curves yield the converged value that matches the maximal value of 1.22 bps/Hz of the second curve ($\gamma_s = 5$) in Fig. 4. This again verifies the reliability of our analysis and CGA implementation.

Table 1 compares the convergence speeds with different combinations of $r_c$ and $r_m$. $\lambda$ is fixed to 100 in this experiment set due to the results in Fig. 4. The Table's values are the average generation numbers at which the target function reaches 95% of the optimal system throughput. CGA needs 73 generations for $r_c = 0.3$ and $r_m = 0.3$, while needing only 12 generations for $r_c = 0.7$ and $r_m = 0.1$. Moreover, the convergence is better with larger crossover rate. The reason is with a large enough crossover ratio, the more diverse population will be created; thus, the evolutionary is more convenient. The mutation scale also affects the speed of convergence process. The scale should be small, e.g., at 0.1, so that the fitness function is able to overcome local optima without slowing down the convergence.

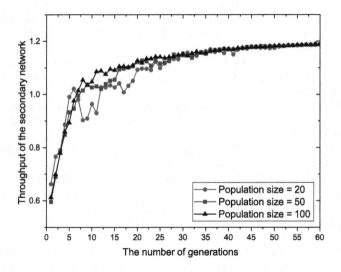

**Fig. 4.** CGA convergence over generations with different population sizes $\lambda = 20$, 50, and 100.

## 6 Conclusions

This paper has studied the system performance of a NOMA CR with the help of multiple URs. Accordingly, the expressions for the OP at the PR and the throughput of the secondary network are defined. Based on that, CGA algorithm has been proposed to apply for determining the optimal power allocation and altitudes of the UR to achieve the best throughput under constraints from the primary network. Finally, the numerical results show that the proposed NOMA CR can satisfy the requirements for system performance.

# References

1. Bao, V.N.Q., Duong, T.Q., Tellambura, C.: On the performance of cognitive underlay multihop networks with imperfect channel state information. IEEE Trans. Commun. **61**(12), 4864–4873 (2013)
2. Chen, Y., Zhao, N., Alouini, Z.D.M.S.: Multiple UAVs as relays: multi-hop single link versus multiple dual-hop links. IEEE Trans. Wireless Commun. **17**(9), 6348–6359 (2018)
3. Chi-Nguyen, D., Pathirana, P.N., Ding, M., Seneviratne, A.: Secrecy performance of the UAV enabled cognitive relay network. In: Proceedings of International Conference on Communications and Information Technology, pp. 117–121 (2018)
4. Do, D.T., Le, A.T., Lee, B.M.: NOMA in cooperative underlay cognitive radio networks under imperfect SIC. IEEE Access **8**, 86180–86195 (2020)
5. Ji, B., Li, Y., Cao, D., Li, C., Mumtaz, S., Wang, D.: Secrecy performance analysis of UAV assisted relay transmission for cognitive network with energy harvesting. IEEE Trans. Veh. Tech. **69**(7), 7404–7415 (2020)
6. Ji, B., Li, Y., Chen, S., Han, C., Li, C., Wen, H.: Secrecy outage analysis of UAV assisted relay and antenna selection for cognitive network under nakagami-$m$ channel. IEEE Trans. Cogn. Commun. Network. **7**, 1–11 (2020). https://doi.org/10.1109/TCCN.2020.2965945
7. Ji, B., Li, Y., Zhou, B., Li, C., Song, K., Wen, H.: Performance analysis of UAV relay assisted IoT communication network enhanced with energy harvesting. IEEE Access **7**, 38738–38747 (2019)
8. Li, Y., Zhang, R., Zhang, J., Gao, S., Yang, L.: Cooperative jamming for secure UAV communications with partial eavesdropper information. IEEE Access **7**, 94593–94603 (2019)
9. Ozger, M., Pehlivanoglu, E.B., Akan, O.B.: Energy-efficient transmission range and duration for cognitive radio sensor networks. IEEE Trans. Cogn. Commun. Network. 1–1 (2021). https://doi.org/10.1109/TCCN.2021.3130986
10. Prajapat, R., Yadav, R.N., Misra, R.: Energy-efficient k-hop clustering in cognitive radio sensor network for internet of things. IEEE Internet Things J. **8**(17), 13593–13607 (2021)
11. Sboui, L., Ghazzai, H., Rezki, Z., Alouini, M.: On the throughput of cognitive radio MIMO systems assisted with UAV relays. In: Proceedings of the International Wireless Communications and Mobile Computing Conference, pp. 939–944 (2017)
12. Sohail, M.F., Leow, C.Y., Won, S.: Non-orthogonal multiple access for unmanned aerial vehicle assisted communication. IEEE Access **6**, 22716–22727 (2018)
13. Vo, V.N., So-In, C., Tran, D.D., Tran, H.: Optimal system performance in multihop energy harvesting WSNs using cooperative NOMA and friendly jammers. IEEE Access **7**, 125494–125510 (2019)
14. Xiang, Z., Yang, W., Pan, G., Cai, Y., Song, Y.: Physical layer security in cognitive radio inspired NOMA network. IEEE J. Select. Top. Signal Process. **13**(3), 700–714 (2019)

# Information Processing and Data Analysis

# An Intelligent Edge System for Face Mask Recognition Application

Tuan Le-Anh[✉], Bao Nguyen-Van, and Quan Le-Trung

UiTiOt Research Group, Department of Computer Networks, University of Information Technology, Vietnam National University – Ho Chi Minh City, Ho Chi Minh City, Vietnam
`tuanla.14@grad.uit.edu.vn`, `{baonv,quanlt}@uit.edu.vn`

**Abstract.** In the modern age, the growth of embedded devices, IoT (Internet of Things), 5G (Fifth Generation) and AI (Artificial Intelligence), has driven edge AI applications. Adopting Edge computing for AI applications intends to deal with power consumption, network capacity, response latency issues. In this paper, we introduce an intelligent edge system. It aims to assist with managing and developing microservices based AI applications on embedded computers with limited hardware resource. The proposed system uses Docker/Containerd and lightweight Kubernetes cluster (K3s) for high availability, self-healing, load balancing, scaling and automated deployment. It also facilitates GPU (Graphics Processing Unit) to speed up AI applications. The centralized cluster management and monitoring features simplify clusters and services administration, especially on a large scale. Meanwhile, container registry and DevOps platform with built-in code repository and CI/CD (Continuous Integration/Continuous Delivery) offer continuous integration and delivery for AI applications running on the cluster. This improves the process of AI applications development and management at the edge. In this experience, we implement the face mask recognition application with the proposed system. This application engages the state-of-the-art and lightweight object detection models with deep learning, observing mask violations to contribute to reducing the spread of COVID-19 disease.

**Keywords:** Edge computing · IoT · AI · Docker/Containerd · Kubernetes · DevOps · CI/CD · Cluster management · Monitoring

## 1 Introduction

In modern times, the figure of devices connected to the network, and the data generated by these devices in many fields have been increasing [1, 2], in which processing data and applying AI majorly occur in the cloud. However, the IoT-Cloud approach encounters with response latency, energy consumption, and network capacity issues. To work out the situation, the IoT-Edge-Cloud approach has been in place. This brings the computation to the edge, close to the IoT devices sending the data. Besides, AI at the edge has become one of the top research trends in recent years [3]. It has strengthened real-time AI applications with the back of modern embedded systems, IoT devices, and state-of-the-art deep learning models. By taking advantage of container-based virtualization

N.-S. Vo et al. (Eds.): INISCOM 2022, LNICST 444, pp. 107–124, 2022.
https://doi.org/10.1007/978-3-031-08878-0_8

and lightweight container orchestration technologies, AI applications run on isolated environments with high availability, self-healing, load balancing, scaling and automated deployment [4, 5]. In addition, applying cluster management and monitoring features makes it effortless to administer clusters and AI applications as services on the cluster. For systems on a large scale, these will be more beneficial. The container registry and DevOps framework with built in Git repository and CI/CD for continuous delivery of AI applications. This speeds up the development and management of AI applications.

In this study, we present an intelligent edge system to aid with managing and developing microservices based AI applications on embedded computers with hardware constraints. The proposed system engages the approaches mentioned above. In which, we apply the proposed system for face mask recognition application.

This paper follows this structure: Sect. 1 introduces the approaches relevant to the proposed system. Section 2 outlines related work. Section 3 presents the proposed system's design and implementation. Section 4 shows the experimental results. Section 5 ends with a conclusion and future work.

## 2   Related Work

This section presents an overview of research on smart COVID-19 pandemic observation systems, edge AI and containerization, and state-of-the-art object detection models for real-time AI applications at the edge.

### 2.1   COVID-19

The need to apply AI to deal with COVID-19 has been huge over the years. In which AI-based observation applications have been used to help mitigate the spread of the disease. These include social distancing, body temperature monitoring, and mask detection [6–8] in the area we cover in this article.

### 2.2   Edge Artificial Intelligence and Containerization

In recent years, Edge AI has been growing, especially for real-time AI applications with low latency, network capacity and energy saving. It favors container-based virtualization for flexible and fast deployment. Some major container-based technologies include Docker, Containerd, CRI-O with GPU support. These platforms run containers with a performance like a bare-metal environment. In addition, container orchestration platforms such as lightweight Kubernetes (K3s) also improve edge AI performance by optimizing workload placement. Nowadays, Kubernetes is one of the top choices for automating deployment, scaling, and management of containerized applications. Some leading managed service and certified Kubernetes include Amazon Elastic Kubernetes Service (EKS), Google Kubernetes Engine (GKE), Azure Kubernetes Service (AKS), etc. For edge or on-premises systems, major distributions are MicroK8s, K3s, and so on. K3s is one of the best candidate for edge systems with lower resource usage than MicroK8s [9]. Some relevant case studies include A Container-Based Edge Computing System for Smart Healthcare Applications [5], Edge Computing and Artificial Intelligence for Landslides Monitoring [10], Edge AI-IoT Pivot Irrigation, Plant Diseases and Pests Identification [11].

### 2.3 Deep Learning-Based Object Detection

In computer vision, there are many studies about real-time object detection models with deep learning. In this section, we conducted a survey of Faster R-CNN, Mask R-CNN, SSD, and YOLO. In which lightweight YOLO models balancing between the performance and accuracy would be our choice to apply for facemask recognition on embedded systems, ARM architecture with limited hardware resources.

#### 2.3.1 Faster R-CNN and Mask R-CNN

Shaoqing Ren et al. introduced Faster R-CNN in 2016 [12]. The model uses Region Proposal Network to predict Region of Interest. Faster R-CNN outperformed with 0.2 s per image, compared to 2.3 and 49 s of Fast R-CNN and R-CNN respectively, using VGG16 network. Kaiming He et al. introduced Mask R-CNN in 2018 [13] with adding a new branch to predict mask and the rest was the same as Faster R-CNN. Although introducing a minor computational cost to detect mask, Mask R-CNN still achieved of 5 FPS.

#### 2.3.2 SSD

Wei Liu et al. proposed SSD (Single Shot MultiBox Detector) in 2016 [14]. The model uses a single stage to predict bounding boxes and class probabilities from the entire image. Meanwhile, Faster R-CNN runs two stages. SSD can achieve high accuracy with relatively low resolution input images, speeding up object detection. SSD300 and SSD512 got performance of 46 FPS and 19 FPS respectively, outperforming Faster R-CNN with 7 FPS. Meanwhile, their accuracy was of 74.3 mAP and 76.8 mAP respectively, higher than Faster R-CNN with 73.2 mAP. Compared to YOLOv1 using VGG-16, SSD300 was more than twice, up to 46 FPS compared to 21 FPS and their accuracy was also higher, reaching 74.3 mAP compared to YOLOv1's 66.4 mAP.

#### 2.3.3 YOLO

Joseph Redmon et al. introduced YOLO (You Look Only Once) in 2016 [15]. Similar to SSD, YOLO is a one-stage object detection model. It outperformed Faster R-CNN, achieving 45 FPS, although its 63.4% mAP sacrificed a bit, compared to Faster R-CNN model. Besides, YOLO-Tiny achieved 155 FPS and 52.7% mAP on PASCAL VOC. Joseph Redmon et al. proposed YOLO9000 and YOLOv2 in 2016 [16]. YOLO9000 could detect 9,000 different objects. YOLOv2 got 76.8% mAP on VOC 2007 at 67 FPS on 2007 and 2012 VOC using Darknet-19 network and new enhancements. This result outperformed Faster R-CNN and SSD. Joseph Redmon et al. introduced YOLOv3 in 2018 [17] with Darknet-53 network. Its major enhancements include multi-label prediction, predictions across scales etc. YOLOv3-320 achieved 45.5 FPS and 51.5% mAP with IoU 0.5 on COCO trainval. YOLOv3-Tiny offered high performance at 220 FPS on COCO, although its 33.1% mAP sacrificed, compared to YOLOv3. Another research, Mini-YOLO [18] got 52.1% mAP at 67 FPS. Alexey Bochkovskiy et al. brought birth to YOLOv4 in 2020 [19]. With the state-of-the-art network architecture, including CSP-Darknet53 backbone, SPP, PAN, and YOLOv3, YOLOv4 optimizes the accuracy and high performance. YOLOv4-416 got 38 FPS and 62.8% mAP, better than YOLOv3-416 with 35 FPS and 55.3% mAP. YOLOv4-Tiny [20], using CSPDarknet53-tiny backbone, and FPN instead of SPP and PAN, provided extreme performance at 270 FPS with 38.1% mAP. The other proposed by Zicong Jiang [21] achieved at 294 FPS with 38.0% mAP. Glenn Jocher et al. introduced YOLOv5 in June 2020 [22], achieving 140 FPS. However, an official paper on the offered model has not yet been available. YOLOv5 uses CSP and PA-NET networks, along with enhancements including mosaic data augmentation, merging multiple images into one set of ratios for training, and automatic learning anchor boxes. Delong Qi et al. introduced YOLO5Face in May 2021 [23]. The author modified the architecture to support face detection with large and small size and landmark supervision.

## 3 Proposed System

This section introduces the proposed system. Section 3.1 presents the system design, and Sect. 3.2 describes the implementation of the proposed model.

### 3.1 System Design

The proposed system architecture includes three layers: Cloud, Edge, and End Devices, as shown below (Fig. 1):

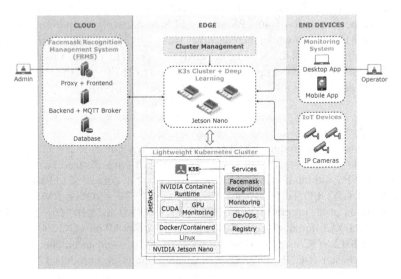

**Fig. 1.** System architecture.

### 3.1.1 Cloud

Facemask Recognition Management System based on MaskCam [24] covers these components: backend, frontend, proxy, MQTT broker and database (Fig. 2).

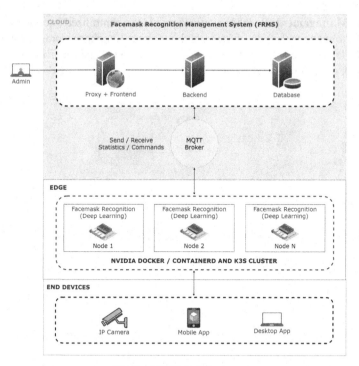

**Fig. 2.** FRMS architecture.

The backend comprises APIs using FastAPI, SQLAlchemy, Paho MQTT, etc. It receives information from facemask recognition services at the edge through MQTT broker running Eclipse Mosquitto, then saves to database and provides information to the frontend using Streamlit, Plotly, Paho MQTT, etc. The dashboard allows administrators to observe face mask recognition information as visual charts or manage facemask recognition services by sending requests through MQTT broker, including update status; start or stop streaming; capture a video. It also provides a function to download saved videos. Nginx acts as a HTTPs reverse proxy for the frontend. MQTT broker transports messages between FRMS and facemask recognition services. Database running PostreSQL stores statistical data and device information.

### 3.1.2  Intelligent Edge

The edge system runs K3s cluster, combining multiple master and worker nodes, to provide high availability, load balancing, scaling, and automated deployment. NVIDIA Docker/Containerd supports GPU to speed up facemask recognition services running modern lightweight YOLO models, etc. The cluster gives external access to its services via Nginx/Traefik Ingress Controller, Load Balancer, NodePort. Services within the cluster communicate with each other through ClusterIP. Theses services include cluster management, monitoring, registry, DevOps, and facemask recognition.

- **Cluster Management:** Rancher platform provides a centralized interface via UI, CLI and API to manage the edge system, and integrates Longhorn storage with no single point of failure (data replication across multiple nodes and recurring snapshot and backups), monitoring service, etc. (Fig. 3).

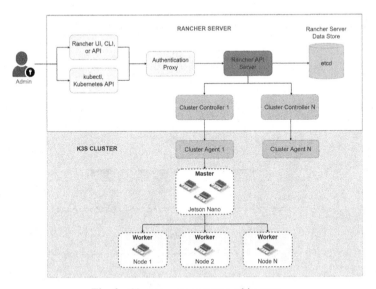

**Fig. 3.** Cluster management architecture.

- **Monitoring:** Prometheus, Grafana and AlertManager integrated with the cluster management system to observe the edge system (Fig. 4).

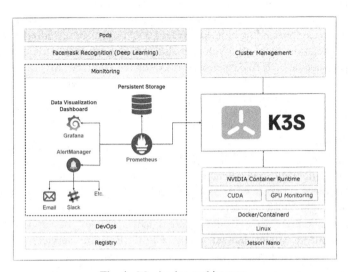

**Fig. 4.** Monitoring architecture.

- **DevOps:** GitLab DevOps platform, which incorporates Git repository, CI/CD management, etc. GitLab Runner works with GitLab CI/CD to run jobs. GitLab supports different Executors, including Docker, Kubernetes, SSH, Shell, etc. Meanwhile, Kubernetes Executor is our choice because it executes jobs on Pods of the cluster. The Pods end when finishing the jobs to free up resources. In this design, we apply CI/CD for facemask recognition services (Fig. 5).

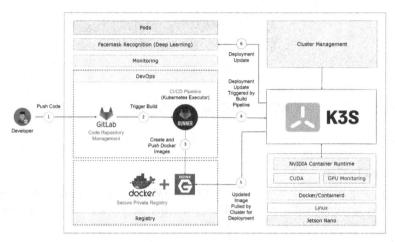

**Fig. 5.** CI/CD architecture.

- **Registry:** Docker Registry manages container images and Docker Credential Pass stores access information. Nginx with SSL/TLS as a reverse proxy. It sits in front of Docker Registry and forwards client requests to that application (Fig. 6).

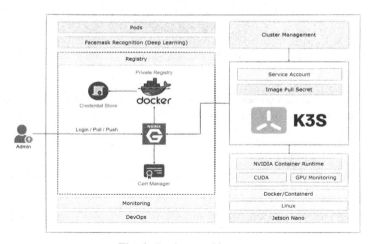

**Fig. 6.** Registry architecture.

- **Facemask Recognition:** Its design includes the orchestrator, facemask recognition inference, streaming server, and file server. The orchestrator coordinates among the processes. The inference uses lightweight YOLO object detection models (Fig. 7).

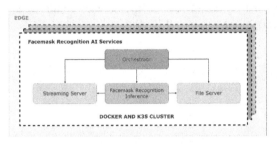

**Fig. 7.** Facemask recognition architecture.

### 3.1.3 End Devices

The IoT devices include ESP32, OV2640 and IMX219-160 cameras, etc. The application is written in C/C++. The mobile application developed with Flutter, Dart and NoSQL Google Firebase (Fig. 8).

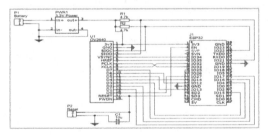

**Fig. 8.** Circuit design.

For COVID-19 design context, facemask recognition applications deploy in public areas, such as airport, schools, and so on (Fig. 9).

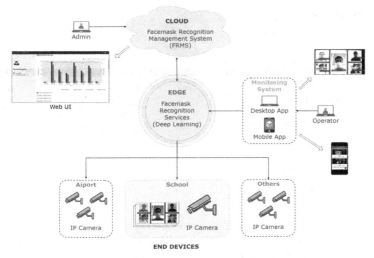

**Fig. 9.** Design context.

## 3.2 System Implementation

In this section, we present the implementation of the proposed system, including FRMS application; cluster management integrating storage and monitoring services; CI/CD pipelines for facemask recognition; IoT, mobile and desktop application. To make it at ease, we also developed a utility to automate the deployment of the proposed system. This will be more beneficial for deployment on a large scale; saving time and avoiding manual installation mistakes.

### 3.2.1  Cloud

See Fig. 10.

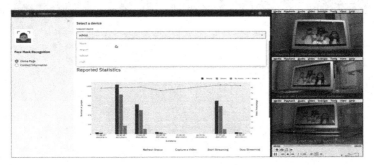

**Fig. 10.** FRMS application.

### 3.2.2  Intelligent Edge

See Figs. 11, 12, 13, 14 and 15.

**Fig. 11.**  Cluster management.

**Fig. 12.**  Volume replicas, snapshots and backups.

**Fig. 13.**  Secondary data backup on Amazon S3.

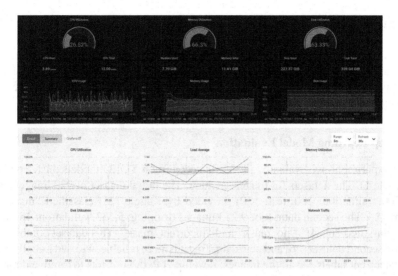

**Fig. 14.** Monitoring.

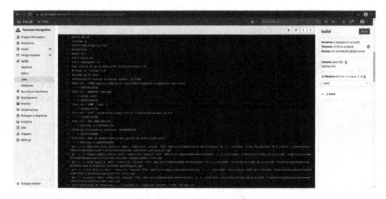

**Fig. 15.** CI/CD pipelines.

### 3.2.3   End Devices

See Figs. 16, 17 and 18.

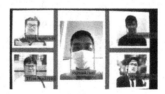

**Fig. 16.** IoT application.     **Fig. 17.** Desktop app (VLC).     **Fig. 18.** Mobile app.

## 4  Experimental Results

This section covers three parts: Sect. 4.1 describes the accuracy assessment and performance analysis of facemask recognition deep learning models. Section 4.2 presents the availability evaluation of the edge services. Section 4.3 shows the hardware resource assessment occupied by the edge system.

### 4.1  Deep Learning Model Evaluation

In this experiment, we evaluated facemask recognition YOLO models on Jetson Nano (see Table 1). The datasets for the test include: The initial dataset of 920 images (training: 700, validation: 100, test: 120) provided by Kaggle [25] classified "mask" and "no_mask". The second dataset of 9,213 images (training: 5,533, validation: 1840, test: 1840) classified "mask", "no_mask" and "incorrect_mask". This dataset combined the first and second dataset [26] and new data. To get it more reliable, we used LabelImg [27] to fix incorrect labels for all the images; developed Python scripts to remove duplicate, missing data and formalize with the same YOLO annotation format; balance data among training, validation, and test (Fig. 19).

**Table 1.** Hardware specification.

| No. | Role | Description |
|---|---|---|
| 1 | Master | Jetson Nano: GPUNVIDIA Maxwell architecture with 128 NVIDIA CUDA® |
| 2 | Worker | cores, CPU Quad-core ARM Cortex-A57 MPCore processor, RAM 4 GB 64-bit LPDDR4, 1600 MHz 25.6 GB/s, SD Card 64 GB |

**Table 2.** Deep learning model evaluation.

| Model | mAP – validation | | | mAP – testing | | |
|---|---|---|---|---|---|---|
| | IoU 0.25 | IoU 0.5 | IoU 0.75 | IoU 0.25 | IoU 0.5 | IoU 0.75 |
| YOLOv3 416 × 416 | 88.6 | 77.9 | 29.5 | 81.7 | 75.9 | 32.8 |
| YOLOv3-Tiny 320 × 320 | 73.3 | 64.1 | 15.5 | 76.8 | 56.1 | 15.3 |
| YOLOv3-Tiny 416 × 416 | 83.8 | 73.3 | 23.5 | 83.1 | 65.5 | 22.0 |
| YOLOv3-Tiny 640 × 640 | 88.1 | 83.0 | 34.1 | 88.1 | 78.5 | 32.9 |
| YOLOv3-Tiny 1024 × 576 | 88.7 | 81.9 | 26.7 | 90.1 | 85.2 | 38.5 |
| YOLOv4 416 × 416 | 92.6 | 87.9 | 42.8 | 93.7 | 91.1 | 50.3 |
| YOLOv4-Tiny-3L 320 × 320 | 88.0 | 80.6 | 33.3 | 86.8 | 78.4 | 35.9 |

*(continued)*

**Table 2.** (*continued*)

| Model | mAP – validation | | | mAP – testing | | |
|---|---|---|---|---|---|---|
| | IoU 0.25 | IoU 0.5 | IoU 0.75 | IoU 0.25 | IoU 0.5 | IoU 0.75 |
| YOLOv4-Tiny-3L 416 × 416 | 88.0 | 83.3 | 34.6 | 89.1 | 85.7 | 41.0 |
| YOLOv4-Tiny-3L 640 × 640 | 89.0 | 85.7 | 35.6 | 89.0 | 87.0 | 38.5 |
| YOLOv4-Tiny-3L 1024 × 576 | 88.6 | 85.0 | 32.9 | 90.8 | 89.4 | 40.7 |
| YOLOv4-Tiny 320 × 320 | 72.6 | 67.7 | 28.0 | 64.2 | 57.0 | 24.0 |
| YOLOv4-Tiny 416 × 416 | 85.3 | 79.8 | 36.4 | 75.4 | 72.3 | 37.6 |
| YOLOv4-Tiny 640 × 640 | 89.4 | 86.0 | 41.5 | 89.2 | 85.9 | 48.9 |
| YOLOv4-Tiny 1024 × 576 | 90.1 | 86.7 | 39.9 | 90.9 | 89.4 | 46.2 |

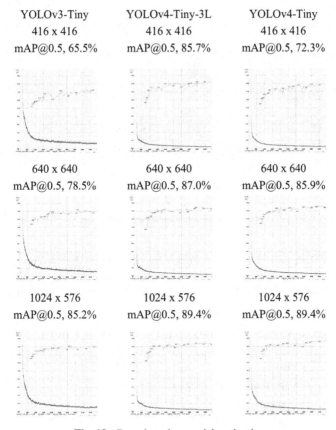

| YOLOv3-Tiny | YOLOv4-Tiny-3L | YOLOv4-Tiny |
|---|---|---|
| 416 x 416 | 416 x 416 | 416 x 416 |
| mAP@0.5, 65.5% | mAP@0.5, 85.7% | mAP@0.5, 72.3% |
| 640 x 640 | 640 x 640 | 640 x 640 |
| mAP@0.5, 78.5% | mAP@0.5, 87.0% | mAP@0.5, 85.9% |
| 1024 x 576 | 1024 x 576 | 1024 x 576 |
| mAP@0.5, 85.2% | mAP@0.5, 89.4% | mAP@0.5, 89.4% |

**Fig. 19.** Deep learning model evaluation.

According to Table 2, it shows that YOLOv4-Tiny-640 and YOLOv4-Tiny-1024 got 85.9% and 89.4% mAP with IoU 0.5. Besides, YOLOv4-Tiny-3L-1024 achieved 89.4% mAP with IoU 0.5 but 40.7% mAP with IoU 0.75, less than YOLOv4-Tiny-640 and YOLOv4-Tiny-1024 models. These results arrived from the initial dataset [25]. Next, we assessed the YOLO models with high accuracy, including YOLOv4-Tiny-3L-1024, YOLOv4-Tiny-640 and YOLOv4-Tiny-1024 on the second dataset. In Table 3, it shows YOLOv4-Tiny-1024 got the highest score with mAP@0.5 83.5% on test data and 85.8% on validation (Fig. 20).

**Table 3.** Deep learning model evaluation.

| Model | mAP – validation | | | mAP – test | | |
|---|---|---|---|---|---|---|
| | IoU 0.25 | IoU 0.5 | IoU 0.75 | IoU 0.25 | IoU 0.5 | IoU 0.75 |
| YOLOv4-Tiny-3L-1024 | 85.5 | 83.0 | 49.5 | 84.7 | 82.6 | 49.2 |
| YOLOv4-Tiny-640 | 85.5 | 83.3 | 54.0 | 85.4 | 83.0 | 52.8 |
| YOLOv4-Tiny-1024 | 87.9 | 85.8 | 52.3 | 86.0 | 83.5 | 52.4 |

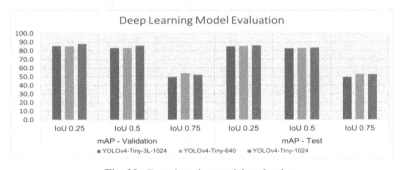

**Fig. 20.** Deep learning model evaluation.

Following Table 4, it shows YOLOv4-Tiny-640 and YOLOv4-Tiny-1024 models did 16.1 and 23.1 BFLOPS, less computation than YOLOv4-Tiny-3L-1024 with 27.3 BFLOPS. Therefore, they would be the choices for face mask recognition application.

**Table 4.** Comparison of BFLOPS for various YOLOv4-Tiny models.

| Model | BFLOPS |
|---|---|
| YOLOv4-Tiny-3L-1024 | 27.3 |
| YOLOv4-Tiny-640 | 16.1 |
| YOLOv4-Tiny-1024 | 23.1 |

For the performance assessment, we conducted the test with YOLOv4-Tiny-1024 and a camera speed of 30 FPS. As a result, facemask recognition service using YOLOv4-Tiny-1024 achieved 13.7, 27.86 and 29.94 FPS with the inference interval of 0, 1 and 2 respectively in 10-W mode with a peak GPU speed of 921.6 MHz. The results show the inference interval of 2 gained the best performance. However, with a maximum GPU speed of 614.4 MHz in 5-W mode, it still achieved a relative performance of 27.16 FPS but less energy consumption (Table 5 and Fig. 21).

**Table 5.** Facemask recognition performance evaluation.

| | Inference interval | | |
|---|---|---|---|
| | 0 | 1 | 2 |
| Performance (FPS) | 13.7 | 27.86 | 29.94 |

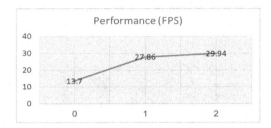

**Fig. 21.** Face mask recognition performance evaluation.

## 4.2  High Availability and Performance Evaluation

In this section, we assessed the high availability of edge services on K3s cluster, including registry, DevOps, and facemask recognition. Table 1 presents the hardware specification under the test. From the kubectl tool, we tried to delete a Pod of these services. As a result, the Pod terminated, and the others were in charge to avoid the downtime. In parallel, K3s cluster created a new Pod as a replacement for the deleted one. For another test, we evaluated the edge platform performance. Table 6 shows how long K3s cluster took to create or remove the edge services.

## 4.3  Hardware Resource Usage Assessment

In this part, we evaluated the hardware resource usage, especially the GPU speeding up face mask recognition service at the edge (Table 7 and Fig. 22).

The results show that the average GPU resource increased from 0.00% to 93.92%, 94.82%, 71.73% after the face mask recognition AI application in operation corresponding to the interval inferences of 0, 1 and 2. The GPU average difference was 86.82%. The average percentage of CPU and memory usage increased by 15.26% and 1018.70 MB.

**Table 6.** Edge platform performance assessment.

| Service | Time | Creation/Removal |
|---|---|---|
| DevOps (GitLab, GitLab Runner) | <30 s | Persistent Volume, Persistent Volume Claim, Deployment, Service, Secret, etc. |
| Registry (Docker Registry, Nginx) | | |
| Facemask Recognition (YOLO) | | |

**Table 7.** Hardware resource usage.

| Component | Before | After | | | Difference |
|---|---|---|---|---|---|
| | | 0 | 1 | 2 | |
| CPU (%) | 19.12 | 35.12 | 35.73 | 32.27 | 15.26% |
| GPU (%) | 0.00 | 93.92 | 94.82 | 71.73 | 86.82% |
| Memory (MB) | 1,538.20 | 2,550.36 | 2,546.48 | 2,573.86 | 1,018.70 |

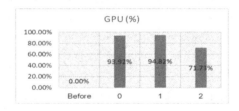

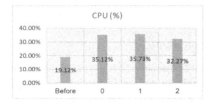
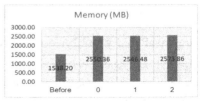

**Fig. 22.** Hardware resource usage chart.

## 5 Conclusion

In this paper, we introduced an intelligent edge system to assist with managing and developing microservices based on AI applications on embedded computers with hardware constraints. In this study, we implemented the face mask recognition application on the proposed system. For future work, we plan to investigate new features to expand the ecosystem of the proposed system; develop new functions for the face mask recognition application; explore new deep learning models capable of accuracy enhancements with optimized speed on embedded systems with limited hardware resources; investigate and develop a software platform to provide fast development to edge AI applications in computer vision.

**Acknowledgement.** This research is funded by the Ho Chi Minh City University of Information Technology, Vietnam National University, under grant number D1-2022-02.

# References

1. Cisco annual internet report (2018–2023) white paper. Cisco. https://www.cisco.com/c/en/us/solutions/collateral/executive-perspectives/annual-internet-report/white-paper-c11-741490.html
2. Lasse Lueth, K.: State of the IoT 2020: 12 billion IoT connections, surpassing non-IoT for the first time. IoT Analytics, 19 November 2020. https://iot-analytics.com/state-of-the-iot-2020-12-billion-iot-connections-surpassing-non-iot-for-the-first-time/
3. Koon, J.: How AI Changes the Future of Edge Computing. EE Times Europe, 24 June 2019. https://www.eetimes.eu/how-ai-changes-the-future-of-edge-computing/
4. Morabito, R.: Virtualization on Internet of Things edge devices with container technologies: a performance evaluation. IEEE Access **5**, 8835–8850 (2017). https://doi.org/10.1109/ACCESS.2017.2704444
5. Le-Anh, T., Ngo-Van, Q., Vo-Huy, P., Huynh-Van, D., Le-Trung, Q.: A container-based edge computing system for smart healthcare applications. In: Vo, N.-S., Hoang, V.-P., Vien, Q.-T. (eds.) INISCOM 2021. LNICSSITE, vol. 379, pp. 324–336. Springer, Cham (2021). https://doi.org/10.1007/978-3-030-77424-0_27
6. Sanjaya, S.A., Adi Rakhmawan, S.: Face mask detection using MobileNetV2 in the era of COVID-19 pandemic. In: 2020 International Conference on Data Analytics for Business and Industry: Way Towards a Sustainable Economy (ICDABI), pp. 1–5, October 2020. https://doi.org/10.1109/ICDABI51230.2020.9325631
7. Suresh, K., Palangappa, M., Bhuvan, S.: Face mask detection by using optimistic convolutional neural network. In: 2021 6th International Conference on Inventive Computation Technologies (ICICT), pp. 1084–1089, January 2021. https://doi.org/10.1109/ICICT50816.2021.9358653
8. Jiang, X., Gao, T., Zhu, Z., Zhao, Y.: Real-time face mask detection method based on YOLOv3. Electronics **10**(7) (2021). Article no. 7. https://doi.org/10.3390/electronics10070837
9. Böhm, S., Wirtz, G.: Profiling lightweight container platforms: MicroK8s and K3s in comparison to Kubernetes, March 2021
10. Elmoulat, M., Debauche, O., Saïd, M., Mahmoudi, S., Manneback, P., Lebeau, F.: Edge computing and artificial intelligence for landslides monitoring. Procedia Comput. Sci. **177**, 480–487 (2020). https://doi.org/10.1016/j.procs.2020.10.066
11. Debauche, O., Saïd, M., Elmoulat, M., Mahmoudi, S., Manneback, P., Lebeau, F.: Edge AI-IoT pivot irrigation, plant diseases and pests identification. Procedia Comput. Sci. **177**, 40–48 (2020). https://doi.org/10.1016/j.procs.2020.10.009
12. Ren, S., He, K., Girshick, R., Sun, J.: Faster R-CNN: towards real-time object detection with region proposal networks. arXiv:1506.01497 Cs, January 2016. http://arxiv.org/abs/1506.01497
13. He, K., Gkioxari, G., Dollár, P., Girshick, R.: Mask R-CNN. arXiv:1703.06870 Cs, January 2018. http://arxiv.org/abs/1703.06870
14. Liu, W., et al.: SSD: single shot multibox detector. In: Leibe, B., Matas, J., Sebe, N., Welling, M. (eds.) ECCV 2016. LNCS, vol. 9905, pp. 21–37. Springer, Cham (2016). https://doi.org/10.1007/978-3-319-46448-0_2
15. Redmon, J., Divvala, S., Girshick, R., Farhadi, A.: You only look once: unified, real-time object detection. arXiv:1506.02640 Cs, May 2016. http://arxiv.org/abs/1506.02640

16. Redmon, J., Farhadi, A.: YOLO9000: better, faster, stronger. arXiv:1612.08242 Cs, December 2016. http://arxiv.org/abs/1612.08242
17. Redmon, J., Farhadi, A.: YOLOv3: an incremental improvement. arXiv:1804.02767 Cs, April 2018. http://arxiv.org/abs/1804.02767
18. Mao, Q.-C., Sun, H.-M., Liu, Y.-B., Jia, R.-S.: Mini-YOLOv3: real-time object detector for embedded applications. IEEE Access 7, 133529–133538 (2019). https://doi.org/10.1109/ACCESS.2019.2941547
19. Bochkovskiy, A., Wang, C.-Y., Liao, H.-Y.M.: YOLOv4: optimal speed and accuracy of object detection. arXiv:2004.10934 Cs Eess, April 2020. http://arxiv.org/abs/2004.10934
20. Bochkovskiy, A.: Darknet (2021). https://github.com/AlexeyAB/darknet
21. Jiang, Z., Zhao, L., Li, S., Jia, Y.: Real-time object detection method based on improved YOLOv4-tiny. arXiv:2011.04244 Cs, December 2020. http://arxiv.org/abs/2011.04244. Accessed 04 Aug 2021
22. Nelson, J.: YOLOv5: state-of-the-art object detection. Roboflow Blog, 10 June 2020. https://blog.roboflow.com/yolov5-is-here/
23. Qi, D., Tan, W., Yao, Q., Liu, J.: YOLO5Face: why reinventing a face detector. arXiv:2105.12931 Cs, May 2021. http://arxiv.org/abs/2105.12931
24. MaskCam. BDTI (2021). https://github.com/bdtinc/maskcam
25. Purohit, A.: Face mask dataset with YOLO format. https://kaggle.com/aditya276/face-mask-dataset-yolo-format
26. ethancvaa: Properly-Wearing-Masked-Detect-Dataset (2021). https://github.com/ethancvaa/Properly-Wearing-Masked-Detect-Dataset
27. Tzutalin, LabelImg (2021). https://github.com/tzutalin/labelImg

# Advanced Joint Model for Vietnamese Intent Detection and Slot Tagging

Nguyen Thi Thu Trang[1($\boxtimes$)], Dang Trung Duc Anh[1], Vu Quoc Viet[1],
and Park Woomyoung[2]

[1] School of Information and Communication Technology,
Hanoi University of Science and Technology, Hanoi, Vietnam
trangntt@soict.hust.edu.vn
[2] Naver Corporation, Gyeonggi, South Korea
max.park@navercorp.com

**Abstract.** This paper aims to propose BiJoint-BERT-NLU, an advanced BERT-based joint model for Vietnamese intent detection and slot tagging, which extends the state-of-the-art JointBERT-CRF model. This model leverages the bi-directional relationships of these two tasks by: (i) adopting an intent-slot attention layer to explicitly incorporate the simple intent output (but with a temporary intent loss) into slot tagging (with a slot tagging loss) from the JointIDSF model, and (ii) introducing an advanced intent classification layer (with a final intent loss) that uses the slot tagging results to improve the accuracy of intent classification. The slot tagging outputs of all tokens, i.e. slot probability, will be summed up for each slot to build the final slot vector for the intent classifier. During the training phase, the coefficients of the three losses are optimized by grid search. The experiments have been done on the recently (and only) published PhoATIS dataset, the Vietnamese version of ATIS. The experimental results show that the proposed model using PhoBERT encoder on word-level on the syllable-level variant of the dataset gives a significant enhancement of Intent accuracy compared to state-of-the-art baseline models, i.e. JointBERT-CRF and JointIDSF. The Sentence accuracy has a considerable improvement on both syllable-level (using XLM-R encoder) and word-level variant.

**Keywords:** Vietnamese · NLU · BiJoint-BERT-NLU · Intent classification · Slot tagging

## 1 Introduction

Dialog systems, such as virtual assistant, chatbot systems, etc. have been increasingly become more and more popular. Natural language understanding (NLU) is one of the most important components in such systems. The two main tasks of this component are intent classification and slot tagging. The goal of intent classification is to understand what users want by classifying users' intents from a given utterance into a given set of intents. Whereas, slot tagging is a sequence

© ICST Institute for Computer Sciences, Social Informatics and Telecommunications Engineering 2022
Published by Springer Nature Switzerland AG 2022. All Rights Reserved
N.-S. Vo et al. (Eds.): INISCOM 2022, LNICST 444, pp. 125–135, 2022.
https://doi.org/10.1007/978-3-031-08878-0_9

labeling task, which aims to tag each token in utterance to correct a defined tag to extract semantic concepts.

Several previous works solved these two tasks independently using modern deep learning methods and achieved high accuracy. For text classification, in both [7] and [20], a Convolutional Neural Network (CNN) is used. Long Short-Term Memory (LSTM) [6] and recently Transformer [16] were proposed to classify the intent of the input sentence. For slot tagging task, in [19], the author used a regression model on top of an LSTM, whereas the work in [8] introduced one LSTM to extract contextual information and then use another LSTM for sequence tagging. These models achieve 95.08% and 95.47% slot F1-score on the ATIS dataset respectively.

Recent research has shown that jointly learning these two tasks helps to boost the performance since information used to solve one task can be useful for the other. Models which learn to solve both of these problems simultaneously are called joint models. [18] designs new Bi-model based Recurrent Neural Network (RNN) semantic frame parsing network structures to consider cross-impact between two tasks. Currently, this is the best performing model on the ATIS dataset with 98.99% intent accuracy and 96.89% slot F1-score. Moreover, some research use pre-trained language models that are trained on a large unlabeled corpus such as BERT [5] to deal with the difficulty of lacking labeled data. [3] proposed a simple joint model based on BERT, on which [14] based on to introduce a Stack-Propagation framework, which can better incorporate the intent semantic information to guide slot tagging and make the model more interpretable.

Vietnamese is a low-resource language in these research topics. Some research done on private Vietnamese datasets made predictions on intent and slots separately [13,15] using LSTM and Conditional Random Field (CRF). Recently, PhoATIS dataset [4] has been publicly available for intent classification and slot tagging. This dataset was translated into Vietnamese from the ATIS dataset, a popular dataset for this field. The joint model that was introduced along with the PhoATIS, i.e. JointIDSF model extending the work of [3], extracted features using a pre-trained language model and used an intent-slot attention layer to explicitly incorporate intent context information into slot tagging.

However, the intent accuracy of the JointIDSF model was not significantly improved over its baseline model (JointBERT-CRF). In JointIDSF, only the intent context was used to enhance the quality of slot tagging. In this paper, we propose a joint model, called BiJoint-BERT-NLU, that leverages the bidirectional relationships of these two tasks. In this model, beside the intent-slot attention layer to explicitly incorporate intent context information into slot tagging, we build an advanced intent classification layer that leverages the tagging slot outputs to improve the intent accuracy of usersays.

The rest of the paper is organized as follows. Section 2 presents the proposed joint model along with the baseline one. Section 3 goes in depth into the related works done in this field of research. In Sect. 4, the experiments and evaluation results on PhoATIS will be reported and discussed with state-of-the-art baseline models. Finally, the paper draws some conclusions of the work in Sect. 5.

## 2   Our Model

In this section, we present our proposed model with extensions from the baseline model JointBERT-CRF [3].

### 2.1   Baseline Model

The baseline model [3] uses BERT encoder followed by a feed-forward layer for Intent classification and a Conditional Random Field layer for Slot tagging (Fig. 1). These 2 tasks are performed separately in this model.

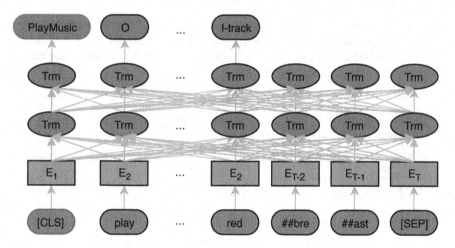

**Fig. 1.** Architecture of the baseline joint model for intent classification and slot tagging

Given an input sentence with n tokens $x_1...x_n$, a special classification token [CLS] is inserted as the first token of the sequence, resulting in the sequence $x_0, x_1...x_n$ ($x_0$ corresponds to the [CLS] token). The sequence is then passed to the BERT encoder to form a contextualized embedding $h_0, h_1...h_n$ with $h_i$ corresponds to token $x_i$.

*Intent Classification.* The contextualized embedding $h_0$ of [CLS] is then fed into a single-layer feed-forward neural network ($FFNN_{IC}$), whose output size is the number of intent labels, to create the probability vector $y^i$

$$y^i = softmax(FFNN_{IC}(h_0))$$

*Slot Tagging.* The contextualized embedding for the other tokens $(h_1...h_n)$ is fed to another feed-forward network ($FFNN_{ST}$) with the output size, i.e. the number of slot labels.

$$y_j^s = softmax(FFNN_{ST}(h_j))$$

The output is then fed into a linear-chain CRF layer to predict slot types of the tokens.

The objective of the model is to maximize the probability $p(y^i, y^s|x)$. The model is trained by minimizing the cross-entropy loss.

$$p(y^i, y^s|x) = p(y^i|x) \prod_{j=1}^{n}(p(y_j^s|x))$$

## 2.2   Proposed Model: BiJoint-BERT-NLU

In this paper, we propose a new model, called BiJoint-BERT-NLU, for the intent classification and slot tagging tasks for Vietnamese, illustrated in Fig. 2. In this model, we introduce mechanisms to incorporate information from one task to help with the performance of the other.

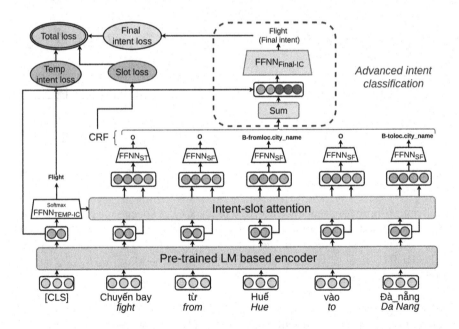

**Fig. 2.** Architecture of the proposed joint model for intent classification and slot tagging

*Intent-Slot Attention Layer.* We adopt the Intent-slot attention proposed by [4] to incorporate intent context information into slot tagging to enhance the performance. We also consider this model as the second baseline model, an extension of the original baseline model presented in Sect. 2.1. However, in this paper, the intent prediction used in this layer is just temporary and only used to provide more context for slot tagging. In other words, this prediction is not part of the output of the model. We compute a separate cross-entropy loss for the intent classification and call it Temporary Intent Loss ($\mathcal{L}_{\text{Temp}-\text{IC}}$).

This layer creates an intent label embedding by multiplying the intent probability vector $y^i$ with a weight matrix $W$. The intent label embedding is then used together with the contextualized embedding $h_i$ to create intent-specific vector $s_i$ (with $i \in 1, 2, ...n$)

$$w = W y^i$$

$$\alpha_i = \frac{exp(w^T h_i)}{\sum_{j=1}^{n} exp(w^T h_i)}$$

$$s_i = \alpha_i w$$

The contextualized embedding of each token $(h_1...h_n)$ is then concatenated with the intent-specific vector $s_i$. The newly created vector is then passed to the feed-forward layer and CRF to produce the slot type prediction

$$v_i = s_i \circ h_i$$

$$y_j^s = softmax(FFNN_{\text{ST}}(v_j))$$

*Advanced Intent Classification Layer.* This component's idea is to use the output of the slot tagging layer to help better improve the accuracy of intent classification. We do not use the previously computed intent vector because that prediction does not take account for the slot types of tokens. The output prediction for slot tagging ($y_j^s$ with $j \in 1, 2...n$) is summed up into a single vector. Note that the vectors being added are probability vectors of tokens presented in the input sequence. We use summation to firstly keep the dimension of the vector unchanged and secondly, adding probability vectors will retain information about the frequency of each slot type in the given utterance. This vector is then concatenated with $h_0$ and then passed into a feed-forward network to produce the final intent prediction. The output of this layer will be the actual intent the model predicts and counted towards intent accuracy.

$$q = \sum_{j=1}^{n} y_j^s$$

$$y_{\text{final}}^i = softmax(FFNN_{\text{final}-\text{IC}}(q \circ h_0))$$

The Final Intent Loss ($\mathcal{L}_{\text{Final}-\text{IC}}$) is then computed for this advanced intent classification layer. The output of this layer will be the final decision for the intent classification task although both cross-entropy losses are calculated for the temporary and final intent classification layers.

*Joint Training.* The cross-entropy losses of the temporary intent classification, the slot tagging and the advanced intent classification are denoted as $\mathcal{L}_{\text{Temp-IC}}$, $\mathcal{L}_{\text{ST}}$, $\mathcal{L}_{\text{Final-IC}}$ respectively. Although the result of temporary intent classification result is not used for the output of intent classification task, the $\mathcal{L}_{\text{Temp-IC}}$ is still calculated as the cross-entropy loss of the temporary intent prediction for slot tagging and contributes to the total loss ($\mathcal{L}_{\text{Total}}$). The final training objective, i.e. Total Loss, is the weighted sum of these losses as follows:

$$\mathcal{L}_{\text{Total}} = \lambda_{\text{Temp-IC}}\mathcal{L}_{\text{Temp-IC}} + \lambda_{ST}\mathcal{L}_{\text{ST}} + \lambda_{\text{Final-IC}}\mathcal{L}_{\text{final-IC}}$$

These three weight coefficients ($\lambda_{\text{Temp-IC}}$, $\lambda_{\text{ST}}$ and $\lambda_{\text{Final-IC}}$) can be tuned as other hyperparameters of the model.

## 3  Related Works

*BERT.* Word embedding has been widely used in many natural language processing tasks, it helps with capturing the semantic meaning of words using a relatively low dimension vector. Since these word embeddings are trained on a very large corpus, this feature representation improves the performance on a variety of NLP tasks, especially when the dataset is small. BERT (Bidirectional Encoder Representations from Transformers) is by far one of the most powerful and most popular pretrained language representation models. Unlike previous language models such as GloVe [12] or FastText [1], BERT can learn contextual relations between words, meaning the same word can have different vector representations in different sentences. This makes BERT exceptional when used to train on down-stream tasks. For that reason, many BERT-based language models are introduced such as RoBERTa [9] and its multilingual variant and Vietnamese monolingual variant, XLM-R and PhoBERT.

*Joint Model.* Recent research shows that constructing and training joint models that handle multiple tasks simultaneously increases the performance significantly, compared to doing so independently. For intent classification and slot tagging tasks, the joint model aims to capture the joint distributions of intent and slot labels, with respect also to the words in the utterance, their local context, and the global context in the sentence. Recurrent neural networks (RNNs) have been frequently used in the field. In more recent years, the transformer architecture has become more and more prominent because of its ability to capture long range dependency. Following that is the task-specific component. For example, the Diet architecture [2], after the input vectors are fed into transformer encoder, the contextualized embedding will be fed into a CRF layer to predict slot types of tokens and similarity block is used to classify the intent label, and these two components work independently. However, in [4], the author feeds the intent prediction to the slot tagging layer instead. In our proposed model BiJoint-BERT-NLU, the prediction of one task is partly determined by that of the other.

# 4 Experiments

In this section, we did the experiments on our proposed model, i.e. BiJoint-BERT-NLU, and on the two baseline ones, i.e. (i) JointBERT-CRF by [3] (Joint BERT model with a CRF layer for slot tagging) and (ii) JointIDSF by [4] (the extension of JointBERT-CRF with an intent-slot attention layer).

## 4.1 Datasets

To evaluate the effectiveness of the proposed method, we use the PhoATIS dataset (Table 1), the only public dataset for Vietnamese. This dataset is a Vietnamese version of ATIS, a popular dataset for this field of research. The dataset was created through three steps according to the original paper. The first step is to manually translate the data into Vietnamese (this is done by one NLP researcher and two research engineers that achieve 7.0+ IELTS score). The second one is to project intent and slot annotations into the translation. The final step is to correct the inconsistencies that appear in the dataset. Since the utterances of PhoATIS are annotated at syllable level (in Vietnamese, white space is not only used as border between words but it's also used as border between syllables that compose words), in the original paper, the word-level variant is obtained through using RDRSegmaneter [11] from VnCoreNLP [17].

**Table 1.** Statistics of PhoATIS dataset

|              | Train | Dev | Test |
|--------------|-------|-----|------|
| Intent #     | 24    | 17  | 21   |
| Slot Types # | 82    | 70  | 71   |
| Utterance #  | 4,478 | 500 | 893  |

The training set, evaluation set and test set contains 4,478, 500 and 893 utterances respectively. The statistics of the PhoATIS dataset is shown by Table 1, which is computed on the dataset on the public github. In the original paper, the dataset is said to consist of 28 intent labels, but according to our observation on the public dataset, the training set (both syllable-level and word-level variants) has only 24 intent labels.

## 4.2 Experiment Preparation

The metrics that we use to measure the effectiveness of our methods are Intent accuracy, Slot F1-score and Sentence accuracy. With regards to Sentence accuracy, a sentence is said to be correctly classified if both the intent as well as all of the slots are correctly predicted.

For experimenting all models including the two baseline models and our proposed model, we use AdamW [10] with $\epsilon = 1e - 8, \beta_1 = 0.9$ and $\beta_2 = 0.999$ as our optimizer and set the batch size to 32. All of the models are trained for 50 epochs using NVIDIA GeForce GTX 2080 Ti.

### 4.3    Experimental Results

We use grid search on the evaluation set to find the best loss weight coefficient combination for the proposed model, as illustrated in Table 2. To be specific, we select the best 3 combinations with the highest average of Intent accuracy and Slot F1-score then apply them to the test set. For each hyper-parameter combination, we train the model for 50 epochs and select the checkpoint achieving the highest average score over the evaluation set to apply to the test set.

**Table 2.** The result of the loss weight coefficients grid search with the loss weight coefficients correspond to $\mathcal{L}_{\text{Temp-IC}}/\mathcal{L}_{\text{ST}}/\mathcal{L}_{\text{Final-IC}}$ respectively. The best combinations are chosen based on Average score of Intent acc and Slot F1 on evaluation set. Intent acc., Slot F1 and Sent acc. are results on test set

| Loss weight co-effs ($\mathcal{L}_{\text{Temp-IC}}/\mathcal{L}_{\text{ST}}/\mathcal{L}_{\text{Final-IC}}$) | Encoder | Average on dev (%) | Intent acc. (%) | Slot F1 (%) | Sent acc. (%) |
|---|---|---|---|---|---|
| **0.2/0.4/0.4** | XLM-R | 97.12 | 97.42 | **95.21** | 86.45 |
| 0.4/0.3/0.3 | XLM-R | 97.11 | 97.42 | 94.74 | 85.89 |
| **0.2/0.3/0.5** | XLM-R | 97.05 | **97.65** | 95.19 | **86.90** |
| **0.4/0.4/0.2** | PhoBert | 97.30 | 97.65 | **95.22** | 86.67 |
| 0.3/0.6/0.1 | PhoBert | 97.22 | 97.65 | 94.76 | 86.23 |
| **0.2/0.3/0.5** | PhoBert | 97.19 | **98.43** | 95.09 | **87.23** |

**Table 3.** Results of the best performing model on PhoATIS test set compare to JointBERT-CRF and JointIDSF on syllable-level (XLM-R) or word-level (PhoBERT) variant of test set

| Model | Encoder | Intent acc. (%) | Slot F1 (%) | Sent acc. (%) |
|---|---|---|---|---|
| Joint-Bert-CRF [3] | XLM-R | 97.42 | 94.62 | 85.39 |
| JointIDSF [4] | XLM-R | 97.56 | 94.95 | 86.17 |
| **BiJoint-BERT-NLU (our model*)** | XLM-R | **97.65** | **95.19** | **87.35** |
| Joint-Bert-CRF [3] | PhoBert | 97.40 | 94.75 | 85.55 |
| JointIDSF [4] | PhoBert | 97.62 | 94.98 | 86.25 |
| **BiJoint-BERT-NLU (our model*)** | PhoBert | **98.43** | **95.01** | **87.23** |

We also initialized our models as well as the baseline using 2 different pretrained language models, in this case, we chose XLM-R and PhoBERT, to see the significance of impact the pretrained language model has on our architecture. When using XLM-R encoder, we conduct experiments on syllable-level variants of PhoATIS while when using PhoBERT, we do so on word-level. The results of this experiment are illustrated by Table 2. The model with the best performance on test set regarding Sentence accuracy for both XLM-R encoder and PhoBERT encoder has $\mathcal{L}_{\text{IC}} = 0.2/\mathcal{L}_{\text{ST}} = 0.3/\mathcal{L}_{\text{final-IC}} = 0.5$, achieving 86.90% and 87.23% respectively. This result will be used to compare with JointBERT-CRF and JointIDSF as illustrated in Table 3 and Fig. 3.

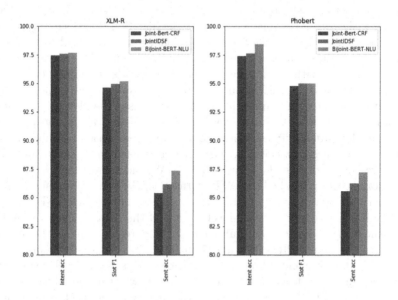

**Fig. 3.** Results of the best performing model on the PhoATIS test set compared to JointBERT-CRF and JointIDSF on syllable-level (XLM-R) and word-level (PhoBERT). The bar representing JointBERT-CRF, JointIDSF and BiJoint-BERT-NLU is colored blue, orange and green respectively. (Color figure online)

For each pretrained encoder, we compare our model (BiJoint-BERT-NLU) with JointBERT-CRF and JointIDSF. All three of these architectures extract semantic meaning from BERT-based language models (BERT, XLM-R), but JointBERT-CRF solves intent classification and slot tagging independently. As illustrated in Table 3 and Fig. 3, our proposed model achieves the best score on all three metrics: Intent accuracy, Slot F1 and Sentence accuracy. The intent accuracy of our model is higher by about 1% compared to both baseline models using the PhoBERT encoder (word-level variant of the dataset). The sentence accuracy of the proposed model is about 2% better than the JointBERT-CRF and about 1% better than the JointIDSF model on both syllable and word level. The slot F1 is slightly better than both baseline models. This result shows that the advanced intent classification layer has a great impact on the quality of intent classification and sentence accuracy, but does not degrade the quality of the slot tagging task.

# 5   Conclusion

In this paper, we introduce an advanced BERT-based joint model, i.e. BiJoint-BERT-NLU, to improve the quality of Vietnamese intent classification and slot tagging. Two baseline state-of-the-art models are: (i) JointBERT-CRF (not explicitly model the relationship between these two tasks) and (ii) JointIDSF (only explicitly utilize the output of intent classification to aid slot tagging). In the proposed model, we model the bi-directional relationships of the two tasks by: (i) adopting an intent-slot attention layer to explicitly incorporate the simple intent output (with a temporary intent loss) into slot tagging (with a slot tagging loss) from the JointIDSF model, and (ii) introducing an advanced intent classification layer (with a final intent loss) that uses the slot tagging results to improve the accuracy of intent classification. The slot tagging outputs of all tokens, i.e. slot probability, will be summed up for each slot to build the final slot vector for the intent classifier. Grid search is used to optimize coefficients of the three losses during the training phase. We did some experiments on the recently (and only) published PhoATIS dataset, the Vietnamese version of ATIS. The experimental results show that the proposed model BiJoint-BERT-NLU using PhoBERT encoder on word-level variant of the dataset gives a significant enhancement of Intent accuracy (about 1%) compared to state-of-the-art baseline models, i.e. JointBERT-CRF and JointIDSF. The Sentence accuracy has a considerable improvement, about 1% to 2%, on both syllable-level (using XLM-R encoder) and word-level variant. This result shows that the advanced intent classification layer has a great impact on the quality of intent classification and sentence accuracy.

**Acknowledgments.** This work is supported by Naver Corporation and School of Information and Communication Technology, Hanoi University of Science and Technology.

# References

1. Bojanowski, P., Grave, E., Joulin, A., Mikolov, T.: Enriching word vectors with subword information. arXiv:1607.04606 [cs], June 2017. http://arxiv.org/abs/1607.04606

2. Bunk, T., Varshneya, D., Vlasov, V., Nichol, A.: DIET: lightweight language understanding for dialogue systems. arXiv:2004.09936 [cs], May 2020. http://arxiv.org/abs/2004.09936

3. Chen, Q., Zhuo, Z., Wang, W.: BERT for joint intent classification and slot filling. arXiv:1902.10909 [cs], February 2019. http://arxiv.org/abs/1902.10909

4. Dao, M.H., Truong, T.H., Nguyen, D.Q.: Intent detection and slot filling for vietnamese. arXiv:2104.02021 [cs], June 2021. http://arxiv.org/abs/2104.02021

5. Devlin, J., Chang, M.W., Lee, K., Toutanova, K.: BERT: Pre-training of deep bidirectional transformers for language understanding. arXiv:1810.04805 [cs], May 2019. http://arxiv.org/abs/1810.04805

6. Hochreiter, S., Schmidhuber, J.: Long short-term memory. Neural Comput. **9**(8), 1735–1780 (1997). https://doi.org/10.1162/neco.1997.9.8.1735

7. Kim, Y.: Convolutional neural networks for sentence classification. In: Proceedings of the 2014 Conference on Empirical Methods in Natural Language Processing (EMNLP), pp. 1746–1751. Association for Computational Linguistics, Doha, Qatar, October 2014. https://doi.org/10.3115/v1/D14-1181, https://aclanthology.org/D14-1181

8. Kurata, G., Xiang, B., Zhou, B., Yu, M.: Leveraging sentence-level information with encoder LSTM for semantic slot filling. arXiv:1601.01530 [cs], August 2016. http://arxiv.org/abs/1601.01530

9. Liu, Y., et al.: RoBERTa: a robustly optimized BERT pretraining approach. arXiv:1907.11692 [cs], July 2019. http://arxiv.org/abs/1907.11692

10. Loshchilov, I., Hutter, F.: Decoupled weight decay regularization. arXiv:1711.05101 [cs, math], January 2019. http://arxiv.org/abs/1711.05101

11. Nguyen, D.Q., Nguyen, D.Q., Vu, T., Dras, M., Johnson, M.: A fast and accurate vietnamese word Segmenter. arXiv:1709.06307 [cs], December 2017. http://arxiv.org/abs/1709.06307

12. Pennington, J., Socher, R., Manning, C.: GloVe: global vectors for word representation. In: Proceedings of the 2014 Conference on Empirical Methods in Natural Language Processing (EMNLP), pp. 1532–1543. Association for Computational Linguistics, Doha, Qatar, October 2014. https://doi.org/10.3115/v1/D14-1162, https://aclanthology.org/D14-1162

13. Pham, D., Le, H., Quan, T.: Transfer learning for a Vietnamese dialogue system. In: 2019 11th International Conference on Knowledge and Systems Engineering (KSE), pp. 1–5, October 2019. https://doi.org/10.1109/KSE.2019.8919425. ISSN: 2164-2508

14. Qin, L., Che, W., Li, Y., Wen, H., Liu, T.: A stack-propagation framework with token-level intent detection for spoken language understanding. arXiv:1909.02188 [cs], September 2019. http://arxiv.org/abs/1909.02188

15. Trang, N.T.T., Ky, N.H., Son, H., Hung, N.T., Huan, N.D.: Natural language understanding in Smartdialog: a platform for Vietnamese intelligent interactions. In: Proceedings of the 2019 3rd International Conference on Natural Language Processing and Information Retrieval, pp. 158–163. NLPIR 2019, Association for Computing Machinery, New York, NY, USA, June 2019. https://doi.org/10.1145/3342827.3342857

16. Vaswani, A., et al.: Attention is all you need. arXiv:1706.03762 [cs], December 2017. http://arxiv.org/abs/1706.03762

17. Vu, T., Nguyen, D.Q., Nguyen, D.Q., Dras, M., Johnson, M.: VnCoreNLP: A Vietnamese natural language processing toolkit. In: Proceedings of the 2018 Conference of the North American Chapter of the Association for Computational Linguistics: Demonstrations, pp. 56–60 (2018). https://doi.org/10.18653/v1/N18-5012, http://arxiv.org/abs/1801.01331, arXiv: 1801.01331

18. Wang, Y., Shen, Y., Jin, H.: A Bi-model based RNN semantic frame parsing model for intent detection and slot filling. arXiv:1812.10235 [cs], December 2018. http://arxiv.org/abs/1812.10235

19. Yao, K., Peng, B., Zhang, Y., Yu, D., Zweig, G., Shi, Y.: Spoken language understanding using long short-term memory neural networks. In: 2014 IEEE Spoken Language Technology Workshop (SLT), pp. 189–194, December 2014. https://doi.org/10.1109/SLT.2014.7078572

20. Zhang, X., Zhao, J., LeCun, Y.: Character-level convolutional networks for text classification. Adv. Neural Inf. Process. Syst. **28** (2015), https://proceedings.neurips.cc/paper/2015/hash/250cf8b51c773f3f8dc8b4be867a9a02-Abstract.html

# Optimising Maritime Big Data by K-means Clustering with Mapreduce Model

Tuan-Anh Pham[1,2], Xuan-Kien Dang[1(✉)], and Nguyen-Son Vo[3]

[1] Ho Chi Minh City University of Transport, Ho Chi Minh City 700000, Vietnam
kien.dang@ut.edu.vn
[2] Southern Vietnam Maritime Safety Corporation,
Ho Chi Minh City 700000, Vietnam
[3] Institute of Fundamental and Applied Sciences, Duy Tan University,
Ho Chi Minh City 700000, Vietnam
vonguyenson@duytan.edu.vn

**Abstract.** During the management and operation, the maritime industry has collected a large amount of data in marine navigation, which has posed a great challenge in terms of resource saving (memory and processing capacity) and utility efficiency. Therefore, the highly specialised nature of the marine navigation and the maritime big data must be analysed to assist the scientists and operational engineers to extract the useful information from this data using algorithms with big data platforms. However, a specific model for big data application, which has a lot of methods for performing such as data visualisation techniques, machine learning, deep learning, etc., has not been extensively studied in the field of marine navigation to provide adequate comparisons. In this paper, we apply Mapreduce (MR) model to the big data of marine navigation. Particularly, we use a standard clustering algorithm called K-means based on the MR model to process the data of marine traffic in the South Vietnam Sea region. According to the main results obtained, we consider making the inference or the prediction of the clustering data which is collected and shown the dashboard of maritime ships traffic, including the scale, the spatial and time-series distribution situation.

**Keywords:** AIS data · Data mining · K-means clustering · Mapreduce model

## 1 Introduction

In recent years, the significant growth of the marine sector has occurred in maritime big data along with a dense network of ships [1], particularly the concentration of large seaports is capable of accepting ships up to 160,000 DWT. Marine data is often used in an automatic identification system (AIS) [2] which offers a wealth of real-time information on a ship's navigation utilised for maritime

© ICST Institute for Computer Sciences, Social Informatics and Telecommunications Engineering 2022
Published by Springer Nature Switzerland AG 2022. All Rights Reserved
N.-S. Vo et al. (Eds.): INISCOM 2022, LNICST 444, pp. 136–151, 2022.
https://doi.org/10.1007/978-3-031-08878-0_10

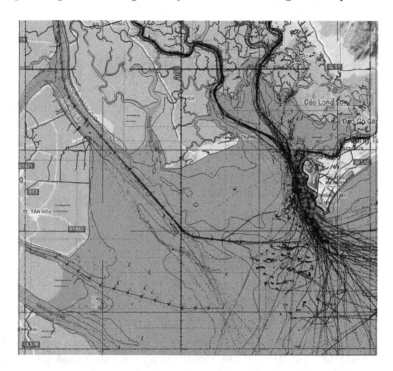

**Fig. 1.** Dynamic visualisation of AIS data, South Vietnam Sea region, January 1st, 2019.

situational awareness and ocean surveillance. According to the statistics on the quantity of data, i.e., more than 2 million notices, collected from the AIS system in the previous years in the South Vietnam Sea region, it is quite important to provide a superb supply of data mining for maritime traffic research. For example, Fig. 1 shows a sample data of dense maps captured on January 1st, 2019.

Generally, the maritime data is collected through the AIS and contains a lot of information like time, name, maritime mobile service identity (MMSI), speed over ground (SOG), course over ground (COG), etc. [3,4]. Moreover, the analysis and investigation of big data can quickly, automatically, and intelligently determine the characteristics of a ship such as position and navigation behavior, thereby orienting the effective development of the maritime industry and contributing to the development of the marine economy. The data acquired, some of which is repeated, along with the tremendous data of the ship's position, performs two obstacles for its use including large-scale data manipulation (e.g., sensor fault identification, data classification [2], data compression, data expansion, data integrity, and data regression [5]) and data complexity mining [6].

Dealing with the aforementioned issues, Hadoop architecture processing engine enables parallel data processing in a cluster [7,8]. It is necessary to design a K-means clustering (KMC) by means of maritime big data based on Hadoop architecture that implements the Mapreduce (MR) model [9]. We further use the Elbow

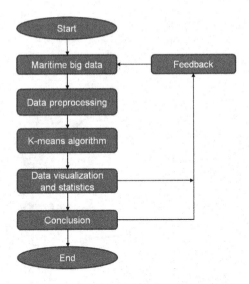

**Fig. 2.** Flowchart of data visualisation and data analysis.

Rule to determine the optimal number of clusters and recalculate the pairs of vectors SOG and COG, i.e., the feature vector when performing clustering, which is better perceived by the statistics and distribution of ships. As a result, the goal of this study is to improve the KMC of maritime data using the MR model (MRM) [10]. To do so, a flowchart of data visualisation and analysis is proposed in Fig. 2. The workflow includes choosing marine data fields, preprocessing data, K-means algorithm (KMA), statistics and data visualisation, conclusion, and feedback. It is noted in Fig. 2 that the data preprocessing step can be omitted if the maritime data is correct. The main contributions of this work are given as follows:

1. We first detect the data errors and remove them, convert the data, and extract the data from the source.
2. We then use the KMA [11–13] to perform the corresponding clustering step after preprocessing the received data and marine data field selection.
3. Finally, through data visualisation, we analyse the results and make some recommendations on the selection of content that displays the information for efficient marine navigation.

The rest of the paper is organised as follows. Section 2 shows the KMA and Hadoop architecture implementation of MRM for analysing the clustered characteristics of the maritime data. In Sect. 3, by using Hadoop architecture to perform the MRM, we determine the optimal number of clusters evaluating the navigation of ship traffic in the South Vietnam Sea. Then, we perform the KMC with two testing cases and analyse the results in Sect. 4. Finally, we conclude the paper in Sect. 5.

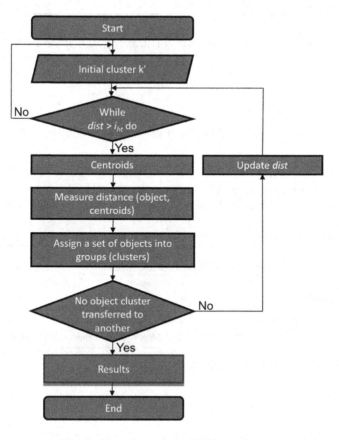

**Fig. 3.** Flowchart of the KMA analysis.

## 2 KMA and Hadoop Architecture Implementation of MRM

### 2.1 KMA

The KMA is used to analysing the clustered characteristics of the data. Figure 3 presents the flowchart of the KMA analysis. In this flowchart, the KMC method utilises the input, standard function $E$, and output. The Pseudo code describing the KMA [14,15] is presented in Algorithm 1. In Algorithm 1, the standard function $E$ using Euclidean distance and the new point of $k'$ clusters are given by

$$E = \sum_{v=1}^{N} \sum_{\substack{i=1 \\ x_v \in C_i}}^{k'} \| x_v - c_i \|^2, \tag{1}$$

$$C_i^{(j)} = \{x_v : \| x_v - c_i^{(j)} \|^2 \leq \| x_v - c_m^{(j)} \|^2, m = 1, 2, ..., k'\}, \tag{2}$$

---

**Algorithm 1.** K-means $(X', k')$

---

**Input:** Data set of $N$ objects $X' = \{x_v | v = 1, 2, ..., N\}, x_v \in R^d$, $d$-dimensional vector
**Output:** Separated clusters $C_i$ $(i = 1, 2, ..., k')$ and minimum standard function $E$ (1)

1: Generate initial parameters
   $j = 1$
   Convergent boundary $i_{ht}$
   $k'$ centers from $X'$ as the initial cluster centers $C^{(0)} = \{c_i^{(j)}\}, i = 1, 2, ..., k'$ using KMC
   $dist \leftarrow E$ using (1)
2: **while** $dist > i_{ht}$ **do**
3:     Form $k'$ clusters by assigning all points in the set $X'$ to the nearest central point
4:     Find the new point of $k'$ clusters $c_1^{(++j)}, c_2^{(++j)}, ..., c_{k'}^{(++j)}$ using (2) and (3)
5:     Update $dist \leftarrow \sum_{i=1}^{k'} \| c_i^{(j)} - c_i^{(j-1)} \|^2$
6: **end while**

---

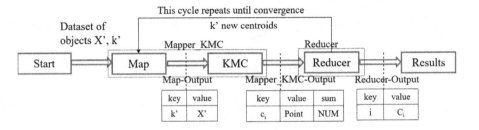

**Fig. 4.** Basic process of MRM with KMC.

$$c_i^{(++j)} = \frac{1}{|C_i^{(j)}|} \sum_{x_v \in C_i^{(j)}} x_v. \tag{3}$$

The Algorithm 1 works on a $d$-dimensional vector set, the data set $X'$ includes $N$ elements. The KMA repeats the process many times including data assignment and centroid update. The KMA assigns each point $c_i$ to the cluster with the nearest center, which is the average for each distinct dimension overall point in the cluster. The process stops when the centroids converge and each object is part of a cluster.

## 2.2   MRM

The problem of ever-increasing data volume generated by technological advancements makes clustering a major undertaking, especially in maritime data. The studies in [7,8] attempt to solve this problem by developing effective clustering methods. Furthermore, the MRM, which is a model exclusively designed by Google, has the ability to programmatically process the large data sets in parallel and distributed algorithms on a cluster of computers. The MRM includes a map

---

**Function 1.** Mapper_KMC($X'$, $k'$)

---

**Input:** A list of $< X', k' >$ pairs and a list of center global centroids, i.e, $k'$ is the index of data point and $X'$ is the content of object and $d$-dimensional array

**Output:** $< i, \text{Point}, NUM >$, i.e., $i$ is the index of cluster (nearest centroid), Point is the value of the sample information series of objects, and $NUM$ is the sum of data points belonging to that cluster

1: Generate initial parameters
   Initialise a sample scenario from $X'$, i.e., the values of the $d$-dimensional array
   nearest_distance ← Double.max_value (1000000000)
   nearest_cluster_id ← None
2: **for** $i = 0$ to length.center **do**
3:     Distance = distance_function(scenario, $c_i$)
4:     **if** Distance $<$ nearest_distance **then**
5:         nearest_distance = Distance
6:         nearest_distance_id = $i$
7:     **end if**
8: **end for**
9: Create an empty dictionary dict() and initialise a cont_index
10: Set the $NUM$ counter record to be the sum of samples scenario belonging to the same cluster
11: Calculate $NUM$ by
    - Adding the nearest_distance as $NUM$ into dict()
    - Adding NUM+ = scenario
    - cont_index++
    - Adding $NUM$ and cont_index into dict()
12: Obtain $< i, \text{Point}, NUM >$

---

function and a reduce function. The map function covers the task of assigning each sample to the nearest center, whereas the reduce function deals with the process of updating the new centers. This paper further considers integrating the process of KMC into the map function of the MRM as shown in Fig. 4 [14,16]. The so-called mapper and KMC function and reducer function [17], which are used in Sect. 4 for the process of testing and analysing, are described in Function 1 and Function 2.

## 2.3   Hadoop Architecture Implementation of MRM

In this section, we focus on a distributed system known as Hadoop architecture that uses commodity machines to create a combined and powerful system. This system is the most popular open-source framework for the process of MRM proposed by Google [9], which is able to process the maritime big data much more efficiently. This framework includes map and reduce functions. The major input for the framework is a key-value pair (key, value) and the map function is performed to process the input in key-value pair (key, value) one by one. The map function is created from more intermediate key-value pairs (key', value'). After that, it groups these intermediate key-value pairs by the key $k'$, so the system

**Function 2.** Reducer($i$, Point, $NUM$)

**Input:** $< i, \text{Point}, NUM >$, where $i$ is the index of cluster (nearest centroid), Point is
　　the value of the sample information series of objects and $NUM$ is the sum of data
　　points belonging to that cluster
**Output:** $< i, C_i >$ pairs, where $i$ is the index of the cluster and $C_i$ is its new global
　　centroid
　1: Initialise an array containing the sum of data points belonging to that cluster from
　　　the list of Point, i.e., the value of the sample information series of objects
　2: Generate $C_i$ from the mean of $NUM$ belonging to the same cluster as a string
　　　value
　3: Obtain $< i, C_i >$ pairs

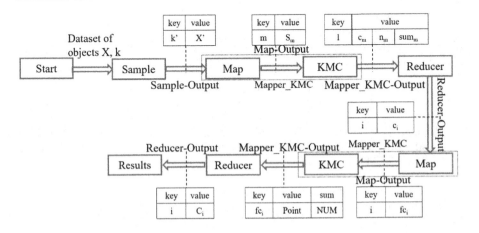

**Fig. 5.** Optimised MRM with KMC.

connects the reduce function for each clustering, which collects and aggregates
into results from the map function. One of the main advantages of this framework
is the important task of defining the map and reduce functions to perform a large-
scale data analysis. However, the I/O performance of the Hadoop architecture
depends on the Hadoop distributed system, which is a major open-source project
to design for high volume and highly reliable storage.

## 3   Optimised MRM with KMC

The optimised MRM with KMC is shown in Fig. 5, which it is improved over
the traditional method [14] by further calculating the total within-cluster sum
of the objects for each cluster. We set $k$ clusters and repeat the process until the
center point of the cluster converges. It is noted in Fig. 5 that $fc_i$ is the final
center $i$. This rule indicates the center point of the cluster to the mean point of
the data set and then splits the elements within it. To determine the number of

**Table 1.** The contents of AIS data [19] and AIS data record.

| Type | Contents | AIS data record |
|---|---|---|
| Static data | imo, mmsi, class, shipname, shiptype, callsign, length, beam, deadweight | Time: 01/01/2019; Data (sample data): 61.091.450 |
| Dynamic data | tagblock_times (UTC), status (navigation status), lon (longitude), lat (latitude), SOG (speed), COG (course), heading, turnrate | Marine objects (*): 943 Data field (**): 25 |
| Auxiliary data | band, destination (port), draught | |

*Marine objects: (ships, AIS is integrated signaling devices, ...)
**Data field (including mobile and static, information of marine objects)

clusters $k$, we use the Elbow Rule to calculate the optimal number of clusters [18], given as below

$$\operatorname*{argmin}_{k} \sum_{i=1}^{k} \sum_{x \in C_i} \|x - c_i\|^2, \tag{4}$$

where $k$ is the number of clusters, $c_i$ is the center point of cluster $C_i$, and $x$ is the feature vector of each ship's trajectory in $X$.

In particular, we calculate the Euclidean interval from every sample to the center point of the cluster by using (4). Then, we proceed to different values of $k$. The total distance decreases as $k$ increases, so it will converge and the position of the largest point is considered as the convergence point, i.e., the elbow.

## 4    Testing and Analysis

The collected AIS data of the Southern Vietnam Sea is very rich. It is a variety of navigation status information for maritime traffic. The trajectory of the ships is determined by linking the ship's position information collected by the AIS to the system operation center. However, the amount of AIS data collected by each ship is not uniform, which can be caused a signal congestion or a failure of the transmitters and conducted by identifying the unique MMSI of each ship. In this case, we remove this AIS data collected because it completely does not represent the sailing pattern of this ship. The standard deviation of the feature SOG and the feature COG of each ship converted from degrees ($^0$) to radians is calculated using the feature $\text{SOG}_{\text{sd}}$ and pairs of vectors ($\text{SOG}_{\text{sd}}$, COG) to assess the stability of the ship. In addition, we normalise the sample before clustering by using logarithmic normalisation [18], expressed as

$$\text{SOG}_{\text{sd}} = \frac{\log_{10}(\text{SOG} + 1)}{\log_{10}(\text{SOG}_{\text{max}} + 1)}. \tag{5}$$

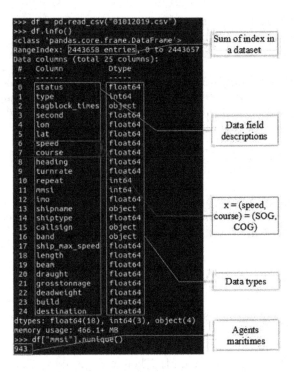

**Fig. 6.** Detail of the framework for the AIS data collected.

## 4.1    Data Input

The contents of AIS data and maritime AIS data sample are described in Table 1. There are three types of data, including static data, dynamic data, and auxiliary data. In addition, the detail of the framework for the collected AIS data is shown in Fig. 6, in which the standard deviation values of SOG are marked in red rectangle. These values are used as the pairs of feature vectors SOG and COG of each object in the implementation of KMC process presented in the sequel.

## 4.2    Implementation of MRM with KMC

In this paper, we implement the MRM with KMC (MRM-KMC) in two scenarios. i.e., randomly taking 3 central points (3CP) and 7 central points (7CP). We also provide the clustering results of these two scenarios to demonstrate the performance of the proposed MRM-KMC solution.

**3CP Scenario.** To implement the 3CP scenario, three initial parameters with the feature vector of SOG and COG of each ship are listed in Table 2. Furthermore, the Hadoop architecture used to build the model is shown in Fig. 7. We receive the result of the 3CP scenario using 3 different starting the pairs of vectors SOG and COG (Table 3) which is applied to the model to find out the

**Table 2.** Selecting three parameters with the feature vector of SOG and COG of each ship.

| $k$ clusters | SOG | COG |
|---|---|---|
| 1 | 0.0 | 104.400001525879 |
| 2 | 0.0 | 160.0 |
| 3 | 0.4000000059604645 | 227.3000030517578 |

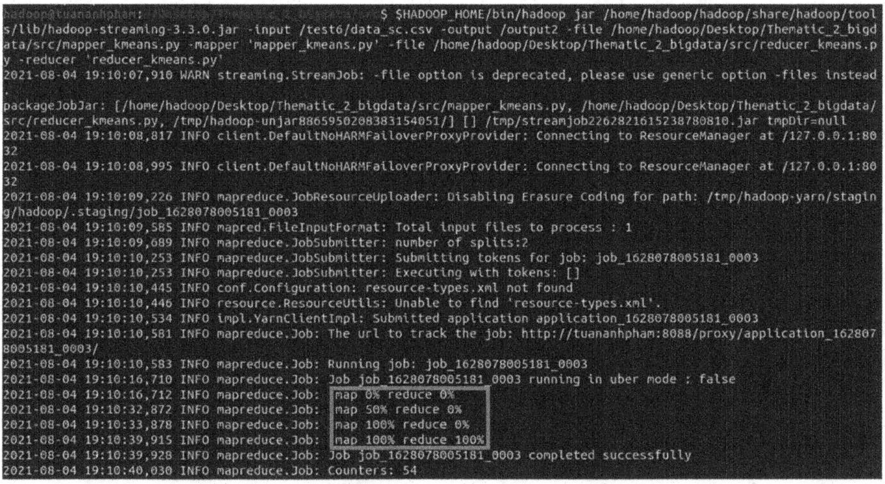

**Fig. 7.** Implementation of MRM-KMC with $k = 3$.

**Table 3.** Result of 3CP scenario.

| $k$ clusters | SOG_new | COG_new |
|---|---|---|
| 1 | 1.1448615977471592 | 66.9534619292097 |
| 2 | 1.4988419143613 | 160.48269968421656 |
| 3 | 2.7800271048373233 | 280.0375339552592 |

characteristics of clusters. The result in Fig. 8 shows that the objective function gets saturated at a minimal value of 2182.00 when $k = 3$. The increase of $k$ cannot improve the result any more. Importantly, as shown in Fig. 9, the majority of the ships is green and blue, which indicates that the ship's navigation is relatively stable. Meanwhile, the orange ones are more unstable, i.e., the pairs of feature vectors SOG and COG are changed over time frequently. In Fig. 9, the results change after each iteration from left to right and top to bottom until the end when $dist$ is less than $i_{ht}$ as mentioned in the flowchart of KMA (Fig. 3).

**7CP Scenario.** Similarly, to implement the 7CP scenario, seven initial parameters with the feature vector of SOG and COG of each ship are listed in Table 4.

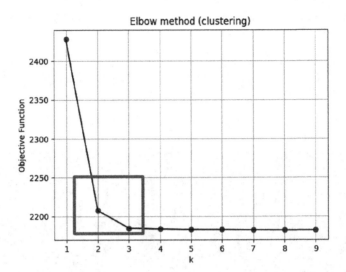

**Fig. 8.** Objective function value with $k = 3$.

**Table 4.** Selecting seven parameters with the feature vector of SOG and COG of each ship.

| $k$ clusters | SOG | COG |
|---|---|---|
| 1 | 0.0 | 41.79999923706055 |
| 2 | 0.0 | 104.400001525879 |
| 3 | 0.0 | 155.0 |
| 4 | 0.0 | 160.0 |
| 5 | 8.699999809265137 | 184.0 |
| 6 | 0.4000000059604645 | 227.3000030517578 |
| 7 | 0.4000000059604645 | 355.20001220703125 |

The Hadoop architecture used to build the model is shown in Fig. 10. We also receive the result of the 7CP scenario using 7 different starting the pairs of vectors SOG and COG (Table 5) which is applied to the model to find out the characteristics of clusters. The result in Fig. 11 shows that the objective function starts getting saturated at a minimal value of 1235.73 when $k = 7$. The increase of $k$ cannot make any further improvements. Importantly, as shown in Fig. 12, the majority of the ships is red, blue, purple, and green, which indicates that the ship's navigation is relatively stable. Meanwhile, the pink and brown ones are more unstable due to more changes in the SOG and the COG over time.

Generally, according to the implemented results in Fig. 8, Fig. 9, Fig. 10, Fig. 11, and Fig. 12, we can see that the majority of the ships is green and blue (with $k = 3$) or red, blue, purple, and green (with $k = 7$), which indicates that the ship's navigation is relatively constant over the period. Meanwhile, the

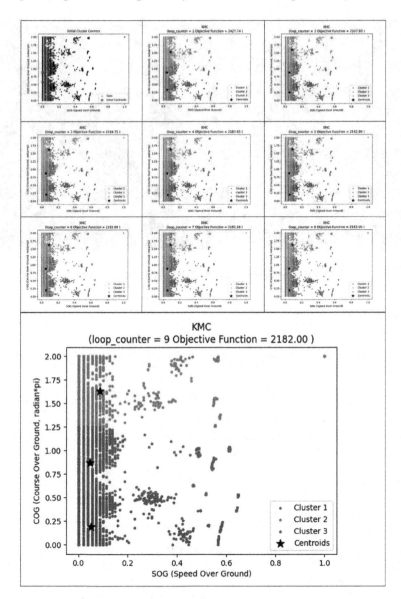

**Fig. 9.** Normalized the KMC results with $k = 3$.

orange, pink, and brown zones are less stable. Based on the obtained results, the standard deviation is a feature of SOG, which means the courses and speeds of ships are unstable and changing frequently. To arrange together with the objective function value, we determine the optimal number of clusters. Thereby, we can evaluate the navigation process of ships more easily.

hadoop@tuananhpham:~/Desktop/Thematic$ $HADOOP_HOME/bin/hadoop jar /home/hadoop/hadoop/share/hadoop/tool
s/lib/hadoop-streaming-3.3.0.jar -input /test6/data_sc.csv -output /output1 -file /home/hadoop/Desktop/Thematic_2_bigd
ata/src/mapper_kmeans.py -mapper 'mapper_kmeans.py' -file /home/hadoop/Desktop/Thematic_2_bigdata/src/reducer_kmeans.p
y -reducer 'reducer_kmeans.py'
2021-08-04 19:07:28,728 WARN streaming.StreamJob: -file option is deprecated, please use generic option -files instead

packageJobJar: [/home/hadoop/Desktop/Thematic_2_bigdata/src/mapper_kmeans.py, /home/hadoop/Desktop/Thematic_2_bigdata/
src/reducer_kmeans.py, /tmp/hadoop-unjar6265058714676650259/] [] /tmp/streamjob7239163228008924271.jar tmpDir=null
2021-08-04 19:07:29,653 INFO client.DefaultNoHARMFailoverProxyProvider: Connecting to ResourceManager at /127.0.0.1:80
32
2021-08-04 19:07:29,850 INFO client.DefaultNoHARMFailoverProxyProvider: Connecting to ResourceManager at /127.0.0.1:80
32
2021-08-04 19:07:30,088 INFO mapreduce.JobResourceUploader: Disabling Erasure Coding for path: /tmp/hadoop-yarn/stagin
g/hadoop/.staging/job_1628078005181_0002
2021-08-04 19:07:30,863 INFO mapred.FileInputFormat: Total input files to process : 1
2021-08-04 19:07:30,961 INFO mapreduce.JobSubmitter: number of splits:2
2021-08-04 19:07:31,113 INFO mapreduce.JobSubmitter: Submitting tokens for job: job_1628078005181_0002
2021-08-04 19:07:31,114 INFO mapreduce.JobSubmitter: Executing with tokens: []
2021-08-04 19:07:31,329 INFO conf.Configuration: resource-types.xml not found
2021-08-04 19:07:31,330 INFO resource.ResourceUtils: Unable to find 'resource-types.xml'.
2021-08-04 19:07:31,414 INFO impl.YarnClientImpl: Submitted application application_1628078005181_0002
2021-08-04 19:07:31,469 INFO mapreduce.Job: The url to track the job: http://tuananhpham:8088/proxy/application_162807
8005181_0002/
2021-08-04 19:07:31,471 INFO mapreduce.Job: Running job: job_1628078005181_0002
2021-08-04 19:07:38,599 INFO mapreduce.Job: Job job_1628078005181_0002 running in uber mode : false
2021-08-04 19:07:38,601 INFO mapreduce.Job:  map 0% reduce 0%
2021-08-04 19:07:55,793 INFO mapreduce.Job:  map 100% reduce 0%
2021-08-04 19:08:01,835 INFO mapreduce.Job:  map 100% reduce 100%
2021-08-04 19:08:02,855 INFO mapreduce.Job: Job job_1628078005181_0002 completed successfully
2021-08-04 19:08:02,937 INFO mapreduce.Job: Counters: 54

**Fig. 10.** Implementation of MRM-KMC with $k = 7$.

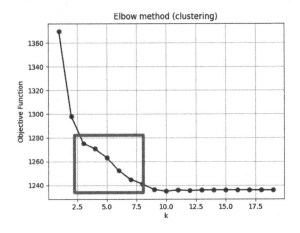

**Fig. 11.** Objective function value with $k = 7$.

**Table 5.** Result of 7CP scenario.

| $k$ clusters | SOG_new | COG_new |
|---|---|---|
| 1 | 0.9424347227602381 | 33.06937842932461 |
| 2 | 1.374841608471513 | 102.5497472633251 |
| 3 | 1.4336294004340628 | 144.46374699151812 |
| 4 | 1.4844708358424163 | 164.190693091593 |
| 5 | 1.1571614708710054 | 190.33812071821583 |
| 6 | 0.6553970429182934 | 249.26870687848287 |
| 7 | 5.574822245091656 | 328.82117546900054 |

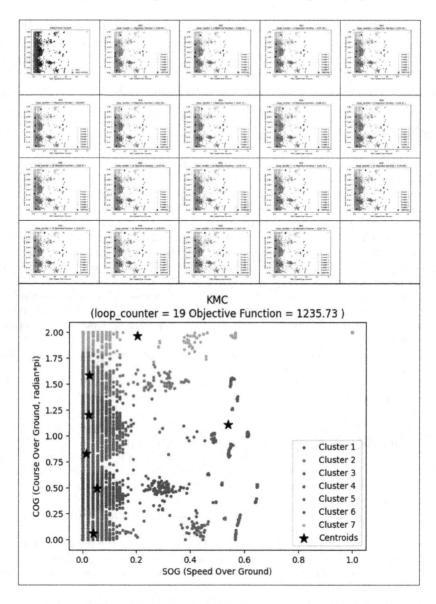

**Fig. 12.** Normalized the KMC results with $k = 7$.

## 5  Conclusion

In this paper, we have performed the analysis of maritime big data by MRM with KMC. This enables us to process the trajectory characteristics (standard deviation of pairs of vectors SOG and COG) for each ship from the AIS data collected and sent to the operating system center to analyse the maritime traffic data in South Vietnam Sea. The proposed method, which evaluates the stability of ship's traffic, is also used to detect the anomaly in the navigation of ships based on the characteristics of the cluster. However, the information collected from AIS data still has many features that we have not fully exploited, and the extracted features need to be enhanced in our future works.

# References

1. Fiorini, M., Capata, A., Bloisi, D.D.: AIS data visualization for maritime spatial planning (MSP). Int. J. e-Navigation Maritime Econ. **5**, 45–60 (2016)
2. Le, V.T., Dang, X.K., Nguyen, D., Pham, T.D.A.: A novel maritime risk assessment model of waterway transportation based on Takagi-Sugeno fuzzy logic: Vietnam case study. IOP Conf. Ser. Earth Environ. Sci. **527**(1), 1–8 (2020)
3. Alba, J.M.M., Dy, G.C., Viriña, N.I.M., Samonte, M.J.C., Cruz, F.R.G.: Localized monitoring mobile application for automatic identification system (AIS) for sea vessels. In: Proceedings of IEEE International Conference on Industrial Engineering and Applications, Bangkok, Thailand, pp. 790–794, April 2020
4. Wakabayashi, N., Jurdana, I.: Maritime communications and remote voyage monitoring. In: Proceedings of International Conference on Broadband Communications for Next Generation Networks and Multimedia Applications, Graz, Austria, pp. 1–8, July 2020
5. Han, J., Kamber, M., Pei, J.: DataMining: Concepts and Techniques, 3rd edn. Morgan Kaufmann, Burlington (2011)
6. Li, Y., Liu, Z., Zheng, Z.: Study on complexity of marine traffic based on traffic intrinsic features and data mining. J. Comput. Methods Sci. Eng. **19**(3), 619–633 (2019)
7. Aji, A., et al.: Hadoop GIS: a high performance spatial data warehousing system over mapreduce. VLDB Endow. **6**(11), 1009–1020 (2013)
8. Mujeeb, S., Sam, R.P., Madhavi, K.: Adaptive hybrid optimization enabled stack autoencoder-based Mapreduce framework for big data classification. In: Proceedings of International Conference on Emerging Trends in Information Technology and Engineering, Vellore, India, pp. 1–5, February 2020
9. Hadoop: Open source implementation of Mapreduce (2021). https://hadoop.apache.org
10. Wang, Z., Xu, A., Zhang, Z., Wang, C., Liu, A., Hu, X.: The parallelization and optimization of k-means algorithm based on spark. In: Proceedings of International Conference on Computer Science & Education, Delft, Netherlands, pp. 457–462, August 2020
11. Lee, S.G., Lee, C.: Developing an improved fingerprint positioning radio map using the K-means clustering algorithm. In: Proceedings of International Conference on Information Networking, Barcelona, Spain, pp. 761–765, January 2020
12. Ng, Y., Pereira, J.M., Garagic, D., Tarokh, V.: Robust marine buoy placement for ship detection using dropout K-means. In: Proceedings of IEEE International Conference on Acoustics, Speech and Signal Processing, Barcelona, Spain, pp. 3757–3761, May 2020
13. Shen, H., Duan, Z.: Application research of clustering algorithm based on K-means in data mining. In: Proceedings of International Conference on Computer Information and Big Data Applications, Guiyang, China, pp. 66–69, April 2020

14. Cui, X., Zhu, P., Yang, X., Li, K., Ji, C.: Optimized big data K-means clustering using Mapreduce. J. Supercomput. **70**, 1249–1259 (2014)
15. Hartigan, J.A., Wong, M.A.: Algorithm AS 136: a K-means clustering algorithm. J. Roy. Stat. Soc.: Ser. C (Appl. Stat.) **28**(1), 100–108 (1979)
16. Lin, Y., Ma, K., Sun, R., Abraham, A.: Toward a MapReduce-based K-means method for multi-dimensional time serial data clustering. In: Abraham, A., Muhuri, P.K., Muda, A.K., Gandhi, N. (eds.) ISDA 2017. AISC, vol. 736, pp. 816–825. Springer, Cham (2018). https://doi.org/10.1007/978-3-319-76348-4_78
17. Zhao, W., Ma, H., He, Q.: Parallel K-means clustering based on Mapreduce. In: Proceedings of International Conference on Cloud Computing, Beijing, China, pp. 674–679, November 2009
18. Hanyang, Z., Xin, S., Zhenguo, Y.: Vessel sailing patterns analysis from S-AIS data dased on $k$-means clustering algorithm. In: Proceedings of IEEE International Conference on Big Data Analytics, Suzhou, China, pp. 10–13, March 2019
19. IMO: Regulations for carriage of AIS, (I. M. Organization, Producer), AIS transponders (2021). https://www.imo.org

# Histopathological Imaging Classification of Breast Tissue for Cancer Diagnosis Support Using Deep Learning Models

Tat-Bao-Thien Nguyen[1]($\boxtimes$), Minh-Vuong Ngo[2], and Van-Phong Nguyen[3]

[1] Vietnam Aviation Academy, Ho Chi Minh City, Vietnam
thienntb@vaa.edu.vn
[2] Ho Chi Minh City Open University, Ho Chi Minh City, Vietnam
vuong.nm@ou.edu.vn
[3] University of Information Technology, VNU-HCM, Ho Chi Minh City, Vietnam
phongnv.13@grad.uit.edu.vn

**Abstract.** According to some medical imaging techniques, breast histopathology images called Hematoxylin and Eosin are considered as the gold standard for cancer diagnoses. Based on the idea of dividing the pathologic image (WSI) into multiple patches, we used the window [512, 512] sliding from left to right and sliding from top to bottom, each sliding step overlapping by 50% to augmented data on a dataset of 400 images which were gathered from the ICIAR 2018 Grand Challenge. Then use the EficientNet model to classify and identify the histopathological images of breast cancer into 4 types: Normal, Benign, Carcinoma, Invasive Carcinoma. The EffficientNet model is a recently developed model that uniformly scales the width, depth, and resolution of the network with a set of fixed scaling factors that are well suited for training images with high resolution. And the results of this model give a rather competitive classification efficiency, achieving 98% accuracy on the training set and 93% on the evaluation set.

**Keywords:** Machine learning · Multi-layer perceptron · Convolutional Neutral Network (CNN) · Biomedical image classification · EfficientNet

## 1 Introduction

Cancer is still one of the most important problems all over the world. According to Globocan cancer statistics in 2020, the situation which people are diagnosed and died of cancer tends to increase around the world. In Vietnam, it is estimated that there are 182,563 new cases of cancer and 122,690 cancer deaths. The people who were diagnosed cancer come with a rate of 159 per 100,000 ones and the cancer mortality is 106 per 100,000 people [1].

Up to now, not only domestic researches but international ones have also frequently based on breast cancer imaging techniques to classify breast cancer which generally focuses on feature engineering before the classifier detects different kinds of breast

© ICST Institute for Computer Sciences, Social Informatics and Telecommunications Engineering 2022
Published by Springer Nature Switzerland AG 2022. All Rights Reserved
N.-S. Vo et al. (Eds.): INISCOM 2022, LNICST 444, pp. 152–164, 2022.
https://doi.org/10.1007/978-3-031-08878-0_11

cancer from the extracted characteristics. These features may be created manually or by the feature descriptor such as Scale Invariant Feature Transform (SIFT) [2], Generative Matrix Computation Library (GMCL) [3], Histogram of Oriented Gradients (HOG) [4], etc. For instance, Zhang and others utilized the manual feature engineering and Principal Component Analysis (PCA) to determine whether the tumor is benign or malignant [5]. Spanhol and others took advantage of machine learning methods based on the means of different feature descriptors for cancer classification [6]. Besides, Wang and others not only made use of 138 characteristic descriptors by text but they also used the Support Vector Machine to detect whether the tumor is benign or malignant [7]. Although these methods based on feature engineering gain proper accuracy for cancer classification, this process requires the wide data preprocessing, Region of Interest and hand-operated extraction which depend upon human and calculation. Furthermore, either features or the manual feature engineering is taken for a low-level feature one which may not analyze all the knowledge for concealed imaging issues such as morphology, tissue structures and other deep-tissue characteristics.

Some of the Convolutional Neutral Networks (CNN) have been demonstrated as the exceeding performance against the computer vision tasks of human. Many CNNs working paradigm are carried out for classification of biomedical images. These networks comprise AlexNet [8], ResNet [9], Inception [10], Inception-V4 and Inception-ResNet [11]. Jaffar suggested utilizing the CNN for the mammogram image classification which attained extraordinary achievement. Qiu and others [12] have operated CNN for identifying the short-term risk of breast cancer which gains the average accuracy of cancer prediction outcome as 71.40%. Rubin and Ertosun [13] have used CNN for the volume visualization observation and breast cancer classification which is up to 85% of accurate outcome. Qui and others [14] have used CNN to classify whether the tumor is benign or malignant in mammogram. Likewise, Jiao and others [15] have attained the high accurate outcome which is up to 96.7% in the same task. Sahiner and others [16] have applied CNN classifier utilizing spatial domain and texture image for mammogram classification which turned out to display 0.87 of AUC. Jadoon and others have classified 3 layers of mammogram including normal, benign and malignant which was based on the described characteristics according to CNN [17].

ConvNet models' scaling are carried out widely to get a better accuracy. For instance, ResNet may be developed from the previous versions, ResNet-18 to ResNet-200, thanks to adding more layers; recently, GPipe has attained the top 1 accuracy on ImageNet by enlarging scaling the base model 4 times up to 84.3%. However, the model scaling process for ConvNet has never been comprehensively perceived and currently there are many ways to carry out. The most popular procedure is to expand the scale of ConvNet through deep dimension or wide dimension (Zagoruyko & Komodakis, 2016). Another procedure which is less popular than the preceding one but it is becoming more and more frequent in usage is image resolution scaling [19]. Heretofore, generally, one of the three dimensions (resolution, depth, and width) was scaled. Although it is possible to scale more than one dimension arbitrarily, the arbitrary scaling is in need of an uninteresting manual scaling. Consistently, manual scaling generates sub-optimal accuracy and efficiency [18].

EfficientNets is significantly better than other ConvNets. Especially, EfficientNet-B7 has been attained the top accuracy as 84.3% which has been the most advanced model. In addition, EfficientNet-B7 is 8.4 times smaller and 6.4 times faster than GPipe. Besides, EfficientNet-B1 is 7.6 times smaller and 5.7 times faster than ResNet-152 [19].

Accordingly, we are going to carry out the research: "Histopathological Imaging Classification of Breast Tissue for Cancer Diagnosis Support" based on EfficientNet model. By using the overlapping patch method through the steps, we have effectively enhanced the image while minimizing the loss of structural and morphological features of the histopathological image. Helps EfficientNet model to be more effective because there is a combination of two factors: the model is suitable for high resolution images and trained with large data sets.

The remaining sections of our study are given as follows. In Sect. 2, the EfficientNet model was presented. Section 3 describes the dataset and the techniques that we used to pre-processing image. Section 4 the process of breast tissue imaging classification and building the software tool for cancer diagnosis support and Sect. 5 highlights the conclusion. Finally, Sect. 6 Acknowledgement.

## 2   EfficientNet Model

### 2.1   Model Scaling of EfficientNet

EfficientNet model, as shown in Fig. 1, has been designed on the scaling principle method of ConvNets which is possible to gain better accuracy and efficiency. Experimental study demonstrates that the most important thing is to balance all the three dimensions: width, depth and resolution. Surprisingly, the balance scaling is attained by scaling each of the three dimensions at a constant scale. Based on the observation, EfficientNet model suggests a dual scaling method which is easily manageable but efficient. Unlike other arbitrarily conventional scaling methods, the technique scales the consistent ratio among width, depth and resolution of the network with a set of permanent scaling factors. As an example, if we expect to utilize $2^N$ times as large as the computational supplies, we can easily rise the depth by $\alpha^N$ times, the width by $\beta^N$ times and the resolution by $\gamma^N$ times in which "$\alpha, \beta, \gamma$" are the invariable coefficients specified by a small matrix on the initial small configuration.

### 2.2   EfficientNet Architecture

The base model of EfficientNet can be described in general in Fig. 2. The processing unit of neural networks called a neuron or a node that carries out the effortless task. The node obtains the preceding input signals or an external source, then utilizes them for calculating the output signals which are propagated to the other units.

Each model contains 7 blocks, which also have a particular quantity of sub-blocks. This quantity is extended in accordance with the model versions from EfficientNet-B0 to EfficientNet-B7. The total layers of EfficientNet-B0 are 237 while EfficientNet-B7 are 813 layers. These layers are made up of the 5 modules as shown in Fig. 3.

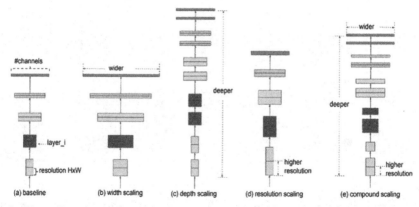

**Fig. 1.** The scaling of networks. (a) is a baseline configuration; (b)-(d) present the are conventional scales in which each model only increases one dimension according to width, depth, and resolution respectively. (e) is our proposed scaling which has uniformly scaling for all three dimensions with a fixed ratio.

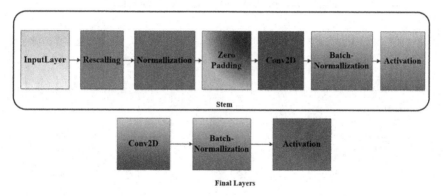

**Fig. 2.** The base model of EfficientNet.

Module 1 is made use for starting points for the sub-blocks, while module 2 is made use for starting points for the first sub-blocks of all 7 main blocks except the first one. Module 3 is utilized for connecting the blocks, while module 4 is utilized for compounding the blocks. Module 5 is utilized for compounding the sub-blocks. These modules are compounded for forming the sub-blocks which would be utilized for blocks in a particular way. The sub-blocks are presented in Fig. 4.

In the first main block, the first sub-block only utilizes Sub-block 1. Sub-block 2 plays a role as the first sub-block for other main blocks. Sub-block 3 is employed for any sub-blocks except the first block in all main blocks. Increasing and compounding sub-blocks could create the EfficientNet models from B0 to B7.

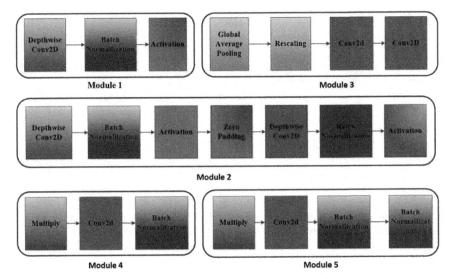

**Fig. 3.** Five modules of EfficientNet model [18].

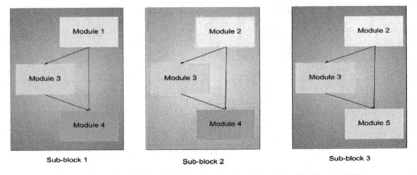

**Fig. 4.** The modules compounded for forming the sub-blocks [18].

## 3   Dataset and Image Pre-processing

### 3.1   Distinctive Features of Diseased Tissue Images

Breast cancer is a heterogeneous disease. This disease comprises many existence with distinct features of biology, histology and clinic. In order to comprehensively analyze malignancy in breast cancer tissues, biopsy techniques are often employed. The biopsy process (see Fig. 5) involves collecting tissue samples, attaching them to microscope slides, then staining these slides to clearly visualize the cytoplasm and nucleus. Next, the conduct microscopic analysis of these slides was taken by pathologists to make a final diagnosis of breast cancer [20].

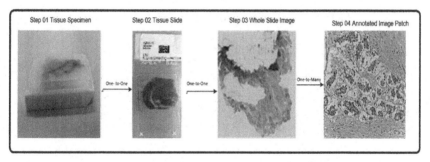

**Fig. 5.** The biopsy procedure for collecting tissue samples.

The breast tissue image is characterized by containing a lot of valuable information which is invisible in the image such as morphological information, structure information of tissues, and other characteristics of deep tissues. Specifically Kowal et al. extracted 42 morphological, topological and structural features from segmented nuclei, similarly, Filipczuk et al. extracted 25 shape and structure-based features from nuclei [20].

### 3.2  Dataset

The dataset of the research contains 400 images from ICIAR 2018. These images are composed of Hematoxylin and eosin (H&E) stained breast histology microscopy and its whole-slide images. These microscopic images are marked into 4 categories as depicted in Fig. 6. They are normal, benign, in situ or invasive carcinoma according to the predominant cancer in each image. This dataset contains a total of 400 microscopy images, which is distributed as given in Table 1.

**Table 1.** The features of our used dataset.

| Images with labels | Quantity | Color type | Staining |
|---|---|---|---|
| Normal (N) | 100 | RGB | H & E |
| Benign (B) | 100 | RGB | H & E |
| In Situ Carcinoma (IS) | 100 | RGB | H & E |
| Invasive Carcinoma (IV) | 100 | RGB | H & E |

We choose 70% of images for training and 20% for evaluation and the remaining 10% for test. Thus, there are 280 images for the training set, 80 images for the evaluation set and 40 images for the test set described in Table 2.

**Table 2.** Dataset division for training, validation, and test.

|  | Number of images | Data percentage |
|---|---|---|
| Training | 280 | 70% |
| Validation | 80 | 20% |
| Test | 40 | 10% |
| Total | 400 | 100% |

### 3.3  Data Augmentation

In during training process, the image data augmentation technique is used to expand a data set by generating modified images. The tensor image data was generated by Pytorch deep learning library with real-time data augmentation. The network models, which are trained with the type of data augmentation, will see new mutations of the data at each and every epochal traversal. With each input image in the batch, the model will generate a series of images through a series of translations, random rotations, etc. We set the width and height change range being 0.2 and the random rotation between $[-40, 40]$ degrees. In the rotation operation, some pixels may be moved out of the image frame and replaced by some empty pixels, then the empty pixel will be filled through a 'reflection mode'. Finally, the batch is randomly transformed and then returned to the calling function. Table 3 presents these parameters combined with their values.

**Table 3.** Parameters of data augmentation.

| Parameters | Values |
|---|---|
| Zoom range | 0.2 |
| Rotation range | 40 |
| Width shift range | 0.2 |
| Height shift range | 0.2 |
| Horizontal flip | True |
| Vertical flip | True |
| Fill mode | Reflect |

Especially based on the method of extracting patches has proven effective in previous studies. In this paper, a sliding window of size $[512 \times 512]$ is applied to slide top to bottom and from left to right with 50% overlap for each step. Thus, from the original image of size $[2048 \times 1536]$, 35 patches were created. Such patch extraction not only collects many features of the original image, but also preserves the structure of the cells.

This data enhancement is applied to insert the image quantity for training which helps pass overfitting and describe features effectively. Especially, the patch extraction method has separated the image to be classified into 35 patches, then the image classification is based on the maximum number of types in those 35 patches.

Besides, the used dataset also contains 10 images of breast tissue collected at Cai Lay Regional General Hospital for model trial after the training. Some of these images are shown in Fig. 7.

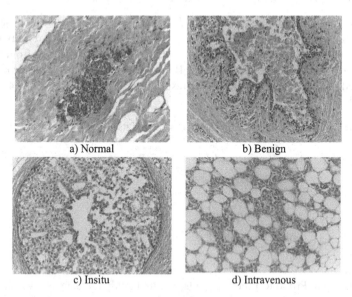

a) Normal          b) Benign

c) Insitu          d) Intravenous

**Fig. 6.** Four categories of the breast histology microscopy images.

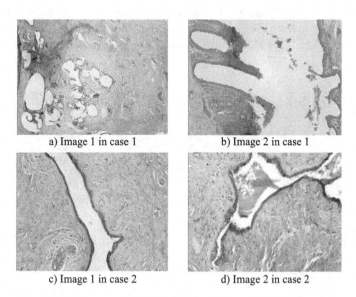

a) Image 1 in case 1          b) Image 2 in case 1

c) Image 1 in case 2          d) Image 2 in case 2

**Fig. 7.** The images collected at Cai Lay Regional General Hospital.

## 4   The Process of Breast Tissue Imaging Classification and Building the Software Tool for Cancer Diagnosis Support

### 4.1   The Process of Breast Tissue Imaging Classification

The imaging classification process is developed by using EfficientNet for the classification. Because the small data set is only suitable for small models, we only run from model B0 to model B3.Through the experimental process of EfficientNet from B0 to B3, the results have been shown that Efficient B3 is at the peak of the accuracy rate which has attained 98% on training dataset. The results are presented in the Table 4.

**Table 4.** EfficentNet models and its precision.

| Deep learning models | Precision |
|---|---|
| EfficientNet B0 | 86% |
| EfficientNet B1 | 90% |
| EfficientNet B2 | 91% |
| EfficientNet B3 | 98% |

We use Colab Pro to test these models. We first study the data set overview and its corresponding labels as shown in Fig. 8. Then, we augment the data which is essential for the learning process. The enhancement method is detailed below in Sect. 4.1. Because learning requires a lot of time and limited hardware resources, we divide the learning into several stages to learn. The code format can be referred as `exp_lr_scheduler = lr_scheduler.StepLR (optimizer_ft, step_size = 30, gamma= 0.5)`.

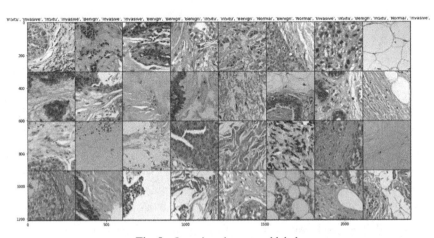

**Fig. 8.** Overview dataset and label.

## 4.2 Evaluation Metrics

The confusion matrix, also called the error matrix or contingency table, is used to evaluate the performance of our proposed model. The matrix includes four categories:

- True Positive (TP): present the number of carcinoma images which were correctly classified as carcinoma.
- False Positive (FP): present the number of non-carcinoma images which were mistakenly classified as carcinoma.
- False Negative (FN): present the number of carcinoma images which were mistakenly classified as non-carcinoma.
- True Negative (TN): present the number of non-carcinoma images which were correctly classified as non-carcinoma images.

We use precision, recall and F1-score to evaluate the classification performance of the proposed model. These measures are based on four categories of the confusion matrix in above. In that:

- Precision (P): It shows the exactness of a model which presents the ratio between the accurately classified carcinoma images to the total of predicted carcinoma images, $P = TP/TP + FP$.
- Recall (R): It shows the completeness of a model which presents the ratio between the accurately classified carcinoma images to all carcinoma images of the dataset, $R = TP/TP + FN$.
- F1-score (F1): It shows the harmonic average of precision and recall, $F1 = 2 * P * R/P + R$.

Table 5 and Fig. 9 present measures and normalized confusion matrix of our proposed model. We use the python scikit-learn module to support in calculating these measures.

**Table 5.** Classification performance of the proposed model.

|          | Precision | Recall | F1-score |
|----------|-----------|--------|----------|
| Normal   | 0.83      | 1      | 0.91     |
| Benign   | 1.00      | 0.80   | 0.89     |
| InSitu   | 0.91      | 1      | 0.95     |
| InVasive | 1.00      | 0.90   | 0.95     |

## 4.3 Building the Application for Cancer Diagnosis Support

The application utilizing framework Django and EfficientNet model was trained above for histopathological imaging classification of breast tissue to support the cancer diagnosis. The application has the input and output data, and its interfaces. The input data is a

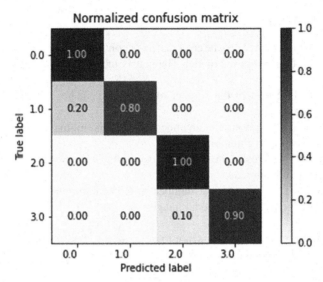

**Fig. 9.** Confusion matrix results of model B3 and measures.

histopathological image of breast tissue. The output data is the image which is included in one of the four layers: Normal (N), Benign (B), In Situ (IS), Intravenous (IV). The steps to execute web apps are as follows:

- Step 1: Enter the patient's full name, year of birth and select a photo.
- Step 2: Click View diagnostics button.

The training process was carried out on the Colab environment. After the process, we have obtained an optimal EfficientNet model in which the capability has been 4 - layer classification with the accuracy of 98%.

Creating a diagnostic support application is very effective for lower-level hospitals. It helps to answer fast results to increase patient satisfaction, in addition, it also helps doctors who are learning to practice their knowledge on the trained dataset.

## 5   Conclusion

The result shows that transfer learning backs us to generate the deep architecture of the networks with a restricted quantity of images in the training process but we have still gained the surprising result.

In addition, the enhancement of the data and the division of the original image into many small pieces stacked by 50% should also be investigated to enrich data for the training process, backing us to get over the overfitting and generating the better efficiency of the characteristics.

In the future, we will continue to enhance the application for breast cancer diagnosis support which could attain the far more accurate results. In addition, we will continue to execute all the rest of the models once more data has been collected and compare our model with other machine learning models. We will also build more features for the application to receive feedback from users and doctors to improve the model.

**Acknowledgement.** We thank University of Information Technology, Vietnam Aviation Academy and Ho Chi Minh City Open University for offering us a unique opportunity to accomplish the research paper.

# References

1. Ministry of health portal. https://moh.gov.vn/hoat-dong-cua-dia-phuong/-/asset_publisher/gHbla8vOQDuS/content/tinh-hinh-ung-thu-tai-viet-nam. Accessed 21 Nov 2021
2. Lowe, D.G.: Object recognition from local scale-invariant features. In: Proceedings of the Seventh IEEE International Conference on Computer Vision (1999)
3. Haralick, R.M., Shanmugam, K. Dinstein, I.: Textural features for image classification. IEEE Trans. Syst. Man Cybern. SMC-**3**(6), 610–621 (1973)
4. Dalal, N., Triggs, B.: Histograms of oriented gradients for human detection. In: 2005 IEEE Computer Society Conference on Computer Vision and Pattern Recognition (CVPR 2005) (2005)
5. Zhang, Y., et al.: One-class kernel subspace ensemble for medical image classification. EURASIP J. Adv. Signal Process. **2014**(1), 17 (2014)
6. Spanhol, F.A., et al.: A dataset for breast cancer histopathological image classification. IEEE Trans. Biomed. Eng. **63**(7), 1455–1462 (2016)
7. Wang, P., et al.: Automatic cell nuclei segmentation and classification of breast cancer histopathology images. Signal Process. **122**, 1–13 (2016)
8. Krizhevsky, A., Sutskever, I., Hinton, G.E.: ImageNet classification with deep convolutional neural networks. Adv. Neural Inf. Process. Syst. **25**, 1097–1105 (2012)
9. He, K., et al.: Deep residual learning for image recognition. In: Proceedings of the IEEE Conference on Computer Vision and Pattern Recognition (2016)
10. Szegedy, C., et al.: Rethinking the inception architecture for computer vision. In: Proceedings of the IEEE Conference on Computer Vision and Pattern Recognition (2016)
11. Szegedy, C., et al.: Inception-v4, inception-resnet and the impact of residual connections on learning. In: Thirty-First AAAI Conference on Artificial Intelligence (2017)
12. Qiu, Y., et al.: An initial investigation on developing a new method to predict short-term breast cancer risk based on deep learning technology. In: Medical Imaging 2016: Computer-Aided Diagnosis. 2016, International Society for Optics and Photonics (2016)
13. Ertosun, M.G., Rubin, D.L.: Probabilistic visual search for masses within mammography images using deep learning. In: 2015 IEEE International Conference on Bioinformatics and Biomedicine (BIBM). IEEE (2015)
14. Qiu, Y., et al.: Computer-aided classification of mammographic masses using the deep learning technology: a preliminary study. In: Medical Imaging 2016: Computer-Aided Diagnosis, International Society for Optics and Photonics (2016)
15. Jiao, Z., et al.: A deep feature based framework for breast masses classification. Neurocomputing **197**, 221–231 (2016)
16. Sahiner, B., et al.: Classification of mass and normal breast tissue: a convolution neural network classifier with spatial domain and texture images. IEEE Trans Med. Imaging **15**(5), 598–610 (1996)
17. Jadoon, M.M., et al.: Three-class mammogram classification based on descriptive CNN features. 2017 (2017)

18. Tan, M., Le, Q.: EfficientNet: rethinking model scaling for convolutional neural networks. In: International Conference on Machine Learning. PMLR (2019)
19. Complete Architectural Details of all EfficientNet Models. https://towardsdatascience.com/complete-architectural-details-of-all-efficientnet-models-5fd5b736142
20. Hameed, Z., et al.: Breast cancer histopathology image classification using an ensemble of deep learning models. Sensors **20**(16), 4373 (2020)

# Industrial Networks and Intelligent Systems

# Navigation for Two-Wheeled Differential Mobile Robot in the Special Environment

Tran Thuan Hoang[1,2], Nguyen Ngo Anh Quan[1], Vo Chi Thanh[1],
and Tran Le Thang Dong[1,2(✉)]

[1] Center of Electrical Engineering, Duy Tan University, Danang 550000, Vietnam
tranthangdong@duytan.edu.vn
[2] Faculty of Electrical-Electronic Engineering, Duy Tan University, Danang 550000, Vietnam

**Abstract.** In this paper, a new navigation method for the two-wheeled differential mobile robot operating in a specific environment is proposed. The orientation angle and position of the mobile robot are estimated by the data collected from the inertial sensors. The encoder sensor at the motor axis is calculated by the Kalman filter algorithm. Further, angular and positional errors are corrected as the robot passes through magnetic reference points installed under the floor on virtual paths. Next, the control function Lyapunov and the program to avoid obstacles by the VFH+ method in local space were also developed to help the robot reach the destination safely. Simulation results and some analysis clarify the correctness of our proposed algorithm. All of the results show promise and applicable.

**Keywords:** Mobile robot · Kalman filter · Robot tracking control · Lyapunov function · VFH+

## 1 Introduction

Nowadays, the world is starting to enter the Industrial Revolution 4.0, mobile robots are increasingly widely used in life. With the function of automatic transportation, flexibility, and ability to replace people to perform jobs more efficiently and effectively, it is widely applied in the manufacturing and warehousing industry. In particular, mobile robots are very important in hazardous environments or isolated areas [1–3].

Ignoring the operation of the parts attached to the robot base, the navigation problem for the safe movement of the base from a starting point to a destination, or called "*navigation for mobile robots*", is considered as major in current robotics research. Navigation is not so different from human behavior. To deal with this problem, the robot needs positioning, mapping if necessary, path planning, and exporting the path control as well as avoiding obstacles on the track.

With today's technology, many navigation solutions have been researched and developed, which can divide the path system for robots into two types: *fixed path* and *free path*.

© ICST Institute for Computer Sciences, Social Informatics and Telecommunications Engineering 2022
Published by Springer Nature Switzerland AG 2022. All Rights Reserved
N.-S. Vo et al. (Eds.): INISCOM 2022, LNICST 444, pp. 167–183, 2022.
https://doi.org/10.1007/978-3-031-08878-0_12

The fixed paths are defined as physical paths including magnetic tapes, wires, paint lines, etc. They are all sticked on the ground where the mobile robot stops by or goes through. This system has the following benefits: low cost, ease of deployment, and high reliability. However, this technology has the disadvantage of being less flexible and adaptable to the environment, particularly in outdoor locations or where there is a lot of dirt, which raises the path's maintenance costs.

The free path is considered as a virtual path that is generated and decided using data from current navigation sensing devices on a computer including ultrasonic sensor, 3D camera, laser sensors., LiDAR sensor, inertial sensor, etc. The advantages of this approach include a flexible and highly efficient operating system. These technologies, on the other hand, have the disadvantage of being expensive and difficult to increase accuracy [4–8].

Due to their great accuracy and versatility, solutions based on laser sensors, LiDAR sensors, or cameras have recently become popular. However, in some settings, such as those that are outside or dusty, the system's accuracy will quickly deteriorate. At current time, the inertial sensor is a viable option because it is adaptable to a wide range of settings. However, because of the nature of the inertial sensor, errors accumulate during operation, lowering the system's accuracy over time [9–12].

In oder to overcome the problems, in this paper, we propose a navigation solution for a two-wheeled differential mobile robot. In the method, the inertial sensor and encoder data are used to estimate the robot's direction angle and location, which is then calculated using the Kalman filter algorithm. Magnetic sensors are added on top of this to remedy the accumulated inaccuracies. When the robot travels over magnetic reference points installed under the floor on virtual routes (known as *trajectories of the robot*), its angular and positional faults are corrected. The content is presented in Sect. 2 of the paper. Based on the established global trajectory with path-continuous control using the Lyapunov function [13–16]. Some theories related to these tests will be presented in Sect. 3. For the task of avoiding close obstacles in the local area, we applied the VFH+ method [26, 27] with a system of ultrasonic sensors, developed a control program that allows avoiding obstacles in the distance area from 0.3 m to 4 m. Obstacle avoidance results during navigation are also presented in Sect. 3 of the paper. Section 4 presents experimental measurement results showing the effectiveness of data aggregation from sensors for autonomous robot navigation, allowing to open up application possibilities with intelligent autonomous vehicles in real life.

## 2   Robot Positioning Using Sensors and Virtual Paths

### 2.1   Kinematic Model of Mobile Robot

In this work, the mobile robot is a two-wheeled moving vehicle with differential drive. Each wheel is connected to an independently controlled electric motor, and the speed of these two motors is used to control the vehicle's movement and orientation.

The dynamic analysis will be influenced by a number of parameters, including vehicle load, control circuitry, engine, and body construction, among others. A somewhat simple robot motion model is described in this paper, omitting certain relatively minor aspects. The following Fig. 1 depicts the robot's structure.

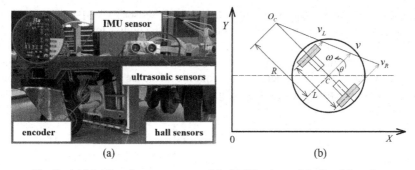

**Fig. 1.** (a) Mobile robot structure model; (b) Kinetic model of mobile robot

The OXY coordinate system associated with the active area plane of the mobile robot is chosen where the origin O is the initiating point of the mobile robot. The gravity center of the robot C is the point among the two-wheeled differential drive. The robot AGV will travel through an arc of the center $O_c$ and the radius $R$. The rotation angle of the center OC will coincide with the center C of the robot when $v_r = v_l$.

Defining $v$, $\omega$ are the translational speed and angular velocity of the robot. Based on the kinetic model of the robot in Fig. 1, we achieve

$$v = \frac{v_r + v_l}{2}. \tag{1}$$

Defining $x$, $y$ are the coordinates of the robot that create the angle between the vertical axis of the robot and the axis OX.

The robot's state is illustrated by the vector $X = \begin{bmatrix} x\ y\ \theta \end{bmatrix}^T$. At the different time of $k$ and time $k-1$, we got the robot's states which are presented as $X_k = \begin{bmatrix} x_k\ y_k\ \theta_k \end{bmatrix}^T$ and $X_{k-1} = \begin{bmatrix} x_{k-1}\ y_{k-1}\ \theta_{k-1} \end{bmatrix}^T$. Where, $X_k$ is determined in terms of $X_{k-1}$ by the following calculation:

$$X_k = \begin{bmatrix} x_k \\ y_k \\ \theta_k \end{bmatrix} = \begin{bmatrix} x_{k-1} \\ y_{k-1} \\ \theta_{k-1} \end{bmatrix} + \begin{bmatrix} cos\theta_{k-1} & 0 \\ sin\theta_{k-1} & 0 \\ 0 & 1 \end{bmatrix} \begin{bmatrix} v_{k-1}T \\ \omega_{k-1}T \end{bmatrix}, \tag{2}$$

where, $T$ is the sampling time from the measuring signal.

### 2.2 Position and Orientation of Mobile Robot Based on Reference Points

Tracking the trajectory of the robot is needed to be able to control it. In our paper, the model uses an inertial sensor (IMU) adn encoders to define either the direction angle or the coordinates of the robot. As a result, the trajectory is determined using the initial input values paired with sensor feedback values, and the cumulative inaccuracy will steadily increase as the robot moves.

When a result, a magnetic sensor is added to detect the waypoints with known coordinates so that the trajectory can be recalibrated as the Robot passes through them. The magnetic sensor is a bar made up of 16 hall sensors arranged in a row and separated by a distance of $l = 10$ mm. As a result, the magnetic sensor's width is 160 mm. At the midway of the sensor bar, it will be perpendicular to the body's longitudinal axis.

The hall sensors traveling above the reference point will be engaged when the robot passes through the magnetic reference points on the floor. The deviation of the longitudinal axis of the body can be determined from the reference point using the position of the activated hall sensors, as shown in Fig. 2.

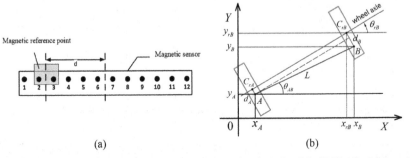

(a)     (b)

**Fig. 2.** (a) The magnetic reference point and the magnetic sensor model; (b) The Position and the orientation of Robot at the reference point calculation.

We assume both reference points, $A(x_A, y_A)$ and $B(x_B, y_B)$ having eithe the distance $L$ or known coordinates. The angle of segment AB considering axis OX is $\theta_{AB}$. The robot will travel through A to B. At the moment, the robot travels through point A, the deviation $d_A$ is detected by the magnetic sensor. When the robot moves to point B, the sensor can determine the deviation $d_B$. Based on Fig. 2(b), it is obvious to be able to calculate both the actual position and the angle of the robot at the point B.

Define $\delta$ as the angle of deviation of the line segment AB and the longitudinal axis of the body, we achieve:

$$\delta = \arcsin[(d_A - d_B)/L] \tag{3}$$

Hence, the actual direction angle of the robot AGV at the point B can be calculated as

$$\theta_{rB} = \theta_{rB} + \delta. \tag{4}$$

Based on that, the coordinates of the actual position of the AGV at point B is defined as

$$\begin{cases} x_{rB} = x_B + d_B \sin(\theta_{rB}) \\ y_{rB} = y_B + d_B \sin(\theta_{rB}) \end{cases} \tag{5}$$

Hence, the the robot AGV's state at point B can be adjusted based on the actual state as follows

$$X_{rB} = \begin{bmatrix} x_{rB} \\ y_{rB} \\ \theta_{rB} \end{bmatrix} = \begin{bmatrix} x_{rB} = x_B + d_B\sin(\theta_{rB}) \\ y_{rB} = y_B + d_B\sin(\theta_{rB}) \\ \theta_{AB} + \arcsin[(d_A - d_B)/L] \end{bmatrix} \tag{6}$$

## 2.3 Application Filter for Mobile Robot

Measured disturbances and system noise frequently alter the robot's signal during operation. The Kalman filter, which is widely used in the field of signal processing and control, is utilized in the article to identify the exact value of the robot's state [4–8].

Based on Eq. (2), the state model system is built and measured following

$$X_k = AX_{k-1} + Bu_{k-1} + w_{k-1}, \\ Z_{k-1} = HX_{k-1} + v_{k-1} \tag{7}$$

where, $X_k$ is defined as the state of the robot at the time $k$, and $Z_{k-1}$ is the measuring state at the time $k - 1$. The system noise and measurement noise are defined as $w$ and $v$. The state transition matrix and the input control matrix are defined as $A$ and $B$, respectively. $H$ denotes the observation transfer matrix. The matrices are calculated in details as

$$A = \begin{bmatrix} 1 & 0 & 0 \\ 0 & 1 & 0 \\ 0 & 0 & 1 \end{bmatrix}, B = \begin{bmatrix} \cos\theta_{k-1} & 0 \\ \sin\theta_{k-1} & 0 \\ 0 & 1 \end{bmatrix}, u_{k-1} = \begin{bmatrix} v_{k-1}T \\ \omega_{k-1}T \end{bmatrix}, H = \begin{bmatrix} 1 & 0 & 0 \\ 0 & 1 & 0 \\ 0 & 0 & 1 \end{bmatrix}. \tag{8}$$

The Kalman filter includes two stages, prediction and correction, that are provided as follows.

Stage 1: Based on the present state and the value of the incoming control signal, predicts the next state:

$$\hat{X}_k^- = A\hat{X}_{k-1}^- + Bu_{k-1} \\ P_k^- = AP_{k-1}A^T + Q \tag{9}$$

Stage 2: Recalibrate the estimated value based on the projected value and the signal value measured:

$$K_k = P_k^- H^T \left( HP_k^- H^T + R \right)^1 \\ \hat{X}_k = \hat{X}_k^- + K_k \left( Z_k - H\hat{X}_k^- \right), \\ P_k = (I_n - K_k H)P_k^- \tag{10}$$

where $Q$ and $R$ denote the system noise correlation matrices. The measurement noise is defined by using the noise variance.

In our work with the robot control system, the measurement values as $Z_k$ are the sum of collected values from the Encoder, IMU, and the time reference while the robot is operating.

# 3 Tracking the Trajectory and Obstacle Avoidance

## 3.1 Trajectory Tracking

The main goal is to control the mobile robot to track a certain trajectory. A different trajectory with a path with time constraints added to it, which makes the control target not only minimize the distance between the robot and the path, but also to ensure the travel time. We define the actual robot state as: $X = \begin{bmatrix} x\ y\ \theta \end{bmatrix}^T$ and according to the pattern trajectory is: $X_r = \begin{bmatrix} x_r\ y_r\ \theta_r \end{bmatrix}^T$.

When the robot moves, the error will appear (Fig. 3):

$$
e = \begin{bmatrix} e_1 \\ e_2 \\ e_3 \end{bmatrix} = \begin{bmatrix} \cos\theta & \sin\theta & 0 \\ -\sin\theta & \cos\theta & 0 \\ 0 & 0 & 1 \end{bmatrix} \begin{bmatrix} x_r - x \\ y_r - y \\ \theta_r - \theta \end{bmatrix} \tag{11}
$$

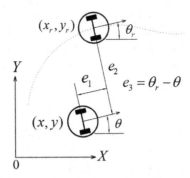

**Fig. 3.** The positional error between the robot's actual coordinates and the reference coordinates in the trajectory.

From the kinetic and derivative model (11), we get the error model as follows:

$$
\begin{bmatrix} \dot{e}_1 \\ \dot{e}_2 \\ \dot{e}_3 \end{bmatrix} = \begin{bmatrix} \cos e_3 & 0 \\ \sin e_3 & 0 \\ 0 & 1 \end{bmatrix} \begin{bmatrix} v_r \\ \omega_r \end{bmatrix} + \begin{bmatrix} -1 & e_2 \\ 0 & -e_1 \\ 0 & -1 \end{bmatrix} \begin{bmatrix} v \\ \omega \end{bmatrix}, \tag{12}
$$

where $v_r$, $\omega_r$ define the linear and angular velocities of the robot according to the trajectory.

The robot controller is built following

$$
\begin{bmatrix} v \\ \omega \end{bmatrix} = \begin{bmatrix} v_r \cos e_3 \\ \omega_r \end{bmatrix} + \begin{bmatrix} v_{fb} \\ \omega_{fb} \end{bmatrix}, \tag{13}
$$

where $v_{fb}$, $\omega_{fb}$ is the feedback signal of the controller.

Substituting (13) into the error model (12), becomes:

$$
\begin{aligned}
\dot{e}_1 &= \omega_r e_2 - v_{fb} + \omega_{fb} e_2 \\
\dot{e}_2 &= -\omega_r e_1 + v_r \sin e_3 - \omega_{fb} e_1 \\
\dot{e}_3 &= -\omega_{fb}
\end{aligned} \tag{14}
$$

The control target is to bring the error of the error model to zero by choosing signals $v_{fb}$ and $\omega_{fb}$ appropriately. Using the Lyapunov stability theorem for stability control design purposes and if asymptotic stabilization is possible. It means that all trajectories finally will be converged to the reference trajectories. The most likely Lyapunov function candidate is calculated as the sum of three square errors:

$$V(e) = (e_1^2 + e_2^2)k_2/2 + (1/2)e_3^2 \tag{15}$$

It is also considered as the weighted sum of the squared error of distance and squared error of direction. The constant $k_2 > 0$ must be added because the units are different. The time derivative of $V$ can be calculated as

$$\dot{V} = k_2 e_1 \dot{e}_1 + k_2 e_2 \dot{e}_2 + e_3 \dot{e}_3. \tag{16}$$

Substitute (14) into (16) to get:

$$\dot{V} = -k_2 e_1 v_{fb} + k_2 v_r e_3 \sin e_3 - e_3 \omega_{fb} \tag{17}$$

The purpose of the Lyapunov-based control design aims to achieve the derivative of the Lyapunov function negative by picking a appropriate control law. The velocity $v_{fb}$ is linearly chosen to have the first term in Eq. (7) negative by squaring the negative term. The angular velocity is chosen to eliminate the second and third terms as well to square the negative term. The control laws include

$$\begin{aligned} v_{fb} &= k_1 e_1 \\ \omega_{fb} &= k_2 v_r (\sin e_3 / e_3) e_2 + k_3 e_3 \end{aligned} \tag{18}$$

Then $\dot{V}$ becomes:

$$\dot{V} = -k_1 k_2 e_x^2 - k_3 e_3^2 \tag{19}$$

It is clear that A is always negative for $k_1 > 0$, $k_2 > 0$, and $k_3 > 0$, satisfying the Lyapunov stability conditions. Then the control law (3) for trajectory tracking will be rewritten as follows:

$$\begin{bmatrix} v \\ \omega \end{bmatrix} = \begin{bmatrix} v_r \cos e_3 + k_1 e_1 \\ \omega_r + k_2 v_r (\sin e_3 / e_3) e_2 + k_3 e_3 \end{bmatrix} \tag{20}$$

## 3.2   Obstacle Avoidance Using VFH+ with Ultrasonic Sensors

Along the way, the robot must be able to detect and avoid unexpected obstacles. In these cases, a proximity sensor system is used. That is 12 ultrasonic distance sensors installed on the robot as shown in Fig. 4, allowing to detect obstacles in front and two sides of the robot.

The VFH+ method uses a histogram grid to map the environment around the robot. This map is continuously updated with distance to obstacle data obtained from the ultrasonic sensors mounted on the robot as shown in Fig. 4. The method will find the

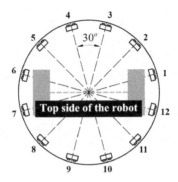

**Fig. 4.** Layout diagram of ultrasonic sensors.

optimal direction of movement when encountering obstacles, and appropriate velocity control for the robot (linear velocity, angular velocity).

### The Histogram Grid

In this step, a two-dimensional Cartesian histogram grid (C) is generated containing the information transmitted from the ultrasonic sensors (the selected C has dimensions of 81 × 81 and a resolution of 0.1 m/cell). Each grid cell $C[i, j]$ contains a value representing the reliability of the existence of an obstacle at the coordinate position $(i, j)$. The grid is filled using distances measured by ultrasonic sensors, each of which updates the value of only one cell at a time (Fig. 5).

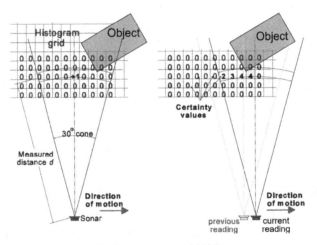

**Fig. 5.** Histogram grid [25].

### The Primary Polar Histogram

In the second step, a window C ∗ has a fixed orientation, whose center is attached to the robot and moves along its motion (the selected C ∗ is 33 × 33). It is called the active window and it overlays the histogram grid C at the robot's current position. The content of each active cell in the map grid is considered as an obstacle vector, its direction $\beta$ being towards the center of the active region (robot center point-RCP)

$$\beta_{i,j} = \tan^{-1}(\frac{y_i - y_o}{x_i - x_0}) \tag{21}$$

The magnitude vector of the active cell $C[i,j]$ is provided by

$$m_{i,j} = c_{i,j}^2(a - bd_{i,j}^2), \tag{22}$$

where both $a$ and $b$ are positive constants; $c_{i,j}$ denotes the certainty value of an active cell $(i, j)$; $d_{i,j}$ is the distance from each cell to the center of the active area (RCP); the magnitude of the obstacle vector at the cell $(i, j)$ is denoted as $m_{i,j}$; $(x_0, y_0)$ is the coordinate of the robot center; $(x_i, y_i)$ is the coordinate of each cell $(i, j)$.

The Primary Polar Histogram $H^p$ is built based on the obstacle vectors. $H^p$ contains an arbitrary angular resolution, denoted as $\alpha$. Hence, $n = 360^o/\alpha$ is an integral number. Specifically, in our work, we choose $\alpha = 5^o$ and $n = 72$ angular sectors. A angular sector $k$ corresponds to a discrete angle $k\alpha$.

For each obstacle cell, the enlargement angle $\gamma_{i,j}$ is defined by:

$$\gamma_{i,j} = \arcsin\frac{r}{d_{i,j}}, \tag{23}$$

where $r$ is the radius of the robot's safe zone (Fig. 6).

For a angular sector $k$, the polar obstacle density is then defined as

$$H_k^p = \sum m_{i,j}h_{i,j}', \tag{24}$$

with

$$h_{i,j}' = \begin{cases} 1 & \text{if } k\alpha \in [\beta_{i,j} - \gamma_{i,j}, \beta_{i,j} + \gamma_{i,j}] \\ 0 & \text{elsewhere} \end{cases} \tag{25}$$

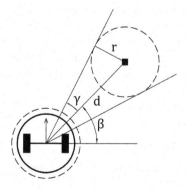

**Fig. 6.** Enlargement angle from robot to the obstacle.

## Binary Polar Histogram

The Binary Polar Histogram $H^b$ shows which directions are free for a robot that can change direction of motion instantly without colliding with obstacles. The following rules are used to update the binary polar histogram.

$$H_{k,i}^b = \begin{cases} 1 & \text{if } H_k^p > \tau_{high} \\ 0 & \text{if } H_k^p < \tau_{low} \\ H_{k,i-1}^b & elsewhere \end{cases} \tag{26}$$

where $\tau_{high}$ and $\tau_{low}$ are high thresholds and low thresholds are chosen to ensure that obstacles too far away from the robot do not affect the robot's movement, even though the obstacle is in front of the moving direction.

## The Masked Polar Histogram

The original VFH technique ignores the robot's dynamics and kinematics. It implicitly presupposes, as shown in Fig. 7(a), that the robot can change its direction of motion at any time. Unless the robot can move in all directions, this assumption is not true for two-wheeled differential robots.

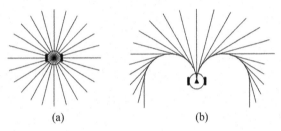

(a)                              (b)

**Fig. 7.** Flexible mobility of the robot: a) omnidirectional, b) limited multidirectional movement [26]

The VFH+ [27] approach uses a simple but more accurate approximation of most mobile robots' trajectory. As shown in Fig. 7(b), the robot's route is based on circular arcs (constant curvature curves) and straight lines.

In the example shown in Fig. 8, because of the robot dynamics, obstacle A blocks all directions to its left. Obstacle B, on the other hand, does not obstruct the directions to its right. The original VFH approach considers the directions to the left of obstacle A to be appropriate motion directions. The original VFH algorithm will instruct the robot to the left and collide with the obstacle A.

The positions of the right and left rotation centers are related to the current position of the robot which are determined by

$$\Delta x_r = R\sin(\theta - \tfrac{\pi}{2}) \quad \Delta x_l = R\cos(\theta + \tfrac{\pi}{2}) \tag{27}$$
$$\Delta y_r = R\cos(\theta - \tfrac{\pi}{2}) \quad \Delta y_l = R\sin(\theta + \tfrac{\pi}{2})$$

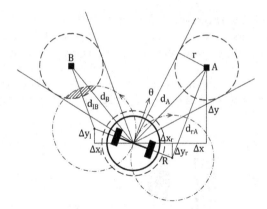

**Fig. 8.** An illustration of blocked directions

Distance from obstacle to robot's right and left rotation centers:

$$d_r = \sqrt{(\Delta x - \Delta x_r)^2 + (\Delta y - \Delta y_r)^2}$$
$$d_l = \sqrt{(\Delta x - \Delta x_l)^2 + (\Delta y - \Delta y_l)^2}.$$

(28)

There is an obstacle blocking the robot's right direction if.

$$d_r < R + r \quad [\text{condition 1}]$$

(29)

Then, an obstacle will block the robot's right direction if

$$d_l < R + r \quad [\text{condition 2}]$$

(30)

The right limit angle $\varphi_r$ and the left $\varphi_l$ are calculated as follows:

- Let: $\varphi_r = \varphi_l = \theta + \pi$. Check the cells in the *active window* with c > threshold:

  – If $\beta$ to the right of $\theta$ and the left of $\varphi_r$, check condition 1. If the condition is satisfied, set $\varphi_r = \beta$.
  – If $\beta$ to the left of $\theta$ and the right of $\varphi_l$, check condition 2. If the condition is satisfied, set $\varphi_l = \beta$.

Based on $\varphi_r$, $\varphi_l$ and binary polar histogram, a masked polar histogram can be built in Eq. (31) and illustrated in Fig. 9.

$$H_k^m = \begin{cases} 0 & \text{if } H_k^b = 0 \text{ and } k\alpha \in \{[\varphi_r, \theta], [\theta, \varphi_l]\} \\ 1 & \text{othewise} \end{cases}$$

(31)

### Selection of the Steering Direction

The VFH+ approach first determines a collection of probable candidate directions by finding all vacancies in the masked polar histogram. These candidate directions are then subjected to a cost function that takes into account more than simply the difference between the candidate and goal directions. The candidate motion $k_n$ with the lowest cost is then selected as the new motion $\varphi_n = \alpha \, k_n$ direction.

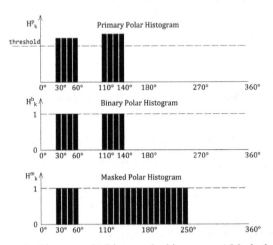

**Fig. 9.** a) Primary polar histogram, b) Binary polar histogram, c) Masked polar histogram.

**Fig. 10.** Selecting the most optimal direction among candidate directions

In the beginning, the right and left borders $k_r$ and $k_r$ of all openings are considered. It is similar to the original VFH method, two kinds of openings are recognized and defined as *wide* and *narrow* ones. If the difference between its two borders is larger than $s_{max}$ time $\alpha$ (in our system $s_{max} = 16$ sectors), then an opening is considered wide. Otherwise, it is considered narrow, as shown in Fig. 10.

The only one candidate direction can be chosen for narrow openings:

$$c_n = (k_r + k_l)/2 \tag{32}$$

For wide openings, 3 candidate directions are selected:

$$\begin{aligned} c_1 &= k_r + s_{max}/2 \\ c_2 &= k_l - s_{max}/2 \\ c_3 &= k_{target} \quad \text{if } k_{target} \in [c_1, c_2] \end{aligned} \tag{33}$$

With $k_{\text{target}}$ is target direction.

We substitute the selected directions into the cost function:

$$g(c) = \mu_1 \Delta(c, k_{\text{target}}) + \mu_2 \Delta(c, k_\theta) + \mu_3 \Delta(c, c^{-1}) \tag{34}$$

With $k_\theta$ is the current direction of the robot.

The function $g(c)$ with the lowest result will be the next optimal direction for the robot to move.

The higher the value of $\mu_1$, the more goal-oriented the robot's behavior will be. The higher $\mu_2$, the more the robot strives to follow an efficient course with the fewest possible changes in motion direction. The higher $\mu_3$, the more the robot strives to follow the previously chosen path, and the smoother the trajectory becomes. To prioritize towards the goal, we choose as follows

$$\mu_1 > \mu_2 + \mu_3 \tag{35}$$

## 4  Simulation and Experimental Results

### 4.1  Track the Trajectory When There Are no Obstacles

The robot in Fig. 1 is used for the experimentation. With a distance between two wheels $L = 0.47$ m, wheel diameter $d = 0.15$ m, maximum translational speed $v_{max} = 1$ m/s. The robot will be controlled to track the reference trajectory according to the control law based on the Lyapunov function as shown in Fig. 11(b). The robot will start from the origin O (0,0) traveling through the magnet points glued on the floor: A, B, C, D, E, F, G, H, and destination I (4.5, 3). The robot will accelerate at point O with an acceleration of $0.15$ m/s$^2$, when it reaches a certain speed as $0.2$ m/s, it can move stably on the trajectory and will begin to decelerate when $0.2$ m away from the destination with an acceleration of $-0.15$ m/s$^2$. The robot will come to a halt when reaching the destination I.

The robot will update the status values of the parameters (including position parameters from the Encoder and orientation angle from the IMU) and a controller based on these parameters to control the robot to track the reference trajectory as it moves through the correction points from A, B, C, D, E, F, G, H.

Figure 11 shows the results of gathering the robot's trajectories in three scenarios, together with a reference trajectory. The path calculated only by odometry (Encoder), the path estimated using a Kalman filter and an IMU sensor (Encoder + IMU), and the predicted path when incorporating additional Hall sensors (Encoder + IMU + Hall) are the three scenarios.

The deviations in the X and Y directions and the position of the robot when following the reference trajectory are shown in Figs. 12, 13 and 14. When combining a fusion of encoder sensors, IMU, and magnetic hall sensors, the trajectory is visually closer to the true path than when using only odometry.

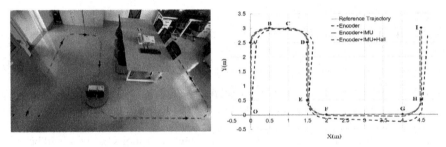

**Fig. 11.** Experimental images & Tracing reference trajectory

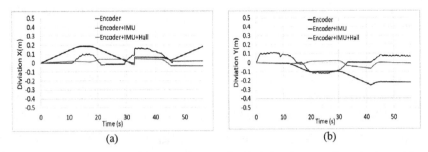

**Fig. 12.** When tracking the reference trajectory, the deviation between the robot's positions is calculated: (a) in X(m) direction; (b) in Y(m) direction

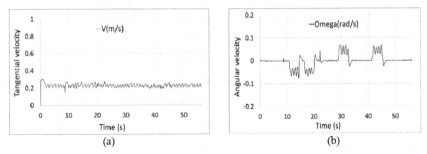

**Fig. 13.** Linear and angular velocities of the robot in case of using three sensors Encoder + IMU + Hall.

## 4.2 Track the Trajectory and Avoid Obstacles

The robot will use all three sensors Encoder + IMU + Hall and be controlled to track the trajectory set up in the laboratory in Fig. 11(b), on the way the robot will encounter unexpected obstacles. The robot will use the VFH+ method to avoid obstacles as shown in Fig. 15.

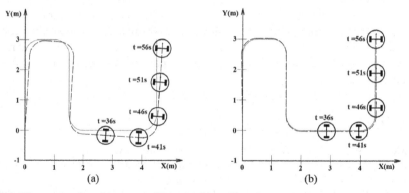

**Fig. 14.** The error of position over time of robot with reference trajectory in case: (a) using Encoder and (b) using all three sensors Encoder + IMU + Hall.

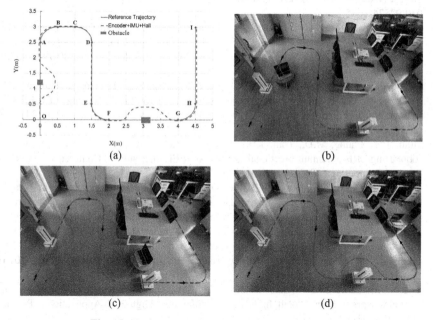

**Fig. 15.** Trajectory path and scene image of the robot.

## 5 Conclusions

The article presents the research process of guiding a mobile robot to operate autonomously through the stages of positioning, tracing the trajectory, and avoiding obstacles appearing unexpectedly on the way. Despite the existence of measurement noise in sensors such as the Encoder and IMU, the simulation results show that the robot follows the reference trajectory and clings to it successfully.

The basis of the reference trajectory is established, with a control law based on the Lyapunov function applied. Although the Lyapunov function method may require a longer distance than the previous method, it will have a continuous trajectory, satisfying the angle of the robot at the destination. The software for controlling robotic obstacle avoidance by potential field method has also been developed with good results in local space. These research results can be developed for the research of navigation of autonomous vehicles in outdoor environments.

# References

1. Meiling, W., Zhen, W., Yi, Y., Mengyin, F.: Model predictive control for UGV trajectory tracking based on dynamic model. In: Proceedings of the IEEE International Conference on Information and Automation Ningbo, pp. 1676–1681 (2016)
2. Thanh, V.C., Quan, N.N.A., Le Thang Dong, T., Hoang, T.T., Nguyen, M.T.: Fusion of inertial and magnetic sensors for autonomous vehicle navigation and freight in distinctive environment. In: Nguyen, D.C., Vu, N.P., Long, B.T., Puta, H., Sattler, K.-U. (eds.) ICERA 2021. LNNS, vol. 366, pp. 431–439. Springer, Cham (2022). https://doi.org/10.1007/978-3-030-92574-1_45
3. Kim, D.H., Kim, S.B.: Path following control of automated guide vehicle using camera sensor. In: Zelinka, I., Brandstetter, P., Trong Dao, T., Hoang Duy, Vo., Kim, S.B. (eds.) AETA 2018. LNEE, vol. 554, pp. 932–938. Springer, Cham (2020). https://doi.org/10.1007/978-3-030-14907-9_90
4. Hoang, T.T., Duong, P.M., Van, N.T.T., Viet, D.A., Vinh, T.Q.: Development of an EKF-based localization algorithm using compass sensor and LRF. In: Proceedings of IEEE 12th International Conference on Control, Automation, Robotics & Vision, ICARCV, pp. 341–346 (2013)
5. Dinh, T.H., Phung, M.D., Tran, T.H., Tran, Q.V.: Localization of a unicycle-like mobile robot using LRF and omni-directional camera. In: IEEE International Conference on Control System, Computing and Engineering, pp. 477–482 (2012)
6. Hoang, T.T., Duong, P.M., Van, N.T.T., Viet, D.A., Vinh, T.Q.: Multi-sensor perceptual system for mobile robot and sensor fusion - based localization. In: IEEE 1st International Conference on Control, Automation and Information Sciences (ICCAIS-2012), pp. 259–264 (2012)
7. Hoang, T.T., Hiep, D.T., Duong, P.M., Van, N.T.T., Duong, B.G., Vinh, T.Q.: Proposal of algorithms for navigation and obstacles avoidance of autonomous mobile robot. In: Proceedings of IEEE 8th Conference on Industrial Electronics and Applications (ICIEA-2013), pp. 1308–1313 (2013)
8. Thanh, V.C., Dong, T.L.T., Quan, N.N.A., Hoang, T.T.: Autonomous vehicle navigation using inertial sensors and virtual path. In: National Conference "High-Tech Application in Practice in 2021" (2021)
9. Yousuf, S., Kadri, M.B.: Sensor fusion of INS, odometer and GPS for robot localization. In: IEEE Conference on Systems, Process and Control (ICSPC 2016), pp. 118–123 (2016)
10. Zhang, M., Li, K., Hu, B., Meng, C.: Comparison of kalman filters for inertial integrated navigation. Sensors 19, 1426 (2019)
11. Kumar, S., Suganthi, M.: Design of accurate navigation system by integrating INS and GPS using extended kalman filter. Int. J. Eng. Res. Technol. (IJERT) 4(5), 803–808 (2015)
12. Anbu, N.A., Jayaprasanth, D.: Integration of inertial navigation system with global positioning system using extended kalman filter. In: IEEE Second International Conference on Smart Systems and Inventive Technology (ICSSIT 2019), pp. 789–794 (2019)
13. Klancar, G., Matko, D., Blazic, S.: Mobile robot control on a reference path. In: Proceedings of the 13th Mediterranean Conference on Control and Automation, Limassol, Cyprus, 27–29 June 2005, pp. 1343–1348 (2005)

14. Widyotriatmo, A., Hong, K.S., Prayudhi, L.H.: Robust stabilization of a wheeled vehicle: hybrid feedback control design and experimental validation. J. Mech. Sci. Technol. **24**(2), 513–520 (2010)
15. Tran, T.H., Phung, M.D., Van Nguyen, T.T., Tran, Q.V.: Stabilization control of the differential mobile robot using lyapunov function and extended kalaman filter. J. Sci. Technol. **50**(4), 441–452 (2012)
16. Aicardi, M., Casalino, G., Bicchi, A., Balestrino, A.: Closed loop steering of unicycle-like vehicles via Lyapunov techniques. IEEE Robot. Autom. Mag. **2**(1), 27–35 (1995)
17. Ryck, D.M., Mark, V., Debrouwere, F.: Automated guided vehicle systems, state-of-the-art control algorithms and techniques. J. Manuf. Syst. **54**, 152–173 (2020)
18. Secchi, H., Carelli, R., Mut, V.: An experience on stable control of mobile robots. J. Latin Am. Appl. Res. **33**(4), 379–385 (2003)
19. Fei, L.: Two-wheel Driven AGV Path Planning and Motion Control. Hebei University of Science and Technology (2016)
20. Son, T.A., et al.: Research and manufacture of automated guided vehicle for the service of storehouse. Sci. Technol. Dev. J. Eng. Technol. **1**(1), 5–12 (2018)
21. Nascimento, T.P., Dórea, C.E.T., Gonçalves, L.M.G.: Nonholonomic mobile robots' trajectory tracking model predictive control: a survey. Robotica **36**, 676–696 (2018)
22. Hasan, H.S., Abidin, M.S.Z., Mahmud, M.S.A., Mohd, F.M.S.: Automated guided vehicle routing: Static, dynamic and free range. J. Int. Eng. Adv. Technol. **8**(5C), 1–7 (2019)
23. Kim, S., Jin, H., Seo, M., Har, D.: Optimal path planning of automated guided vehicle using dijkstra algorithm under dynamic conditions. In: 7th International Conference on Robot Intelligence Technology and Applications (RiTA). IEEE (2019)
24. Moshayedi, A.J., Roy, A.S., Liao, L.: PID tuning method on AGV (automated guided vehicle) industrial robot. J. Simul. Anal. Novel Technol. Mech. Eng. **12**(4), 53–66 (2020)
25. Borenstein, J., Koren, Y.: The vector field histogram - fast obstacle avoidance for mobile robots. IEEE J. Robot. Autom. **7**(3), 278–288 (1991)
26. Ulrich, I., Borenstein, J.: VFH+: reliable obstacle avoidance for fast mobile robots. In: Proceedings of the IEEE International Conference on Robotics and Automation, Leuven, Belgium, pp. 1572–1577 (1998)
27. Diaz, D., Marın, L.: VFH+D: an improvement on the VFH+ algorithm for dynamic obstacle avoidance and local planning. IFAC PapersOnLine **53**(2), 9590–9595 (2020)

# Improving the Control Performance of Jacking System of Jack-Up Rig Using Self-adaptive Fuzzy Controller Based on Particle Swarm Optimization

Tien-Dat Tran[1], Viet-Dung Do[1,2], Xuan-Kien Dang[1(✉)], and Ba-Linh Mai[3]

[1] Ho Chi Minh City University of Transport, Ho Chi Minh City, Vietnam
`kien.dang@ut.edu.vn`
[2] Dong An Polytechnic, Binh Duong, Vietnam
[3] Ministry of Transportation, Ha Noi, Vietnam

**Abstract.** Oil and gas Jack-up Rig is a type of offshore production for exploitation with complex structure and working modes, capable of operating independently at sea. Although Vietnam has rich petroleum resources, the exploitation equipment, particularly jack-up rigs, almost depends on international technologies. Therefore, the subject of an advanced control theory for the jacking system of Jack-up Rig is a critical issue. In this work, we study the Particle swarm optimization approach based on a Fuzzy controller to adapt to the effects of environmental forces and hydrodynamic amplification. The designed Fuzzy Particle Swarm Optimization controller is compared with the Fuzzy Proportional Integral Derivative controller in order to verify the advantage of the proposed method. By using Matlab software, the simulation results show the advantages of the suggested approach.

**Keywords:** Hydrodynamic amplification · Environmental forces · Fuzzy particle swarm optimization · Jacking system

## 1 Introduction

For decades, Jack-up drilling platforms have been utilized for offshore oil and gas exploration, drilling, and work-over. There are several techniques [1–4] for stable control and decreasing influencing factors in the jacking process of a Jack-up Rig (JuR). Even while each technique has its benefits, the study of advanced control algorithms continuously motivates researchers to develop theory and practice solutions to assist the system function more reliably and securely control system and has many more operations that were not possible previously.

In general, the rig move system and the jacking system are the two most significant control systems for JuR. For these two systems' outstanding advantages, many researchers are committed to creating enhanced technology and artificial intelligence [5–10]. Several suggested advanced control methods, such as Fuzzy [5], Hybrid Fuzzy

N.-S. Vo et al. (Eds.): INISCOM 2022, LNICST 444, pp. 184–200, 2022.
https://doi.org/10.1007/978-3-031-08878-0_13

[6], Fuzzy Adaptive [7], Neural Network [8], Genetic Algorithm (GA) [9], and Particle swarm optimization (PSO) [10], have shown their effectiveness and stability. In the meanwhile, several traditional controllers like the PID and the Linear Quadratic Regulator (LQR) are still in use for the jacking systems. Furthermore, there are few research on the application of current control theory to improve the quality and performance of controllers, particularly jacking systems.

Recently, the Fuzzy Control (FC) has received plenty of innovative results in achievements of literature [6, 7] to cope with problems of unpredictability and disturbance. The FC method preserves all closed-loop signals within the constraints of a class of switching signals with typical dead-time. The Adaptive Fuzzy Control (AFC) is also seen to be an effective technique for improving the control performance of the fuzzy controller [11, 12], especially for the self-adaptive fuzzy control (SAFC) [13–15]. On the other hand, optimal algorithms such as GA and PSO are being studied and applied in combination with fuzzy logic to increase the adaptability and stability of the SAFC. By the way, the controller does not only ensures the control performance but also enhances the robustness. Finally, this is the motivating factor for our choice to employ the innovative technique for JuR's jacking control system, as it must operate in harsh environmental conditions.

Related to the Rig building in Vietnam, the automatic controller does not play an important role in rig construction. Due to the fuzzy system's capacity to simulate a nonlinear composition, the hierarchical fuzzy model fits out a suitable approach for the JuR with unpredictable affects. In this study, we used the SAFC based on the PSO called Fuzzy Particle Swarm Optimization (FPSO) to improve the control performance of the Jacking system of the JuR. The following are the primary contributions of this paper: (i) We constructed the mathematical modeling of the Jacking system after performing movements of the JuR in the axis; (ii) We realize that the Fuzzy PID (FPID) controller designed for the Jacking system is not highly feasible under the influence of internal and external loads by simulation results. Therefore, our suggested controller, one kind of the SAFC, is the FPSO aiming to solve the aforementioned issue; (iii) Finally, the simulation of the designed FPSO is compared with the FPID controller in order to verify the advantage of the proposed approach.

This paper is organized as follows. The mathematical modeling of the Jacking system is presented in Sect. 2, and Sect. 3 analyzes the affected factors including internal and external load. Section 4 represents the JuR control methods. The simulation results and discussion of the three case studies are expressed in Sect. 5, followed by the concluding remarks of this study in Sect. 6.

## 2 Mathematical Modeling of Jacking System

### 2.1 The Movements of the Jack-Up Rig

The movements of the Jack-up Rig are shown in Fig. 1. The rig moves along the X direction, transversely vibrates in the Y direction, and moves up and down in the Z direction. However, vertical and horizontal shaking of the rig body oscillates around the X-axis, Y-axis while rotating around the vertical Z-axis. In lifting mode, the jacking system is driven by electric motors mounted on the body of the truss. The motors on each axis operate synchronously and are the same type and parameters.

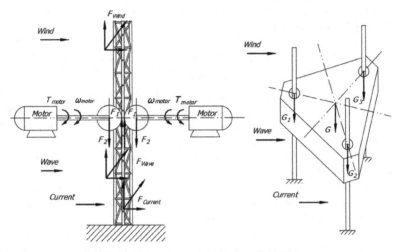

**Fig. 1.** Movement of the Jack-up Rig [16].

## 2.2 Mathematical Model of the Jacking Control System

In actual operating conditions, the sensor system determines the current displacement position of the JuR under the influence of disturbances. Based on the error between the desired position and the actual position, the controller computes the value of the control signal to transmit to the thrust allocation. Here, the thrust allocation converts the control signal into control commands (such as the direction of rotation, speed, and torque on the motor shaft) for distribution to thruster dynamics. The motors at the rig legs will operate according to the control command to carry out the process of lifting and lowering the platform. From there, the JuR's kinematic model will move, and the sensor system continues to determine the new position of the JuR. The overall diagram of the Jacking control system is shown in Fig. 2. The system of differential equations describing the JuR's kinematics is given as [17–20]

$$M\frac{d^2x(t)}{dt^2} + C\frac{dx(t)}{dt} + Kx(t) = \tau_m(t) + \tau_d(t) \tag{1}$$

where $M = \sum_{i=0}^{n} m_i$ is total weight of JuR, $C$ and $K$ are damping and stiffness of the single degree of freedom (SDOF) system, $\tau(t) = \tau_m(t) + \tau_d(t)$, $\tau_m(t) = \sum_{i=0}^{n} \tau_i(t)$ is the total torque on motor shafts, $x(t)$ is the displacement of the hull.

The total effect of load including wave, wind, current, and external load, respectively

$$\tau_d(t) = \tau_{wave}(t) + \tau_{wind}(t) + \tau_{current}(t) + \tau_1(t) \tag{2}$$

The displacement of the hull is calculated by

$$x(t) = R\theta(t) \tag{3}$$

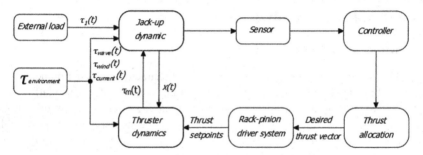

**Fig. 2.** An overall diagram of the Jacking control system.

therein, $R$ expresses the effective radius of the pinion, and $\theta(t)$ is the angular of the pinion. From the Eqs. (1) and (3), the JuR's hull kinematics is written as

$$Rs^2\theta(s)\sum_{i=1}^{n} m_i + RCs\theta(s) + KR\theta(s) = \tau(s) \tag{4}$$

The transfer function of the JuR kinematics model (the Jack-up dynamic block expresses in Fig. 2) is given as

$$G_{JuR} = \frac{\theta(s)}{\tau(s)} = \frac{k_e}{Ms^2 + Cs + K} \tag{5}$$

with $k_e = 1/R$ is the conversion factor in rotary translational transmission (including the number of motors and transmission coefficient). The rig body is raised through the rack and pinion systems. By using DC motors, the thruster dynamics provide torque for the drivetrain. The driving DC motor torque is calculated as [21]

$$L_a \dot{I}_a + R_a I_a + K_b W_m = V$$
$$\tau_m = K_t I_a \tag{6}$$

where $K_t$ is torque constant, $K_b$ is back emf constant, $V$ is input voltage, $I_a$ is armature current, $R_a$ is armature resistance, $J$ is rotor inertia, $D_a$ is viscous friction constant, $W_m$ is angular velocity and $L_a$ is inductance. Therefore, the transfer function of the thruster dynamics is performed as

$$G_{Th} = \frac{W(s)}{V(s)} = \frac{k_t}{JL_as^2 + (R_aJ + L_aD_a)s + (R_aD_a + K_bK_t)} \tag{7}$$

The jacking system consists of a jack-up dynamic and thruster dynamic (shown in Fig. 2). From the Eqs. (5) and (7), the transfer function of the jacking system is determined as

$$G = G_{JuR}.G_{Th} = \frac{k_e}{Ms^2 + Cs + K} \frac{k_t}{JL_as^2 + (R_aJ + L_aD_a)s + (R_aD_a + K_bK_t)} \tag{8}$$

## 3 Effected Factors Analysis

### 3.1 Environmental Factors

The jacking system control was impacted by seabed characteristics, environmental conditions, and the depth of the water layer. Furthermore, a variety of marine platforms are used in offshore locations for the exploration and making of energy from oil and gas. Thus, the scope of this research is restricted to areas of oceanographic ambient variables that impact the control process of JuR's jacking system. As a result, the jacking system must be capable of withstanding the following loads:

$$F_{envi} = F_{wave} + F_{wind} + F_{current} \tag{9}$$

**The Wave Force.** In offshore operation, the most characteristic impact is the wave. In six degrees of freedom, they attack an offshore structure to surge, sway, heave, roll, pitch and yaw. They are the primary source of workplace inefficiencies and downtime. In jacking systems, the pressures which are produced by waves play an important role in the design process. Wave factor affecting the jacking system is determined by equation [5, 7, 22, 23]:

$$F_{wave} = \xi(x, y, t) = \sum_{q=1}^{N} \sum_{r=1}^{M} \sqrt{2S(\omega_q \psi_r) \Delta\omega \Delta\psi} \sin(\omega_q t + \phi_{qr} - k_q(x\cos\psi_r + y\sin\psi_r)) \tag{10}$$

where the phase angle $\phi_{qr} \in [0 - 2\pi]$, $\psi_r$ denote direction, $\omega_q$ frequency, and $S$ wave spectrum. The $\Delta\omega$ and $\Delta\psi$ factors represent the harmonic amplitudes of wave frequency $\omega_q$. Besides that, $k_q = 2\pi/\lambda_q$ is the number of waves, in which $\lambda_q$ is the wavelength.

**The Wind Force.** Wind force affects the floating stability of the truss and it depends on the windbreak area, velocity, structure shape, height. There are four methods of calculating wind load: numerical simulation, using the combined formula from experiment, field test, and wind tunnel [3, 9]. However, if the system works under the condition that the wind frequency and direction are modeled as slowly changing quantities, the wind force can be calculated by the formula [7]:

$$F_{wind} = [X_{wind}, Y_{wind}]^T$$
$$X_{wind} = 0.5C_X g_R \rho_w V_R^2 A_T \tag{11}$$
$$Y_{wind} = 0.5C_Y g_R \rho_w V_R^2 A_T$$

The wind traction into the ichnography region $A_T$ is represented by $C_X$ and $C_Y$. $V_R$, $g_R$ is the speed and direction of wind acting on the truss.

**The Current Force.** The flow is considered to be stable even though the flow velocity varies with time, space, depth, and vortex vibration [24]. Assume that the direction and amplitude of the current are unchanged, thus correcting the current speed $V_c$ and the direction $\beta_c$ are modeled as the slow variable quantities according to the earth coordinates. Equation (12) presents the current relative speed of Jack-up coordinates [25]:

$$
\begin{aligned}
u_c &= V_c \cos(\beta_c - \psi_L - \psi_H) \\
v_c &= V_c \sin(\beta_c - \psi_L - \psi_H) \\
\tau_{current} &= [u_c, v_c, 0]^T
\end{aligned}
\tag{12}
$$

where $u_c$ and $v_c$ represent current speed compositions, while $\psi_L$ and $\psi_H$ designate the angular configurations impacted by low and high-frequency values, respectively.

### 3.2 Internal Factors

The internal factors affect to the jacking control system, in which vibrations for the JuR's hull [3, 4, 26] are mainly caused by the periodic action of waves and currents. We have suitable methods such as dynamic factor amplification, frequency domain analysis, or time-domain analysis [27] for vibration analysis of marine structures. Using the Dynamic Amplification Factor (DAF) method [28] where the inertial load is used to represent dynamic load, the ratio between dynamic response amplification and static response amplification is calculated as follows:

$$
DAF = \frac{1}{\sqrt{\left[1 - \left(\frac{T_N}{T}\right)^2\right]^2 + \left(2\varepsilon \frac{T_N}{T}\right)^2}}
\tag{13}
$$

with $T_N$ is a natural period of the platform and $T$ is a wave excitation period, and $\varepsilon$ is the platform damp ratio taken as 0.07. Based on the weight of JuR (M > 2500 ton), the DAF coefficient is chosen to be 1.1 [29].

## 4    Self-adaptive Fuzzy Controller for Jacking System

### 4.1    Fuzzy PID Controller

To control the nonlinear model, a popular strategy combines the linear control method with the intelligent control method to promote the flexible structure and fast-response time. Moreover, the FPID control is often chosen in the industrial application's control. In this paper, authors introduce the FPID controller as follow [30]:

$$u_{FPID}(s) = K_p(s)e(s) + K_i(s)\int_0^s e(s)ds + K_d(s)\frac{de}{ds} \qquad (14)$$

The coefficients $K_p(s)$, $K_i(s)$, and $K_d(s)$ have a flexible structure according to the input variable error instead of the fixed coefficients $K_p$, $K_i$, and $K_d$, respectively. Thus, the normal PID controller is given by [31]:

$$u_{PID}(s) = K_p + \frac{K_i}{s} + K_d s \qquad (15)$$

The flexible coefficients $K_p(s)$, $K_i(s)$, and $K_d(s)$ are updated after each control cycle according to the erroneous amplitude. Then, the PID coefficient is updated by:

$$\begin{cases} K_p(s) = K_p(s-1) + u_f(\Delta kp) \\ K_i(s) = K_i(s-1) + u_f(\Delta ki) \\ K_d(s) = K_d(s-1) + u_f(\Delta kd) \end{cases} \qquad (16)$$

The updated coefficients $u_f\left(u_f(\Delta kp), u_f(\Delta ki), u_f(\Delta kd)\right)$ are defined by the fuzzy system. The notation of membership functions (MFs) for NB is Large Negative, for NBB is Near Big Negative, for NS is Small Negative, for NSS is Near Small Negative, for ZE is Zero, for PSS is Near Small Positive, for PS is Small Positive, for PBB is Near Big Positive, and for PB is Large Positive. In addition, we use a fuzzy system with a double-input $e(t)${NB NBB NS NSS ZE PSS PS PBB PB}, $de/d(t)${NB NS ZE PS PB}, and a triple-output $K_p${ZE PSS PS PBB PB}, $K_i${ZE PSS PS PBB PB} and $K_d${ZE PSS PS PBB PB} to calibrate the coefficients $K_p(s)$, $K_i(s)$, and $K_d(s)$ [22]. Moreover, $B^i$, the rule designation form in Eq. (17), is a binary variable representing the rule outcome.

$$R_i : if\ \hat{e}_1\ is\ A_1^i...and\ \hat{e}_n\ is\ A_n^i\ then\ u\ is\ B^i \qquad (17)$$

for $A_1^i$, $A_2^i$, ... $A_n^i$ and $B^i$ denote the fuzzy sets. The update coefficient can be generated by using the center average defuzzifier as follows:

$$u_f = \frac{\sum_{i=1}^h B^i [\prod_{j=1}^n \mu_{A_j^i}(\hat{e}_j)]}{\sum_{i=1}^h [\prod_{j=1}^n \mu_{A_j^i}(\hat{e}_j)]} \qquad (18)$$

where $\mu_{A_j^i}(\hat{e}_j)$ express the MFs, $h$ indicates the amount of if-then rules [9, 32]. However, the FPID algorithm controls the jacking system in time-varying environmental conditions, the results are not feasible. Therefore, we suggest the optimal solution, named fuzzy particle swarm optimization, to improve the process control quality under extreme weather conditions. Finally, the FPSO operation mechanism is introduced in the next section.

## 4.2 Fuzzy Particle Swarm Optimization Controller

The time-varying influences of the environmental conditions cause the jacking system's position to be inaccurate. To overcome the incorrect position, we proposed the FPSO controller with a flexible structure and optimum parameter values. As a result, the proposed solution's purpose is to adapt the control structure to react to the systematic error caused by the coefficient's environmental impact $\delta_\lambda$. In addition, the PSO algorithm $(\lambda_i)$ is employed to find the best parameters for enhancing response quality. Figure 3 illustrates the suggested model's mechanism, which is divided into two main stages [10]:

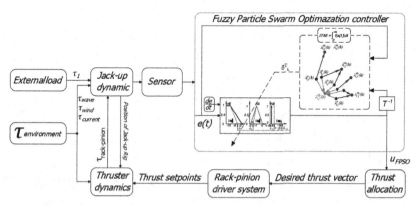

**Fig. 3.** The FPSO controller structure for the jacking system.

**The First Stage.** We establish a fuzzy structure on m.file format with the MFs flexible value to improve flexible structure. Therefore, the fuzzy modulator has a single-output $u_F(t)$ and a double-input $e(t)$, $de/dt$ calibrating by a $\delta_\lambda$ coefficient to maximize the effectiveness of the fuzzy structure. The fuzzy output performance is represented as

$$u_{FPSO} = \frac{\sum_{i=1}^{h} B^i [\prod_{j=1}^{n} \mu_{A_{\lambda j}^i}(\hat{e}_j)]}{\sum_{i=1}^{h} [\prod_{j=1}^{n} \mu_{A_{\lambda j}^i}(\hat{e}_j)]} \tag{19}$$

where $\mu_{A_1^j}(\hat{e}_1) = [\lambda_1(A_1^1, A_1^2, \ldots A_1^j)]$ is the fuzzy set of the error $e(t)$, $\mu_{A_2^j}(\hat{e}_2) = [\lambda_2(A_2^1, A_2^2, \ldots A_2^j)]$ is the fuzzy set of the error-velocity $de/dt$, and $\delta_\lambda = [(\lambda_3 + \lambda_4/s)(B^1, B^2, \ldots B^i)]$ is the adaptive adjustable coefficient corresponding the fuzzy set of output $u_F(t)$. The fuzzy inference $i$ is represented by the $j$ coefficient, which is an index of the fuzzy set. Then, $\varphi_\lambda(\hat{e}) = [\varphi^1, \varphi^2, \ldots, \varphi^h] \in R^h$ expresses the fuzzy basis vector which is determined as [7]

$$\varphi_\lambda(\hat{e}) = \frac{[\prod_{j=1}^{n} \mu_{A_{\lambda j}^i}(\hat{e}_j)]}{\sum_{i=1}^{h}[\prod_{j=1}^{n} \mu_{A_{\lambda j}^i}(\hat{e}_j)]} \tag{20}$$

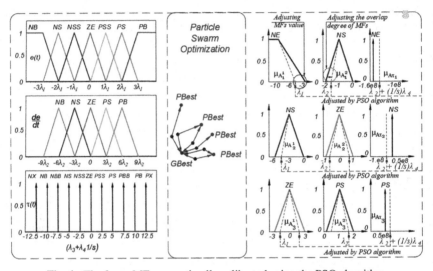

**Fig. 4.** The fuzzy MFs are optimally calibrated using the PSO algorithm.

**The Second Stage.** Aiming to determine the optimal calibration coefficient $\lambda_i$, the PSO algorithm completes the correction of fuzzy set values with coefficient $\lambda_i(\lambda_1, \lambda_2, \lambda_3, \lambda_4)$ to achieve the optimal parameters. Figure 4 represents the calibrating fuzzy MFs using the PSO algorithm. Following Eq. (20), the FPSO response can be described as

$$u_{FPSO} = \delta_\lambda \varphi_\lambda(\hat{e}) \tag{21}$$

The determination of optimal coefficient $\lambda_i$ based on the PSO algorithm [10], to deal with the improving control quality in the time-varying environmental condition is represented in Algorithm 1.

---

**Algorithm 1**: The PSO algorithm calibrates the fuzzy parameter optimally [10]

---

Initialization:

**for each** particle $i$ $(1 \leq i \leq s)$ **do**

    Randomly initialize the position $\lambda_i^p(k)$

    Randomly initialize the velocity $v_i(k)$

    Initialize calibration coefficient $\lambda_i$ $(\lambda_1, \lambda_2, \lambda_3, \lambda_4)$

**end for**

**for each** iteration $k$ **do**

    (a) Each particle $\lambda_i^p(k)$ update the values of $\lambda_{i,j}^p(k)$ and $\lambda_{i,j}^{Gb}(k)$

$$\lambda_{i,j}^p(k+1) = \begin{cases} \lambda_{i,j}^p(k), if\ J\left(\lambda_{i,j}^p(k+1)\right) \geq J\left(\lambda_{i,j}^p(k)\right) \\ \lambda_{i,j}^p(k+1), \qquad\qquad otherwise \end{cases} \quad (22)$$

$$\lambda_{i,j}^{Gb}(k+1) = argmin_{\lambda_{i,j}^{Pb}} J\left(\lambda_{i,j}^{Pb}(k+1)\right), 1 \leq i \leq s \quad (23)$$

    (b) Initialize the particle attribute $v_i(k)$

$$v_{i,j}(k+1) = w(k)v_{i,j}(k) + c_1 r_1 \left[\lambda_{i,j}^{Pb}(k) - \lambda_{i,j}^p(k)\right] + c_2 r_2 \left[\lambda_j^{Gb}(k) - \lambda_{i,j}^p(k)\right]$$

$$(24)$$

    where

$$w(g) = \frac{(iter_{max} - g)(w_{max} - w_{min})}{iter_{max}} + w_{min} \quad (25)$$

    (c) Determine the new position $\lambda_{i,j}^p(k)$

$$\lambda_{i,j}^p(k+1) = \lambda_{i,j}^p(k) + v_{i,j}(k+1) \quad (26)$$

    (d) Apply newly coefficient $\lambda_{i,j}^p(k)$ to adjust the amplitude values of the MFs and compute a fitness value according to the criteria efficiency.

$$ITAE = \int_0^\infty t|e(t)|dt \quad (27)$$

    (f) A suitable point to start is to compare the obtained value to the termination condition. If the convergence criteria do not fulfill the criterion, raise $k$ and return to step 1. (a).

**end for**

---

## 5   Simulation and Evaluation

### 5.1   Configuration Parameter

To evaluate the efficiency of the proposed method, performance comparisons between the proposed FPSO controller and the FPID controller [21] are carried out by simulation. Moreover, the parameters of the TamDao05 JuR model are used in this study. The parameter dimensions scale down by the ratio of 1:100 shown in Table 1.

**Table 1.** Parameters of TAMDAO05 JuR model

| Description | Specifications |
|---|---|
| Type of offshore | Jack-up |
| Length overall | 1.62 m |
| Breadth overall | 0.96 m |
| Hull depth at side | 0.232 m |
| Hull weight | 0.0327 ton |
| Weight of a leg of the rig | 0.012 ton |
| Number of DC motor | 06 |
| Jack-up weight | 0.0928 ton |
| Conversion factor $k_e$ | 33.33 |
| Torque constant $K_t$ | 1.28 |
| Back emf constant $K_b$ | 0.0045 |
| Armature resistance $R_a$ | 11.4 |
| Inductance $L_a$ | 0.1214 |
| Rotor inertia J | 0.02215 |
| Viscous friction constant $D_a$ | 0.002953 |

**Table 2.** The parameters setting of the environmental impact [9]

| Description | Symbol | Specifications |
|---|---|---|
| Wave height | $H_s$ | 0.8 m |
| Wave spectrum peak frequency | $\omega_0$ | 0 rad/s |
| Wave direction | $\psi_0$ | $30^0$ |
| Spreading factor | $s$ | 2 |
| Number of frequencies | $N$ | 20 |
| Number of directions | $M$ | 10 |
| Cutoff frequency factor | $\xi$ | 3 |
| Wave component energy limit | $k$ | 0.005 |
| Wave direction limit | $\psi_{lim}$ | 0 |
| Wind traction into the ichnography region | $A_T$ | 2.4 |
| Wind speed | $V_\omega$ | 2 m/s |
| Angle of impact wind | $\beta_\omega$ | $20^0$ |
| Current speed | $V_c$ | 2 m/s |
| Jack-up direction | $\beta_c$ | $30^0$ |
| Low frequency and high frequency of rotation | $\psi_L, \psi_H$ | $0^0$ |
| Dominating wave frequency | $w_0$ | 0.8976 rad/s |
| Damping coefficient | $\lambda$ | 0.1 |
| Wave intensity | $\sigma$ | $\sqrt{2}$ |

We used the Matlab 2019a software to simulate the designed controllers under the same environmental conditions and parameters of the jacking system. Similarly, the PSO searching algorithm identifies the optimal value of the fuzzy controller to attain the best convergence on control by using the m.file interacted to Simulink. Nevertheless, these optimal coefficients support adjusting the MFs value of the fuzzy controller to fulfill the control requirement. The parameters of the environmental impact are given in Table 2 [9].

## 5.2  Simulation Results

We compare the achievement of the FPID and FPSO controllers in this section. The simulation schematic is shown in Fig. 5. Then, the simulation results present in Figs. 6, 7, and 8 demonstrated how the control force performs the jacking system's actual position responses (FPID in blue and FPSO in red) under the effect of environmental disturbances. In this case, the control forces acting on the legs are transformed into a certain amount of torque on the motor shaft.

The proposed FPSO controller (presented in Sect. 4.2) is carried out on the Tam-Dao05 JuR model in three case studies corresponding to levels 1, 5, and 7 of the sea state. In the simulation pocess, the FPSO controller with the optimal coefficient $\lambda_k \left( 1.279 \times 10^{18}, 1.828 \times 10^{18}, 1.225 \times 10^{18}, 8.743 \times 10^{17} \right)$ and the limitations of adaptive coefficient $\delta_{min} \left( -1.7053 \times 10^{17} \right) \leq \delta_\lambda \leq \delta_{max} \left( 1.7053 \times 10^{17} \right)$ is used to force the jacking system to arrive at the 10 cm position in around 48 s.

### 5.2.1  Case Study 1

The FPID and FPSO controllers perform on the jacking system under environmental force similar to the level 1 sea state. The simulation results that apply the FPID and FPSO controllers are pointed out in Fig. 6. The simulation results showed positions of the JuR hull satisfy the overshoot, response time, and fluctuation requirements. Maximum overshoots are 2.9 cm and 0.15 cm, respectively, of the FPSO and FPID in the details. The

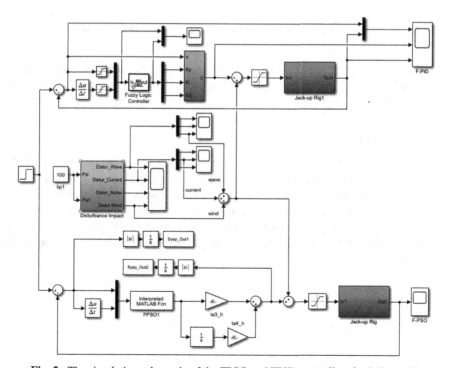

**Fig. 5.** The simulation schematic of the FPSO and FPID controllers for JuR model.

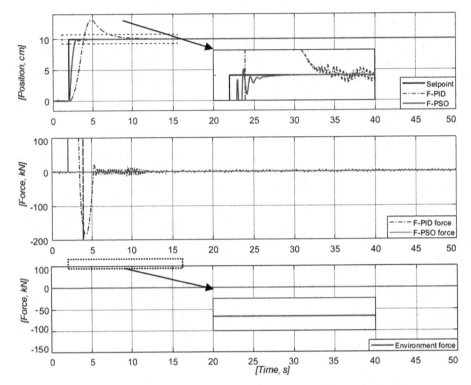

**Fig. 6.** The actual position, control forces, and environmental forces in the level 1 sea state.

proposed FPSO controller has a response time of around 3.5 s, which is faster than the FPID controller. Furthermore, the FPSO has a significantly smaller fluctuation amplitude than the FPID.

### 5.2.2   Case Study 2

In this case, the proposed solution controls the jacking system operation to reach the desired position of environmental force similar to the level 5 sea state. From the Fig. 7, the overshoot amplitude of the FPSO controller is lower than the FPID controller approximately 3.2 cm. On the other hand, the comparison results also show that the FPSO solution is satisfactory in terms of response time and fluctuation. Obviously, the FPSO solution can maintain the response quality for jacking system under changing environmental conditions.

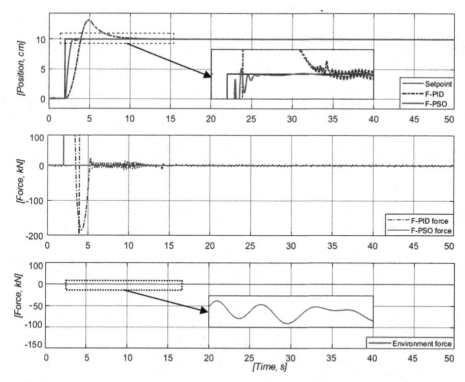

**Fig. 7.** The actual position, control forces, and environmental forces in the level 5 sea state.

### 5.2.3 Case Study 3

In this subsection, the FPSO solution are used to control stability of the JuR hull position in the extreme weather conditions (the environmental force comparable to the level 7 sea state). Figure 8 shows the fluctuation amplitude and response time when using the FPSO solution is 0.16 cm lower, 4.8 s faster, respectively, compared to the FPID controller. Futhermore, the overshoot amplitude of the proposed solution has outstanding quality over the FPID controller under the same operating conditions. The feasibility results indicate that the proposed solution is capable of adaptability disturbances caused by the environmental force.

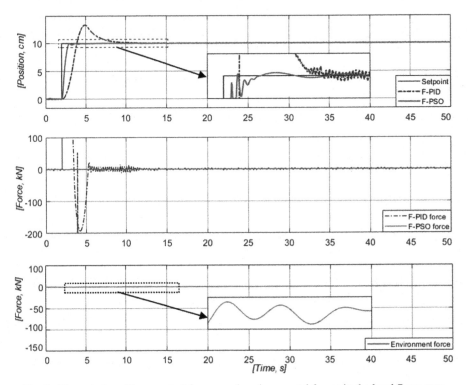

**Fig. 8.** The actual position, control forces, and environmental forces in the level 7 sea state.

In sum, the jacking system performance of the FPID controller is satisfactory in case 1, but unsatisfactory in cases 2 and 3, whereas the FPSO controller exhibits the similar satisfactory control performance in each case. This is because the FPID controller with control force hasn't the adaptability to the time-varying environmental forces, whereas the proposed controller has the adaptability due to exploiting the adaptive ability of $\delta_\lambda$ coefficient. In addition, the response of the jacking system can be enhanced by the optimal coefficient $\lambda_k$ in the proposed FPSO controller. Though, the proposed solution necessitates testing in other actual working conditions to verify its advantage.

## 6   Conclusion

This paper has an overview of the control method for JuRs, especially in the jacking system. The movements of the JuR in the axis are analyzed and used to build the mathematical modeling of the Jacking system. Moreover, to improve the control performance of the fuzzy controller, the PSO algorithm is considered an effective solution for fuzzy self-adaptive control methods. The increase of adaptability and stability of the proposed controller for the jacking system demonstrated the effectiveness of the FPSO compared to the FPID controller in simulation. The JuR jacking control system can be enhanced performance by improving a robust algorithm in harsh conditions in the next study.

# References

1. Yi, J.T., Liu, F., Zhang, T.B., Qiu, Z.Z., Zhang, X.Y.: Determination of the ultimate consolidation settlement of jack-up spudcan footings embedded in clays. Ocean Eng. **236**, 1–13 (2021)
2. Yin, Q., et al.: Field experimental investigation of punch-through for different operational conditions during the jack-up rig spudcan penetration in sand overlying clay. J. Petrol. Sci. Eng. **195**, 1–21 (2020)
3. Wang, F., Xiao, W., Yao, Y., Liu, Q., Li, C.: An analytical procedure to predict transverse vibration response of Jack-Up Riser under the random wave load. Shock. Vib. **2020**, 1–9 (2020)
4. Xie, Y., Huang, J., Li, X., Tian, X., Liu, G., Leng, D.: Experimental study on hydrodynamic characteristics of three truss-type legs of jack-up offshore platform. Ocean Eng. **234**, 1–15 (2021)
5. Dang, X.K., Ho, L.A.H., Do, V.D.: Analyzing the sea weather effects to the ship maneuvering in Vietnam's Sea from Binh Thuan Province to Ca Mau Province based on fuzzy control method. TELKOMNIKA (Telecommun. Comput. Electron. Control) **16**(2), 533–543 (2018)
6. Pashna, M., Yusof, R., Ismail, Z.H., Namerikawa, T., Yazdani, S.: Autonomous multi-robot tracking system for oil spills on sea surface based on hybrid fuzzy distribution and potential field approach. Ocean Eng. **207**, 1–11 (2020)
7. Dang, X.K., Do, V.D., Nguyen, X.P.: Robust adaptive fuzzy control using genetic algorithm for dynamic positioning system. IEEE Access **8**, 222077–222092 (2020)
8. Wang, S., Yin, X., Li, P., Zhang, Y., Wang, X., Tong, S.: Cognitive control using adaptive RBF neural networks and reinforcement learning for networked control system subject to time-varying delay and packet losses. Arab. J. Sci. Eng. **46**(10), 10245–10259 (2021). https://doi.org/10.1007/s13369-021-05752-y
9. Do, V.-D., Dang, X.-K., Huynh, L.-T., Ho, V.-C.: Optimized multi-cascade fuzzy model for ship dynamic positioning system based on genetic algorithm. In: Duong, T.Q., Vo, N.-S., Nguyen, L.K., Vien, Q.-T., Nguyen, V.-D. (eds.) INISCOM 2019. LNICSSITE, vol. 293, pp. 165–180. Springer, Cham (2019). https://doi.org/10.1007/978-3-030-30149-1_14
10. Do, V.-D., Dang, X.-K.: The fuzzy particle swarm optimization algorithm design for dynamic positioning system under unexpected impacts. J. Mechan. Eng. Sci. **13**(3), 5407–5423 (2019)
11. Dang, X.-K., Do, V.-D., Do, V.-T., Ho, L.-H.: Enhancing the control performance of automatic voltage regulator for marine synchronous generator by using interactive adaptive fuzzy algorithm. In: Vo, N.-S., Hoang, V.-P., Vien, Q.-T. (eds.) INISCOM 2021. LNICSSITE, vol. 379, pp. 379–392. Springer, Cham (2021). https://doi.org/10.1007/978-3-030-77424-0_31
12. Fateh, S., Fateh, M.M.: Adaptive fuzzy control of robot manipulators with asymptotic tracking performance. J. Control Autom. Electr. Syst. **31**(1), 52–61 (2019). https://doi.org/10.1007/s40313-019-00496-5
13. Xiaowei, G., Shen, Q.: A self-adaptive fuzzy learning system for streaming data prediction. Inf. Sci. **579**, 623–647 (2021)
14. Buzura, S., Dadarlat, V., Iancu, B., Peculea, A., Cebuc, E., Kovacs, R.: Self-adaptive fuzzy QoS algorithm for a distributed control plane with application in SDWSN. In: 2020 IEEE International Conference on Automation, Quality and Testing, Robotics (AQTR), pp. 1–6 (2020)
15. Thomas, V.K.S., Ashok, S.: Fuzzy controller-based self-adaptive virtual synchronous machine for microgrid application. IEEE Trans. Energy Conv. **36**(3), 2427–2437 (2021)
16. Dang, X.-K., Tran, T.-D.: Modeling techniques and control strategies for jack-up rig: a state of the art and challenges. IEEE Access **9**, 155763–155787 (2021)

17. Dokainish, M.A., Subbaraj, K.: A survey of direct time-integration methods in computational structural dynamics—I explicit methods. Comput. Struct. **32**(6), 1371–1386 (1989)
18. Veletsos, A.S., Ventura, C.E.: Modal analysis of non-classically damped linear systems. Earthq. Eng. Struct. Dynam. **14**, 217–243 (1986)
19. Jong-Shyong, W., Chang, C.-Y.: Structural simplification of jackup rig and its dynamic responses in regular waves. J. Ship Res. **32**(2), 134–153 (1988)
20. Ben, C.: Gerwick: Construction of Marine & Offshore Structures. 3rd edn. Taylor & Francis Group, LLC (2007)
21. Do, V.D., Dang, X.K., Le, A.T.: Fuzzy adaptive interactive algorithm for rig balancing optimization. In: International Conference on Recent Advances in Signal Processing, Telecommunication and Computing, Danang, Vietnam, pp. 143–148 (2017)
22. Dang, X.-K.: Le Anh-Hoang Ho: Joint fuzzy controller and fuzzy disturbance compensator in ship autopilot system: investigate stability in environmental conditions. J. Curr. Sci.Technol. **11**, 114–126 (2021)
23. Fossen, T.I.: A survey on nonlinear ship control: from theory to practice. IFAC Conf. Manoeu. Control Marine Craft **33**(21), 1–16 (2000)
24. American Bureau of Shipping: ABS Rules For Building and Classing Mobile Offshore Drilling Units. American Bureau of Shipping, New York (2014)
25. Fossen, T.I.: Handbook of Marine Craft Hydrodynamics and Motion Control. John Wiley & Sons, Ltd., Chichester (2011)
26. Abdulrahman, M.: Reyad: environmental load effects at offhore Jack-up unit. Int. J. Sci. Eng. Res. **9**(10), 1349–1369 (2018)
27. Zhen, W., Zhigao, Z.: Damage detection of offshore platform structures using time domain response Data. In: IEEE/International Conference on Intelligent Computation Technology and Automation, pp. 1079–1084 (2010)
28. Society of Naval Architects and Marine Engineers: SNAME Technical and Research Bulletin 5–5A Site Specific Assessment of Jack-up Units. Society of Naval Ar-chitects and Marine Engineers, New Jersey (2012)
29. Subrata, K.: Chakrabarti: Handbook of Offshore Engineering-Offshore Structure Analysis, 1st edn. Plainfield, Illinois (2005)
30. Dang, X.K., Guan, Z.H., Li, T., Zhang, D.X.: Joint Smith predictor and neural network estimation scheme for compensating randomly varying time-delay in networked control system. In: Proceedings of the 24th Chinese Control and Decision Conference, Tai Yuan, China, pp. 512–517 (2012)
31. Salih, A.M., Humod, A.Th., Hasan, F.A.: Optimum design for PID-ANN controller for automatic voltage regulator of synchronous generator. In: Proceedings of 4th Scientific International Conference Najaf (SICN), Al-Najef, Iraq, pp. 74–79 (2016)
32. Sharma, R., Gopal, M.: A Markov game-adaptive fuzzy controller for robot manipulators. IEEE Trans. Fuzzy Syst. **16**(1), 171–186 (2008)

# Stabilization Controller Design for Differential Mobile Robot Using Lyapunov Function and Extended Kalman Filter

Tran Thuan Hoang[1,2], Vo Chi Thanh[1], Nguyen Ngo Anh Quan[1],
and Tran Le Thang Dong[1,2(✉)]

[1] Center of Electrical Engineering, Duy Tan University, Danang 550000, Vietnam
nguyennanhquan@dtu.edu.vn, tranthangdong@duytan.edu.vn
[2] Faculty of Electrical-Electronic Engineering, Duy Tan University, Danang 550000, Vietnam

**Abstract.** This paper presents the design of a stability controller according to Lyapunov criteria in the presence of noises for a differential two-wheeled mobile robot built in the laboratory. Two Lyapunov functions are constructed that allow a hybrid feedback to control law to execute the robot movements to the desired destination from an arbitrary initial position. The asymptotical stability and robustness of the closed loop system are assured. Then, the position estimates of the Kalman filter are better than usual and designed to be inserted into the feedback control loop to improve the motion control quality. The asymptotic stability of the closed-loop control system has been proven theoretically. A variety of simulations and experiments have been carried out to prove the effectiveness and applicability of the proposed method.

**Keywords:** Kalman filter · Lyapunov function · Mobile robot control · Stabilization of mobile robot

## 1 Introduction

Researching the navigation problem for mobile robots has been interested by many authors for many years [1–11]. Success in navigation requires success at the four building blocks of navigation: perception, the robot must interpret its sensors to extract meaningful data; localization, the robot must determine its position in the environment; cognition, the robot must decide how to act to achieve its goals; and motion control, the robot must modulate its motor outputs to achieve the desired trajectory [12]. For the task of controlling the robot to track a predetermined trajectory, a simple method often used is to divide the trajectory into a set of points. Then that task will become a stable point-to-point motion control: The robot will go from the starting point to the neighboring point (sub-destination) and continue until the destination is reached. A differential mobile robot with a kinematic model as described in [13–16] is a non-holonomic system, so it will be difficult to design a static state-feedback motion control law smoothly. In addition, that control law will be invariant with time because Brockett's condition is not

© ICST Institute for Computer Sciences, Social Informatics and Telecommunications Engineering 2022
Published by Springer Nature Switzerland AG 2022. All Rights Reserved
N.-S. Vo et al. (Eds.): INISCOM 2022, LNICST 444, pp. 201–213, 2022.
https://doi.org/10.1007/978-3-031-08878-0_14

satisfied [17]. Some studies have tackled this problem by using the method of converting the kinematic model to a polar coordinate system associated with navigation variables. Then, the smooth feedback control laws are introduced to control the robot to move stably from any position (coordinates and direction of the robot) to the destination position as the authors Aicardi [18], Secchi [19], ... However, those studies solely consider the ideal case when the robot model is not affected by noise, while the reality shows that the control law will no longer be stable asymptotically to the destination when there is noise, especially for input is the angular velocity. The authors [20] mentioned this problem when solving the problem of noise for a three-wheeled autonomous vehicle. Accordingly, to address the differential two-wheeled mobile robot model built with noise conditions, we also divide the robot operation configuration sets (coordinates and directions) into 2 domains: the configuration near the destination location $(x_d, y_d, \theta_d)$ is called the local configuration set and the configuration far from the destination location is called the global configuration set [21, 22]. These results are far from perfect, especially when the robot converges to the finish line. Therefore, a new Control Law corresponding to those two configurations is proposed. Then, a Kalman filter with better position estimates is usually designed to feed into the simulated and tested feedback control loop. The result allows improving the quality of motion control.

## 2  Problem Description

Figure 1 depicts the robot's posture when it is controlled to move through 2 reference positions in the OXY global coordinate system. Attached to the robot are the $OX_RY_R$ local coordinate systems. The robot starts from an arbitrary position $O_1$, where it has coordinates $(x, y)$ and direction angle $\theta$. The robot to be driven goes to the destination position $O_2$ where it needs to have the coordinates $(x_d, y_d)$ and the direction angle $\theta_d$ known.

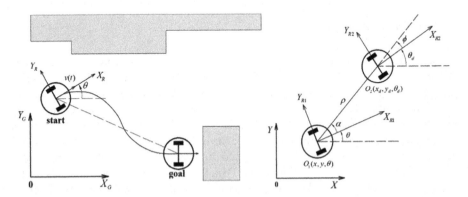

**Fig. 1.** Posture and parameters of the robot.

The kinematics of the robot is described as follows:

$$\dot{x} = v\cos\theta; \ \dot{y} = v\sin\theta; \ \theta = \omega \tag{1}$$

where $\omega$ and $v$ are the control inputs which are respectively the rotational angular and the translational speed of the robot. Let $O_1$ and $O_2$ be the equilibrium points of the system of Eq. (1).

The control law according to the Lyapunov stability criterion obtained when converting the configuration variables $(x, y, \theta)$ into navigation variables $(\rho, \varphi, \alpha)$. With $\rho$ be the distance between $O_1$ and $O_2$, $\phi$ be the angular made by the vector connecting $O_1$ and $O_2$ and the vector connection $O_2$ and $X_{R2}$, $\alpha = (\phi + \theta_d) - \theta$ be the angular made by the vector connection $O_1$ and $O_2$ and the vector connection $O_1$ and $X_{R1}$.

If $\alpha$ is in the range $\alpha \in (-\pi/2, \pi/2)$:

$$
\begin{aligned}
\rho &= \sqrt{(x_d - x)^2 + (y_d - y)^2} \\
\phi &= \text{atan2}(y_d - y, x_d - x) - \theta_d \\
\alpha &= \text{atan2}(y_d - y, x_d - x) - \theta
\end{aligned}
\tag{2}
$$

Then the kinematic model of the robot is described through the navigation variables:

$$
\begin{aligned}
\dot{\rho} &= -v \cos \alpha \\
\dot{\phi} &= v \sin \alpha / \rho \\
\dot{\alpha} &= -\omega + v \sin \alpha / \rho
\end{aligned}
\tag{3}
$$

In case $\alpha$ is in the remaining interval $\alpha \in (-\pi, -\pi/2] \cup (\pi/2, \pi]$, it's possible to redefine the robot's forward direction by setting $v = -v$.

When there's noise, let $\varepsilon_x, \varepsilon_y, \varepsilon_\theta$ be measured noises affecting the nominal values of coordinates $(x, y)$ and direction angle $\theta$. The measured position estimates feedback to the controller will be: $\hat{x} = x + \varepsilon_x, \hat{y} = y + \varepsilon_y$ and $\hat{\theta} = \theta + \varepsilon_\theta$. Where $|\varepsilon_x| \leq \varepsilon_x^{\max}$, $|\varepsilon_y| \leq \varepsilon_y^{\max}$ and $|\varepsilon_\theta| \leq \varepsilon_\theta^{\max}$ are bounded and $\varepsilon_x^{\max}, \varepsilon_y^{\max}, \varepsilon_\theta^{\max}$ are the upper bounds of $\varepsilon_x, \varepsilon_y, \varepsilon_\theta$.

The navigation variables $\rho, \phi, \alpha$ are also affected by the state feedback noises $\varepsilon_\rho, \varepsilon_\phi, \varepsilon_\alpha$ as follows:

$$
\begin{aligned}
\varepsilon_\rho &= \sqrt{(x_d - \hat{x})^2 + (y_d - \hat{y})^2} - \sqrt{(x_d - x)^2 + (y_d - y)^2} \\
\varepsilon_\phi &= \text{atan2}(x_d - \hat{x})^2 + (y_d - \hat{y})^2 - \text{atan2}(x_d - x)^2 + (y_d - y)^2 \\
\varepsilon_\alpha &= \varepsilon_\phi - \varepsilon_\theta
\end{aligned}
\tag{4}
$$

where $|\varepsilon_\rho| \leq \varepsilon_\rho^{\max}, |\varepsilon_\phi| \leq \varepsilon_\phi^{\max}, |\varepsilon_\alpha| \leq \varepsilon_\alpha^{\max}$ are bounded and $\varepsilon_\rho^{\max}, \varepsilon_\phi^{\max}, \varepsilon_\alpha^{\max}$ are the upper bounds of $\varepsilon_\rho, \varepsilon_\phi, \varepsilon_\alpha$.

Similarly, let $|\varepsilon_v| \leq \varepsilon_v^{\max}, |\varepsilon_\omega| \leq \varepsilon_\omega^{\max}$ be the input noises of the control signals $v$ and $\omega$, where are the upper bounds of $\varepsilon_v^{\max}, \varepsilon_\omega^{\max}$,

System of Eqs. (4) when there is input noise, it will become:

$$
\begin{aligned}
\dot{\rho} &= -(v + \varepsilon_v) \cos \alpha \\
\dot{\phi} &= (v + \varepsilon_v) \sin \alpha / \rho \\
\dot{\alpha} &= -(\omega + \varepsilon_\omega) + (v + \varepsilon_v) \sin \alpha / \rho
\end{aligned}
\tag{5}
$$

## 3  Controller Design

Let $\Omega = \{(x, y, \theta) : \rho, \alpha, \phi \in R\}$ be the set of all accessible configurations of the robot in the configuration space. Let $\Omega_L = \{(x, y, \theta) : \rho(x, y) - \alpha(x, y, \phi) < \varepsilon_\theta\}$ be defined as the local configuration set of the robot close to the goal configuration. Let $\Omega_G = \Omega - \Omega_L$ be the global configuration set of the robot distant from the goal configuration.

### 3.1  Stability Control in the Global Configuration $\Omega_G$

Choose a Lyapunov function (positive definite function) built on navigation variables of the form:

$$V = V_{G1} + V_{G2} = \frac{\rho^2}{2} + \frac{\alpha^2 + h\phi^2}{2} > 0 \tag{6}$$

Notice (3), the first derivative of $V$ is:

$$\dot{V} = \dot{V}_{G1} + \dot{V}_{G2} = \rho\dot{\rho} + (\alpha\dot{\alpha} + h\phi\dot{\phi}) = -\rho v \cos\alpha + \alpha\left[-\omega + v\frac{\sin\alpha\,(\alpha + h\phi)}{\alpha}\frac{}{\rho}\right] \tag{7}$$

To satisfy the stability condition according to the Lyapunov criterion, the first derivative of $V$ must be negative. Based on that, the control law for $v$ and $\omega$ is chosen as follows:

$$\begin{aligned} v &= k_v\rho\cos\alpha \\ \omega &= k_\alpha\alpha + k_v\frac{\cos\alpha\sin\alpha}{\alpha}(\alpha + h\phi) \end{aligned} \tag{8}$$

where $k_v > 0, k > 0$ and $k_\alpha > 0$. This control law, provided that the effect of state feedback noise $\varepsilon_\rho$ and $\varepsilon_\alpha$ has the form:

$$\begin{aligned} v &= k_v(\rho + \varepsilon_\rho)\cos(\alpha + \varepsilon_\alpha) \\ \omega &= k_\alpha(\alpha + \varepsilon_\alpha) + k_v\frac{\cos(\alpha + \varepsilon_\alpha)\sin(\alpha + \varepsilon_\alpha)}{(\alpha + \varepsilon_\alpha)}\left[(\alpha + \varepsilon_\alpha) + h(\phi + \varepsilon_\phi)\right] \end{aligned} \tag{9}$$

Substitute $\dot{\rho}$ in (7) into (8), consider $\dot{V}_{G1}$:

$$\begin{aligned} \dot{V}_{G1} &= \rho\dot{\rho} = -\rho(v + \varepsilon_v)\cos\alpha \\ &= -k_v\rho\cos\alpha\cos(\alpha + \varepsilon_\alpha)(\rho + \varepsilon_\rho) - \rho\varepsilon_v\cos\alpha \end{aligned} \tag{10}$$

Consider angles $\alpha$ and $\alpha + \varepsilon_\alpha$ in the range $\alpha, \alpha + \varepsilon_\alpha \in (-\pi/2, \pi/2]$, so the components $\cos\alpha > 0, \cos(\alpha + \varepsilon_\alpha) > 0$. In the global configuration set, there are $\rho > 0$, $\rho > |\varepsilon_\alpha|$ so $\rho + \varepsilon_\alpha > 0$.

Continue to consider $\dot{V}_{G2}$:

$$\dot{V}_{G2} = \alpha\dot{\alpha} + h\phi\dot{\phi} = \alpha[-(\omega + \varepsilon_\omega) + (v + \varepsilon_v)\sin\alpha/\rho] + h\phi(v + \varepsilon_v)\sin\alpha/\rho \tag{11}$$

Let: $A = \alpha[-(\omega + \varepsilon_\omega) + (v + \varepsilon_v)\sin\alpha/\rho]$; $B = h\phi(v + \varepsilon_v)\sin\alpha/\rho$.

Substitute the Control Law (8) when affected by state feedback noise into $A$ and $B$:

$$A = \alpha \left\{ [k_v(\rho + \varepsilon_\rho)\cos(\alpha + \varepsilon_\alpha) + \varepsilon_v] \frac{\sin \alpha}{\rho} - (\omega + \varepsilon_\omega) \right\}$$

$$= -k_\alpha \alpha^2 - k_\alpha \alpha \varepsilon_\alpha - \alpha \varepsilon_\omega + k_v \alpha \cos(\alpha + \varepsilon_\alpha)[\sin \alpha - \sin(\alpha + \varepsilon_\alpha)]$$

$$+ k_v \alpha \varepsilon_\rho \cos(\alpha + \varepsilon_\alpha) \frac{\sin \alpha}{\rho} + \alpha \varepsilon_v \frac{\sin \alpha}{\rho} - k_v h\alpha \phi \frac{\sin(\alpha + \varepsilon_\alpha)}{(\alpha + \varepsilon_\alpha)} \cos(\alpha + \varepsilon_\alpha) \tag{12}$$

$$- k_v h\alpha \varepsilon_\phi \frac{\sin(\alpha + \varepsilon_\alpha)}{(\alpha + \varepsilon_\alpha)} \cos(\alpha + \varepsilon_\alpha)$$

$$B = h\phi(v + \varepsilon_v) \frac{\sin \alpha}{\rho} = h\phi \frac{\sin \alpha}{\rho} [k_v(\rho + \varepsilon_\rho)\cos(\alpha + \varepsilon_\alpha) + \varepsilon_v]$$

$$= k_v h\phi \frac{\sin \alpha}{\rho}(\rho + \varepsilon_\rho)\cos(\alpha + \varepsilon_\alpha) + h\phi \varepsilon_v \frac{\sin \alpha}{\rho} \tag{13}$$

$$= k_v h\phi \sin \alpha \cos(\alpha + \varepsilon_\alpha) + k_v h\phi \varepsilon_\rho \frac{\sin \alpha}{\rho}\cos(\alpha + \varepsilon_\alpha) + h\phi \varepsilon_v \frac{\sin \alpha}{\rho}$$

$$\dot{V}_{G2} = A + B = -k_\alpha \alpha^2 - k_\alpha \varepsilon_\alpha \alpha - \alpha \varepsilon_\omega + k_v \alpha \cos(\alpha + \varepsilon_\alpha)[\sin \alpha - \sin(\alpha + \varepsilon_\alpha)]$$

$$+ k_v h\phi \cos(\alpha + \varepsilon_\alpha) \left[ \sin \alpha - \frac{\alpha}{(\alpha + \varepsilon_\alpha)}\sin(\alpha + \varepsilon_\alpha) \right] + \varepsilon_v \frac{\sin \alpha}{\rho}(h\phi + \alpha)$$

$$+ k_v \varepsilon_\rho (\frac{\alpha}{\rho} + \frac{h\phi}{\rho})\sin \alpha \cos(\alpha + \varepsilon_\alpha) - k_v h\alpha \varepsilon_\phi \frac{\sin(\alpha + \varepsilon_\alpha)}{(\alpha + \varepsilon_\alpha)}\cos(\alpha + \varepsilon_\alpha)$$

$$\tag{14}$$

Since a is very small, the two expressions in square brackets can be approximated when $\cos \varepsilon_\alpha \approx 1$ and $\sin \varepsilon_\alpha \approx \varepsilon_\alpha$.

$$[\sin \alpha - \sin(\alpha + \varepsilon_\alpha)] \approx -\varepsilon_\alpha \cos \alpha$$

$$[\sin \alpha - \alpha \sin(\alpha + \varepsilon_\alpha)/(\alpha + \varepsilon_\alpha)] \approx \varepsilon_\alpha(\sin \alpha - \alpha \cos \alpha(\alpha + \varepsilon_\alpha))$$

Therefore (14) can be rewritten as:

$$\dot{V}_{G2} = A + B \approx -k_\alpha \alpha^2 - k_\alpha \varepsilon_\alpha \alpha - \alpha \varepsilon_\omega - k_v \alpha \varepsilon_\alpha \cos(\alpha + \varepsilon_\alpha)\cos \alpha$$

$$+ k_v h\phi \varepsilon_\alpha \cos(\alpha + \varepsilon_\alpha) \left( \frac{\sin \alpha - \alpha \cos \alpha}{\alpha + \varepsilon_\alpha} \right) + \varepsilon_v \frac{\sin \alpha}{\rho}(h\phi + \alpha) \tag{15}$$

$$+ k_v \varepsilon_\rho \left( \frac{\alpha}{\rho} + \frac{h\phi}{\rho} \right)\sin \alpha \cos(\alpha + \varepsilon_\alpha) - k_v h\alpha \varepsilon_\phi \frac{\sin(\alpha + \varepsilon_\alpha)}{(\alpha + \varepsilon_\alpha)}\cos(\alpha + \varepsilon_\alpha)$$

From (15) we can choose a coefficient $k_\alpha$ large enough to ignore the noise $\varepsilon_\alpha, \varepsilon_v, \varepsilon_\rho$ and $\varepsilon_\phi$ (rear components) so that $\dot{V}_{G2} < 0$ in the global configuration $\Omega_G$. Hence $V_{G2}$ will converge to a non-negative finite limit and $\alpha$ will approach a small value.

So, with the control law chosen at (8), then $\dot{V}_G = \dot{V}_{G1} + \dot{V}_{G2} \leq 0$ is a negative semi-deterministic function and the Lyapunov function $V_G$ is a positive function. The system will start in the global configuration and proceed in the local configuration $\Omega_L$.

The system Eq. (5) with the control law (7) with noise becomes:

$$\dot{\rho} = -\left[k_v(\rho + \varepsilon_\rho)\cos\alpha\cos(\alpha + \varepsilon_\alpha) + \varepsilon_v\cos\alpha\right]$$
$$\dot{\phi} = \left[k_v(\rho + \varepsilon_\rho)\cos(\alpha + \varepsilon_\alpha) + \varepsilon_v\right]\sin\alpha/\rho$$
$$\dot{\alpha} = \left[k_v(\rho + \varepsilon_\rho)\cos(\alpha + \varepsilon_\alpha) + \varepsilon_v\right]\sin\alpha/\rho$$
$$- \left\{ k_\alpha(\alpha + \varepsilon_\alpha) + k_v\frac{\sin(\alpha + \varepsilon_\alpha)}{(\alpha + \varepsilon_\alpha)}\cos(\alpha + \varepsilon_\alpha)\left[(\alpha + \varepsilon_\alpha) + h(\phi + \varepsilon_\phi)\right] + \varepsilon_\omega \right\}$$
$$(16)$$

## 3.2  Stable Control in Local Configuration $\Omega_L$

The control law (8) is asymptotically stable in the global configuration $\Omega_G$. It however is not stable in the local configuration $\Omega_L$. This can be proven as follows.

Assume that the navigation variable $\rho$ goes to small parameters $\varepsilon_P$ ($\varepsilon_P$ same as $\rho$, always positive). The variables $(\alpha, \phi)$ go to their small disturbances $(\varepsilon_\alpha, \varepsilon_\phi)$. The system kinematics (15) becomes:

$$\dot{\rho} = -\left[k_v(\varepsilon_P + \varepsilon_\rho) + \varepsilon_v\right] \tag{17}$$

$$\dot{\phi} = k_v\varepsilon_\alpha\left(1 + \varepsilon_\rho/\varepsilon_P\right) \tag{18}$$

$$\dot{\alpha} = k_v\varepsilon_\alpha\left(1 + \varepsilon_\rho/\varepsilon_P\right) - 2\varepsilon_\alpha(k_\alpha + k_v) - 2k_vh\varepsilon_\phi - \varepsilon_\omega \tag{19}$$

Consider the Lyapunov function and the control law remains the same as in the global configuration $\Omega_G$. Substitute $\dot{\rho}$ in (17) into (10) and consider $\dot{V}_{G1}$:

$$\dot{V}_{G1} = \rho\dot{\rho} = k_v(-\varepsilon_P^2 - \varepsilon_P\varepsilon_\rho) - \varepsilon_P\varepsilon_v \tag{20}$$

Choose $\varepsilon_P > |\varepsilon_\rho| + (|\varepsilon_v|/k_v)$ so that $\dot{V}_{G1}$ is at the boundary between the global configuration and local configuration sets. When $\rho$ approaches a small value of $\varepsilon_P$, the system begins to approach the boundary region and local region.

In (13), with $k_v > 0$ as preselected and $V_{G1} = \rho^2/2$ is bounded so $\rho$ is also bound. Therefore, the control law of $v$ still holds valid in the local configuration.

Let:

$$\dot{V}_{G2} = \alpha\dot{\alpha} + h\phi\dot{\phi} = \dot{V}_{G2'} + \dot{V}_{G2''} \tag{21}$$

Consider:

$$\dot{V}_{G2''} = h\phi\dot{\phi} = hk_v\varepsilon_\phi\varepsilon_\alpha\left(1 + \varepsilon_\rho/\varepsilon_P\right) \tag{22}$$

In (18) there is a finite-escape-time (there exists a finite time $t_1$ at which $\phi(t_1) = \infty$ when $\varepsilon_\alpha\left(1 + |\varepsilon_\rho|/\varepsilon_P\right) > 0$, and (19) has the same condition as (18) because $\alpha$ is proportional to $\phi$.

When $\varepsilon_\alpha, \varepsilon_\phi > 0$ then $\dot{V}_{G2''} > 0$, $\phi$ cannot be directed to zero, which means the system will be *unstable*. Therefore, we need to redesign the controller so that the closed-loop system works stably and sustainably. With $\alpha = (\phi + \theta_d) - \theta$, let $\theta_e = \theta - \theta_d$, or from (2) has $\theta_e = \phi - \alpha$.

The Lyapunov function in the local configuration is otherwise selected as follows:

$$V_L = V_{L1} + V_{L2} = \frac{\rho^2}{2} + \frac{(\phi - \alpha)^2}{2} = \frac{\rho^2}{2} + \frac{\theta_e^2}{2} > 0 \qquad (23)$$

The control law $\omega$ in the local configuration of $\Omega_L$ is re-selected as follows:

$$\begin{aligned} v &= k_v(\rho + \varepsilon_\rho)\cos(\alpha + \varepsilon_\alpha) \\ \omega &= -k_\theta \theta_e \end{aligned} \qquad (24)$$

As selected in (20) (the control law $v$ is still valid for the local configuration), $\dot{V}_{L1} = \dot{V}_{G1} \leq 0$ and $\alpha, \rho, \phi$ are bounded. Consider $\dot{V}_{L2}$:

$$\dot{V}_{L2} = \theta_e \dot{\theta}_e = \theta_e(\omega + \varepsilon_\omega) = \theta_e(-k_\theta \theta_e + \varepsilon_\omega) = -k_\theta \theta_e^2 + \theta_e \varepsilon_\omega \qquad (25)$$

From (25) choose $k_\theta$ large enough for $\dot{V}_{L2} \leq 0$ or $\dot{V}_L = \dot{V}_{L1} + \dot{V}_{L2} \leq 0$. In the global configuration with control law (8), the system will star from the global configuration and move into the local configuration. When the value of $\rho$ approaches a small value of $\varepsilon_P$, the system starts to switch to a local configuration with control laws (24). Since $\dot{V}_L \leq 0$ are bounded at the boundary between the global configuration $\Omega_G$ and local configuration $\Omega_L$ sets, so $\Omega_L = \{x \in R^n | V_L \leq C\}$ are bounded and the limit of $V_L$ is $C > 0$ when $t \to \infty$. Then set $\dot{V}_{L2} \leq 0$ with $\Omega_L = \{x \in R^n | V(x) \leq C\}$ for every $x \in \Omega_L$ are positive invariant because every solution starting from $\Omega_L$ will stay in $\Omega_L$ for every $t \geq 0$. In other words, each trajectory starting in $\Omega_L$ must stay in $\Omega_L$ and converge asymptotically to the equilibrium point $O_2$ when $t \to \infty$. The local configuration $\Omega_L$ is also called region of attraction or region of asymptotic stability [23]. Then $\rho \to 0; \theta_e \to 0; x \to x_d; y \to y_d; \theta \to \theta_d$.

### 3.3  Using Kalman Filter for Feedback Control Loop

In [13–16], the author and research team used sensor fusion using Kalman filter to accurately position differential mobile robots. The results reveal that the estimated value of the position received from the Extended Kalman filter is closer to the nominal value of the robot than usual. This is like minimizing the effect of measurement noise.

In the motion control phase, the input noise $(\varepsilon_v, \varepsilon_\omega)$ and the measurement noise $(\varepsilon_x, \varepsilon_y, \varepsilon_\theta)$ significantly affect the performance of the control model such as trajectory tracking and converge to the destination domain. The author and colleagues tested the design of a closed feedback control loop in the program as shown in Fig. 2 in which a Kalman filter was introduced into the feedback line to improve the reliability of the robot position estimation. Since the state estimates at the output with the Extended Kalman filter are more reliable than those without, the deviations from the comparator output from the destination value feed to the stable controller input will have higher reliability. The result has better control quality.

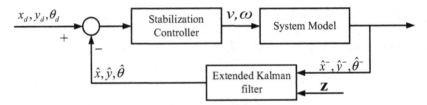

**Fig. 2.** Feedback control loop with Kalman filter.

Simulation and experimental results indicate that using the Extended Kalman filter in the feedback loop of the motion control system allows increasing the accuracy of the feedback value, or reducing the error and controlling the limit of the feedback noise compared to the normal case.

## 4 Simulation and Experiment

The simulation is performed in MATLAB where the parameters are extracted from the real robot built in the laboratory. The control law satisfying the Lyapunov stability criterion in both configuration sets $\Omega_G$ and $\Omega_L$ has been applied.

The maximum speed of the robot is $1.3\,\text{m/s}$, the sampling time of the system is $\Delta t = 100\,\text{ms}$. The system error when reaching the destination is $\rho = 10^{-2}\,\text{m}$.

The parameter values are selected as follows: $k_v = 1$; $k_\alpha = 2$; $k_\theta = 1$ and $h = 5$. The measured noise values are selected based on the largest deviation in the estimate of the EKF word for the real robot which are $\varepsilon_x^{\max} = 0.1\,\text{m}$, $\varepsilon_y^{\max} = 0.1\,\text{m}$ and $\varepsilon_\theta^{\max} = 0.0036\,\text{m}$. The system noise is based on the experimental investigation with real robot controlling motor by PID algorithm with the error of angular velocity $\omega_L$ and $\omega_R$ are $\pm 5\%$. So, for $v_{\max} = 1.3\,\text{m/s}$ then $\varepsilon_y^{\max} = 0.065$ and $\varepsilon_x^{\max} = 0.2167$. The $\varepsilon_P$ value to switch to the local configuration is selected so that the condition $\varepsilon_P \geq |\varepsilon_\rho| + (|\varepsilon_v|/k_v)$ is satisfied.

In simulation 1 when investigating the stability, we choose a robot whose destination configuration is $(0, 0, 0°)$, starting configuration is $(-2, 3.5, -60°)$. The robot is controlled to move stably from the starting position to the destination position. The results obtained when using only one control law (8) for both configurations are shown in Figs. 3(a), 4(a). Although the path coordinates are stable to the destination after 150 sampling time steps with coordinates $(x, y) = (0.0032\,\text{m}, 0.0013\,\text{m})$, the direction angle $\theta$ still exists non-zero and fluctuates strongly. While the results in Figs. 3(b), 4(b) show the efficiency when separating two configurations using control law (25) for the local configuration, all three variables have stabilized asymptotically to the destination and return to 0 for both $(x, y, \theta) = (0.0086\,\text{m}, 0.0035\,\text{m}, -0.0031\,\text{rad})$.

In simulation 2, the starting position of the robot is $(0, 0, 0°)$ and the three non-zero destination positions are: $(2, 2, 30°)$, $(2, 2, 60°)$ and $(2, 2, 90°)$. Figure 5(a) shows the simulation results where the destination configurations of the robot are converged to coordinates $(2, 2)$ with three different orientation angles. This shows the feasibility of the controller.

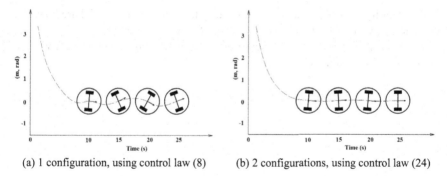

(a) 1 configuration, using control law (8)    (b) 2 configurations, using control law (24)

**Fig. 3.** Stabilization results with the assumption of constant measurement noises and input disturbances.

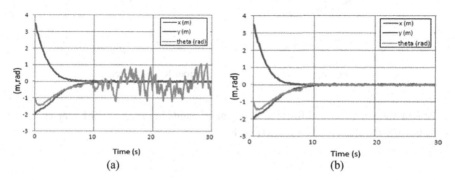

**Fig. 4.** Result response to control laws using 1 configuration (a) and 2 configurations (b).

The navigation experiment was conducted on the differential two-wheeled robot in the laboratory from the starting position to the destination position and gave satisfactory results as shown in Fig. 5(b), almost simulated.

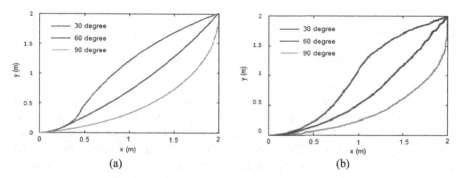

**Fig. 5.** Simulation results (a) and experimental results (b).

The stability control results of the trajectory tracking control model are convergent and the stability in the destination domain is tested in two cases:

When not using Kalman filter: measurement results in Fig. 6(a) for linear velocity $v$ and Fig. 6(b) for angular velocity $\omega$.

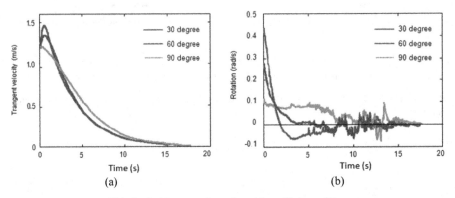

**Fig. 6.** Stable control results without Kalman filter.

When not using Kalman filter: measurement results in Fig. 7(a) for linear velocity $v$ and Fig. 7(b) for angular velocity $\omega$ (Fig. 8).

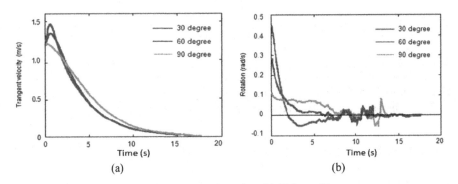

**Fig. 7.** Stable control results with Kalman filter.

The Fig. 9 graph extracted from the Figs. 6(b) and 7(b) graphs is a visual comparison of the variation of the velocity of angle $\omega$ over time with and without Kalman filter when destination position is $(0, 0, 30°)$. It can be seen that, through the Kalman filter with the sensor data fusion (red line), the estimation of the robot state (especially the direction angle) will be better, so the velocity of angle $\omega$ of the controlled robot near the destination neighborhood is stabler than the case without Kalman filter (blue line).

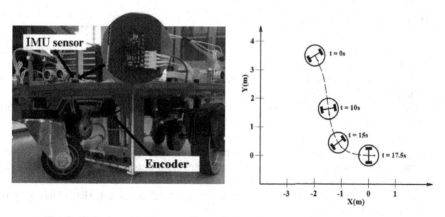

**Fig. 8.** Robot used in the experiment & Experiment result: *X-Y* coordinates.

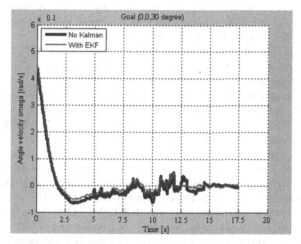

**Fig. 9.** The angular velocity $\omega$ stably asymptote to the destination without the EKF (blue line) and with the EKF (red line) (Color figure online).

## 5  Conclusion

This paper presents studies on the implementation of the tracking stability control process by using the positioning values by merging the sensor's data with the EKF for motion control. As a result, the combination of using stable motion control laws in 2 sets of configurations according to Lyapunov standards with EKF allows to increase the accuracy and stability of the motion trajectory. Although the Lyapunov method may require a longer distance, in return, a continuous trajectory will be obtained, satisfying both the angle and the direction of the robot at the destination.

# References

1. Ngo, Q.H., Hong, K.-S., Jung, I.H.: Adaptive control of an axially moving system. J. Mech. Sci. Technol. **23**, 3071–3078 (2009)
2. Michalek, M., Kozlowski, K.: Vector-field orientation feedback control method for a differentially driven vehicle. IEEE Trans. Contr. Syst. Technol. **18**(1), 45–65 (2010)
3. Liang, Z., Wang, C.: Robust exponential stabilization of nonholonomic wheeled mobile robots with unknown visual parameters. J. Control Theory. **9**(2), 295–301 (2011)
4. Trung, T.D., Vinh, N.Q., Thuan, T.D., Hung, N.Q.: Building an algorithm to determine the navigation parameters for moving vehicles on the basis of combining angular speed gyroscope with magnetometer, speedometer and accelerometer. J. Military Sci. Technol. Res. **09**, 13–27 (2013)
5. Fei, L.: Two-wheel Driven AGV Path Planning and Motion Control. Hebei University of Science and Technology (2016)
6. Viet, D.T.: Autonomous vehicles applied with the algorithm of motion trajectory recognition and motion trajectory prediction. In: Proceedings of The 5th National Conference on Mechanical Science and Technology (VCME), pp. 110–119, Hanoi, Vietnam (2018)
7. Son, T.A., et al.: Research and manufacture of automated guided vehicle for the service ofstorehouse. Sci. Technol. Dev. J. Eng. Technol. **1**(1), 5–12 (2018)
8. Kim, S., Jin, H., Seo, M., Har, D.: Optimal path planning of automated guided vehicle using Dijkstra algorithm under dynamic conditions. In: 7th International Conference on Robot Intelligence Technology and Applications (RiTA). IEEE (2019)
9. Hasan, H.S., Abidin, M.S.Z., Mahmud, M.S.A., Mohd, M.F.M.S.: Automated guided vehicle routing: static, dynamic and free range. J. Int. Eng. Adv. Technol. **8**(5C), 1–7 (2019)
10. Ryck, D.M., Mark., V., Debrouwere, F.: Automated guided vehicle systems, state-of-the-art control algorithms and techniques. J. Manuf. Syst. **54**, 152–173 (2020)
11. Moshayedi, A.J., Roy, A.S., Liao, L.: PID tuning method on AGV (automated guided vehicle) industrial robot. J. Simul. Anal. Novel Technol. Mech. Eng. **12**(4), 53–66 (2020)
12. Roland, S., Nourbakhsh Illah, R.: Introduction to Autonomous Mobile Robots, pp. 291–298. The MIT Press Cambridge, Massachusetts London, England (2004)
13. Hoang, T.T., Hiep, D.T., Duong, P.M., Van, N.T.T., Viet, D.A., Vinh, T.Q.: Development of an EKF-based localization algorithm using compass sensor and LRF. In: Proceeding of IEEE 12th International Conference on Control, Automation, Robotics and Vision, ICARCV, pp. 341–346 (2013)
14. Hoang, T.T., Hiep, D.T., Duong, P.M., Van, N.T.T., Viet, D.A., Vinh, T.Q.: Multi-sensor perceptual system for mobile robot and sensor fusion - based localization. In: IEEE 1st International Conference on Control, Automation and Information Sciences (ICCAIS-2012), pp. 259–264 (2012)
15. Hoang, T.T., Hiep, D.T., Duong, P.M., Van, N.T.T., Duong, B.G., Vinh, T.Q.: Proposal of algorithms for navigation and obstacles avoidance of autonomous mobile robot. In: Proceedings of IEEE 8th Conference on Industrial Electronics and Applications (ICIEA-2013), pp. 1308–1313 (2013)
16. Thanh, V.C., Dong, T.L.T., Quan, N.N.A., Hoang, T.T.: Autonomous vehicle navigation using inertial sensors and virtual path. In: National Conference "High- Tech Application in Practice in 2021" (2021)
17. Brockett, R.W.: Asymptotic stability and feedback stabilization, In: Differential Geometric Control Theory, Boston, Birkhauser, pp. 181–191 (1983)
18. Aicardi, M., Casalino, G., Bicchi, A., Balestrino, A.: Closed loop steering of unicycle-like vehicles via Lyapunov techniques. IEEE Robot. Autom. Mag. **2**(1), 27–35 (1995)

19. Secchi, H., Carelli, R., Mut, V.: An experience on stable control of mobile robots. J. Latin Am. Appl. Res. **33**(4), 379–385 (2003)
20. Widyotriatmo, A., Keum-Shik, H., Prayudhi Lafin, H.: Robust stabilization of a wheeled vehicle: hybrid feedback control design and experimental validation. J. Mech. Sci. Technol. **24**(2), 513–520 (2010)
21. Hoang, T.T., Duong, P.M., Tinh, N.V., Vinh, T.Q.: A path following algorithm for wheeled mobile robot using extended Kalman Filter. In: IEICE Proceedings of the 3rd International Conference on Integrated Circuit Design, pp. 179–183 (2012)
22. Tran, T.H., Phung, M.D., Van Nguyen, T.T., Tran, Q.V.: Stabilization control of the differential mobile robot using Lyapunov function and extended Kalaman Filter. J. Sci. Technol. **50**(4), 441–452 (2012)
23. Khalil, H.K.: Chapter 3-Lyapunov Stability. Nonlinear System, Prentice Hall. Inc, New Jersey, p. 114 (1996)

# Red-Light Running Violation Detection of Vehicles in Video Using Deep Learning Methods

Nam Nguyen Van[1,2(✉)], Hanh Le Thi[1], Minh Phan Nhat[3],
and Long Lai Ngoc Thang[4]

[1] Department of Data Governance, Viettel Group, 7 Alley, TonThatThuyet Street,
CauGiay, Hanoi, Vietnam
{namnv78,hanhlt87}@viettel.com.vn
[2] Thuyloi University, 175 Tayson, DongDa, Hanoi, Vietnam
nvnam@tlu.edu.vn
[3] Fontbonne University, 6800 Wydown Blvd., St. Louis, MO 63105, USA
phanm@fontbonne.edu
[4] Hanoi University of Science and Technology, 1 DaiCoViet, HaiBaTrung,
Hanoi, Vietnam
long.lnt183581@sis.hust.edu.vn

**Abstract.** Recently, Traffic Monitoring Systems (TMS) based on camera are widespread used in many large cities thanks to advances in artificial intelligence especially in deep learning and computer vision. Detection of traffic violation of vehicles is a critical problem for law enforcement in such TMS due to complicated trajectories of different vehicle types in road. Existing methods based on computer vision techniques for detecting, tracking vehicles and then applying violation rules on the perceived path of every vehicles. In this paper, we present a novel approach which is based on the flexible LSTM recurrent neural networks in addition to the traditional fixed rules to detect red-light running violation of vehicles. We also present our improvements on the existing DeepSort tracking algorithm for faster and more accurate ID matching. We evaluate our deep LSTM with attention mechanism on a dataset (Dataset and code are available here: https://github.com/namnv78/RunningRedlight) of 108 traffic videos captured from three road intersections in Vietnam including 628 red-light running violated vehicles. Our method achieved a precision, recall and F1-score of more than 99% which is 3% higher than the traditional rule-based method.

**Keywords:** Traffic violation detection · Vehicle detection and tracking · Recurrent neural networks

## 1 Introduction

Robust detection and identification of law-violating vehicles from monitoring camera in cross-roads are critical for ensuring road safety and enforcing the laws.

© ICST Institute for Computer Sciences, Social Informatics and Telecommunications Engineering 2022
Published by Springer Nature Switzerland AG 2022. All Rights Reserved
N.-S. Vo et al. (Eds.): INISCOM 2022, LNICST 444, pp. 214–227, 2022.
https://doi.org/10.1007/978-3-031-08878-0_15

The task is highly challenging under a full range of traffic, lighting and weather conditions. Solving this problem necessitates solving and integrating solutions of multiple difficult sub-tasks, including (a) detection, embedding and tracking of vehicles, and (b) automatic violation detection. Although effective techniques for sub-tasks exist, there is a large gap on building an integrated solution that works in real time and filling this gap demands novel adaptation and systematic thinking.

We based our method on the efficient YOLOv4 [2] and the light-weight Select-SLS [8] for vehicle detection and embedding. Once the vehicles are detected and embedded, tracking can be carried out using several methods such as DeepSORT [16], JDE [15] and DeepMOT [17]. Typically these methods work by extracting features from bounding boxes of the vehicles and associating them with the existing trajectories. This strategy works well for a small number of vehicles, but the computation cost quickly grows prohibitive in crowded roads and with tracking duration.

Our main contributions are as follows. We considerably reduce the computation burden as well as ID missing ratio compared to the original DeepSort tracking algorithm by matching the new detection and tracks by group, involving and approximating only the Mahalanobis distance of the centroid coordinates but not the size of the bounding boxes. We then, proposed Deep LSTM and Dense LSTM to detect running red-light violations of the vehicles from the their trajectories. We also found that the Deep LSTM with attention mechanism produces the best accuracy in our dataset including 108 traffic videos in Vietnam. This is because the model can learn and keep the most important weights corresponding to the essential evidences for the violations.

The rest of the paper is as follows. Section 2 reviews related works. Section 3 describes our tracking algorithm named WAYS. Section 4 briefly summarize the rule-based method for violation detection. Section 5 presents in detail our recurrent-based methods. In Sect. 6, we demonstrate our experimental results on real dataset. Finally, the last section concludes our works.

## 2   Related Works

Here we briefly review recent methods that solve the three main sub-tasks of identification of law violation vehicles: vehicles detection, tracking and traffic law violation recognition. Although they differ in specific architectures, they are all trained deep neural networks.

*Vehicles Detection:* There is a rich set of powerful deep learning techniques for detecting objects in traffic scene like cars, bikes and drivers. One of the most used methods is Faster-RCNN [11] which consists of two two-stages. The first stage employs a Regional Proposal Network (RPN) to regress the rectangular bounding box of the objects. The second stage is to classify objects in the these bounding box using a convolutional neural network (CNN). This two-stage strategy is accurate but at the cost of running time due to a high number of proposal regions. Faster-RCNN can only predict at 5 fps using GPU while achieving an accuracy of 73.4% and 70.4% mAP on PASCAL VOC 2007 and 2012, respectively with 300 proposals per image.

One-shot techniques avoid the cost by regressing the bounding boxes and predicting objects at the same time, e.g., those proposed in SSD [7] and YOLO [10]. Here input image is divided into a grid of cells, each of which is mapped to a point of the feature map resulting from the image via a multi-channel CNN such as Resnet [3] or VGGNet [12]. Several anchor boxes are proposed to regress a bounding box as well as to predict the probabilities of objects. With fewer number of proposals, one-shot models are much faster. Over the years, the accuracy of one-shot methods has improved. The latest version of YOLO [2] utilizes data augmentation and achieves an impressive accuracy of 43.5% AP (65.7% AP50) on MS COCO dataset and a frame rate of 65 fps on GPU Tesla V100.

*Vehicles Tracking:* Tracking moving vehicles boils down to matching features extracted from the recognized object bounding boxes to existing trajectories. At present, there are several powerful online tracking methods including DeepSORT [16], JDE [15] and DeepMOT [17]. However, feature matching using the default Hungarian algorithm is expensive for a large number of objects, which is often the case at busy intersection of the roads.

### Recognition of Traffic Law Violation

Very few works have been proposed to automatically reason the traffic violation of vehicles given that they can be detected and tracked in videos. In [14], the authors proposed a flowchart for identifying the violation of over speed, of running over red light, of crossing the line and of retrograde after detecting the stop lines, the lanes and the traffic lights. They tracked the center of the vehicles and detected rules violations using certain thresholds. For instance, if the red light is on and the y-coordinate of the center is greater than a threshold then the vehicle runs the red light. However, at a high density of traffic, there is a long queue of vehicles waiting at the stop lines with various values of y-coordinate but none breaks the rule. Similarly, their flowchart for detecting other violations is not reasonable. The work in [1] aims to detect the violation of crosswalk at signal, and of no helmet, but this is also very limited without any explanation to cover all possible situations in reality.

Due to the complicated traffic situation in Vietnam with majority of motorbikes, we propose an comprehensive approach for this issue including vehicle detection, embedding, tracking and law violation recognition using deep learning methods.

## 3   Vehicle Tracking Algorithm

We improved the original DeepSORT tracking algorithm to adapt to the city traffic as shown in Fig. 1. Our algorithm firstly detects the vehicles and embeds them. Then, we calculate the Mahalanobis distance as well as the cosine similarity between the newly detected bounding boxes and the ones from the existing tracks. Finally, our group-based matching algorithm divides the bounding boxes

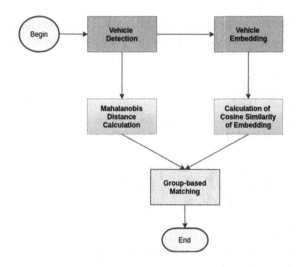

**Fig. 1.** Improved vehicle tracking algorithm

into two groups according their labels. The first group includes cars, trucks and buses and the second includes motorbikes and bicycles. Since the time complexity of Hungarian algorithm is $O(n^3)$ in the worst case for $n$ objects, the matching within each group will considerably decrease the processing time. For example, if there are two equal groups, the complexity will be reduced by 4 times.

The matching algorithm is based on a matrix of costs relating to both the feature and the location of the boxes. The location metric is the squared Mahalanobis distance and calculated as

$$d_{maha}[i,j] = (l_j - m_i)^T C_i^{-1} (l_j - m_i)$$

where $l_j = (x, y, a, h)$ corresponding to coordinates of the center, aspect ratio and height of the newly $j^{th}$ detected box, respectively; $m_i$ and $C_i$ are the mean and covariance of the previous measurements for the $i_{th}$ track estimated by Kalman filter. Since we estimate only the future position of the vehicles, $d_{maha}$ can be approximated as follows [9]:

$$d_{maha}[i,j] \approx \frac{v_1^2}{c_{11}} + \frac{v_2^2}{c_{22}} \tag{1}$$

where $[c_{11}, c_{22}]$ is the diagonal of matrix C and $v = [v_1, v_2] = l_j - m_i$. As shown in [9], this approximation can decrease the processing time without loss of accuracy.

Given the embedding $e_j^*$ of the $j^{th}$ detected bounding box with detected label $L_j^*$ of the group $L$, and the embedding of the $i^{th}$ track at the age of $k$ with the label $L_j^k$, the cosine distance between them is:

$$d_{embed}[i,j] = \begin{cases} 1 - \frac{e_i^k \cdot e_j^*}{\|e_i^k\| \|e_j^*\|}, & \text{if } L_j^k \in L \\ \infty, & \text{if } L_j^k \notin L \end{cases} \tag{2}$$

The new detection is admissible to the track if the following condition holds $b = (d_{maha} \leq t_{maha})\&(d_{embed} \leq t_{embed})$ for pre-defined thresholds $t_{maha}$ and $t_{embed}$.

**Input** :

A group of labels: L ;

Tracking IDs: Track_IDs={1,..,N} ;

Detected Bounding Box IDs including their labels: Box_IDs={1,..,M} ;

Age of tracks A: ={1,..,K} ;

**Output:**

Matched = {(i,j)}, $i \in \overline{1,N}, j \in \overline{1,M}$ and

Unmatched= {j, $(j \in Box\_IDs)\&(j \notin Matched)$ }

| | |
|---|---|
| 1 | $D_{maha}^{L} \leftarrow \{d_{maha}[i,j]\}^{NxM}$ Eq. 1 on L ; |
| 2 | $D_{embed}^{L} \leftarrow \{d_{embed}[i,j]\}^{NxM}$ Eq. 2 on L ; |
| 3 | $Matched \leftarrow \emptyset$ ; |
| 4 | $Box\_IDs\_L \leftarrow \{j \in Box\_IDs | (Label(j) \in L)\}$ ; |
| 5 | $Unmatched \leftarrow Box\_IDs\_L$ ; |
| 6 | **for** $k = 1; k < K; k + +$ **do** |
| 7 | $\quad Track\_IDs\_k\_L \leftarrow \{i \in Track\_IDs | (A(i) = k)\&(Label(i) \in L)\}$ ; |
| 8 | $\quad$ **for** $i \in Track\_IDs\_k\_L$ **do** |
| 9 | $\quad\quad d_{embed}[i,j*] = 0$ ; |
| 10 | $\quad\quad$ **for** $j \in Unmatched$ **do** |
| 11 | $\quad\quad\quad$ **if** $(d_{embed}[i,j*] < D_{embed}^{L}[i,j])$ **then** |
| 12 | $\quad\quad\quad\quad d_{embed}[i,j*] = D_{embed}^{L}[i,j]$ ; |
| 13 | $\quad\quad\quad\quad j^* = j$ ; |
| 14 | $\quad\quad\quad$ **end** |
| 15 | $\quad\quad$ **end** |
| 16 | $\quad\quad$ **if** $(d_{embed}[i,j*] \leq t_{embed})\&(D_{maha}^{L}[i,j*] \leq t_{maha})$ **then** |
| 17 | $\quad\quad\quad Matched \leftarrow Matched \cup \{(i,j*)\}$ ; |
| 18 | $\quad\quad\quad Unmatched \leftarrow Unmatched \setminus \{j*\}$ ; |
| 19 | $\quad\quad$ **end** |
| 20 | $\quad$ **end** |
| 21 | **end** |

**Algorithm 1:** Group-based Tracking Algorithm

The group-based matching algorithm works as follows (see Algorithm 1 for pseudo-code). The input consists of the group of labels $L$, a list of track indices $Track\_IDs$ including their corresponding ages $A$ and labels, a list of detected bounding boxes with their labels. The output of the algorithm will be a set of matching $(i,j)$ between the $i_{th}$ track and the $j_{th}$ detected bounding box and a set of unmatched detected boxes. From line 1 to line 5, we compute the matrices of cosine similarity and of Mahalanobis distance between the detected bounding boxes and the tracks of all ages of which their labels belong to $L$. From line 6 to 21, we iterate over the tracks from the youngest to the oldest ones. For a given track $i$, we find a $j$ among $M$ detected bounding boxes in the same label group so that the cosine distance between $i$ and $j$ is minimal. If the cosine distance and the corresponding Mahalanobis distance between them are small enough then the matching is admissible. Otherwise, it is rejected.

The above tracking algorithm can produces accurate vehicle' states including their identity, label, four coordinates of their bounding box as well as the frame's sequential number during a time interval with the same traffic light (i.e. red, green or yellow). These are then used for red-light running violations of the vehicles.

## 4    Rule-Based Method

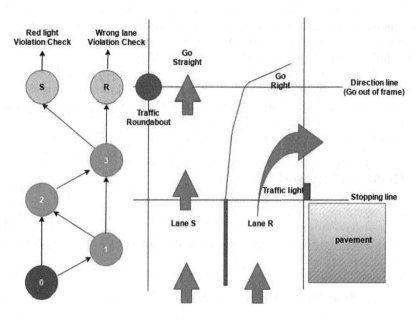

**Fig. 2.** The violation detection's diagram. Six states of vehicles are: 0: initial state, 1: under red line, 2: cross line, 3: over red line, S: straight, R: right. (Color figure online)

Based on a simple diagram, we can apply the rule of red-light running violation at an typical intersection: if a vehicle runs over the stop line while the red-light is on then it is violated. The violation detection's state transition diagram is therefore shown in Fig. 2. At a typical cross-road, a camera is configured to monitor one traffic flow as well as the corresponding red light signals. There is an additional green arrow light permitting vehicles to turn right even if the red light is on. The road thus has two or more lanes: lane S for going straight forward and lane R for turning right. A stopping line and a direction line are drawn to determine the states of the vehicles. Six possible states of a moving vehicle on the intersection are defined as follows:

- 0: the initial state when the vehicle is detected and tracked.
- 1: the state denotes whether the vehicle enters the region under the red line in lane S or R.
- 2: the state indicates whether the vehicle crosses the stopping line in lane S or R.
- 3: the state lets us know that the vehicle has entered the violation region if the red light is on.
- S: the state notifies that the vehicle is going straight, and
- R: this state indicates that the vehicle is turning right.

Based on the final states $(S, R)$ and the passing ones $(0, 1, 2, 3)$, we can decide whether the vehicle violates the traffic laws. If a vehicle is at the final state $S$ while the red light is on then a running a red light violation is detected. In case the vehicle is currently at $R$ and it has been detected passing the lane S then a wrong lane violation is recognized.

The rule-based method can work fast in real time deployment. However, due to the limited and fixed states, violations can be missed in cases of occlusion or truncation. We, therefore, propose recurrent-based methods which use recurrent neural networks to learn the violation from all the perceived time-series states of the vehicles.

## 5    Recurrent-Based Methods

Using recurrent neural networks, our recurrent-based methods can take as input a sequential data of every vehicles' states. The networks are mainly based on the Long-Short-Term-Memory (LSTM) thanks to their ability of learning long sequence.

### 5.1    Long Short Term Memory (LSTM)

LSTM [4] are improved recurrent neural networks (RNN) which can mitigate exploding and vanishing gradients with three interactive gates instead of one as in Fig. 3. These are the forget gate $(f)$, the input modulated gate $(i)$ and the output gate $(o)$. As in original RNN, the $x$ input is a sequence and $h$ and $c$ are the hidden and cell states, respectively. The forget gate decides whether the states are memorized or not aiming to save memory for important information.

In detail, the gates function as the following formula

$$f_t = \sigma(U_f x_t + W_f h_{t-1} + b_f)$$
$$i_t = \sigma(U_i x_t + W_i h_{t-1} + b_i)$$
$$o_t = \sigma(U_o x_t + W_o h_{t-1} + b_o)$$
$$\tilde{c}_t = \tanh(U_c x_t + W_c h_{t-1} + b_c)$$
$$c_t = f_t c_{t-1} + i_t \tilde{c}_{t-1}$$
$$h_t = o_t \tanh(c_t)$$

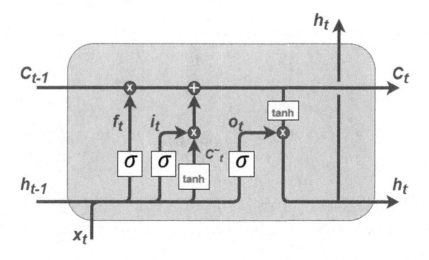

**Fig. 3.** Long short term memory

where $U_f, U_i, U_o, U_c, W_f, W_i, W_o, W_c$ are the weight matrices and tanh is the activation function. In fact, the early and strong LSTM works similarly to the skip connection used in recent ResNet [3] network to avoid vanishing gradient in deep networks. However, the attention mechanism results in wider networks instead of deep ones.

### 5.2 Attention Layer

Recently, the attention layer [13] can keep important weights of the network and therefore considerably reduce the size of the network. As shown in Fig. 4, the inputs of this attention layer are the hidden vectors $h_1, h_2, \ldots, h_n$ and the context $c$ from the previous LSTM layer. The layer returns a vector $z$ summarizing all hidden states that are relevant to context $c$ as in the following equations.

$$m_i = \tanh(W h_i + U c + b)$$
$$p_i = softmax(<v, m_i>)$$
$$z = \sum_i p_i h_i$$

where $W, H$ are the weight matrices corresponding to the input $h_i, c$ and $v$ is the learnable weight of $h_i$.

Inspired from LSTM and the attention mechanism, we build two robust networks for classification of input sequences representing the consecutive states of the vehicles while the red-light is on or off.

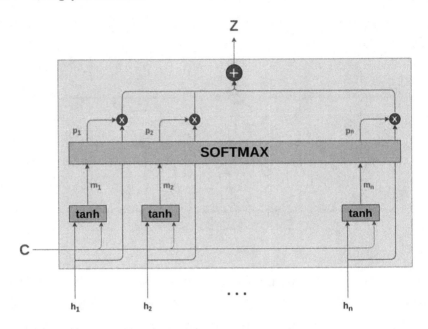

**Fig. 4.** The attention layer

### 5.3  Deep LSTM with Attention Mechanism

The Deep LSTM model (Fig. 5) contains three stacked LSTM layers, followed by an attention layer. The use of LSTM cells instead of RNN cells mitigates some of the exploding and vanishing gradient problems. However, LSTM is still struggling with longer sequences in the training data. Combine the output from LSTM layers with the attention mechanism helps the model focus on the more important information in the sequence, thus creating a more powerful and robust model.

The input for the model has size $(B, N, D)$, where batch size $B = 64$, a fixed sequence length $N = 147$ (consecutive frames), and $D = 4$ represents the upper left/lower right coordinates of the bounding box. The Deep-LSTM module contains three stacked LSTM layers with hidden states $h$ and cell states $c$ of size 100 for each layer. The attention mechanism takes in both cell state $c$ and hidden states $h$ from the last LSTM layer and outputs a 128-dimension vector $z$. $z$ is then passed through a classification layer with two nodes, representing if the vehicle ran red light or not.

### 5.4  Dense LSTM with CNN1D Method

Our Dense LSTM (Fig. 6) consists of 8 LSTM layers which are densely connected. This is inspired from Densenet [5] which establishes skip connections from any layer to all of its later ones to avoid vanishing gradient. Dense LSTM are therefore fast converged and really robust. We also add a CNN1D and max pooling layers

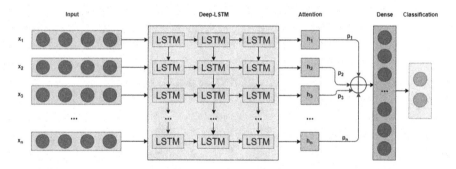

**Fig. 5.** Deep LSTM with attention mechanism model

to Dense LSTM so that the output can aggregate features from all LSTM layers. Usually, CNN (Convolutional Neural Networks) are used for feature extraction of images. However, one-dimensional CNN (CNN1D) [6] are really efficient for sequential input such as time series, text and speech.

The model has inputs similar to the Dense LSTM model in Sect. 5.3. Both hidden state $h$ and cell state $c$ have the size of 256 in each LSTM cell. Concatenating the hidden states $h$ from 8 LSTM layers results in a tensor of size $(B, 2048, N)$. The convolution filter in the CNN1D layer has the filter size of 3, $padding = 1$ and $stride = 1$. The CNN1D layer takes this tensor in as input and produces an output tensor of size $(B, 128, N)$. The max pooling layer then reduces the feature map size to $(B, 128, 1)$, and fully connects with a 2-neuron classification layer.

# 6 Experiments

## 6.1 Dataset

The traffic dataset is captured from three intersections, consists of 105 videos in the training set and 14 videos in the test set. Each video was taken from one of three surveillance cameras in Vietnam, has a resolution of $2560 \times 1980$ px, with a length of approximately 15 s, and a sampling rate of 10 frames per second. Each video also has a list of vehicle ids and their bounding boxes location across the frames resulted from the above vehicle tracking algorithm.

After filtering to get vehicles that go forward in the videos, the valid samples are labeled as violating (True) or not violating (False) the traffic light. The dataset statistics is shown in Table 1. The bounding boxes are normalized, and the bounding box list for each sample is zero-padded to have the same sequence length $N = 147$ before being taken as input for the models.

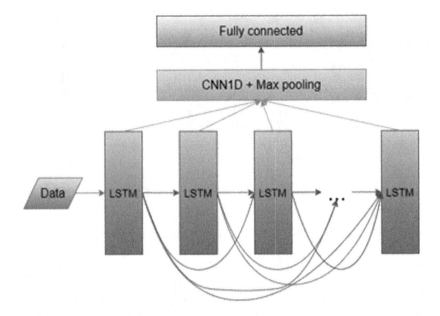

**Fig. 6.** Dense LSTM with CNN1D model

**Table 1.** Traffic dataset statistics

|       | Vehicle counts | Violate | Not violate |
|-------|----------------|---------|-------------|
| Train | 1315           | 628     | 687         |
| Test  | 254            | 44      | 210         |

## 6.2   Evaluation Metrics

The main evaluation metrics for detecting traffic violations is F1-score. F1-score is the harmonic mean of Precision and Recall metrics, where Precision summarizes the exactness of the model and Recall represents the completeness of the predictions.

$$Precision = \frac{TP}{TP + FP}$$
$$Recall = \frac{TP}{TP + FN}$$
$$F1 = 2 * \frac{Precision * Recall}{Precision + Recall}$$

where $TP$ = True Positive, $FP$ = False Positive, $FN$ = False Negative.

## 6.3   Results

After training the Dense LSTM with cross validation of 100 epochs on GPU K8 (8G), we achieved the curves as shown in Fig. 7. The curves show that the model fit very well to the training and validation dataset. We also found similar curves with Deep LSTM. The accuracy of the models is demonstrated in the Table 2. The test precision, recall and f1-score indicate that Dense LSTM with CNN1D exhibits better accuracy than pure LSTM pure LSTM with CNN1D and LSTM with skip connections (Dense LSTM). These are all 98.63%. However, Deep LSTM with Attention Layer expresses the best among all with the precision, recall and f1-score are of 98.85%, 100% and 99.33%, respectively. This is because the model is optimized both in depth and width. We notice that the rule-based method can not detect red-light running violations in which the vehicles do not reach the states $S$ or $R$. This accounts about 3% in our dataset.

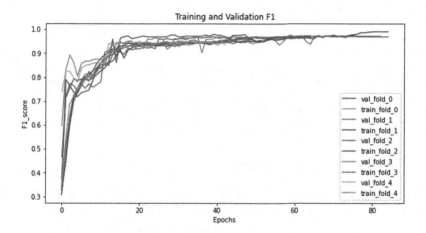

**Fig. 7.** Training and validation curves of the Dense LSTM with CNN1D

**Table 2.** Violation detection models results

| Model | Test precision | Test recall | Test F1 |
|---|---|---|---|
| LSTM | 0.8699 | 0.9439 | 0.9004 |
| Dense LSTM (LSTM + Skip connections) | 0.9420 | 0.9654 | 0.9531 |
| LSTM + CNN1D | 0.9455 | 0.9767 | 0.9602 |
| Dense LSTM + CNN1D | 0.9863 | 0.9863 | 0.9863 |
| Deep LSTM + Attention | **0.9885** | **1.0000** | **0.9933** |

## 6.4   Performance

In Figs. 8 and 9, we demonstrate the time improved by Mahalanobis distance approximation and cosine distance calculation by group in our tracking algorithm compared to the original one on a traffic video of ten minute long captured at an intersection of roads. The x-axis denotes the number of calculations and the y-axis is the total processing time for matching (in seconds) of WAYS and the original DeepSORT. We notice that, in this case, DeepSORT and WAYS are all configured with *nn_budget* of 100. From the figures, we find that the time of calculations of Mahalanobis distance and of cosine distance can be saved by nearly 60% and 30%, respectively. Moreover, the time for cosine distance calculation always accounts for nearly 99% of the total matching time. Thus, this shows valuable improvements of the proposed matching algorithm.

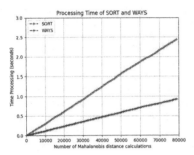

**Fig. 8.** Matching time due to Mahalanobis distance calculations.

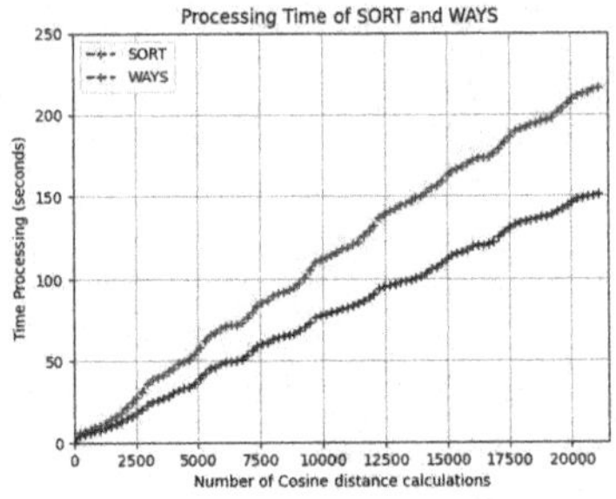

**Fig. 9.** Matching time due to cosine distance calculations.

## 7 Conclusion and Perspectives

In this paper, we address the recognition of red light running violations of vehicles in traffic videos using deep learning networks. We improved the traditional Deep-Sort for 30% faster tracking. Our tracking methods with group-based matching resulted in accurate sequences of states for corresponding vehicles in video. Our classifier of sequences combine LSTM and attention achieved 99.33% of f1-score which higher than the rule-based method thanks to its deep and wide optimization. In the future, we continue apply our classifier for more classes such as reverse direction, stopping and wrong lane violations of the vehicles.

## References

1. Bewoor, L.A., Tonge, A., Khiste, R., Chandak, S., Khan, U.: Traffic rules violation detection. Int. J. Adv. Sci. Technol. **29**(4s), 1153–1157 (2020). http://sersc.org/journals/index.php/IJAST/article/view/6667
2. Bochkovskiy, A., Wang, C.Y., Liao, H.Y.M.: YOLOv4: optimal speed and accuracy of object detection. arXiv preprint arXiv:2004.10934 (2020)
3. He, K., Zhang, X., Ren, S., Sun, J.: Deep residual learning for image recognition. CoRR abs/1512.03385 (2015). http://arxiv.org/abs/1512.03385
4. Hochreiter, S., Schmidhuber, J.: Long short-term memory. Neural Comput. **9**(8), 1735–1780 (1997). https://doi.org/10.1162/neco.1997.9.8.1735

5. Huang, G., Liu, Z., van der Maaten, L., Weinberger, K.Q.: Densely connected convolutional networks. In: Proceedings of the IEEE Conference on Computer Vision and Pattern Recognition (CVPR), July 2017
6. Kiranyaz, S., Avci, O., Abdeljaber, O., Ince, T., Gabbouj, M., Inman, D.J.: 1D convolutional neural networks and applications: a survey (2019)
7. Liu, W., et al.: SSD: single shot multibox detector. CoRR abs/1512.02325 (2015). http://arxiv.org/abs/1512.02325
8. Mehta, D., et al.: XNect: real-time multi-person 3D human pose estimation with a single RGB camera. CoRR abs/1907.00837 (2019). http://arxiv.org/abs/1907. 00837
9. Pinho, R., Tavares, J., Correia, M.: Efficient approximation of the Mahalanobis distance for tracking with the Kalman filter. Int. J. Simul. Model. **6**, 84–92 (2007). https://doi.org/10.2507/IJSIMM06(2)S.03
10. Redmon, J., Farhadi, A.: YOLO9000: better, faster, stronger. CoRR abs/1612.08242 (2016). http://arxiv.org/abs/1612.08242
11. Ren, S., He, K., Girshick, R., Sun, J.: Faster R-CNN: towards real-time object detection with region proposal networks. In: Proceedings of the 28th International Conference on Neural Information Processing Systems, NIPS 2015, vol. 1, pp. 91–99. MIT Press, Cambridge (2015)
12. Simonyan, K., Zisserman, A.: Very deep convolutional networks for large-scale image recognition (2015)
13. Vaswani, A., et al.: Attention is all you need. In: Proceedings of the 31st International Conference on Neural Information Processing Systems, NIPS 2017, pp. 6000–6010. Curran Associates Inc., Red Hook (2017)
14. Wang, X., Meng, L.M., Zhang, B., Lu, J., Du, K.L.: A video-based traffic violation detection system, pp. 1191–1194 (2013). https://doi.org/10.1109/MEC.2013. 6885246
15. Wang, Z., Zheng, L., Liu, Y., Li, Y., Wang, S.: Towards real-time multi-object tracking. arXiv preprint arXiv:1909.12605 (2019)
16. Wojke, N., Bewley, A., Paulus, D.: Simple online and realtime tracking with a deep association metric. In: 2017 IEEE International Conference on Image Processing (ICIP), pp. 3645–3649. IEEE (2017)
17. Xu, Y., Osep, A., Ban, Y., Horaud, R., Leal-Taixe, L., Alameda-Pineda, X.: How to train your deep multi-object tracker. In: Proceedings of the IEEE/CVF Conference on Computer Vision and Pattern Recognition (CVPR), June 2020

# Security and Privacy

# Impact of Wireless Backhaul and Imperfect Channel Estimation on Secure Communication Networks

Cheng Yin[1(✉)], Xinkai Cheng[2], Yijiu Li[1], and Haoran Liu[1]

[1] Queen's University Belfast, Belfast, UK
{cyin01,yli84,hliu18}@qub.ac.uk
[2] Wuhan University of Science and Technology, Wuhan, China

**Abstract.** This paper investigates the system performance of secure communication networks under unreliable backhaul and imperfect channel estimation. We first incorporate a transmitter selection approach that could achieve maximize signal-to-noise ratio at the receiver to improve secrecy performance. Then we derive the closed-form expressions of the secrecy outage performance under the impact of wireless backhaul and imperfect channel estimation. Our Monte-Carlo simulations verify that the analytical results match the simulation well, therefore validating the correctness of our expressions. Our theoretical analysis and simulations reveal the influence of the number of transmitters, the backhaul reliability, the channel estimation errors and the position of the eavesdropper on the secrecy system performance.

**Keywords:** Wireless backhaul · Imperfect channel estimation · Secure communication network

## 1 Introduction

In the fifth generation (5G) and beyond, there is a significant demand for massive connections among people, machines, and environments. A large number of wireless devices bring threats to network security. According to the broadcast nature, transmission is vulnerable to be attacked [3]. Therefore, it is a challenge to secure wireless network. The conventional approach to secure systems is mainly based on cryptography applied in high layers and assuming perfect physical layer with zero-error. In addition, the conventional method requires a large amount of power for encrypting and decrypting, which is not desirable for lightweight devices. Thus, physical layer security (PLS) has attracted increasing attention to meet the challenges in wireless communications.

Several studies have made a remarkable contribution to the literature by investigating the secrecy system performance in the presence of an eavesdropper [1,2,5–8,14,16,18–21]. However, all these works assume that the backhaul and

---

Supported by organization x.

N.-S. Vo et al. (Eds.): INISCOM 2022, LNICST 444, pp. 231–240, 2022.
https://doi.org/10.1007/978-3-031-08878-0_16

the channel estimation are perfect, which is ideal and unrealistic in practical future wireless communication systems. For instance, the authors investigated energy harvesting relay networks with an eavesdropper without considering the impact of unreliable backhaul and channel estimation on the system secrecy performance [14].

Wireless backhaul connections need to be deployed for future high dense networks. Conventional backhaul, such as copper and optical fibre, are highly reliable, but the deployment cost is high [4,17]. Wireless backhaul is a promising alternative to wired ones with lower cost. However, it suffers from unreliability because of non-LOS propagation, and channel fading [12]. There has been research considering wireless backhaul in cooperative system [11] and PLS scenarios [10,23] and the results prove that backhaul unreliability has shown negatively impact on the system performance [9]. Therefore, it is crucial to take undesirable outcomes of the wireless backhaul into account in the performance analysis in future wireless systems.

Several existing works in secure communications considered unreliable backhaul in performance analysis [10,23], however the authors assume that the channel estimation is perfect at the receiver side, which is not achievable in practical wireless systems [24]. The impact of imperfect channel state information (CSI) on system performance has been studied in secure communication systems [13,15,22]. In [13], the authors considered the influence of imperfect CSI in a wireless powered communication network with multiple eavesdroppers. Furthermore, a secure cellular vehicle-to-everything network was proposed, and the impact of imperfect CSI on system performance was considered [15]. In addition, a secure massive MIMO system with imperfect CSI has been proposed, and the authors analysed the impacts of imperfect CSI on the system secrecy performance [22].

Motivated by the above research, we study the system performance with the impact of both wireless backhaul unreliability and imperfect channel estimation in this work. As far as we know, this work, for the first time, addresses both the wireless backhaul unreliability and channel estimation uncertainties in wireless system performance analysis.

## 2   System Model

We investigate a secure communication network, consisting of a macro base station $S$ connected to $K$ small-cell transmitters, $T_{\{1,\cdots,K\}}$, via unreliable backhaul links, a receiver, $D$, in presence of an eavesdropper, $E$, as in Fig. 1. A selected transmitter $T_k^*$ sends its information to $D$ while $E$ is listening to the transmission from the transmitter to the destination. Reliability of the $k^{th}$ backhaul is modelled as a Bernoulli process $\mathbb{I}_k$. The success probability is defined as $s_k$, where $\mathbb{P}(\mathbb{I}_{k^*} = 1) = s_k$ and $\mathbb{P}(\mathbb{I}_{k^*} = 0) = 1 - s_k$, which demonstrates that $T_k$ forwards the message to the destination via the wireless backhaul with success probability $s_k$ and unsuccessful probability $1 - s_k$. All the channels are supposed to undergo Rayleigh fading. In addition, the transmitters and the receiver are equipped with single antenna.

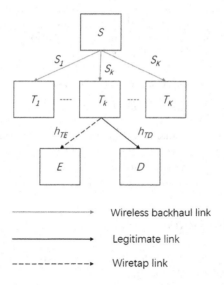

**Fig. 1.** System model

An sub-optimal transmitter selection approach is applied, the transmitter $T_k^*$ with the largest SNR at $D$ is selected as the best to forward the information to $D$, i.e.,

$$k^* = \arg \max_{1 \le k \le K} \text{SNR}_{T_k D}, \tag{1}$$

where $k^*$ indicates the index of the selected transmitter and $\text{SNR}_{T_k D}$ is the SNR of the link from $T_k$ to $D$. In addition, $h_{T_{k^*} D}$, $h_{T_{k^*} E}$ are the channel coefficient link from the selected transmitter $T_k^*$ to $D$ and $E$.

In practical systems, channel state information (CSI) cannot be perfectly obtained at $D$. We assume that the receiver $D$ and the eavesdropper $E$ estimate the CSI of $\widehat{h}_{T_{k^*} D}$, $\widehat{h}_{T_{k^*} E}$ and perform imperfect channel estimation of $h_{T_{k^*} D}$, $h_{T_{k^*} E}$ as follow,

$$h_{T_{k^*} D} = \widehat{h}_{T_{k^*} D} + e_{TD}, \tag{2}$$

$$h_{T_{k^*} E} = \widehat{h}_{T_{k^*} E} + e_{TE}, \tag{3}$$

where $e_{TD}$ and $e_{TE}$ represent the estimation error, i.e., $e_{TD} \sim CN(0, \epsilon_D^2)$, $e_{TE} \sim CN(0, \epsilon_E^2)$. According to channel estimation, $\epsilon_D = E[|h_{T_{k^*} D}|^2] - E[|\widehat{h}_{T_{k^*} D}|^2]$, similarly, $\epsilon_E = E[|h_{T_{k^*} E}|^2] - E[|\widehat{h}_{T_{k^*} E}|^2]$, where $E[\cdot]$ represents the expectation. We assume that all the channel estimation errors follow the same distribution, $e \sim CN(0, \epsilon^2)$.

Taking into account the selected transmitter $T_k^*$, $E$ experiences the SNR without wireless backhaul. Therefore, the received information at the receiver $D$ and eavesdropper $E$ are of the following forms,

$$y_D = \sqrt{P_T}(\widehat{h}_{T_{k^*}D} + e)\mathbb{I}_{k^*}x + z, \tag{4}$$

$$y_E = \sqrt{P_T}(\widehat{h}_{T_{k^*}E} + e)x + z, \tag{5}$$

where $x$ is the unit power transmitted symbol of the transmission and $P_T$ is the transmitted power of $T_{k^*}$. We assumed that $D$ and $E$ are experienced by the same noise indicated by $z$, which represents the complex additive white Gaussian noise (AWGN) with zero mean and variance $\sigma$, i.e., $z \sim CN(0, \sigma^2)$.

## 3    SNR Distributions

To assess the secrecy system performance, the SNR distributions at $E$ and $D$ need to be firstly derived. According to Eqs. 4 and 5, the received SNRs at $E$ and $D$ from the selected transmitter $T_k^*$ can be written as,

$$SNR_{k^*D} = \frac{P_0\widehat{h}_{T_{k^*}D}\mathbb{I}_{k^*}}{P_0\epsilon\mathbb{I}_{k^*} + 1}, \tag{6}$$

$$SNR_{T_{k^*}E} = \frac{P_0\widehat{h}_{T_{k^*}E}}{P_0\epsilon + 1}, \tag{7}$$

where $P_0 = P_T/\sigma^2$. As all the channels follow Rayleigh fading, the cumulative distribution function (CDF) and probability density function (PDF) of the channel associated with the unreliable backhaul are,

$$F(x) = 1 - s_k \exp(-\lambda x), \tag{8}$$

$$f(x) = s_k\lambda \exp(\lambda x), \tag{9}$$

where $s_k$ indicates the backhaul unreliability from the macro base station to the selected transmitter $T_k^*$. Therefore, the CDF of $SNR_{kD}$ are derived utilizing Eq. 8,

$$F_{SNR_{kD}}(x) = 1 - s_k \exp(-\frac{\lambda_D(P_0\epsilon\mathbb{I}_k + 1)x}{P_0}). \tag{10}$$

The best transmitter $T_k^*$ is selected according to the sub-optimal selection rule described in Eq. 1, thus the CDF of $SNR_{k^*D}$ with the best transmitter is,

$$F_{SNR_{k^*D}}(x) = F_{SNR_{kD}}(x)^K. \tag{11}$$

Similarly, the CDF and PDF of $E$ are can be obtained as follows,

$$F_{SNR_{T_{k*E}}}(x) = 1 - \exp(-\frac{-\lambda_E(P_0\epsilon + 1)x}{P_0}), \tag{12}$$

$$f_{SNR_{T_{k*E}}}(x) = \frac{-\lambda_E(P_0\epsilon + 1)x}{P_0} \exp(-\frac{-\lambda_E(P_0\epsilon + 1)x}{P_0}). \tag{13}$$

In this section, we obtain the SNR distributions of the links from the selected transmitter $T_k^*$ to $D$ and $E$. Then, we derive the CDF of PDF of the related SNR distributions under the impact of wireless backhaul and channel estimation imperfections. In the next section, we will assess the system secrecy performance.

## 4   Secrecy Performance Analysis

In this section, we investigate the secrecy system performance under the impact of wireless backhaul and imperfect channel estimation. We derive the secrecy outage probability (SOP) utilizing the SNR distributions given in the above section. SOP is an metric which has been widely used to assess the system performance, it is defined as the secrecy capacity being below a certain threshold $\theta$. To achieve the general results working in most cases with wireless backhaul and imperfect channel estimation in practice, we measure the SOP in terms of two scenarios: (1) single transmitter and (2) multiple $K$ transmitters.

Firstly, we derive the SOP with a single transmitter with both wireless backhaul and channel estimation imperfection. The expression is derived as follows,

$$F(\theta) = \int_0^\infty F_{SNR_{kD}}(2^{2\theta}(1+x) - 1)f_{SNR_{T_kE}}(x)dx$$
$$= s_k \exp(-\frac{\lambda_D(P_0\epsilon\mathbb{I}_k + 1)(2^{2\theta} - 1)}{P_0}) \tag{14}$$
$$\frac{\lambda_E(P_0\epsilon + 1)}{\lambda_D(P_0\epsilon\mathbb{I}_k + 1)2^{2\theta} + \lambda_E(P_0\epsilon + 1)}.$$

Next, we consider a more practical scenario that multiple transmitter exist. According to the sub-optimal selection rule introduced in Eq. 11, the SOP can be derived as,

$$F_k(\theta) = \int_0^\infty F_{SNR_{k*D}}(2^{2\theta}(1+x) - 1)f_{SNR_{T_{k*E}}}(x)dx$$
$$= 1 + \sum_1^K \binom{K}{k}(-1)^k s_k{}^k \exp(-\frac{\lambda_D(P_0\epsilon\mathbb{I}_k + 1)k(2^{2\theta} - 1)}{P_0}) \tag{15}$$
$$\frac{\lambda_E(P_0\epsilon + 1)}{\lambda_D(P_0\epsilon\mathbb{I}_k + 1)k2^{2\theta} + \lambda_E(P_0\epsilon + 1)}.$$

Compare with Eq. 14, Eq. 15 is power to the number of transmitter $K$, due to Eq. 14 is smaller than 1, Eq. 15 is smaller than Eq. 14 on the condition that $K$ is larger than 1. This illustrates that increasing the number of transmitter leads to a lower SOP and better system secrecy performance.

## 5  Numerical Results

We evaluate the numerical results with Monte-Carlo simulations. The threshold $\theta$ of SOP is assumed to be 1 bits/s/Hz. We also assume that the positions of transmitters, receiver and eavesdropper are located in Cartesian coordinate system, which are $T_k = (0,0)$, $D = (1,0)$ and $E = (4,1)$. The distance between every two nodes is written as $d_{ab} = \sqrt{(x_a - x_b)^2 + (y_a - y_b)^2}$, where $a, b = \{T_k, D, E\}$. It is also assumed that the average SNR of transmission link depends on the pass loss $pl$: $1/\lambda = 1/d_{ab}^{pl}$, and $pl$ is 4. The variance of channel estimation errors is modelled as $\epsilon^2 = \frac{\omega}{1+\delta p \omega}$, where $\omega$ and $p$ are the variance of channel gains and the average transmit SNR, and $\delta$ indicates the channel quality parameter. In the following figures, we use 'Sim' to indicate the simulation results, and 'Ana' to indicate the analytical results.

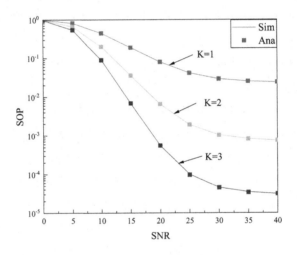

**Fig. 2.** The influence of the number of transmitter $K$ on the SOP

Figure 2 illustrates the influence of the number of transmitter $K$ on the SOP. Wireless backhaul reliability $s$ is assumed to be 0.99, the position of $E$ is (4,1) and $K$ is an integer ranging from 1 to 3. As shown in the figure, with the increase of $K$, SOP decreases significantly. This is because with the increase number of transmitters, there are more choices to transmit to the destination, thus showing better secrecy system performance. In another aspect, the reason of presenting increasing performance can be refereed to Sect. 4. The SOP of the scenario with multiple transmitter is powered to $K$ compared with the SOP with single transmitter, and SOP is smaller than 1, so the SOP becomes smaller after powering to $K$ when $K$ is greater than 1. Therefore, when the number of transmitter grows, the system achieves better performance.

Figure 3 shows the impact of backhaul unreliability on SOP. The position of E is (4,1) and $K = 3$. As shown in the figure, the system has a lower SOP

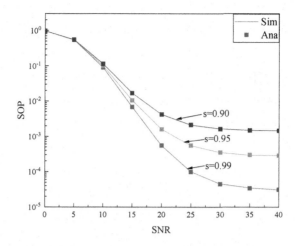

**Fig. 3.** The influence of backhaul reliability $s$ on the SOP

when $s$ becomes larger. This indicates that when the wireless backhaul is more reliable, the system has better performance.

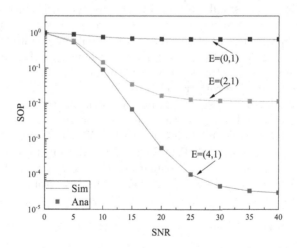

**Fig. 4.** The influence of the position of the eavesdropper $E$ on the SOP

Figure 4 presents the impact the position of the eavesdropper $E$ on SOP. The number of transmitter $K$ equals 3 and $s = 0.99$. We consider two scenarios: 1) The distance between the transmitter and the receiver is the same as that from the transmitter to the eavesdropper; 2) The eavesdropper locates further than the receiver. The position of $E$ is assumed to dynamic from $(0,1)$, $(2,1)$ to $(4,1)$. The eavesdropper locates at $(0,1)$ indicates that the distance between

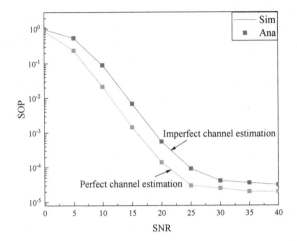

**Fig. 5.** Comparison of perfect channel estimation and imperfect channel estimation

the transmitter and the receiver is the same as that from the transmitter to the eavesdropper. The figure shows that the SOP almost achieve 1 no matter how the SNR changes. This means that when the distance between the transmitter and the eavesdropper is smaller or equal to the distance between the transmitter and the receiver, it is difficult to secure the wireless security in physical layer aspects, more approaches need to be applied to enhance security. In addition, when E locates (2,1) and (4,1), the SOP decreases obviously. This illustrates that the system could obtain better secrecy performance when the distance between the transmitter and eavesdropper increases.

Figure 5 shows the impact of channel estimation imperfection on system secrecy performance and compares the differences between perfect and imperfect channel estimations in secure wireless networks. We could observe a clearly gap between these two cases, the SOP with the perfect channel estimation is lower than that with imperfect channel estimation. The figure demonstrates that the SOP is significantly affected by the channel estimation errors.

## 6   Conclusion

This paper fills the gap in exploring the system secrecy performance of secure communication network under unreliable backhaul and imperfect channel estimation. The remarkable contribution is the novel derivation of the closed-form expressions of secrecy outage probability under both wireless backhaul and channel estimation imperfections. In addition, we reveal the impact of backhaul unreliability and channel uncertainty on system secrecy performance. Our results show that when the wireless backhaul is more reliable, the system has better performance. The system secrecy performance with perfect and imperfect channel estimation is also compared, the SOP with perfect channel estimation is lower than that of imperfect channel estimation. Moreover, we discuss the influence of the number of transmitters and the location of the eavesdropper on the secrecy outage probability. The results show that the system performs better when the number of transmitter increase. Furthermore, when the distance between the transmitter to the eavesdropper is larger, the system presents better performance. However, when the distance between the transmitter to the eavesdropper is equal or smaller than that from the transmitter to the destination, the system cannot be secured. In this situation, more approaches needs to be deployed to secure the wireless system.

# References

1. Fan, L., Lei, X., Duong, T.Q., Elkashlan, M., Karagiannidis, G.K.: Secure multiuser communications in multiple amplify-and-forward relay networks. IEEE Trans. Commun. **62**(9), 3299–3310 (2014)
2. Fan, L., Yang, N., Duong, T.Q., Elkashlan, M., Karagiannidis, G.K.: Exploiting direct links for physical layer security in multiuser multirelay networks. IEEE Trans. Wirel. Commun. **15**(6), 3856–3867 (2016)
3. Fan, L., Zhang, S., Duong, T.Q., Karagiannidis, G.K.: Secure switch-and-stay combining (SSSC) for cognitive relay networks. IEEE Trans. Commun **64**(1), 70–82 (2015)
4. Ge, X., Cheng, H., Guizani, M., Han, T.: 5G wireless backhaul networks: challenges and research advances. IEEE Netw. **28**(6), 6–11 (2014)
5. Hoang, T.M., Duong, T.Q., Suraweera, H.A., Tellambura, C., Poor, H.V.: Cooperative beamforming and user selection for improving the security of relay-aided systems. IEEE Trans. Commun. **63**(12), 5039–5051 (2015)
6. Hu, J., Shu, F., Li, J.: Robust synthesis method for secure directional modulation with imperfect angle information. IEEE Commun. Lett. **20**(16), 1084–1087 (2016)
7. Hu, J., Yan, S., Shu, F., Wang, J., Li, J., Zhang, Y.: Artificial-noise-aided secure transmission with directional modulation based on random frequency diverse arrays. IEEE Access **5**, 1658–1667 (2017)
8. Huang, Y., Wang, J., Zhong, C., Duong, T.Q., Karagiannidis, G.K.: Secure transmission in cooperative relaying networks with multiple antennas. IEEE Trans. Wirel. Commun. **15**(10), 6843–6856 (2016)
9. Khan, T.A., Orlik, P., Kim, K.J., Heath, R.W.: Performance analysis of cooperative wireless networks with unreliable backhaul links. IEEE Commun. Lett. **19**(8), 1386–1389 (2015)
10. Kim, K.J., Khan, T.A., Orlik, P.V.: Performance analysis of cooperative systems with unreliable backhauls and selection combining. IEEE Trans. Veh. Technol. **66**(3), 2448–2461 (2017)
11. Kim, K.J., Orlik, P.V., Khan, T.A.: Performance analysis of finite-sized cooperative systems with unreliable backhauls. IEEE Trans. Wirel. Commun. **15**(7), 5001–5015 (2016)
12. Kim, K.J., Yeoh, P.L., Orlik, P.V., Poor, H.V.: Secrecy performance of finite-sized cooperative single carrier systems with unreliable backhaul connections. IEEE Trans. Signal Process. **64**(17), 4403–4416 (2016)
13. Li, M., Yin, H., Huang, Y., Wang, Y., Yu, R.: Physical layer security of WPCNs with imperfect CSI and full-duplex receiver aided jamming. IEEE Access **7**, 55318–55328 (2019)

14. Nguyen, N.P., Duong, T.Q., Ngo, H.Q., Hadzi-Velkov, Z., Shu, L.: Secure 5g wireless communications: a joint relay selection and wireless power transfer approach. IEEE Access **4**, 3349–3359 (2016)
15. Qiu, B., Xiao, H., Chronopoulos, A.T., Zhou, D., Ouyang, S.: Optimal access scheme for security provisioning of C-V2X computation offloading network with imperfect CSI. IEEE Access **8**, 9680–9691 (2020)
16. Shu, F., Wu, X., Li, J., Chen, R., Vunetic, B.: Robust synthesis scheme for multbeam directional modulation in broadcasting systems. IEEE Access **5**, 6614–6623 (2016)
17. Tipmongkolsilp, O., Zaghloul, S., Jukan, A.: The evolution of cellular backhaul technologies: current issues and future trends. IEEE Commun. Surv. Tutor. **13**(1), 97–113 (2011)
18. Wang, L., Elkashlan, M., Huang, J., Tran, N.H., Duong, T.Q.: Secure transmission with optimal power allocation in untrusted relay networks. IEEE Wirel. Commun. Lett. **3**(3), 289–292 (2014)
19. Wang, L., Kim, K.J., Duong, T.Q., Elkashlan, M., Poor, H.V.: Security enhancement of cooperative single carrier systems. IEEE Trans. Inf. Forensics Secur. **10**(1), 90–103 (2015)
20. Yan, S., Yang, N., Geraci, G., Malaney, R., Yuan, J.: Optimization of code rates in SISOME wiretap channels. IEEE Trans. Wirel. Commun. **14**(11), 6377–6388 (2015)
21. Yan, S., Yang, N., Malaney, R., Yuan, J.: Transmit antenna selection with Alamouti coding and power allocation in MIMO wiretap channels. IEEE Trans. Wirel. Commun. **13**(3), 1656–1667 (2014)
22. Yang, T., Zhang, R., Cheng, X., Yang, L.: Secure massive MIMO under imperfect CSI: performance analysis and channel prediction. IEEE Trans. Inf. Forensics Secur. **14**(6), 1610–1623 (2018)
23. Yin, C., Nguyen, H.T., Kundu, C., Kaleem, Z., Garcia-Palacios, E., Duong, T.Q.: Secure energy harvesting relay networks with unreliable backhaul connections. IEEE Access **6**, 12074–12084 (2018)
24. Yoo, T., Goldsmith, A.: Capacity and power allocation for fading MIMO channels with channel estimation error. IEEE Trans. Inf. Theory **52**(5), 2203–2214 (2006)

# Performance Analysis of Non-profiled Side Channel Attack Based on Multi-layer Perceptron Using Significant Hamming Weight Labeling

Ngoc-Tuan Do[1], Van-Phuc Hoang[1]([✉]), and Van Sang Doan[2]

[1] Institute of System Integration, Le Quy Don Technical University, Hanoi, Vietnam
phuchv@lqdtu.edu.vn
[2] Faculty of Communications and Radar, Vietnam Naval Academy,
Nha Trang, Vietnam

**Abstract.** Deep learning (DL) techniques have become popular for side-channel analysis (SCA) in the recent years. This paper proposes and evaluates the applications of multilayer perceptron (MLP) models for non-profiled attacks on the AES-128 encryption implementation in different scenarios, such as high dimensional data, imbalanced classes, and the impact of additive noise. Along with the designed models, a labeling technique called significant Hamming weight (SHW) and dataset reconstruction method are introduced for solving the imbalanced dataset problem. In addition, using SHW in the non-profiled context can reduce the number of measurements needed by approximately 30%. The experimental results show that the DL based SCA with our reconstructed dataset for different targets of ASCAD, RISC-V microcontroller has achieved a higher performance of non-profiled attacks. Comparing to the binary labeling technique, SHW labeling provides better results with the presence of the additive noise.

**Keywords:** Hardware security · Non-profile side channel attack · Advanced Encryption Standard (AES) · Multilayer perceptron (MLP) · Imbalanced classes

## 1 Introduction

Side channel attack (SCA) is a serious threat, which exploits weaknesses in the physical implementation of cryptographic system. Recently, the hardware security research communities have focused their attention on deep learning (DL) based SCA (DLSCA). This is a promising technique for implementing powerful attacks against cryptographic devices. In general, DL based SCA is divided into profiling attacks and non-profiling attacks according to the attack environment [2].

Profiling DLSCA is an attack that can be implemented when the clone device, which is the same device as the target device, is available. In this case, the

© ICST Institute for Computer Sciences, Social Informatics and Telecommunications Engineering 2022
Published by Springer Nature Switzerland AG 2022. All Rights Reserved
N.-S. Vo et al. (Eds.): INISCOM 2022, LNICST 444, pp. 241–254, 2022.
https://doi.org/10.1007/978-3-031-08878-0_17

attacker has a full control over the clone device. In particular, profiled DLSCA functions in two phases:

- *Profiled phase:* For the profiling phase, the power traces of the clone device are obtained for training a neural network. A template model is then constructed, which is able to identify the correlation between the intermediate values of the cryptography algorithm and the power traces of the target device.

- *Attack phase:* the trained model is used to analyze the power trace recorded from the actual target device.

In contrast, the non-profiled DLSCA can be performed directly on the target device without profiled phase and clone device. Indeed, the authors in TCHES 2019 [15] presented the efficiency of DL based SCA in the non-profiled attack. Accordingly, they introduced the metrics based on sensitivity analysis to extract the confidential key value and the POIs (such as masks and leaks positions in power traces). This attack technique was so-called differential DL analysis (DDLA). More especially, the authors provided two labeling techniques like Hamming weight labeling and Binary labeling. The efficiency of this technique was proved on both types of synchronized and non-synchronized power traces.

Even thought profiled attacks are considered the most powerful form of side-channel attacks, the profiling phase requires to have access to a profiling device, which is a strong assumption that cannot be always met in practice. Interestingly, non-profiled attacks like DDLA can still threaten the device. Therefore, we are more interested in DL based non-profiled attacks, especially DDLA technique.

## 1.1   Related Works and Motivation

While proven as a successful attack, DDLA has some problems that need to take into account.

Firstly, DDLA is necessary to perform a DL training for each key guess. It means a complex architecture will cause the time-consuming for taking the secret key, especially in the case of high dimension data input. The authors in [15] have not considered the high dimension data in DL based non-profiled SCA context. Their experiments used a small number of measurements with a few hundred samples per trace that contained the copies of S-box function in memory. Moreover, the authors introduced a technique called sensitivity analysis based on network input to reveal the correct key. Therefore, the higher the dimension data input, the more complex the model. It leads to an increased computation time for each hypothesis key.

In general, several techniques have been proposed to deal with high dimension data input problem in DLSCA. Picek *et al.* [13] used the correlation analysis to extract the most relevant samples. This technique exploits the correlation between power traces with a power consumption model. Another technique called principle component analysis (PCA) which is usually used in deep learning. However, the main drawback of PCA is that the calculation time increases quadratically relative to the number of samples on a power trace. Despite the efficiency of reducing the data dimension, these techniques mentioned above are only applied in a profiled context.

Secondly, the effectiveness of DDLA depends on data labeling techniques. As indicated in [15], two main labeling techniques (Hamming weight and binary) have been applied in a non-profiled context. In which, the efficiency of binary labeling method is proven in many works [1,15,16]. In contrast, HW labeling has not been considered. Moreover, the authors in [16] have also indicated that HW model in non-profiled SCA causes the imbalance dataset problem. To the best of our knowledge, only one report of using HW labeling method has been published in non-profile deep learning context [4].

Finally, DL based non-profiled SCA technique is sensitive with the additive noise. In profiling DLSCA context, several works have investigated the effect of noise addition [8,11]. Kim et al. have demonstrated in [8] that adding the artificial noise on the input signal can actually improve the performance of neural networks. In [11], Maghrebi has proved that noise addition can avoid over-fitting in DL-based SCA techniques. In contrast, the authors in [1] have indicated that a additive noise may provide higher protection against non-profiled DLSCA. Therefore, it is necessary to proposed a DL model against noise generation countermeasure in a non-profiled context.

Due to the mentioned issues above, the motivation of this research is to introduce a new type of HW labeling technique which can deal with the imbalanced dataset problems. Furthermore, based on the correlation between HW labels and the raw data input, we can reduce the dimension of data input significantly. Consequently, a new multi-layer perceptron model working on new dataset reconstructed is proposed.

The contributions of this paper can be summarized as follows:

- We proposed a new type of HW label based on significant Hamming weight (SHW) to fight against imbalance classes in a non-profiled context. We demonstrate SHW labeling works in both TCHES 2019 model and our proposed architecture. More interestingly, by using SHW labeling, the number of measurements needed for DLSCA attack reduces approximately 30% compared to Binary labeling.

- We introduce a new multi-layer perceptron model instance that applied SHW labeling to reveal the correct key in a non-profiled context. Compared to the state-of-the-art non-profiled DLSCA model (TCHES 2019), our proposed shows better results in discriminating correct key.

- The balancing technique based on SHW enables us to reach better results than Binary labeling with the presence of additive noise.

## 1.2 Paper Outline

The rest of this paper is organized as follows. In Sect. 2, data preparation, including test platforms, imbalanced data problems, dataset reconstruction based on SHW labeling are described in detail. Section 3 presents our proposed MLP architectures which applied SHW labeling to reveal the correct key. In Sect. 4, we will give detailed results from various experiments implemented on raw power traces collected from RISC-V MCU or ASCAD database. Finally, we conclude the paper in Sect. 5.

## 2   Data Preparation

### 2.1   Attack Datasets

As we dealing with the imbalanced classes in DL based non-profiled SCA context. Our proposed labeling method is based on leakage function. We are more interested in the first-order leakage rather than higher order. Therefore, countermeasures like masking are out of scope in this paper. For experimental validation, we use two first-order leakage datasets like unmasked ASCAD and RISC-V data.

**Unmasked ASCAD Dataset:** ASCAD is a public dataset which is introduced by Prouff *et al.* [14]. This database provides side-channel power traces of an 8-bit ATMega8515 board with a first-order protected software AES implementation. The main database ASCAD is composed of two sets of traces: a profiling set of 50,000 traces to train Deep Learning architectures and an attack set of 10,000 traces to test the efficiency of the trained neural networks. It is worth noting that 700 samples corresponding to the output of the third Sbox being processed during the first round. As we are interested in an unmasked implementation, we consider the mask to be known and thus can easily turn it into an unprotected scenario. Accordingly, the leakage model is calculated as follows:

$$H_{p_3,k} = HW \left( Sbox\,[p_3 \oplus \boldsymbol{k^*}] \oplus \underbrace{m_3}_{\text{known mask}} \right) \tag{1}$$

where $p_3$, $\boldsymbol{k^*}$ and $m_3$ are respectively the third byte of plaintext, the key and the third byte of known mask.

**RISC-V Dataset:** Next, the power traces of Sakura-G board with unprotected AES-128 are captured using an oscilloscope at sampling rate of 250 MS/s. It is worth noting that the target device is a 32-bit RISC-V MCU Murax operating at 48 MHz, as shown in Fig. 1. Accordingly, 10,000 power traces of the Sakura-G board are collected. Each power trace contains 9,919 samples. In this platform, we chose the sixth byte for investigating proposed techniques. The leakage model on RISC-V power traces is similar to (1) without mask value, see (2):

$$H_{p_6,k} = HW \left( Sbox\,[p_6 \oplus \boldsymbol{k^*}] \right) \tag{2}$$

### 2.2   Imbalanced Data Problem

Imbalanced data is an issue often occurring in classification applications where the distribution of classes is not balanced. In such a case, deep learning classification algorithms (e.g., multi-layer perceptron, convolutional neural network, etc.) have difficulties since they will be biased towards the majority class.

In profiling SCA context, Pikek *et al.* in [12] indicated that the commonly used Hamming weight model leads to imbalanced training datasets. Indeed, by observing Table 1, it is obvious that the distribution of intermediate values

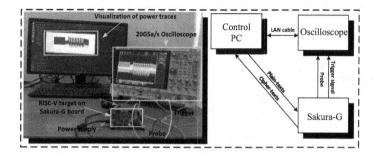

**Fig. 1.** Test platform: RISC-V power traces acquisition on Sakura-G board.

on each $HW$ is imbalanced and symmetric about $HW4$ in the case of AES-128. To tackle this problem, the authors in [12] proposed a method based on the data re-sampling technique. Accordingly, they used a random oversampling method called SMOTE to oversamples for each class. In practice, SMOTE can be considered as a general case of the data augmentation (AU) technique proposed in [3].

**Table 1.** Probability distribution of the $HW$ of a uniformly distributed 8-bit value.

| HW | 0 | 1 | 2 | 3 | 4 | 5 | 6 | 7 | 8 |
|---|---|---|---|---|---|---|---|---|---|
| Probability | $\frac{1}{256}$ | $\frac{8}{256}$ | $\frac{28}{256}$ | $\frac{56}{256}$ | $\frac{70}{256}$ | $\frac{56}{256}$ | $\frac{28}{256}$ | $\frac{8}{256}$ | $\frac{1}{256}$ |

### 2.3 Significant HW Labeling

Similarly, non-profiling SCA like DDLA used HW model also suffers from imbalanced data problems. However, unlike profiled DL based SCA, DDLA uses the training metrics instead of the model's output for discriminating the correct key. According to [15], training with the correct key always has better learning ability than incorrect ones. It means that if we use only three classes for training instead of nine classes, the DL model using correct key still has better training metrics than wrong key. As shown in Table 1, there are three significant HW ($HW =$ 3, 4, 5) that contain the most distribution of intermediate values. Moreover, the distribution of three significant HWs (SHW) are nearly the same. Therefore, we assume that it is possible to use SHW for classification in a non-profiled context.

Apart from balancing data, SHW labeling reduces significant measurements needed for the attack. Indeed, from Table 1, it is clearly shown that SHW discards the intermediate values corresponding to $HW = 0, 1, 2, 6, 7, 8$. It is meaningful in the case of using adaptive chosen plaintext method in a non-profiled context [7]. Next, we will present the procedure in order to reconstruct new datasets from original ones for using SHW labeling.

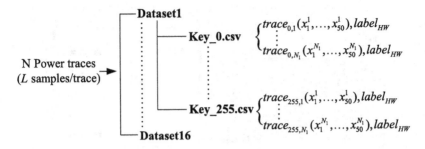

**Fig. 2.** Structure of the new datasets: There are 16 folders (**Dataset1 to Dataset16**) corresponding to 16 bytes of secret key, each folder contains 256 files in **.csv** format which correspond to 256 hypothesis keys. $N$ original power traces ($L$ samples/trace) are calculated to form $N_1$ new traces and labeled ($HW = \{3, 4, 5\}$). Each new trace contains 50 samples which are highest correlation values.

### 2.4  Dataset Reconstruction

As mentioned in the previous section, non-profiled attacks do not need the profiling phase as profiled attacks; therefore, the datasets that are used for deep learning in non-profiled attacks are different. It means that we can use power trace values as input for training neural networks, which can learn to classify the power traces in the group that corresponds to the power consumption model. However, a power trace often contains thousands of samples, whereas only a part of them serves for key prediction. Therefore, using all of these samples as the input features of ML model leads to an increment in the ML complexity and the time-consuming [6,10,13].

In order to handle this issue, we use the correlation characteristic to find the most useful samples on a power trace to feed up the neural network. Recently, in our previous work [5], correlation coefficients are employed for taking the most relevant samples in the power trace by computing correlation between real traces with their model. This method is suitable for a large number of samples because attackers do not need to know detail about the AES implementation. Accordingly, the samples which have high correlation values with the power model will be selected as strong features for training a neural network. As mentioned above, HW model is used as a power consumption model. However, we use formula (1) and (2) for ASCAD dataset and RISC-V data, respectively.

To select the useful features, Pearson correlation coefficients formula is applied:

$$\rho_{k,i} = \frac{\sum\limits_{n=1}^{N'} (h_{n,k} - \bar{h}_k)(t_{n,i} - \bar{t}_i)}{\sqrt{\sum\limits_{n=1}^{N'} (h_{n,k} - \bar{h}_k)^2 \sum\limits_{n=1}^{N'} (t_{n,i} - \bar{t}_i)^2}} \tag{3}$$

where $\bar{h}_k$ and $\bar{t}_i$ are the average values of the power consumption model and real power at instant $i$, respectively.

Let's consider $N$ random plaintexts corresponding to $N$ power traces in which each power trace has $L$ samples. It is noted that $t_{i,j}$ is the value of $j^{th}$ sample in the $i^{th}$ trace ($1 \leq j \leq L$, $1 \leq i \leq N$), $d_{i,B}$ is the byte value of byte $B$ ($B \in [1; 16]$) in the $i^{th}$ plain-text. In order to collect the useful features from the power traces, a half of power traces is used and denoted as $N'(N' = \frac{1}{2}N)$. Afterward, the formula (3) is applied to select the samples of high correlation from all guess keys ($Key = [0; 255]$).

For determining the positions of high correlation, the correlation value of real power trace with its model is calculated on half of power traces. As a result, a matrix of correlation coefficients with a size of $256 \times L$ is produced, in which each row corresponds to a hypothesis key. By determining 50 useful sample points based on the 50-top highest correlation values, a smaller dataset of power traces is generated and reconstructed follows hypothesis keys and $HW$ values, in which $HW$s plays a role of labels as shown in Fig. 2. By this way, a numerous power traces corresponding to other remain $HW$ values can be ignored; therefore, the dataset continues to be reduced (about one-third). Three new datasets are reconstructed from the original ASCAD database and RISC-V data as presented in Table 2.

**Table 2.** The details of reconstructed dataset.

| Dataset | Unmasked ASCAD | | RISC-V data | | Labeling technique |
|---|---|---|---|---|---|
| | Number of traces | Dimension | Number of traces | Dimension | |
| Original | 3000 | 700 | 10000 | 9919 | LSB |
| Dataset 1 | ≈2000 | 700 | x | x | SHW |
| Dataset 2 | ≈2000 | 50 | x | x | SHW |
| Dataset 3 | x | x | ≈7000 | 50 | SHW |

## 3 Proposed Deep Learning Architecture

As demonstrated in [15], multi-layer perceptron (MLP) is the simple and efficient architecture to perform DDLA on synchronous power traces. In this work, we propose a new MLP instance for non-profiled SCA attack. Our novelty is to apply the SHW labeling technique. In addition, we used Exponential Linear Unit (ELU) activation function instead of RELU as in TCHES2019. The details of the proposed architecture are depicted in Fig. 3.

Our proposed network comprises an input layer, output layers, and six hidden layers. As presented in Sect. 2, the reconstructed dataset consists of 50 samples each power trace. The number of nodes in the input layer is assigned according to the number of samples in a power trace. Therefore, the input layer of the proposed MLP has 50 nodes corresponding to 50 features of the extracted power trace. As depicted in Fig. 3, all arrows represent the weights. Prior to implement training phase, the values of weights and bias are randomly chosen from a normal distribution using Xavier scheme.

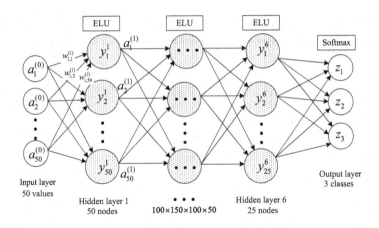

**Fig. 3.** The proposed multi-layer perceptron architecture.

To obtain the output, a procedure called *forward propagation* is performed. *Forward propagation* can be implemented as illustrated in Fig. 3, the weighted sum is calculated as follows:

$$y_i^{(l)} = b_i + \sum_{j=1}^{l^{(l-1)}} a_j^{(l-1)} \times w_{ji}^l \qquad (4)$$

where $b_i$ is the bias of node $i^{th}$, $w_{ji}^l$ is the weight which connect node $i^{th}$ of layer $l-1$ to node $j^{th}$ of layer $l$, $a_j^{(l-1)}$ is the output of activation function $\boldsymbol{F}(y)$ on node $j^{th}$ of layer $l-1$ and calculated as (5).

$$a_j^{(l)} = \boldsymbol{F}(y_j^{(l)}) \qquad (5)$$

It is worth noting that formula (5) does not apply on the input layer. The output $a_j^{(l)}$ is then used as the input of the next neuron on next layer. This procedure is performed from the input layer to the output layer.

In DL based SCA context, the popular activation functions used in hidden layer are ELU and RELU which are computed as formula (6) and (7), respectively. Our proposed model used ELU instead of ReLU to avoid the vanishing problem and produce negative outputs for each node in the hidden layer.

$$\text{ReLU} : F_{(y)} = \left\{ \begin{matrix} y : & y > 0 \\ 0 : & y \le 0 \end{matrix} \right\} \qquad (6)$$

$$\text{ELU} : F_{(y)} = \left\{ \begin{matrix} y : & y > 0 \\ \alpha \cdot (e^y - 1) : & y \le 0 \end{matrix} \right\} \qquad (7)$$

For classification, the Softmax function is used in the output layer for calculating the probability of each HW label. This function is calculated as

$$\text{SoftMax} : z\,(y)\,[i] = \frac{e^{y[i]}}{\sum_{j=1}^K e^{y[j]}} \qquad (8)$$

where $K$ is number of classes, in our case, $K = 3$ since our proposed model uses SHW label.

Finally, *backward propagation* is implemented in order to update the weights to obtain the expected results. Since we have three labels, the categorical crossentropy loss between the labels and predictions are computed as

$$\mathcal{L}_X(\boldsymbol{w}) = - \sum_{j=1}^{3} y_{true} \ln(z) \qquad (9)$$

where $y_{true}$ is the encoded values of HW.

Then, we use Adam optimizer to find the optimal minimizing the loss function. Deep learning will do a series of iteration $t$, and in each iteration, the gradient of loss function $\nabla \mathcal{L}_X(\boldsymbol{w})$ is computed. After that, $\boldsymbol{w}$ is updated by using the following formula described in [9]:

$$\boldsymbol{w}_t = \boldsymbol{w}_{t-1} - \alpha \cdot \hat{m}_t / \left( \sqrt{\hat{v}_t} + \varepsilon \right) \qquad (10)$$

where $\alpha$ is called the learning rate. In our case, $\alpha$ is chosen equal 0.001, other parameters are chosen as recommended in [9] ($\beta_1 = 0.9$, $\beta_2 = 0.999$ and $\varepsilon = 10^{-8}$)

When the correct hypothesis key $\boldsymbol{k}^*$ is used, the series of intermediate results will be correctly computed. Consequently, the partition and the labels used for our model will be consistent with the corresponding traces. In contrast, for all the incorrect guess keys, the labels used for the training will be incompatible with the traces. By analyzing and optimizing the model, we decided to use six layers with the number of nodes as depicted in Fig. 3. Consequently, our model provide better results like lower loss or higher accuracy than the other candidates. Therefore, the correct key can be obtained easily.

## 4    Experimental Results

In our experiment, the reconstructed datasets in Sect. 2 are used to perform training the proposed models. We use three models to obtain the results. Firstly, we reconstruct the MLP architecture in [15] called $MLP_{ref1}$. Next, we use the same as $MLP_{ref1}$, but SHW labeling is used instead of Binary labeling, denotes as $MLP_{ref2}$. Finally, we use proposed MLP called $MLP_{proposed}$. To demonstrate the effectiveness of reconstructed datasets and neural networks, the training metrics such as accuracy and loss are used as criterion. All experiments are performed on Keras framework running on a personal computer (Intel Core i5-9500 CPU, DDR4 24GB memory). We provide the detailed experiment setup in Table 3.

Firstly, we use the unmasked ASCAD database to validate the efficiency of SHW labeling techniques. It is important to note that the dimension of data input of $MLP_{ref1}$ is the same as the original one, while $MLP_{ref2}$ and $MLP_{proposed}$ use the reconstruction data. According to Table 2, $MLP_{ref1}$ is

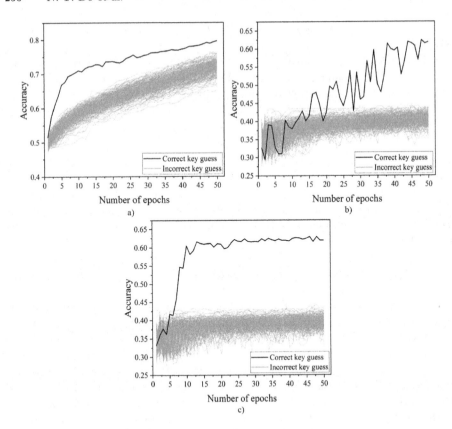

**Fig. 4.** The attack results on ASCAD database with different models using SHW and LSB labeling a) $MLP_{ref1}$ using LSB; b) $MLP_{ref2}$ using SHW; c) $MLP_{proposed}$ using SHW.

trained by original unmasked ASCAD data, $MLP_{ref2}$ and $MLP_{proposed}$ are trained by Dataset1 and Dataset2, respectively. The attack results on the third byte are illustrated in Fig. 4 where we can see that by using the SHW labels, the model has lower accuracy than $MLP_{ref1}$ because they using only two labels, which leads to results for classification is at least 50%. Despite lower accuracy, SHW labeling method gives a high probability for discriminating the correct key than the model in $MLP_{ref1}$. Moreover, the result presented in Fig. 4a shows that $MLP_{ref1}$ adapts to the training set too well on both correct key and incorrect key. In contrast, $MLP_{ref2}$ and $MLP_{proposed}$ only adjust training metric on the correct key. More interestingly, the result of $MLP_{ref2}$ indicates that SHW works for TCHES 2019 architecture. However, the accuracy is fluctuate and it takes more epochs (about 20 epochs) to discriminate correct key compared to $MLP_{ref1}$ and $MLP_{proposed}$ (first 5 epochs).

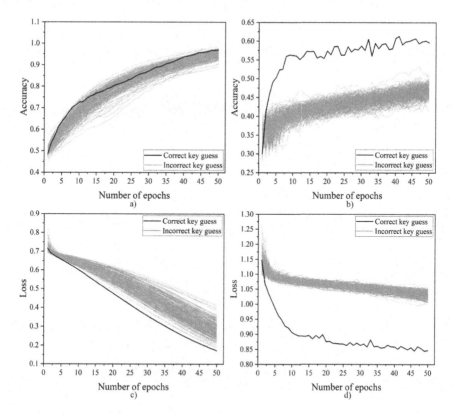

**Fig. 5.** The attack results of models using LSB and SHW labeling technique on Gaussian noise added ASCAD data (Standard deviation of noise= 3.0) a,c) Accuracy and loss of $MLP_{ref1}$ using LSB label; b,d) Accuracy and loss of $MLP_{proposed}$ using SHW label.

For investigating the effect of noise, we performed further experiments, including adding Gaussian noise to power traces and training our model again. We assume raw power traces from ASCAD database are low noise, and they have no impact of measurement equipment. Our method for adding noise is different with [8,11] that the Gaussian noise is added directly on the power traces. It means that we try to simulate the real scenario when an attacker performs the power measurements. The experiment results are shown in Fig. 5. In this case, we observe both the accuracy and loss metrics. It clearly shows that $MLP_{ref1}$ can not distinguish correct key based on accuracy. In contrast, $MLP_{proposed}$ using SHW label provides good performance. As depicted in Fig. 5(b,d), the correct key is easy to be discriminated from the rest. In addition, we can observe that the loss metric gives better results. Therefore, loss metric is the main criterion in our next experiments.

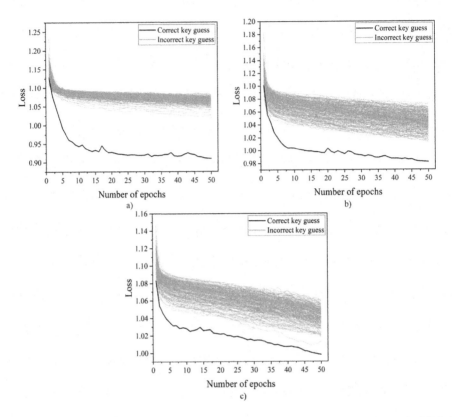

**Fig. 6.** The attack results on RISC-V data with different standard deviation of additive noise a) 0; b) 0.002; c) 0.004.

To prove the efficiency of SHW labeling and proposed ML architecture on different platforms, we perform the same experiment above on the power trace collected from a 32-bit RISC-V processor, as described in Sect. 2. We will investigate the adaption of those techniques for the new dataset. As a result shown in Fig. 6., it is clear that our proposed MLP models have good performance in discriminating the correct key, even with the presence of small level of noise. Besides the efficiency of SHW labeling technique, we can see that additive noise adversely affects the performance of non-profiling DL-based SCA attacks. The more noise added on power traces, DL is more adaptive with the wrong hypothesis key as depicted in Fig. 6c. It leads to more difficulty in discriminating the correct key.

**Table 3.** Hyperparameters of MLP models using in experiments.

| Hyperparameters | $MLP_{ref1}$ | $MLP_{ref2}$ | $MLP_{Proposed}$ |
|---|---|---|---|
| Input | 700 | 700 | 50 |
| Hidden layer | 2 | 2 | 6 |
| Neuron | $20 \times 10$ | $20 \times 10$ | $50 \times 100 \times 150 \times 100 \times 50 \times 25$ |
| Label | LSB | SHW | SHW |
| Optimizer | Adam | | |
| Activation | RELU | RELU | ELU |
| Learning rate | 0.001 | | |
| Batch size | 1000 | | |
| Initializing | Xavier Initialization | | |

## 5  Conclusion

In this paper, we have proposed a new MLP instance using the SHW labeling technique to overcome the practical issue like imbalanced classes, high dimensional data in non-profiled DL based SCA context. Our experiments were performed for both types of the original power trace and the power trace with the added Gaussian noise. The results have clarified that our data preparation technique is capable of extracting the useful features for the non-profiled SCA based on neural networks. Furthermore, our proposed model architecture provides reliable results for non-profiled attacks on variety datasets like ASCAD, RISC-V MCU. Significantly, the proposed MLP model using SHW labeling provides better performance than that of Binary labeling with the presence of additive noise. Additionally, the results have shown that the Gaussian noise added on power traces becomes a serious problem compared to the benefits of noise added in the profiling attack. In future work, we will investigate several other activation functions and pre-processing methods to increase neural networks' performance for non-profiled attacks.

**Acknowledgment.** This research is funded by Vietnam National Foundation for Science and Technology Development (NAFOSTED) under grant number 102.02-2020.14.

## References

1. Alipour, A., Papadimitriou, A., Beroulle, V., Aerabi, E., Hély, D.: On the performance of non-profiled differential deep learning attacks against an AES encryption algorithm protected using a correlated noise generation based hiding countermeasure. In: 2020 Design, Automation Test in Europe Conference Exhibition (DATE), pp. 614–617 (2020). https://doi.org/10.23919/DATE48585.2020.9116387
2. Hettwer, B., Gehrer, S., Güneysu, T.: Applications of machine learning techniques in side-channel attacks: a survey. J. Cryptogr. Eng. **10**(2), 135–162 (2019). https://doi.org/10.1007/s13389-019-00212-8

3. Cagli, E., Dumas, C., Prouff, E.: Convolutional neural networks with data augmentation against jitter-based countermeasures. In: Fischer, W., Homma, N. (eds.) CHES 2017. LNCS, vol. 10529, pp. 45–68. Springer, Cham (2017). https://doi.org/10.1007/978-3-319-66787-4_3

4. Do, N.T., Hoang, V.P., Doan, V.S.: Performance analysis of non-profiled side channel attacks based on convolutional neural networks. In: 2020 IEEE Asia Pacific Conference on Circuits and Systems (APCCAS), pp. 66–69 (2020). https://doi.org/10.1109/APCCAS50809.2020.9301673

5. Do, N.-T., Hoang, V.-P.: An efficient side channel attack technique with improved correlation power analysis. In: Vo, N.-S., Hoang, V.-P. (eds.) INISCOM 2020. LNICST, vol. 334, pp. 291–300. Springer, Cham (2020). https://doi.org/10.1007/978-3-030-63083-6_22

6. Gilmore, R., Hanley, N., O'Neill, M.: Neural network based attack on a masked implementation of AES. In: 2015 IEEE International Symposium on Hardware Oriented Security and Trust (HOST), pp. 106–111 (2015). https://doi.org/10.1109/HST.2015.7140247

7. Hu, W., Wu, L., Wang, A., Xie, X., Zhu, Z., Luo, S.: Adaptive chosen-plaintext correlation power analysis. In: 2014 Tenth International Conference on Computational Intelligence and Security, pp. 494–498 (2014). https://doi.org/10.1109/CIS.2014.94

8. Kim, J., Picek, S., Heuser, A., Bhasin, S., Hanjalic, A.: Make some noise. unleashing the power of convolutional neural networks for profiled side-channel analysis. IACR Transactions on Cryptographic Hardware and Embedded Systems, pp. 148–179, May 2019. https://doi.org/10.46586/tches.v2019.i3.148-179

9. Kingma, D., Ba, J.: Adam: a method for stochastic optimization. In: International Conference on Learning Representations, December 2014

10. Lerman, L., Bontempi, G., Markowitch, O.: A machine learning approach against a masked AES. J. Cryptogr. Eng. 5, 123–139 (2014)

11. Maghrebi, H.: Deep learning based side channel attacks in practice. IACR Cryptol. ePrint Arch. 2019, 578 (2019)

12. Picek, S., Heuser, A., Jovic, A., Bhasin, S., Regazzoni, F.: The curse of class imbalance and conflicting metrics with machine learning for side-channel evaluations (2018). https://ia.cr/2018/476

13. Picek, S., Samiotis, I.P., Kim, J., Heuser, A., Bhasin, S., Legay, A.: On the performance of convolutional neural networks for side-channel analysis. In: Chattopadhyay, A., Rebeiro, C., Yarom, Y. (eds.) SPACE 2018. LNCS, vol. 11348, pp. 157–176. Springer, Cham (2018). https://doi.org/10.1007/978-3-030-05072-6_10

14. Prouff, E., Strullu, R., Benadjila, R., Cagli, E., Canovas, C.: Study of deep learning techniques for side-channel analysis and introduction to ASCAD database. IACR Cryptol. ePrint Arch. 10, 53 (2018)

15. Timon, B.: Non-profiled deep learning-based side-channel attacks. IACR Cryptol. ePrint Arch. 2018, 196 (2018)

16. Won, Y.S., Han, D.G., Jap, D., Bhasin, S., Park, J.Y.: Non-profiled side-channel attack based on deep learning using picture trace. IEEE Access 9, 22480–22492 (2021). https://doi.org/10.1109/ACCESS.2021.3055833

# Full-Duplex UAV Aided Communication in the Presence of Multiple Malicious Jammers

Zhiyu Huang[1], Zhichao Sheng[1(✉)], Huabo Fu[1], Lin Ye[2], Hao Wei[3], and Yong Fang[1]

[1] Key Laboratory of Specialty Fiber Optics and Optical Access Networks, Shanghai University, Shanghai 200444, China
{rain-huang,zcsheng,huabfff,yfang}@shu.edu.cn
[2] Enjoymove Technology, Shanghai 200032, China
lin.ye@enjoymove.com
[3] ZTE Coperation, Shenzhen 518055, China
wei.hao@zte.com.cn

**Abstract.** This paper studies a hybrid communication system, where the full-duplex unmanned aerial vehicle (UAV) communicates with the downlink users (DLUs) and uplink users (ULUs) simultaneously in the presence of multiple jammers. To improve quality of service of both ULUs and DLUs, we formulate an optimization problem, which maximizes the sum throughput of downlink and uplink by jointly designing the UAV trajectory , the scheduling of ULUs/DLUs, and the ULUs'transmit power. Notwithstanding, the formulated problem is non-convex hence computationally insoluble. We propose a low-complexity algorithm that is based on block coordinate descend and successive convex approximation techniques to effectively solve this problem. Numerical outcomes demonstrate that the proposed algorithm can improve throughput significantly comparing to the existing algorithm.

**Keywords:** Unmanned aerial vehicle (UAV) · Malicious jammer · Full-duplex · Non-convex

## 1 Introduction

Due to the adaptable capability and high maneuverability, unmanned aerial vehicle (UAV) has played an important role in the B5G/6G mobile network. Because the line-of-sight (LoS) links [1] is dominant when UAV works in the certain altitude, the channel path-loss is smaller than the one in the terrestrial communication. In addition, full-duplex (FD) technique providing approaches

---

This work was supported in part by the National Natural Science Foundation of China (NSFC) under Grant 61901254 and in part by the Aeronautical Science Foundation of China under Grant 2020Z0660S6001.

N.-S. Vo et al. (Eds.): INISCOM 2022, LNICST 444, pp. 255–266, 2022.
https://doi.org/10.1007/978-3-031-08878-0_18

for simultaneous signal transmission and reception (STR), will be promising to combine with UAV to flexibly perform high-performance STR.

In [2], the FD secrecy communication for the UAV was studied, where the aim of the reseachers was to maximize the UAV's energy efficiency through jointly optimizing the UAV trajectory and transmit powers during a given duration. In [3], the authors studied FD UAV relaying multiple nodes to maximize the network's throughput by jointly optimizing the user scheduling, the UAV trajactory and the UAV transmit power. In [4], FD UAV aided uplink and downlink communication system was studied, where the UAV simultaneously communicates with ULUs and DLUs. An iterative algorithm has been propounded to maximize the throughput of the system through optimizing the UAV trajectory, DLU/ULU scheduling, and ULU transmit power. In [5], the authors studied the UAV that simultaneously communicated with DLUs and ULUs and propounded an iterative algorithm for throughput maximization through optimizing the communication scheduling, UAV transmit power and 3D UAV trajectory. The antecedent researches, nevertheless, have not investigated the transmission among the FD UAV, DLUs and ULUs in the existence of malicious jammers.

In this paper, we investigate FD UAV aided STR with time division Multiple Access (TDMA) manner in the existence of multiple malicious jammers. To improve the performance under malicious jammers, we concentrate on maximizing the aggregate throughput of both DLUs and ULUs through jointly optimizing DLU/ULU scheduling, the UAV trajectory, ULU transmit power. The formulated problem is a non-convex problem hence computationally insoluble. A low-complexity algorithm is proposed by utilizing both the block coordinate descent (BCD) and successive convex approximation (SCA) techniques. Numerical results illustrate that our propounded algorithm's performance is more effective than the existent solutions.

## 2    System Model and Problem Formulation

We suppose a UAV aided communication system, as demonstrated in Fig. 1, where the UAV tends to transmit signal to $K_D$ single-antenna DLUs and receive signal from $K_U$ single-antenna ULUs under $M$ malicious jammers. Define $\mathcal{K}_D = \{1,2,...,K_D\}$, $\mathcal{K}_U = \{1,2,...,K_U\}$ and $\mathcal{M} = \{1,2,...,M\}$ as the series of DLUs, ULUs and malicious jammers, respectively. On the horizon, the location of DLU $j$ is denoted as $w_j$, $j \in \mathcal{K}_D$, the location of ULU $i$ is denoted as $w_i$, $i \in \mathcal{K}_U$, and the location of jammer $m$ is denoted as $w_m$, $m \in \mathcal{M}$. The UAV is considered to fly at a fixed altitude $H$. The total flight duration $T$ is equally divided into $N$ time slots (TSs) $\delta$. Let $Q_{start}$ denotes the start point while $Q_{end}$ denotes the end point, and the horizontal coordinate of UAV $Q[n]$ at TS $n$ is supposed to satisfy the constrains:

$$\|Q[n] - Q[n-1]\| \leq V_{\max}\delta, \; n = 1, 2, 3, \ldots, N, \qquad (1)$$

$$Q_{start} = Q[0], Q_{end} = Q[N], \qquad (2)$$

where $V_{\max}$ is the maximum horizontal speed of the UAV.

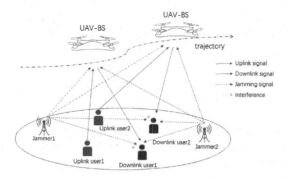

**Fig. 1.** Full-duplex UAV aided STR system under malicious jamming.

As shown in the 3GPP, The air-to-ground communication channel between the UAV and the user is mostly influenced by LoS, particularly in rural and suburban area [1]. Consequently, the channel power gains from the UAV to the $j$-th DLU, $i$-th ULU, $m$-th jammer, respectively, can be given by

$$g_{b,j} = \frac{\beta_0}{\|Q[n] - w_j\|^2 + H^2}, j \in \mathcal{K}_D, \tag{3}$$

$$g_{i,b} = \frac{\beta_0}{\|Q[n] - w_i\|^2 + H^2}, i \in \mathcal{K}_U, \tag{4}$$

$$g_{m,b} = \frac{\beta_0}{\|Q[n] - w_m\|^2 + H^2}, m \in \mathcal{M}, \tag{5}$$

where $\beta_0$ denotes the channel power gain at the reference distance and $H$ is the altitude of the UAV.

The channel model between the $m$-th jammer and $j$-th DLU is influenced by Rayleigh fading, and the channel gain is set as $h_{m,j}[n] = \beta_0 d_{m,j}^{-\alpha} \varrho$ [7], where $d_{m,j}$ is the distance between the $m$-th jammer and the $j$-th DLU, $\varrho$ is a random variable, and $\alpha$ denotes the path loss exponent. Also, the channel gain between the $i$-th ULU and the $j$-th DLU is denoted as $h_{i,j}[n] = \beta_0 d_{i,j}^{-\alpha} \varrho$.

To mitigate interference, a TDMA protocol based transmission is considered where the UAV can communicate with a DLU and a ULU over single TS. Such a protocol has to satisfy:

$$\sum_{j=1}^{K_D} x_j^d[n] \leq 1, \forall n, \tag{6}$$

$$x_j^d[n] \in \{0, 1\}, \forall j, n, \tag{7}$$

$$\sum_{i=1}^{K_U} x_i^u[n] \leq 1, \forall n, \tag{8}$$

$$x_i^u[n] \in \{0, 1\}, \forall i, n, \tag{9}$$

where (6) and (7) denote the scheduling constrains of the DLUs, while (8) and (9) denote the scheduling constrains of the ULUs.

The achievable throughput of the $j$-th DLU over TS $n$ is given by

$$R_j^d[n] = \log_2(1 + \frac{p_b g_{b,j}[n]}{\sum_{i=1}^{K_U} x_i^u[n]\beta_0 d_{i,j}^{-\alpha} p_i[n] + \sum_{m=1}^{M} P_m \beta_0 d_{m,j}^{-\alpha} + \sigma^2}), \quad (10)$$

where $\sigma^2$ denotes the value of white Gaussian noise power, $p_b$ represents UAV transmit power and $P_m$ is the transmit power of $m$-th jammer. Again, the throughput of the UAV from $i$-th ULU is as follows

$$R_i^u[n] = \log_2(1 + \frac{p_i[n]g_{i,b}[n]}{f_b[n] + \sum_{m=1}^{M} P_m g_{m,b} + \sigma^2}), \quad (11)$$

where $f_b[n]$ is the self-interference over TS $n$ from other ULUs to the FD UAV [4]. $p_i[n]$ denotes the uplink transmit power of $i$-th ULU at TS $n$.

Define $\mathcal{X}_D = \{x_j^d[n], \forall j, n\}$, $\mathcal{X}_U = \{x_i^u[n], \forall i, n\}$, $\mathcal{P} = \{p_i[n], \forall i, n\}$, $\mathcal{Q} = \{Q[n], \forall n\}$, then a throughput maximization problem subject to the UAV mobility constrains, the transmit power of ULUs constrains and the scheduling constrains is formulated as:

$$\max_{\mathcal{X}_D, \mathcal{X}_U, \mathcal{Q}, \mathcal{P}} \sum_{n=1}^{N} \sum_{j=1}^{K_D} x_j^d[n] R_j^d[n] + \sum_{n=1}^{N} \sum_{i=1}^{K_U} x_i^u[n] R_i^u[n] \quad (12a)$$

$$\text{s.t.} \quad 0 \le p_i[n] \le P_{\max}, \forall i, n, \quad (12b)$$

$$(1), (2), (6) - (9), \quad (12c)$$

where $P_{\max}$ denotes the transmit power budget of ULUs.

## 3    Proposed Algorithm

By virtue of the non-concave objective function, the problem is non-convex and is not solvable efficiently. Besides, the existence of the binary constrains (7) and (9) makes the problem computationally intractable. Firstly, we transform the constrains into the linear constrains [6], which can be expressed as follows

$$0 \le x_j^d[n] \le 1, \forall j, n, \quad (13)$$

$$0 \le x_i^u[n] \le 1, \forall i, n. \quad (14)$$

Subsequently by applying BCD, we propound an algorithm to solve the problem (12a) through alternatively optimizing $\mathcal{X}_D$, $\mathcal{X}_U$, $\mathcal{Q}$, and $\mathcal{P}$.

## 3.1 Design for DLU Scheduling

We suppose that ULU scheduling $\mathcal{X}_U$, UAV trajectory $\mathcal{Q}$, and ULU transmit power $\mathcal{P}$ have been given. And, the problem is given by

$$\max_{\mathcal{X}_D} \sum_{n=1}^{N} \sum_{j=1}^{K_D} x_j^d[n] R_j^d[n] \tag{15a}$$

$$\text{s.t. } (6), (13). \tag{15b}$$

The problem (15) has satisfied the condition of the linear programming and we can obtain the solution efficiently.

## 3.2 Design for ULU Scheduling

Similarly, we assume that DLU scheduling $\mathcal{X}_D$, trajectory of UAV $\mathcal{Q}$, and ULU transmit power $\mathcal{P}$ have been given, the problem for DLU scheduling is written as

$$\max_{\mathcal{X}_U} \sum_{n=1}^{N} \sum_{j=1}^{K_D} x_j^d[n] R_j^d[n] + \sum_{n=1}^{N} \sum_{i=1}^{K_U} x_i^u[n] R_i^u[n] \tag{16a}$$

$$\text{s.t. } (8), (14). \tag{16b}$$

With respect to the variable $x_i^u[n]$, the throughput of downlink $R_j^d[n]$ is non-concave so that problem (16) cannot be solved effectively. In the sequel, we adopt SCA to derive the lower bound with a feasible point $\{x_i^{u,r}\}$,

$$R_j^d[n] \geq \log_2(1 + \frac{p_b g_{b,j}}{T_j^r[n]}) - \sum_{i=1}^{K_U} \frac{\beta_0 d_{i,j}^{-\alpha} p_i[n] p_b g_{b,j} \log_2^e}{T_j^r[n](T_j^r[n] + p_b g_{b,j})} (x_i^u[n] - x_i^{u,r}[n]),$$

$$\triangleq \mathcal{R}_j^d[n] \tag{17}$$

where $T_j^r[n] = \sum_{i=1}^{K_U} x_i^{u,r} \beta_0 d_{i,j}^{-\alpha} p_i[n] + \sum_{m=1}^{M} P_m \beta_0 d_{m,j}^{-\alpha} + \sigma^2$. Then, the problem (16) can be reconstruct as:

$$\max_{\mathcal{X}_U} \sum_{n=1}^{N} \sum_{j=1}^{K_D} x_j^d[n] \mathcal{R}_j^d[n] + \sum_{n=1}^{N} \sum_{i=1}^{K_U} x_i^u[n] R_i^u[n] \tag{18a}$$

$$\text{s.t. } (8), (14). \tag{18b}$$

We can update the ULU scheduling $\mathcal{X}_U$ by optimizing problem (18).

### 3.3  Design for UAV Trajectory

In like manner, with the given DLU scheduling $\mathcal{X}_D$, ULU scheduling $\mathcal{X}_U$, and ULU transmit power $P$, the problem for the UAV trajectory is formulated as follows

$$\max_{\mathcal{Q}} \sum_{n=1}^{N} \sum_{j=1}^{K_D} x_j^d[n] R_j^d[n] + \sum_{n=1}^{N} \sum_{i=1}^{K_U} x_i^u[n] R_i^u[n] \tag{19a}$$

$$\text{s.t. } (1),(2). \tag{19b}$$

In the first part, the downlink throughput expression of problem (19) is non-convex. Then, we take the first-order Taylor expansion at TS $n$ $\|Q^r[n] - w_j\|$ to get the lower bound:

$$R_j^d[n] \geq \log_2(1 + \frac{D_j[n]}{\|Q^r[n] - w_j\|^2 + H^2}) - \Gamma_j[n] \times (\|Q[n] - w_j\|^2 - \|Q^r[n] - w_j\|^2)$$

$$\triangleq \Phi^{lb}(R_j^d[n]), \tag{20}$$

where

$$\Gamma_j[n] = \frac{D_j[n] \log_2^e}{(D_j[n] + \|Q^r[n] - w_j\|^2 + H^2)(\|Q^r[n] - w_j\|^2 + H^2)}$$

and

$$D_j[n] = \frac{p_b \beta_0}{\sum_{i=1}^{K_U} x_i^u[n] \beta_0 d_{i,j}^{-\alpha} p_i[n] + \sum_{m=1}^{M} P_m \beta_0 d_{m,j}^{-\alpha} + \sigma^2}.$$

The uplink throughput expression of problem (19) is also non-convex. Introduce slack variables $L_{i,b}[n]$ and $I_b[n]$ then the uplink throughput expression is rewritten as

$$\bar{R}_i^u[n] = \log_2(1 + \frac{1}{L_{i,b}[n] I_b[n]}), \forall n, \tag{21}$$

with additional constraints

$$p_i[n] g_{i,b}[n] \geq L_{i,b}[n]^{-1}, \forall n, \tag{22}$$

and

$$f_b[n] + \sum_{m=1}^{M} P_m g_{m,b}[n] + \sigma^2 \leq I_b[n], \forall n. \tag{23}$$

However, the problem (21) cannot be solved effectively due to the non-concave objective function and the non-convex constrains (23). To handle the problem (21), we apply the following lemma to derive an approximate result.

**Lemma.** *With any given achievable point* $(L_{i,b}^r[n], I_b^r[n])$, *$\bar{R}_{i,b}$ should be lower bounded by*

$$\bar{R}_{i,b}^{lb}[n] = \log_2\left(\frac{1}{L_{i,b}^r[n]I_b^r[n]}\right) + \phi_{i,b}(L_{i,b}[n] - L_{i,b}^r[n]) + \psi_{i,b}(I_b[n] - I_b^r[n]), \quad (24)$$

where $\phi_{i,b} = -\frac{\log_2^e}{(L_{i,b}^r[n]+(L_{i,b}^r[n])^2 I_b^r[n])}$ and $\psi_{i,b} = -\frac{\log_2^e}{(I_b^r[n]+(I_b^r[n])^2 L_{i,b}^r[n])}$

Through introducing slack variable $d_m[n]$, the constrains (23) can be substituted by

$$f_b[n] + \sum_{m=1}^{M} P_m \beta_0 d_m[n]^{-1} + \sigma^2 \leq I_b[n], \forall n, \quad (25)$$

$$d_m[n] \leq ||Q[n] - w_m||^2 + H^2, \forall n, \quad (26)$$

$$d_m[n] \geq 0, \forall n. \quad (27)$$

Next, by taking the first-order Taylor expansion, we can derive the lower bound of right hand side (RHS) of constrains (26)

$$C_{m,b}^l = ||Q^r[n] - w_m||^2 + 2(Q^r[n] - w_m)^T(Q[n] - Q^r[n]) + H^2, \quad (28)$$

then, the constrains (26) can be rebuilt as

$$d_m[n] \leq C_{m,b}^l, \forall n, \quad (29)$$

As a result, the original problem (19) is approached as follows:

$$\max_{\mathcal{Q}} \sum_{n=1}^{N}\sum_{j=1}^{K_D} x_j^d[n]\Phi^{lb}(R_j^d[n]) + \sum_{n=1}^{N}\sum_{i=1}^{K_U} x_i^u[n]\bar{R}_{i,b}^{lb}[n] \quad (30a)$$

$$\text{s.t. } (1), (2), (22), (25), (27), (29). \quad (30b)$$

Solve the convex problem (30) to update the UAV trajectory $Q$.

### 3.4 Design for ULU Transmit Power Control

With the given DLU scheduling $\mathcal{X}_D$, ULU scheduling $\mathcal{X}_U$, and the UAV trajectory $\mathcal{Q}$, the problem for the ULU transmit power $P$ is written as:

$$\max_{\mathcal{P}} \sum_{n=1}^{N}\sum_{j=1}^{K_D} x_j^d[n]R_j^d[n] + \sum_{n=1}^{N}\sum_{i=1}^{K_U} x_i^u[n]R_i^u[n] \quad (31a)$$

$$\text{s.t. } (12b). \quad (31b)$$

With respect to $p_i[n]$, the expression $R_j^d[n]$ in the first part is convex. Thus, the problem (31) is a non-convex problem. We also apply the first-order Taylor expansion at achievable point $\{p_i^r[n]\}$ to be approximated as:

$$R_j^d[n] \geq \log_2(1 + \frac{p_b g_{b,j}[n]}{E_j^r[n]}) - \sum_{i=1}^{K_U} \frac{\beta_0 d_{i,j}^{-\alpha} x_i^u[n] p_b g_{b,j} \log_2^e}{E_j^r[n](E_j^r[n] + p_b g_{b,j}[n])}(p_i[n] - p_i^r[n]),$$

$$\triangleq \Upsilon^{lb}(R_j^d[n]) \tag{32}$$

where $E_j^r[n] = \sum_{i=1}^{K_U} x_i^u[n] \beta_0 d_{i,j}^{-\alpha} p_i^r[n] + \sum_{m=1}^M P_m \beta_0 d_{m,j}^{-\alpha} + \sigma^2$.
The objective function (31a) can be rewritten as:

$$\max_{\mathcal{P}} \sum_{n=1}^N \sum_{j=1}^{K_D} x_j^d[n] \Upsilon^{lb}(R_j^d[n]) + \sum_{n=1}^N \sum_{i=1}^{K_U} x_i^u[n] R_i^u[n] \tag{33a}$$

$$\text{s.t. } (12c). \tag{33b}$$

Then, the problem (31) can be approximately solved by solving problem (33).

---

**Algorithm 1.** Algorithm Proposed for Solving (12)

---

1: **Initialization:** Set $r = 0$. Find initial feasible points $\{Q^r[n]\}$, $\{x_i^{u,r}[n]\}$, $\{x_j^{d,r}[n]\}$, $\{p_i^r[n]\}$ for (12), set $\epsilon > 0$.
2: **repeat.**
3: Solve the problem (15) to update the optimum point as $\{x_j^{d,r+1}[n]\}$ with $\{Q^r[n]\}$, $\{x_i^{u,r}[n]\}$, $\{p_i^r[n]\}$.
4: Solve the problem (16) to update the optimum point as $\{x_i^{u,r+1}[n]\}$ with $\{Q^r[n]\}$, $\{x_j^{d,r+1}[n]\}$, $\{p_i^r[n]\}$.
5: Solve the problem (19) to update the optimum point as $\{Q^{r+1}[n]\}$ with $\{x_i^{u,r+1}[n]\}$, $\{x_j^{d,r+1}[n]\}$, $\{p_i^r[n]\}$.
6: Solve the problem (31) to update the optimum point as $\{p_i^{r+1}[n]\}$ with $\{x_i^{u,r+1}[n]\}$, $\{x_j^{d,r+1}[n]\}$, $\{Q^{r+1}[n]\}$.
7: Set $r := r + 1$
8: **Until** the fractional growth of the objective value of (12) is within the tolerance $\epsilon$

---

## 4    Numerical Results

In this segment, numerical outcomes are obtained to demonstrate our proposed algorithm's performance. We think about multiple ULUs, jammers and DLUs. Locations of DLUs and ULUs are set as $D_1 = (200, 700)$, $D_2 = (600, 200)$, $U_1 = (200, 800)$ and $U_2 = (600, 150)$, jammers in $(200, 200)$ and $(700, 700)$. The value of the self-interference is $f_b[n] - 130 \, \text{dB}$ and the value of the tolerance is $\epsilon = 10^{-3}$ [4]. Besides, the UAV altitude is fixed at $H = 100 \, \text{m}$. The bandwidth is $B = 1 \, \text{MHz}$ and the UAV maximal horizontal speed is $V_{max} = 50 \, \text{m/s}$. The UAV maximal transmit power, the ULU maximal transmit power and the transmit power of jammers are respectively assumed as $p_b = 0.1 \, \text{W}$, $P_{max} = 0.1 \, \text{W}$ and $P_m = 0.05 \, \text{W}$. We assume that $\alpha = 3, \delta = 0.5, \beta_0 = -60 \, \text{dB}$ and $\sigma^2 = -110 \, \text{dBm}$ [6].

Figure 2 plots the UAV trajectories based on our algorithm versus flight time $T$. The UAV flight start point and end point respectively are set as $Q_s = (0, 500)$

and $Q_e = (1000, 500)$. Apparently, UAV flies away from jammer1 and reaches $D_1$ in three cases. However, when flight time is small, i.e., $T = 30$ s, $T = 50$ s, it can be observed that UAV has to reach final point in an arc path due to the constrains of the trajectory design after passing $D_1$. If $T$ is sufficiently large, i.e., $T = 110$ s, UAV not only flies to the $D_1$, but also flies to the $U_2$ away from jammer2 and finally reaches the final point for maximizing the throughput.

In following simulations, "Our proposed Algorithm 1" refers to the proposed algorithm, while "Baseline algorithm" refers to the benchmark algorithm without the presence of jammers. Figure 3 shows that the throughput of both downlink and uplink versus flight time $T$. As the time $T$ increasing, the performance of our algorithm is better than the benchmark algorithm. Figure 4 and 5 show the UAV throughput of algorithms versus the number of jammers $M$ and jammers transmit power $P_m$. Observe that the throughput of algorithms decrease gradually, because the denominator of objective function (12a) increases when the number of jammers or the transmit power of jammers increases. The simulation outcomes illustrate that our proposed algorithm is superior over the benchmark algorithm.

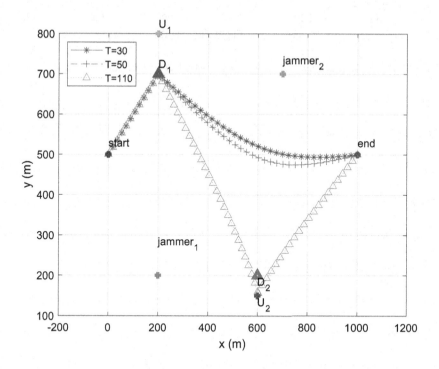

**Fig. 2.** Trajectory of UAV for different period T.

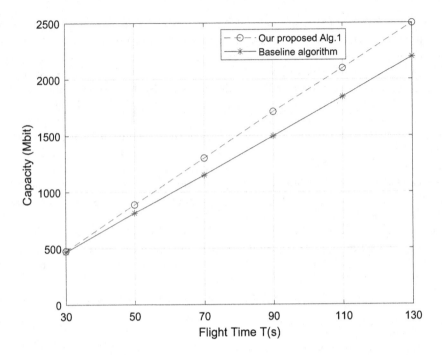

**Fig. 3.** Capacity of UAV versus different period T.

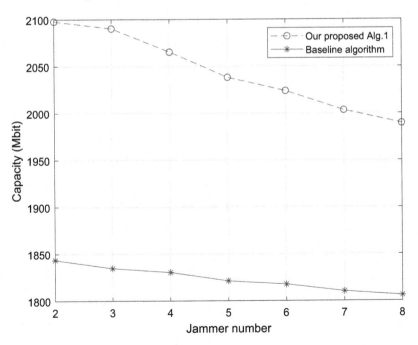

**Fig. 4.** Capacity of UAV versus the number of malicious jammers.

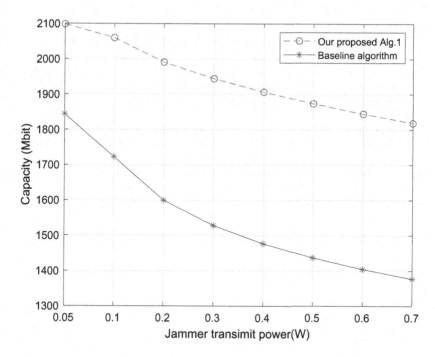

**Fig. 5.** Capacity of UAV versus the transmit power of malicious jammers.

## 5    Conclusion

In this research, a FD UAV communication scheme has been studied, where a FD UAV is used to communicate with DLUs and ULUs in the presence of malicious jammers. A throughput maximization problem has been formulated by iteratively optimizing the scheduling of ULUs/DLUs, the UAV trajectory, and the transmit power of ULUs. Because the proposed problem is non-convex and computationally insoluble, a low-complexity algorithm based on BCD and SCA techniques has been propounded. Our numerical results have illustrated that our algorithm outperforms than the existent algorithm.

## References

1. Lin, X., et al.: The sky is not the limit: LTE for unmanned aerial vehicles. IEEE Commun. Mag. **56**(4), 204–210 (2018). https://doi.org/10.1109/MCOM.2018. 1700643
2. Duo, B., Wu, Q., Yuan, X., Zhang, R.: Energy efficiency maximization for full-duplex UAV secrecy communication. IEEE Trans. Veh. Technol. **69**(4), 4590–4595 (2020). https://doi.org/10.1109/TVT.2020.2977948
3. Li, B., Zhao, S., Zhang, R., Yang, L.: Full-duplex UAV relaying for multiple user pairs. IEEE Internet Things. J. **8**(6), 4657–4667 (2021). https://doi.org/10.1109/ JIOT.2020.3027621

4. Hua, M., Yang, L., Pan, C., Nallanathan, A.: Throughput maximization for full-duplex UAV aided small cell wireless systems. IEEE Wireless Commun. Lett. **9**(4), 475–479 (2020). https://doi.org/10.1109/LWC.2019.2959527

5. Hua, M., Yang, L., Wu, Q., Swindlehurst, A.L.: 3D UAV trajectory and communication design for simultaneous uplink and downlink transmission. IEEE Trans. Wirel. Commun. **68**(9), 5908–5923 (2020). https://doi.org/10.1109/TCOMM.2020.3003662

6. Wu, Q., Zeng, Y., Zhang, R.: Joint trajectory and communication design for Multi-UAV enabled wireless networks. IEEE Trans. Wirel. Commun. **17**(3), 2109–2121 (2018). https://doi.org/10.1109/TWC.2017.2789293

7. Zeng, Y., Zhang, R.: Energy-efficient UAV communication with trajectory optimization. IEEE Trans. Wirel. Commun. **16**(6), 3747–3760 (2017). https://doi.org/10.1109/TWC.2017.2688328

# On Secrecy Analysis of UAV-Enabled Relaying NOMA Systems with RF Energy Harvesting

Anh-Nhat Nguyen[1]($\boxtimes$), Dac-Binh Ha[2], Van-Truong Truong[2], Chakchai So-In[1], Phet Aimtongkham[1], Chinapat Sakunrasrisuay[1], and Chatchai Punriboon[1]

[1] Department of Computer Science, Khon Kaen University,
Khon Kaen 40002, Thailand
{nguyenanhnhat,chinapat.s,chatchai}@kkumail.com,
{chakso,phetim}@kku.ac.th
[2] Faculty of Electrical-Electronics Engineering, Duy Tan University,
Danang 550000, Vietnam
hadacbinh@duytan.edu.vn, truongvantruong@dtu.edu.vn

**Abstract.** This paper investigates the physical-layer security (PLS) for the Internet of Things (IoT) using nonorthogonal multiple access (NOMA) with an unmanned aerial vehicle (UAV)-enabled relaying (UR) cluster in an urban environment. Consider a scenario where two energy-limited IoT device (ID) clusters can use radio frequency (RF) energy harvesting (EH) to send messages to a destination with the help of a UR cluster in the presence of a passive eavesdropper. We propose a UR and ID selection scheme, as well as the usage of artificial noise (AN), to increase the PLS performance of system. As a result, closed-form closed-form secrecy outage probability (SOP) expressions are derived. The effects of network parameters on secrecy performance are also investigated to better understand the NOMA UR system with NOMA UR. Finally, the accuracy of our analysis is verified by Monte-Carlo simulation results.

**Keywords:** Internet of Things · Unmanned aerial vehicles · Radio frequency energy harvesting · Nonorthogonal multiple access · Physical layer security

## 1 Introduction

Unmanned aerial vehicles (UAVs) can provide advanced services for edge-enabled Internet of Things (IoT) applications, such as communication relays for ubiquitous connectivity to ground IDs, due to their advantages of controllable mobility, flexible deployment, and strong Line-of-Sight (LoS) channels [1–3]. For example, the authors of [2] proposed a UAV-enabled relaying (UR) network with a UAV acting as a decode-and-forward (DF) relay. In [3], Liang *et al.* studied an amplify-and-forward (AF) UR network with the channels between the UR and ground devices modeled as LoS propagation.

© ICST Institute for Computer Sciences, Social Informatics and Telecommunications Engineering 2022
Published by Springer Nature Switzerland AG 2022. All Rights Reserved
N.-S. Vo et al. (Eds.): INISCOM 2022, LNICST 444, pp. 267–281, 2022.
https://doi.org/10.1007/978-3-031-08878-0_19

IDs often use rechargeable batteries to keep networks connected. Batteries must be recharged regularly to ensure continuous operation. For energy-limited devices, a new technology is known as radio frequency (RF) energy harvesting [4,5] has emerged to extend and increase battery life [6]. Because of their mobility and adaptability, UR provides wireless power transfer (WPT) to ID while also collecting and transmitting data to the target [7,8]. In [7] investigated UR use DF scheme in IoT network network, in which UR first power many IDs via WPT, and then IDs harvest energy to transmit data to UR. Similar to the model in [7,8] employed both DF and AF schemes to UR.

Recently, nonorthogonal multiple access (NOMA) has much potential to improve IDs' transmission efficiency and connectivity [9]. Through superposition coding and successive interference cancellation (SIC), NOMA improves system throughput and spectral efficiency by enabling multi-user spectrum sharing [10]. NOMA has been applied in several scenarios, with UAV-assisted NOMA being a promising IoT solution [11]. Jiang et al. employ a NOMA DF UR to ferry data from a remote base station (BS) to multiple ground IDs. Moreover, in [12] analyzed the performance of a NOMA DF UR-assisted WPT network, where the UR is used as RF power transmitter and as a communication relay between EH IDs and a BS.

In addition, the communication between the UAV and IDs may be eavesdropped on by nearby eavesdroppers, and the communication links may be attacked due to wireless signal propagation characteristics. Thus, the secrecy of UAV-based communication is a significant aspect affecting system performance [13]. In this context, PLS can protect wireless data transmissions without requiring secret keys or sophisticated algorithms, making it more suited for low cost IDs [14]. For example, Wang et al. suggested a mobile relaying strategy with four nodes: source, destination, UR, and eavesdropper [15]. In [16], the secrecy performance of simultaneous wireless information and power transfer UR system was studied using both AF and DF schemes.

Motivated by the above discussion, the secrecy performance for IoT systems deploying RF EH NOMA UR over Rayleigh fading channels is studied in this paper. In addition, we consider the probability of LoS and non-LoS (NLoS) for UR-ground device wireless channels. Furthermore, we consider the imperfect SIC (iSIC) component to ensure that the model is as close to reality. The following are our paper's main contributions:

- We propose the UR-ID selection scheme to improve system secrecy performance by using the (AN) generated by the selected UR to enhance the PLS.
- We derive closed-form expressions of SOP for each ID cluster and the entire system.
- The system secrecy performance is examined by numerical results to verify the efficiency of our system.

The remainder of this paper is organized as follows. In Section 2, the system model, the communication protocol are introduced. In Sect. 3, the SOPs are analyzed. In Sect. 4, numerical results are presented and discussed. Finally, conclusions are presented in Sect. 5.

## 2     System Model and Communication Protocol

### 2.1     System and Channel Model

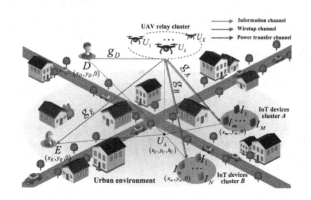

**Fig. 1.** System model for an RF EH NOMA UR system.

As illustrated in Fig. 1, we consider an RF EH NOMA UR system in which two clusters of energy-limited ID (i.e. cluster $A$ has $M$ high-priority devices, denoted by $I_m, 1 \leq m \leq M$ and cluster $B$ has $N$ low-priority devices, denoted by $I_n, 1 \leq n \leq N$) wish to send confidential information to a ground destination $D$ through a UR cluster of $K$ elements, denoted by $U_k, 1 \leq k \leq K$, in the presence of a passive eavesdropper $E$. There are no direct links between the IDs and $D$ because of the presence of barriers in the urban environment. We assume that all devices with a single antenna operate in half-duplex mode and that the URs use the DF scheme [17]. The Rayleigh distribution is used to characterize the small-scale fading of the channel coefficient $h_{ab}$, i.e., the channel power gain $|h_{ab}|^2$ is a random variable (RV) that follows an exponential distribution with parameter $\lambda_{ab}$, where $ab$ is the link $a \rightarrow b$, $ab \in \{I_m U_k, I_n U_k, U_k D, U_k E\}$. For clarity, we define the notations adopted throughout the remainder of this paper in Table 1.

Without loss of generality, we use a three-dimensional Cartesian coordinate system where $D$, $E$, and $I_i, i \in (m, n)$ are on the ground with coordinates $D(x_D, y_D, 0)$, $E(x_E, x_E, 0)$, and $I_i(x_i, x_i, 0)$, respectively. The $U_k$ is fixed at $H_{U_k} > 0$ [13], and its location is $U_k(x_{U_k}, y_{U_k}, H_{U_k})$. Assume that the large-scale fading of the channel between the UAV and ground devices is based on the probabilistic LoS and NLoS model [18], which is influenced by building density and distance between the $U_k$ and ground devices. The likelihood of devices seeing a LoS link is expressed as [18]

$$\begin{cases} P_{LoS}(ab) &= \dfrac{1}{1 + \nu \exp(-\upsilon[\theta_{ab} - \nu])}, \\ P_{NLoS}(ab) &= 1 - P_{LoS}(ab), \end{cases} \tag{1}$$

**Table 1.** Notation

| Notation | Meaning | Notation | Meaning |
|---|---|---|---|
| $M$ | Number of IDs in cluster $A$ | $I_A^*$ | The best ID in cluster $A$ |
| $N$ | Number of IDs in cluster $B$ | $I_B^*$ | The best ID in cluster $B$ |
| $K$ | Number of URs in cluster UR | $U^*$ | The best UR in cluster UR |
| $T$ | Transmission block time | $\alpha$ | Time switching ratio (TSR) |
| $P_U$ | Transmit power of UR | $\eta$ | Energy conversion efficiency |
| $\rho_0, 1 - \rho_0$ | Power allocation coefficient for transmitted signal from $I_A^*$ and $I_B^*$ to $U^*$ | $\rho_A, \rho_B, \rho_J$ | Power allocation coefficient for signal $x_A$, signal $x_B$, and AN from $U^*$ to $D$ |
| $\epsilon_0$ | The cancellation error factor with iSIC at UR | $\epsilon_1$ | The cancellation error factor with iSIC at $D$ |
| $\gamma_U, \gamma_E$ | Average transmit SNR at $U^*$ and $E$ | $\bar{L}_{(.)}$ | The mean path loss |

where $\nu$ and $\upsilon$ are constant values that vary according to the surrounding environment (such as suburban, urban, dense-urban) [19], the elevation angle $\theta_{ab} = \frac{180}{\pi} \arcsin\left(\frac{H_U}{d_{ab}}\right)$, and the distance between the UR and the ground device $d_{ab} = \sqrt{(x_b - x_a)^2 + (y_b - y_a)^2 + H_U{}^2}$. We were using the path-loss model in [18] to accurately present the air-to-ground channels of UR networks, which takes LoS and NLoS of $a \to b$ channels into consideration. The expressions are as follows [13]:

$$L_l\,(ab) = \kappa_l^{-1} d_{ab}^{-\sigma}, \tag{2}$$

where $l \in \{LoS, NLoS\}$, $\kappa_l$ is parameters depend on environment and carrier frequency, which can be expressed as $\kappa_l = \xi_l (4\pi f_c/c)^2$. $f_c$ is the carrier frequency, $c$ is the speed of light, and $\xi_l$ is the excessive path losses of the LoS and NLoS propagation, and $\sigma$ is the path-loss exponent. The mean path loss, taking into account the probability of both LoS and NLoS linkages from the UAV to the ground devices is thus calculated as [18]

$$\bar{L}_{ab} = P_{LoS}\,(ab)\,L_{LoS}\,(ab) + P_{NLoS}\,(ab)\,L_{NLoS}\,(ab). \tag{3}$$

In this work, the URs first send their pilot signals to the $D$ simultaneously. Once the signal-to-noise ratios (SNRs) of all $U_k$ to $D$ channels have been estimated [11], the $D$ selects the best UR, denoted by the symbol $U^*$, which is the one with the highest received SNR at the $D$. Thus, the indices and channel power gain of a selected UAV $U^*$ in a UR cluster are represented as follow:

$$U^* = \arg \max_{1 \le k \le K} \left\{ |h_{U_k D}|^2 \right\}, \tag{4}$$

$$|h_D|^2 = \max_{1 \le k \le K} \left\{ |h_{U_k D}|^2 \right\}. \tag{5}$$

Next, the IDs concurrently transmit pilot signals to the selected UAV. $U^*$ estimates the SNRs of all transmission channels from two clusters and then selects the best ID in cluster $A$, denoted $I_A^*$, and the best ID in cluster $B$, denoted $I_B^*$, as the ones with the greatest received SNRs at the selected UAV terminal. Therefore, the indices and channel power gains of the selected ID in clusters $A$ and $B$ are as follows:

$$I_O^* = \arg \max_{i \in (m,n)} \left\{ |h_{I_i U^*}|^2 \right\}, \tag{6}$$

$$|h_O|^2 = \max_{i \in (m,n)} \left\{ |h_{I_i U^*}|^2 \right\}, \tag{7}$$

where $O \in (A, B)$.

## 2.2 Communication Protocol

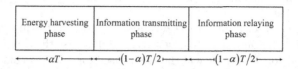

**Fig. 2.** Time flowchart of the considered RF EH NOMA UR network.

In the considered system, we use a time switching (TS) communication protocol as shown in Fig. 2. This communication protocol is described as follows:

- In the first phase, during the duration of $\alpha T$, $I_O^*$ harvests energy from $U^*$, where $\alpha$ $(0 < \alpha < 1)$ indicates the TSR [20], and $T$ represents transmission block time. Thus, the energy harvested at $I_O^*$ can be expressed as follows:

$$E_O = \frac{\eta P_U g_O \alpha T}{\bar{L}_O}, \tag{8}$$

where, $\eta$ is the EH efficiency coefficient, which depends on the rectification $(0 < \eta < 1)$, $P_U$ is the transmit power of $U^*$, $g_O = |h_O|^2$. Noted that all harvested energies are used for their transmission.
- In the second phase, $I_O^*$ sends their own messages to $U^*$ during the period of $(1 - \alpha) T/2$. Thus, the received signal at $U^*$ is written as

$$y_U = \sqrt{\frac{P_A}{\bar{L}_A}} \rho_0 g_A x_A + \sqrt{\frac{P_B}{\bar{L}_B}} (1 - \rho_0) g_B x_B + n_U, \tag{9}$$

where $P_A = \frac{E_A}{(1-\alpha)T/2} = \frac{\beta P_U g_A}{L_A}$, $P_B = \frac{E_B}{(1-\alpha)T/2} = \frac{\beta P_U g_B}{L_B}$, $\beta = \frac{2\eta\alpha}{(1-\alpha)}$, $\rho_0$ denotes the power allocation coefficient for transmitted signal from $I_A^*$ to $U^*$ and $n_U \sim \mathcal{CN}(0, N_0)$ is additive white Gaussian noise (AWGN) at $U^*$ [11]. Because the UR uses the DF transmission scheme, $U^*$ must first decode both $x_A$ and $x_B$ before forwarding. $U^*$ decodes $x_A$ first by treating the signal corresponding to $x_B$ as interference. After successfully decoding $x_A$, $U^*$ decodes $x_B$ by canceling the known $x_A$ using the SIC method [10]. The signal-to-interference-plus-noise ratio (SINR) for detect $x_A$ at $U^*$ is given by

$$\gamma_U^{x_A} = \frac{\beta\gamma_U\rho_0 g_A^2 \bar{L}_B^2}{\left[(1-\rho_0)\beta\gamma_U g_B^2 + \bar{L}_B^2\right]\bar{L}_A^2}, \tag{10}$$

where $\gamma_U = P_U/N_0$. The SIC principle states that $x_B$ is decoded by subtracting $x_A$ from $\gamma_U^{x_A}$; the SIC is perfect when $x_A$ is totally deleted. Otherwise, $x_B$ will be decoded in the presence of residual interference due to iSIC [21]. We investigate the scenario of iSIC in this paper, therefore SINR at $U^*$ to detect $x_B$ is given by

$$\gamma_U^{x_B} = \frac{(1-\rho_0)\beta\gamma_U g_B^2 \bar{L}_A^2}{\bar{L}_B^2 \left(\epsilon_0\beta\gamma_U\rho_0 g_A^2 + \bar{L}_A^2\right)}, \tag{11}$$

where $\epsilon_0$ represents the residual interference due to iSIC, $0 \le \epsilon_0 \le 1$, and $\epsilon_0$ refer to perfect SIC (pSIC).

– In the third phase, $U^*$ uses the downlink NOMA technique to forward the correctly decoded messages to destination $D$. Because the channel state information (CSI) of $E$ is unknown, the AN is used for relaying communication in order to increase information security [22]. It is a strategy that permits the usable signals and the AN to transmit at the same time in order to degrade the received signal of $E$ while without impairing that of $D$. As a result, the message sent from $U^*$ takes the following form:

$$x_U = \sqrt{\rho_A}x_A + \sqrt{\rho_B}x_B + \sqrt{\rho_J}x_J, \tag{12}$$

where $\rho_A$, $\rho_B$, and $\rho_J$ ($\rho_A+\rho_B+\rho_J = 1$ and $\rho_A > \rho_B$) are the power allocation coefficient for messages $x_A$, $x_B$, and AN $x_J$, respectively. Thus, the received signal at $D$ is as follows:

$$y_D = \sqrt{\frac{\rho_A P_U}{\bar{L}_D}}g_D x_A + \sqrt{\frac{\rho_B P_U}{\bar{L}_D}}g_D x_B + \sqrt{\frac{\rho_J P_U}{\bar{L}_D}}g_D x_J + n_D, \tag{13}$$

where $g_D = |h_D|^2$ and $n_D \sim \mathcal{CN}(0, N_0)$ is AWGN at $D$. Assuming the AN can be removed at $D$ [23]. Thus, the SINR to detect $x_A$ and $x_B$ at $D$ are expressed as follows:

$$\gamma_D^{x_A} = \frac{\rho_A\gamma_U g_D}{\rho_B\gamma_U g_D + \bar{L}_U}, \tag{14}$$

$$\gamma_D^{x_B} = \frac{\rho_B\gamma_U g_D}{\epsilon_1\rho_A\gamma_U g_D + \bar{L}_U}, \tag{15}$$

where $\epsilon_1$ represents residual interference due to the iSIC at the $D$. Similarly, the expression of signal received at $E$ is as follows:

$$y_E = \sqrt{\frac{\rho_A P_U}{\bar{L}_E}}g_E x_A + \sqrt{\frac{\rho_B P_U}{\bar{L}_E}}g_E x_B + \sqrt{\frac{\rho_J P_U}{\bar{L}_E}}g_E x_J + n_E, \tag{16}$$

where $g_E = |h_E|^2$ and $n_E \sim \mathcal{CN}(0, N_0)$ is AWGN at $E$. We suppose $E$ is a low-capacity passive eavesdropping device, so $E$ can only eavesdrop on the communication from $U^*$ to $D$. Assuming the AN cannot be removed at $E$ [22]. The SINR to detect $x_A$ and $x_B$ at $E$ is given by

$$\gamma_E^{x_A} = \frac{\rho_A \gamma_E g_E}{(\rho_B + \rho_J)\gamma_E g_E + \bar{L}_E}, \tag{17}$$

$$\gamma_E^{x_B} = \frac{\rho_B \gamma_E g_E}{(\rho_A + \rho_J)\gamma_E g_E + \bar{L}_E}, \tag{18}$$

where $\gamma_E = P_U / N_0$.

Under Rayleigh fading [14], the corresponding cumulative distribution function (CDF) and probability density function (PDF) of channel power gains, $g_X$, ($X \in \{A, B, D\}$) are respectively given by

$$F_{g_X}(x) = \left(1 - e^{-\frac{x}{\lambda_X}}\right)^\Psi = \sum_{\psi=0}^{\Psi} \binom{\Psi}{\psi}(-1)^\psi e^{-\frac{\psi x}{\lambda_X}}, \tag{19}$$

$$f_{g_X}(x) = \sum_{\psi=1}^{\Psi} \binom{\Psi}{\psi} \frac{(-1)^{\psi+1}\psi}{\lambda_X} e^{-\frac{\psi x}{\lambda_X}}, \tag{20}$$

where $\Psi \in \{K, M, N\}$.

The CDF and PDF of channel power gains $g_E$ are respectively expressed as

$$F_{g_E}(x) = 1 - e^{-\frac{x}{\lambda_E}}, \tag{21}$$

$$f_{g_E}(x) = \frac{1}{\lambda_E} e^{-\frac{x}{\lambda_E}}. \tag{22}$$

According to the above results, the CDFs of $\gamma_D^{x_A}$ and $\gamma_D^{x_B}$ are determined as follows:

$$F_{\gamma_D^{x_A}}(x) = \begin{cases} 1, & x \geq \rho_A / \rho_B \\ \sum_{l=0}^{K} \binom{K}{l}(-1)^l e^{-\frac{x l L_U}{\lambda_D(\rho_A - \rho_B x)\gamma_U}}, & x < \rho_A / \rho_B \end{cases}, \tag{23}$$

$$F_{\gamma_D^{x_B}}(x) = \begin{cases} 1, & x \geq \rho_B / \epsilon_1 \rho_A \\ \sum_{l=0}^{K} \binom{K}{l}(-1)^l e^{-\frac{x l L_U}{\lambda_D \gamma_U(\rho_B - \epsilon_1 \rho_A x)}}, & x < \rho_B / \epsilon_1 \rho_A \end{cases}. \tag{24}$$

The CDFs and PDFs of $\gamma_E^{x_A}$ and $\gamma_E^{x_B}$ are respectively given by:

$$F_{\gamma_E^{x_A}}(x) = \begin{cases} 1, & x \geq \rho_A/\rho_B+\rho_J \\ 1 - e^{-\frac{xL_E}{\lambda_E[\rho_A-(\rho_B+\rho_J)x]\gamma_E}}, & x < \rho_A/\rho_B+\rho_J \end{cases}, \tag{25}$$

$$f_{\gamma_E^{x_A}}(x) = \begin{cases} 0, & x \geq \rho_A/\rho_B+\rho_J \\ \frac{\rho_A \bar{L}_E}{\lambda_E \gamma_E [\rho_A-(\rho_B+\rho_J)x]^2} e^{-\frac{xL_E}{\lambda_E \gamma_E [\rho_A-(\rho_B+\rho_J)x]}}, & x < \rho_A/\rho_B+\rho_J \end{cases}, \tag{26}$$

$$F_{\gamma_E^{x_B}}(x) = \begin{cases} 1, & x \geq \rho_B/\rho_A+\rho_J \\ 1 - e^{-\frac{xL_E}{\lambda_E \gamma_E [\rho_B-(\rho_A+\rho_J)x]}}, & x < \rho_B/\rho_A+\rho_J \end{cases}, \tag{27}$$

$$f_{\gamma_E^{x_B}}(x) = \begin{cases} 0, & x \geq \rho_B/\rho_A+\rho_J \\ \frac{\rho_B \bar{L}_E}{\lambda_E \gamma_E [\rho_B-(\rho_A+\rho_J)x]^2} e^{-\frac{xL_E}{\lambda_E \gamma_E [\rho_B-(\rho_A+\rho_J)x]}}, & x < \rho_B/\rho_A+\rho_J \end{cases}. \tag{28}$$

## 3    Secrecy Performance Analysis

In this section, we derive the expressions for the SOPs to evaluate the secrecy performance of the considered system. It is possible for the proposed system to experience a security outage event if the instantaneous secrecy capacity, denoted by $C_S^{x_O}$, falls below a preset secrecy rate threshold, denoted by $C_{th}^O$, which is expressed as

$$\mathbb{S}_O = \Pr\left(C_S^{x_O} < C_{th}^O\right), \tag{29}$$

where $C_S^{x_O}$ is expressed as follows [14]:

$$C_S^{x_O} = [C_D^{x_O} - C_E^{x_O}]^+ = \begin{cases} \frac{(1-\alpha)}{2} W \log_2\left(\frac{1+\gamma_D^{x_O}}{1+\gamma_E^{x_O}}\right), & \gamma_D^{x_O} > \gamma_E^{x_O} \\ 0, & \gamma_D^{x_O} \leq \gamma_E^{x_O} \end{cases}, \tag{30}$$

where $W$ is the system bandwidth, $C_D^{x_O}$ and $C_E^{x_O}$ are the capacities of $D$ and $E$ to detect $x_O$. The following lemmas are provided to characterize the secrecy performance of an RF EH NOMA UR system.

**Lemma 1.** *The closed-form expression of the (OP) $\mathbb{P}_A$ of the considered system in the second phase to detect $x_A$ is provided by*

$$\mathbb{P}_A = \frac{\pi}{2Q\lambda_B} \sum_{i=0}^{M} \sum_{j=1}^{N} \sum_{q=1}^{Q} \binom{M}{i}\binom{N}{j}$$

$$\times \frac{(-1)^{i+j+1} j \sqrt{1-\zeta_q^2}}{\omega_q \ln^2(\omega_q)} e^{-\frac{i\sqrt{\theta_1 \ln^{-2}(\omega_q)+\theta_2}}{\lambda_A} \omega_q - \frac{j \ln^{-2}(\omega_q)}{\lambda_B}}, \tag{31}$$

*where $\theta_1 = \frac{\gamma_{th} \bar{L}_A^2 (1-\rho_0)}{\rho_0 L_B^2}$, $\theta_2 = \frac{\gamma_{th} \bar{L}_A^2}{\beta \gamma_U \rho_0}$, $\zeta_q = \cos\left(\frac{\pi(2q-1)}{2Q}\right)$, $\omega_q = \frac{(\zeta_q+1)}{2}$, $\gamma_{th}^A = 2^{\frac{2R_A}{W(1-\alpha)}} - 1$, and $R_A$ denote the data rate threshold.*

*Proof.* See Appendix A.

**Lemma 2.** *The closed-form expression of the OP* $\mathbb{P}_B$ *of the considered system in the second phase to detect* $x_B$ *is provided by*

$$\mathbb{P}_B = \frac{\pi}{2Q\lambda_A} \sum_{i=1}^{M} \sum_{j=0}^{N} \sum_{q=1}^{Q} \binom{M}{i}\binom{N}{j}$$

$$\times \frac{(-1)^{i+j+1}i\sqrt{1-\zeta_q^{\;2}}}{\omega_q \ln^2(\omega_q)} e^{-\frac{j\sqrt{\theta_1 \ln^{-2}(\omega_q)+\theta_2}}{\lambda_B}} \omega_q^{\frac{i\ln^{-2}(\omega_q)}{\lambda_A}}, \tag{32}$$

*where* $\theta_3 = \frac{\gamma_{th}^B \epsilon_0 \rho_0 \bar{L}_B^2}{(1-\rho_0)\bar{L}_A^2}$, $\theta_4 = \frac{\gamma_{th}^B \bar{L}_B^2}{(1-\rho_0)\beta\gamma_U}$, $\gamma_{th}^B = 2^{\frac{2R_B}{W(1-\alpha)}} - 1$, *and* $R_B$ *denote the data rate threshold.*

*Proof.* Similar to the proof of Lemma 1.

**Lemma 3.** *The closed-form expression of the SOP* $\mathbb{S}_A$ *to detect* $x_A$ *of the third phase is given by*

$$\mathbb{S}_A = \begin{cases} I_A, & b_1 \geq b_2 \\ I_A + e^{-\frac{b_1 \bar{L}_E}{\lambda_E \gamma_E [\rho_A - (\rho_B + \rho_J)b_1]}}, & b_1 < b_2 \end{cases}, \tag{33}$$

*where* $I_A = \frac{\pi\tau\rho_A \bar{L}_E}{2Q\lambda_E\gamma_E} \sum_{l=0}^{K} \sum_{q=1}^{Q} \binom{K}{l} \frac{(-1)^l\sqrt{1-\zeta_q^{\;2}}}{[\rho_A-(\rho_B+\rho_J)b\tau\omega_q]^2} e^{-\frac{[\phi_A(1+\tau\omega_q)-1]t\bar{L}_U}{\lambda_D\gamma_U(\rho_A-\rho_B[\phi_A(1+\tau\omega_q)-1])}}$

$\times e^{-\frac{\tau\omega_q \bar{L}_E}{\lambda_E\gamma_E[\rho_A-(\rho_B+\rho_J)\tau\omega_q]}}$, $\phi_A = 2^{\frac{2C_{th}^A}{W(1-\alpha)}}$, $b_1 = \frac{\rho_A-\rho_B(\phi_A-1)}{\rho_B C_{th}}$, $b_2 = \frac{\rho_A}{\rho_B+\rho_J}$, *and* $\tau = \min(b_1, b_2)$.

*Proof.* See Appendix B.

**Lemma 4.** *The closed-form expression of the SOP* $\mathbb{S}_B$ *to detect* $x_B$ *of the third phase is given by*

$$\mathbb{S}_B = \begin{cases} I_B, & c_1 \geq c_2 \\ I_B + e^{-\frac{c_1 \bar{L}_E}{\lambda_E \gamma_E [\rho_B - (\rho_A + \rho_J)c_1]}}, & c_1 < c_2 \end{cases},$$

*where* $I_B = \frac{\pi\mu\rho_B \bar{L}_E}{2Q\lambda_E\gamma_E} \sum_{l=0}^{K} \sum_{q=1}^{Q} \binom{K}{l} \frac{(-1)^l\sqrt{1-\zeta_q^{\;2}}}{[\rho_B-(\rho_A+\rho_J)\mu\omega_q]^2} e^{-\frac{[\phi_B(1+\mu\omega_q)-1]t\bar{L}_U}{\lambda_D\gamma_U(\rho_B-\epsilon_1\rho_A[\phi_B(1+\mu\omega_q)-1])}}$

$\times e^{-\frac{\mu\omega_q \bar{L}_E}{\lambda_E\gamma_E[\rho_B-(\rho_A+\rho_J)\mu\omega_q]}}$, $\phi_B = 2^{\frac{2C_{th}^B}{W(1-\alpha)}}$, $c_1 = \frac{\rho_B-\epsilon_1\rho_A(C_{th}-1)}{\epsilon_1\rho_A C_{th}}$, $c_2 = \frac{\rho_B}{\rho_A+\rho_J}$, *and* $\mu = \min(c_1, c_2)$.

*Proof.* Similar to the proof of Lemma 3.

According to the proposed RF EH NOMA UR system, the system experiences a secrecy outage when the signal $x_A$ or $x_B$ is not successfully decoded at $U^*$ in phase 2, or when the secrecy rate falls below the predefined threshold. As a result, the SOP for detecting $x_O$, represented by $\Theta_O$, is derived as

$$\Theta_O = \mathbb{P}_O + (1 - \mathbb{P}_O)\, \mathbb{S}_O. \tag{34}$$

And the SOP of considered system is as follow:

$$\Theta_S = 1 - (1 - \Theta_A)(1 - \Theta_B). \tag{35}$$

## 4  Numerical Result

In this section, we describe the numerical results used to validate the analytical expression of the SOP described in Sect. 3 for the RF EH NOMA UR system. Specifically, we consider the following system parameters in all simulations [18]: transmit SNR $\gamma_U \in (0, 20)$ (dB); $f_c = 2.10^8$ (Hz), $c = 3.10^8$; $\alpha \in (0.1, 0.9)$; $\eta = 0.75$; $\sigma = 2$; $\rho_0 = 0.75$, $\rho_A = 0.5$, $\rho_B = 0.3$, $\rho_E = 0.2$; $\epsilon_0 = \epsilon_1 = 0.3$; the coordinates $D(0,0,0)$, $I_A(5,2,0)$, $I_B(4,1,0)$, $E(1,3,0)$, $U(2,2,H_{U^*})$, where $H_{U^*} \in (0,20)$ (m); $W = 10^2$ (Hz); $C_{th}^A = C_{th}^B = 0.05$, $R_A = R_B = 0.05$ (bit/s/Hz); $\nu = 0.1581$, $\upsilon = 9.6177$, $\xi_{los} = 1$ and $\xi_{nlos} = 20$.

The impact of the average SNR $\gamma_U$ and the number of UR $(K)$ on the SOP of the IDs and the entire system is depicted in Fig. 3a. We discover that as $\gamma_U$ increases, the SOP for each ID and the entire system decreases. In other words, raising the UR's' transmit power can improve the SOP. Furthermore, the figure demonstrates that when $K$ increases, the SOP reduces dramatically. This mean that the more URs that permit signal transfer, the more probable the system is to find the best UR to participate in the communication process.

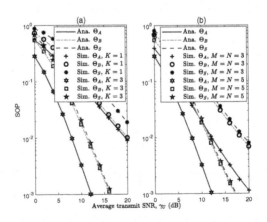

**Fig. 3.** Impact of average transmit SNR on SOP with different number of UR $(K)$ in (a) and numbers of ID in two clusters $(M, N)$ in (b).

Figure 3b depicts the impact of the number of IDs in two clusters $(M, N)$ on the SOP of the IDs and the entire system. The findings indicate that increasing the number of IDs can reduce the SOP of each cluster and the entire system. The results show that increasing the number of IDs in clusters can improve the secrecy performance of the selected IDs as well as the entire system. This is due to the fact that the selected IDs have better channel conditions in this scenario.

The influence of height of $U^*$ on the SOP of the IDs and the entire system is depicted in Fig. 4a. As we can see, there appears to be an optimum $H_{U^*}^*$ value for which the SOP value is minimized. This is due to the fact that while the height of $U^*$ is low, the LoS probability is low, whereas the NLoS probability is large; nonetheless, a high $H_{U^*}$ results in a high path loss. As a result, there is a point where the optimum SOP is reached.

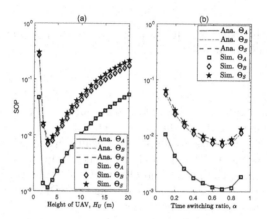

**Fig. 4.** Impact of height of UR ($H_{U^*}$) in (a) and time switching ratio ($\alpha$) in (b) on SOP.

Figure 4b shows the effect of TSR $\alpha$ on the SOP of the IDs and the entire system. The SOP reduces when $\alpha$ increases from 0.5 to 0.8. Then, as $\alpha$ continues to rise, the SOP rises again. Because $\alpha$ is small, less time is spent in the EH phase, resulting in less energy harvested by IDs. When $\alpha$ is larger, IDs can gather more energy, resulting in optimal secrecy performance. However, when $\alpha$ increases, less time is available for phase 2 and phase 3, reducing system reliability and increasing SOP. Based on these findings, we infer that $\alpha^*$ is the ideal value for minimizing SOP.

We investigating a residual interference in Fig. 5a for two cases pSIC and iSIC. The pSIC case $\epsilon_0 = \epsilon_1 = 0$ and the iSIC case $\epsilon_0 = \epsilon_1 = 0.3$. It is clear that $\epsilon_0$ and $\epsilon_1$ harm on system secrecy performance, i.e., when they increase, the higher values of the SOP can be observed. Increasing the values of $\epsilon_0$ and $\epsilon_1$ reduces the SINR for decoding the $x_B$ signal at $U^*$ and $D$, hence increasing the SOP.

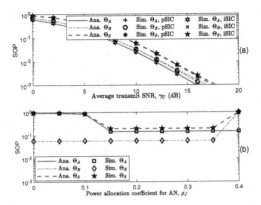

**Fig. 5.** Impact of the pSIC and iSIC ($\epsilon_0, \epsilon_1$) in (a) and the power allocation coefficient for artificial noise in (b) on SOP.

Figure 5b depicts the impact of the AN on the SOP of the IDs and the entire system. In this experiment, we set $\rho_J = 0.6$ and investigate the effect of the AN. We can see is that the SOP of the system tends to decrease gradually, reach a minimum, and then grow as $\rho_J$ increases. Because when $\rho_J = 0$, $U^*$ interacts with $D$ without using AN, the probability that $E$ can decode the signal from $U^*$ is high, leading to the high value of the SOP. As the AN power increases, the interference at $E$ increases, hence reducing the SOP. Increasing $\rho_J$ makes it harder for $E$ to eavesdrop, but it reduces the power available for useful signal transmission, increasing the SOP. So, while $\rho_J$ can improve system SOP, it is necessary to find the optimal $\rho_J^*$ value for minimum SOP.

## 5 Conclusion

In this paper, we investigated the secrecy outage performance of an RF EH NOMA UR system over Rayleigh fading channel. We propose a three-phase system operating protocol based on UR-ID selection, focusing RF EH and AN techniques to increase secrecy outage performance. As a result, we obtain closed-form expressions of SOP for each ID cluster and the entire system. We provided numerical results to verify the proposed system secrecy performance.

**Acknowledgment.** This work was supported by Thailand Science Research and Innovation (TSRI) and the National Research Council of Thailand (NRCT) via the International Research Network Program (IRN61W0006) and by Khon Kaen University.

# A    Proof of Lemma 1

Here, we derive the closed-form expression of $\mathbb{P}_A$ as follows

$$\mathbb{P}_A = \Pr\left(\gamma_{U^*}^{x_A} < \gamma_{th}^A\right)$$

$$= \int_0^\infty F_{g_A}\left(\sqrt{\theta_1 x^2 + \theta_2}\right) f_{g_B}(x)\, dx$$

$$= \sum_{i=0}^M \sum_{j=1}^N \binom{M}{i}\binom{N}{j}\frac{(-1)^{i+j+1} j}{\lambda_B}\int_0^\infty e^{-\frac{i\sqrt{\theta_1 x^2 + \theta_2}}{\lambda_A} - \frac{jx}{\lambda_B}}\, dx$$

$$\stackrel{(a)}{=} \frac{\pi}{2Q\lambda_B}\sum_{i=0}^M \sum_{j=1}^N \sum_{q=1}^Q \binom{M}{i}\binom{N}{j}\frac{(-1)^{i+j+1} j\sqrt{1-\zeta_q^2}}{\omega_q \ln^2(\omega_q)}$$

$$\times\, e^{-\frac{i\sqrt{\theta_1 \ln^{-2}(\omega_q) + \theta_2}}{\lambda_A}}\omega_q^{-\frac{j\ln^{-2}(\omega_q)}{\lambda_B}}, \tag{36}$$

where $\theta_1 = \frac{\gamma_{th}\bar{L}_A^2(1-\rho_0)}{\rho_0 \bar{L}_B^2}$, $\theta_2 = \frac{\gamma_{th}\bar{L}_A^2}{\beta\gamma_U\rho_0}$, $\zeta_q = \cos\left(\frac{\pi(2q-1)}{2Q}\right)$, and $\omega_q = \frac{(\zeta_q+1)}{2}$. Note that step $(a)$ is obtained by applying the Gaussian-Chebyshev quadrature method with $Q$ is the complexity-vs-accuracy trade-off coefficient. This ends our proof.

# B    Proof of Lemma 2

From Eq. (29) we derive closed-form expression of the SOP $\mathbb{S}_A$ as follow

$$\mathbb{S}_A = \int_0^\infty \int_0^{\phi_A(1+y)-1} f_{\gamma_D^{x_A}}(x) f_{\gamma_E^{x_A}}(y)\, dx\, dy$$

$$= \int_0^\infty F_{\gamma_D^{x_A}}\left[\phi_A(1+y)-1\right] f_{\gamma_E^{x_A}}(y)\, dy$$

$$= \begin{cases} \dfrac{\rho_A \bar{L}_E}{\lambda_E \gamma_E}\displaystyle\sum_{l=0}^K \binom{K}{l}(-1)^l \int_0^{b_2} \dfrac{e^{-\frac{[\phi_A(1+y)-1]lL_U}{\lambda_D\gamma_U(\rho_A-\rho_B[\phi_A(1+y)-1])} - \frac{yL_E}{\lambda_E\gamma_E[\rho_A-(\rho_B+\rho_J)y]}}}{[\rho_A-(\rho_B+\rho_J)y]^2}\, dy \\ \qquad\qquad\qquad\qquad\qquad ,\, b_1 \geq b_2 \\[2mm] \dfrac{\rho_A \bar{L}_E}{\lambda_E \gamma_E}\displaystyle\sum_{l=0}^K \binom{K}{l}(-1)^l \int_0^{b_1} \dfrac{e^{-\frac{[\phi_A(1+y)-1]lL_U}{\lambda_D\gamma_U(\rho_A-\rho_B[\phi_A(1+y)-1])} - \frac{xL_E}{\lambda_E\gamma_E[\rho_A-(\rho_B+\rho_J)x]}}}{[\rho_A-(\rho_B+\rho_J)y]^2}\, dy \\[2mm] \qquad\qquad + \int_{b_1}^{b_2} f_{\gamma_E^{x_A}}(y)\, dy \qquad\quad ,\, b_1 < b_2 \end{cases}$$

$$= \begin{cases} I_A, & b_1 \geq b_2 \\ I_A + e^{-\frac{b_1 L_E}{\lambda_E\gamma_E[\rho_A-(\rho_B+\rho_J)b_1]}}, & b_1 < b_2 \end{cases} \tag{37}$$

where $I_A \overset{(b)}{=} \frac{\pi \tau \rho_A \bar{L}_E}{2Q \lambda_E \gamma_E} \sum_{l=0}^{K} \sum_{q=1}^{Q} \binom{K}{l} \frac{(-1)^l \sqrt{1-\zeta_q^2}}{[\rho_A-(\rho_B+\rho_J)b\tau\omega_q]^2} e^{-\frac{[\phi_A(1+\tau\omega_q)-1]lL_U}{\lambda_D \gamma_U (\rho_A-\rho_B[\phi_A(1+\tau\omega_q)-1])}}$

$\times e^{-\frac{\tau\omega_q \bar{L}_E}{\lambda_E \gamma_E [\rho_A-(\rho_B+\rho_J)\tau\omega_q]}}$, $\phi_A = 2^{\frac{2C_{th}^A}{W(1-\alpha)}}$, $b_1 = \frac{\rho_A-\rho_B(\phi_A-1)}{\rho_B C_{th}}$, $b_2 = \frac{\rho_A}{\rho_B+\rho_J}$, and $\tau = $ min $(b_1, b_2)$. Note that step $(b)$ is obtained by applying the Gaussian-Chebyshev quadrature method with $Q$ is the complexity-vs-accuracy trade-off coefficient. This ends our proof.

# References

1. Li, B., Fei, Z., Zhang, Y.: UAV communications for 5G and beyond: recent advances and future trends. IEEE Internet Things J. **6**(2), 2241–2263 (2019)
2. Zeng, S., Zhang, H., Bian, K., Song, L.: UAV relaying: powerallocation and trajectory optimization using decode-and-forward protocol. In: Proceedings of IEEE ICC, pp. 1–6. Kansas City, MO, USA (2018)
3. Yang, L., Chen, J., Hasna, M.O., Yang, H.: Outage performance of UAV-assisted relaying systems with RF energy harvesting. IEEE Commun. Lett. **22**(12), 2471–2474 (2018)
4. Tam, H.H.M., Tuan, H.D., Nasir, A.A., Duong, T.Q., Poor, H.V.: MIMO energy harvesting in full-duplex multi-user networks. IEEE Trans. Wireless Commun. **16**(5), 3282–3297 (2017)
5. Nguyen, M.-N., Nguyen, L.D., Duong, T.Q., Tuan, H.D.: Real-time optimal resource allocation for embedded UAV communication systems. IEEE Wireless Commun. Lett. **8**(1), 225–228 (2019)
6. Feng, W., Zhao, N., Ao, S., Tang, J., Zhang, X., Fu, Y., So, D.K.C., Wong, K.-K.: Joint 3D trajectory design and time allocation for UAV-enabled wireless power transfer networks. IEEE Trans. Veh. Technol. **69**(9), 9265–9278 (2020)
7. Li, Y., Yang, D., Xu, Y., Xiao, L., Chen, H.: Throughput maximization for UAV-enabled relaying in wireless powered communication networks. Sensors **19**(13) (2019)
8. Jia, H., Wang, Y., Liu, M., Chen, Y.: Sum-rate maximization for UAV aided wireless power transfer in space-air-ground networks. IEEE Access **8**, 216 231–216 244 (2020)
9. Ding, Z., Fan, P., Poor, H.V.: Impact of user pairing on 5G nonorthogonal multiple-access downlink transmissions. IEEE Trans. Veh. Technol. **65**(8), 6010–6023 (2016)
10. Vo, V.N., et al.: On security and throughput for energy harvesting untrusted relays in IoT systems using NOMA. IEEE Access **7**, 149 341–149 354 (2019)
11. Nguyen, A.-N., Vo, V.N., So-In, C., Ha, D.: System performance analysis for an energy harvesting IoT system using a DF/AF UAV-enabled relay with downlink NOMA under nakagami-$m$ fading. Sensors **21**(1) (2021)
12. Hadzi-Velkov, Z., Pejoski, S., Zlatanov, N., Schober, R.: UAV-assisted wireless powered relay networks with cyclical NOMA-TDMA. IEEE Wireless Commun. Lett. **9**(12), 2088–2092 (2020)
13. Vo, V.N., So-In, C., Tran, H., Tran, D.-D., Huu, T.P.: Performance analysis of an energy-harvesting IoT system using a UAV friendly jammer and NOMA under cooperative attack. IEEE Access **8**, 221 986–222 000 (2020)
14. Nguyen, A.-N., Vo, V.N., So-In, C., Ha, D., Sanguanpong, S., Baig, Z.A.: On secure wireless sensor networks with cooperative energy harvesting relaying. IEEE Access **7**, 139 212–139 225 (2019)

15. Wang, Q., Chen, Z., Mei, W., Fang, J.: Improving physical layer security using UAV-enabled mobile relaying. IEEE Wireless Commun. Lett. **6**(3), 310–313 (2017)
16. Sun, X., Yang, W., Cai, Y., Ma, R., Tao, L.: Physical layer security in millimeter wave SWIPT UAV-based relay networks. IEEE Access **7**, 35 851–35 862 (2019)
17. Duong, T.-Q., Bao, V.-N.-Q.: Performance analysis of selection decode-and-forward relay networks. Electronics Lett. **44**(12), 1206–1207 (2008)
18. Nguyen, A.-N., Vo, V.N., So-In, C., Ha, D., Truong, V.-T.: Performance analysis in UAV-enabled relay with NOMA under nakagami-$m$ fading considering adaptive power splitting. In: Proceedings, pp. 1–6. Lampang, Thailand, JCSSE (2021)
19. Sohail, M.F., Leow, C.Y., Won, S.: Non-orthogonal multiple access for unmanned aerial vehicle assisted communication. IEEE Access **6**, 22 716–22 727 (2018)
20. Ji, B., Li, Y., Chen, S., Han, C., Li, C., Wen, H.: Secrecy outage analysis of UAV assisted relay and antenna selection for cognitive network under nakagami-$m$ channel. IEEE Trans. Cognitive Commun. Networking **6**(3), 904–914 (2020)
21. Kara, F., Kaya, H.: Improved user fairness in decode-forward relaying non-orthogonal multiple access schemes with imperfect SIC and CSI. IEEE Access **8**, 97 540–97 556 (2020)
22. Nguyen, V.-L., Ha, D.-B., Tran, D.-D., Lee, Y.: Enhancing physical layer security for cooperative non-orthogonal multiple access networks with artificial noise. EAI Endorsed Trans. Indust. Netw. Intellig. Syst. **6**(20) (2019)
23. Liu, Y., Qin, Z., Elkashlan, M., Gao, Y., Hanzo, L.: Enhancing the physical layer security of non-orthogonal multiple access in large-scale networks. IEEE Trans. Wireless Commun. **16**(3), 1656–1672 (2017)

# Author Index

Printed in the United States
by Baker & Taylor Publisher Services